The European Health Data Space

This timely volume provides a comprehensive examination of how the proposed new European Health Data Space (EHDS) legislation will impact upon health and genetic data, individual privacy and providers of health services.

With the current legal framework recognised as insufficient in protecting data-related rights, the book spotlights the opportunities and challenges posed by the EHDS in balancing the interests of individuals with policymakers and researchers. It considers the impact on individual EU member states while highlighting issues such as changes to patients' rights, wearable technology, developments in e-health and the secondary use of medical data. Critically, it also examines how the EHDS will operate within existing legal frameworks, including the General Data Protection Regulation, the Data Governance Act and the Data Act.

Including contributions from some of the leading scholars in this area, this groundbreaking book will be key reading for students and researchers across law and public health.

Santa Slokenberga is Associate Professor in medical law and Senior Lecturer in administrative law at the Faculty of Law, Uppsala University, Sweden.

Katharina Ó Cathaoir is Associate Professor of Law at the Faculty of Law, University of Copenhagen, and Pro Futura Scientia Fellow at the Swedish Collegium for Advanced Studies, Sweden.

Mahsa Shabani is Associate Professor in health privacy law and innovation at the University of Amsterdam.

The European Health Data Space

Examining A New Era in Data Protection

Edited by Santa Slokenberga, Katharina Ó Cathaoir and Mahsa Shabani

Routledge
Taylor & Francis Group
LONDON AND NEW YORK

Designed cover image: Taylor and Francis

First published 2025
by Routledge
4 Park Square, Milton Park, Abingdon, Oxon OX14 4RN

and by Routledge
605 Third Avenue, New York, NY 10158

Routledge is an imprint of the Taylor & Francis Group, an informa business

Chapters 2, 5, 10 and 11 are funded by Justitierådet Edvard Cassels stiftelse, Europe Framework Programme.

British Library Cataloguing-in-Publication Data
A catalogue record for this book is available from the British Library

Library of Congress Cataloging-in-Publication Data
Names: Slokenberga, Santa, 1987- editor. | Ó Cathaoir, Katharina, editor. | Shabani, Masha, editor.
Title: The European Health Data Space : examining a new era in data protection / edited by Santa Slokenberga, Katharina Ó Cathaoir, and Masha Shabani.
Description: Abingdon, Oxon ; New York, NY : Routledge, 2025. | / Mahsa Shabani, Santa Slokenberga, Katharina Ó Cathaoir.
Identifiers: LCCN 2024032593 | ISBN 9781032822884 (hardback) | ISBN 9781032896847 (paperback) | ISBN 9781003544111 (ebook)
Subjects: MESH: European Parliament. European Health Data Space Regulation. | Electronic Health Records--legislation & jurisprudence | Public Health--legislation & jurisprudence | Data Management--legislation & jurisprudence | Patient Rights--legislation & jurisprudence | Legislation as Topic | Europe
Classification: LCC R859.7.E43 | NLM WX 33 GA1 | DDC 610.285094--dc23/eng/20240913
LC record available at https://lccn.loc.gov/2024032593

ISBN: 978-1-032-82288-4 (hbk)
ISBN: 978-1-032-89684-7 (pbk)
ISBN: 978-1-003-54411-1 (ebk)

DOI: 10.4324/9781003544111

Typeset in Times New Roman
by SPi Technologies India Pvt Ltd (Straive)

Contents

Contributor biographies

Eila El Asry is Senior Attorney at Dittmar & Indrenius.

Patricia Cervera de la Cruz is a PhD candidate at Ghent University, Belgium, and a member of the METAMEDICA research group.

Hrefna D. Gunnarsdóttir, Mag. Juris, MA, PhD, is a researcher at Welma – Legal Studies in Welfare and EU Market Integration, Faculty of Law, University of Copenhagen, and Assistant Professor in Welfare and Health Law at the Faculty of Law, University of Iceland.

Magdalena Kogut-Czarkowska is a legal researcher at the Faculty of Law and Criminology, Metamedica, Ghent University, Belgium, and an attorney at Timelex.

Sandra Liede is an LL.D. candidate at the University of Helsinki and a Senior Legal Specialist at Healthtech Finland.

Juli Mansnérus, LL.D., is a postdoctoral researcher at the University of Helsinki and a partner and Head of Patents and Life Sciences at Dittmar & Indrenius. She has acted as a doctoral thesis supervisor and post-doctoral researcher in DECIDER project that has received funding from the European Union Horizon 2020 research and innovation programme under grant agreement No 965193". It would ve very important for us to add this text to the electronic version of the article.

Petra Holmberg, PhD, is a postdoctoral researcher in medical law at the Faculty of Law, Lund University. She holds a double PhD from the Université Toulouse 1 Capitole and Charles University in Prague in European Law.

Katharina Ó Cathaoir, PhD, is Associate Professor of Law at the Faculty of Law, University of Copenhagen, and Pro Futura Scientia Fellow at the Swedish Collegium for Advanced Studies, Sweden.

Tjaša Petročnik is a PhD researcher at the Tilburg Institute for Law, Technology, and Society (TILT), Tilburg University.

Andelka M. Phillips, PhD, is Academic Affiliate at the Centre for Health, Law, and Emerging Technologies (HeLEX), University of Oxford, UK, and an affiliate with the Bioethics Institute Ghent, University of Ghent, Belgium.

Jane Reichel is Professor of Administrative Law at the Faculty of Law, Stockholm University.

Enrique Santamaría Echeverría is Assistant Professor at the Department of Law and Markets, Faculty of Law, Erasmus University Rotterdam.

Mahsa Shabani, PhD, is Associate Professor of Health Privacy Law and Innovation at the University of Amsterdam, The Netherlands.

Santa Slokenberga, LL.D., is Associate Professor of Medical Law and Senior Lecturer in administrative law at the Faculty of Law, Uppsala University, Sweden.

Daniela Spajić, PhD, is a postdoctoral researcher at the KU Leuven Centre for IT & IP Law – imec in Leuven, Belgium.

Part I

Primary use: Control and access

1 Introduction

Transformation of electronic health data governance through the EHDS

Santa Slokenberga, Katharina Ó Cathaoir and Mahsa Shabani

1.1 Introductory remarks

The European Health Data Space Regulation (EHDS) was adopted in 2025. It sets out common rules, standards, infrastructures, and a governance framework with a view to facilitating access to electronic health data for their use in patients' healthcare (primary use) as well as for a number of objectives defined for realising societal benefits (secondary use).[1] In that regard, the rights of patients and obligations of healthcare actors are delineated, electronic health record (EHR) systems are regulated, common rules, practices, and infrastructures are set, and a governance and coordination mechanism is created.[2] Once fully implemented, it can be expected to have transformed the governance and management of electronic health data, including data management practices in healthcare and data access rules for research, innovation, and regulatory and public policy purposes anchored in public health objectives.[3] That, in turn, has implications for patients and their rights, healthcare providers and their obligations, public and industry researchers, as well as diverse market actors and authorities. On a larger scale, the EHDS has implications for the balance of competencies and authorities between the EU and the member states within the domain of health and data, and it marks the EU's position in the field in relation to third countries and international organisations.

1.2 Background to the EHDS

1.2.1 Policy perspective

The EHDS is the first data space of several to come.[4] It is anchored in the European Strategy for Data[5] and is a means to further different, larger, and smaller interrelated policy ambitions.[6] These form a complex policy and legal background for the EHDS.

One of the EHDS nucleus facets is the ambition to further the data market economy, which in turn seeks to achieve other diverse objectives, including contributing to the realisation of AI's potential in medicine. To achieve that in the health sector, large quantities of high-quality data are crucial for both

DOI: 10.4324/9781003544111-2

public and private entities. The EHDS creates a mechanism to enhance the availability and facilitate accessibility of electronic health data (EHD), while also strengthening the rights of the data subjects in regard to their EHD in healthcare.

Enhancing the availability and facilitating access to health data have not been straightforward tasks for the EU legislature. One starting point for such discussions is the state of play since 2018 when the GDPR became applicable. The GDPR has been both praised and criticised.[7] For example, one central criticism is the GDPR's impact on secondary uses of health data and the fragmented regulatory landscape's implications for scientific research. At the core of data governance of scientific research remained member state law as the member states – to a large degree – held autonomy in designing laws that decide to whom, based on which legal bases prescribed in the GDPR, and under what circumstances access to health data should be given. Another contributing factor is the lessons learned during the COVID-19 pandemic regarding hurdles in timely access to vital data for public health governance and product innovation. The EHDS now changes this. Mechanisms are prescribed to access EHD in a more streamlined and open manner for scientific research and other specified purposes aimed at furthering the public interest.

In 2022, the European Parliament and Commission launched the Digital Decade Policy Programme 2030.[8] It sets out a number of objectives, including having a digitally skilled population, securing and performing digital infrastructures, digital transformations of businesses, and digitalising public services. These objectives now are built into the EHDS. In the pursuit of the ambition to digitalise public services, the primary use mechanism enhances patient access to their electronic health data and is designed to further the availability of electronic health data.[9]

In line with the Digital Decade Policy, actors in the healthcare domain will inevitably face further digitalisation. That applies not only to the healthcare providers ensuring the capability to carry out the new tasks that the EHDS places on them but also to actors that aspire to capitalise on electronic health data, who will need to develop the necessary digital infrastructure and adopt the necessary skills. The EHDS leaves it to the market actors to develop these necessary skills so that they can take advantage of the enhanced availability of electronic health data for research, development, and innovation purposes. On the other hand, in regard to the patients and healthcare providers, particular requirements are prescribed in the EHDS. After all, these two actors are at the centre of the primary use mechanism, the engine generating data that cater to the secondary purpose aspirations.

Enabling the availability and enhancing the accessibility of electronic health data are not measures that need to be done at all costs. The European approach can be contrasted with that of other major market actors, such as China and the US. As emphasised in the European Strategy for Data, China combines government surveillance over massive amounts of data with strong control of Big Tech companies without providing sufficient safeguards for individuals.

In the US, on the other hand, the organisation of the data space is generally left to the private sector, with considerable concentration effects.[10] In contrast, in the EU, the ambition is to further digitalisation in the health data sector, just as in other sectors too, in what the European Commission calls 'a European way'.[11] This should be a manner that is anchored in European values, rights, and principles. Among the central facets is the balance between privacy protection and market objectives, as well as empowerment through data rights.[12] While it is clear that the data of individuals are essential for the mechanism to function, enable rapid reactions and informed policy choices to public health challenges, and further research, development, and innovation, among others, enabling and enhancing availability have to be done in a way that is respectful to individuals. Values, principles, and rights that are at the core of the EU legal order are a point of departure for the field of EHD governance. How they are balanced against each other and what expressions they take in the EHDS are a result of different factors and considerations, including difficult policy choices and priorities, and trade-offs made in the legislative process to achieve pressing Union objectives.

When it comes concretely to individuals and their rights set out in the EHDS, the GDPR and the fragmented approach to health data governance at the national level are the points of departure. Examples include challenges in realising the rights set out in the GDPR,[13] as well as differing levels of digitalisation and diverse approaches to covering the content requirements for electronic health data. The EHDS enhances the GDPR data subject's rights in the context of electronic health data and at times goes beyond that. It accounts for other data-related questions, such as the role and scope of an individual's autonomy regarding diverse processing aspects in primary use, the control of data in regard to secondary use, and the balance between self-determination and public interest in the primary and secondary use contexts. These questions are related to informational self-determination, but simultaneously, they have implications for public health and human rights. Matters that previously have commonly been regulated by national legal orders and have been the objects of interest of different human rights actors, including the Council of Europe[14] and UNESCO,[15] are now part of the market and data policy of the EU too.

Content-wise, the EHDS is made from scratch, with some previous workpieces created under the existing EU legal frameworks. They include, for example, the eHealth framework and the voluntary cooperation mechanism under the Patients' Rights Directive, and the previously existing MyHealth@EU platform, as well as eHealth network guidelines.[16] Moreover, the EHDS relates to a number of other existing and emerging legal solutions, for example, in the data field, medical devices, AI, and cybersecurity governance.[17]

The EU's approach to EHD governance inevitably furthers the EU as a health actor. It plays out in the relationship and the balance of powers between the EU and the member states, as well as between the member states and the EU jointly vis-à-vis other actors in the public health arena, including the prominent global public health actor, the World Health Organization. The COVID-19 pandemic clearly showed the need for greater regional leadership in the arena and the need for strong global actions. The EHDS, through the policies it pursues, is inevitably a piece in the larger puzzle of (public) health governance set out in the central policy documents, such as the European Health Union[18] and EU Global Health Strategy.[19]

1.2.2 Legal basis

The EU's ambitions in the field of electronic health data realised through the EHDS rest on a dual legal basis – the internal market under Article 114 and data protection under Article 16 Treaty on the Functioning of the European Union (TFEU). Once fully realised, the framework will considerably impact health policies, raising questions regarding the role of Article 168 TFEU – the public health provision in the treaty.[20] The questions that emerge are diverse, including the impact on public health and whether it is a necessity to invoke Article 168 TFEU as a legal basis in a manner comparable to the Patients' Rights Directive, or it is sufficient that a high level of health is considered under Article 114(3) TFEU, as well as the limits that are prescribed to EU action under the principle of conferral, and the competencies that remain with the member states.

The challenge of legal basis and a potential competence tension were spotted soon after the Commission launched the proposal to the EHDS in 2022.[21] While there were discussions regarding whether Article 168 TFEU – the public health basis – should be included as a legal basis,[22] that did not result in action from the Council and the Parliament. On the surface, of course, questions remain about the extent to which market and data policies may justify interferences with public health governance, in which, save for explicit cases prescribed in Article 168(4) TFEU, the EU enjoys only supportive, coordination and supplementing competence. Arguably, a central highlight in this is Article 168(7), which states that 'Union action shall respect the responsibilities of the Member States for the definition of their health policy and for the organisation and delivery of health services and medical care'. The current approach implies that digitalisation of health data is considerably excluded from the scope of member states' responsibilities in defining health policy and delivering the medical services and care that the EU committed to respect.

Arguments in defence of the EU's policy can be anchored in the case law of the Court of Justice of the European Union (CJEU) that legitimises the EU's approach of legislating through the back doors.[23] For example, once it is established that the conditions for legislating under Article 114 TFEU are met, the EU is not prevented from pursuing policies, including in those areas in which the EU does not enjoy legislative competence.[24] The same argument could be made about data protection and responsible governance of health data under Article 16 TFEU. This could justify the legislature's approach and would not sit at odds with the view pursued in the scholarship regarding the web of competencies to regulate health.[25] Thus, in the same way as in the earlier days of

EU law when the free movement of goods and services encroached on Article 168(7) TFEU, requiring a rethink of the remaining member state competence in the field, now it is the turn of digitalisation through data and market doors to push this rethink. Nonetheless, two notes need to be made. First, directive 2011/24 remains a black swan in the health policy lake. Since then, the EU legislature does not seem to have repeated legislating under Article 168 TFEU in the same way. Second, it is difficult to see the rationale behind the non-involvement of Article 168, other than policy-motivated, sending a clear signal regarding how far the EU legislature may – and gets support to – go, and how much – or little – the member states are ready to accept.

1.3 EHDS in a nutshell

The EHDS is centred around EHD, as a point of departure, adhering to the definitions provided in the GDPR on health data and genetic data.[26] It distinguishes between personal electronic health data – health and genetic data as defined in the GDPR when processed in an electronic form – and non-personal electronic health data. The category of non-personal electronic health data encompasses two further categories. First is electronic health data other than personal electronic health data, e.g., anonymised data. Second is data that has never related to a data subject.[27] However, where the borders between personal and non-personal electronic health data lie is not necessarily easy to draw in light of post-Breyer case law.[28]

To steer the generation and movement of these data, the EHDS sets up a primary use mechanism – namely, the storage of electronic health data obtained from various sources to provide healthcare to a patient – as well as a secondary use mechanism – the use of electronic health data for a number of objectives anchored in the common good. These two then form central pillars of the EHDS, and in order to ensure their functioning, rules, common standards and practices, infrastructures, and a governance framework are prescribed.[29]

In the primary use mechanism, patients are given a set of rights in regard to the control over and use of their electronic health data. Healthcare actors are prescribed a number of obligations so that the patients can enjoy their rights. Moreover, technical and administrative solutions are prescribed. These include a technical platform and designation of a Digital Health Authority – or authorities, should a member state choose to have more than one.[30] Interestingly, the Digital Health Authority is assigned to carry out a range of tasks, including dealing with complaints from individuals, but the general Data Protection Authorities remain competent for those rights that build on the GDPR.[31] In practice, this means that the two will co-exist and collaborate tightly. As the EHDS primary-use mechanism builds on the GDPR rights, difficult questions could emerge regarding the split of competences.

The primary use mechanism focuses on EHR. Moreover, the realisation of patient empowerment by adding information to electronic health records is linked to wellness applications. Those, too, are potentially valuable sources of data for secondary use. Therefore, the EHR systems intended for the primary use of priority categories of electronic health data are subjected to interoperability requirements.[32] The aim is to ensure compliance with the requirements set out in the EHDS so that the systems fully support the EHDS ambitions. Wellness applications, on the other hand, are subjected to voluntary requirements. They apply – as envisioned by the Commission – if manufacturers claim interoperability of an EHR system.[33]

The secondary use mechanism is designed with the goal of enabling accessing electronic health data for a range of purposes in connection to a potential societal benefit. The EHDS prescribes categories of electronic health data subject to secondary uses and lists permitted as well as prohibited uses. Generally, access is to be ensured by national authorities in their function as health data access bodies, and a function is assigned to trusted health bodies too.[34] Health data access bodies, in turn, have a multitiered close collaboration with data holders to enable data sharing. This includes providing information on datasets, as well as ensuring access to the requested datasets through a secure processing environment.

For the secondary use mechanism to function, the EHDS establishes administrative tools and mechanisms, procedural rules, and technical solutions so that the secondary use of electronic health data can take place. These include such administrative tools as a health data access application, a data permit, and a health data request. Each member state shall establish (at least) one national health data access body responsible for granting access to electronic health data for secondary use, the ability to establish various trusted data holders, and a technical solution, HealthData@EU. It also prescribes procedures for granting a data permit in a rather elaborate way,[35] powers to set out conditions for the data user,[36] as well as timelines and sanctions.[37]

The EHDS does not stop here. For the EHDS to function fully, a European governance and coordination mechanism is set up. In that, the European Health Data Space Board is central. In its structure and tasks, it resembles the European Data Protection Board, with a range of tasks and administrative tools to ensure the effective functioning of the EHDS.[38] Moreover, in order to facilitate the exchange of information and promote cooperation with stakeholders in relation to the implementation of the EHDS, a stakeholder forum is established.[39] To ensure adequate development and functioning of the technical platforms, the Steering Groups for the infrastructures MyHealth@EU and HealthData@EU are created.[40] Finally, the European Commission assumes several roles and responsibilities so that the EHDS is fully operational.[41]

1.4 Legislative process, key battles, and compromise

1.4.1 Some remarks on the legislative process

The EHDS has been subject to significant transformations during the legislative process. The adopted EHDS rests on the central pillars set by the European Commission, namely, the primary and secondary use of electronic health data, the involvement of market players in order to provide the infrastructure for EHRs, as well as the technical, administrative, and procedural setup for the EHDS to function. The specifics of how these mechanisms should function have been subject to intense discussions during the legislative process, and – at times – their outcomes differ significantly from what the Commission had envisaged.

By way of illustration, some central battles of relevance to issues covered in this volume are introduced. These are discussed further in later chapters.

1.4.2 Battles and compromise on the rights and obligations in primary use

A central question cutting across the primary use mechanism has been the scope of patient autonomy in connection to EHR, and the implications that different regulatory choices suggested by the Commission bring along, including for patient safety and healthcare professionals' responsibility and liability.[42] This concerns, for example, a proposal for patients to be able to restrict access to information without medical professionals knowing that such restrictions exist, as well as patients being empowered to insert information into their medical records without clearly marking it.[43] A natural implication of this is a question about the competences of the EU and the extent to which such significant healthcare questions should be regulated through data protection and the internal market legal basis.

In relation to considerations such as these, one central question was the scope of member state law to determine exceptions to the rights enshrined in Chapter II of the EHDS, in order to preserve the variety of approaches among member states. Across the EU, there are differences when it comes to medical ethics, such as the balance between autonomy and paternalism. This variety is better preserved in the final text, which also addresses many documented concerns, such as negative effects attributed to enhanced patient self-determination regarding their data. However, the offered solutions also carry the likelihood of fragmentation of the field.

1.4.3 Telemedicine – to be or not to be included in the primary-use mechanism?

Telemedicine has been on the EU regulatory agenda for a considerable time. Already in 2011, in the provisions of the EU Patient's Rights Directive, telemedicine was indicated as one way to provide cross-border healthcare services.[44] The European Commission had envisaged that not only should telemedicine be clearly defined but also that it would be placed under the primary use of electronic health data. After all, telemedicine, in its modern form, is an output of health digitalisation, and the provision of telemedicine services is intrinsically linked to the processing of health data in an electronic form. Substantively, however, the European Commission did not propose any revolution in the field. Minding the EU's limitations under Article 168(7) TFEU, it merely proposed that cross-border telemedicine services shall be accepted, should a member state accept telemedicine services. Where it does so, cross-border telemedicine shall be accepted under the same conditions.[45] From the free movement of services perspective, this was an affirmation of Decker/Kohl case law, albeit in the telemedicine context. Among others, stakeholders argued challenges from the point of view of the principle of conferral.[46]

In the final form of the EHDS, telemedicine is mentioned in its recitals. It now reiterates Article 168(7) TFEU and states:

> Member States are responsible for their health policy, in particular for the organisation and delivery of health services and medical care, including regulation of activities such as online pharmacies, telemedicine and other services that they provide and reimburse, in line with their national legislation. Different healthcare policies should not, however, constitute barriers to the free movement of electronic health data in the context of cross-border healthcare, including telemedicine, such as online pharmacy services.[47]

In the substantive provisions of the regulation, telemedicine is only named in Article 24, where the member states are allowed to provide supplementary services through the MyHealth@EU platform. The removal of telemedicine from the body text of the regulation does not present any substantial changes for the issue. If anything, it merely makes it strongly and clearly visible that telemedicine is part of medical services, and all relevant provisions apply to it as to any other type of medical service.

1.4.4 Wellness applications as a data source

The EU's aspiration to include wellness systems in the EHDS can be seen as a recognition of a transformational element of modern medicine. As put by Gilbert et al., the EHDS builds on the premise that 'health and data on health do not start at the clinic gate', and wellness data 'describes, in intricate detail, the health of individuals'. This contributes to the shifting of the centre of gravity 'away from the clinic perimeter and towards the sofa, the pocket, the wrist and the sensor skin patch of the citizen'. On the condition that 'acceptable and workable approaches are found to link this data to personal EHR data', not only can the understanding of medicine be increased but also the development of novel approaches for preventive and medical care, and enhanced public health and medical care delivery.[48] To support this transformation, wellness data have been included in the secondary use regime, and wellness application labelling and interoperability rules have been prescribed. In regard to this, the control of the wellness application user over their data can be said to be at the core of the issue, in particular, whether voluntary use of wellness applications should automatically lead to compulsory participation in the data sharing regime in the name of the common good. The final text of the EHDS has leaned towards responding to the calls for clarity[49] with other minor precisions.[50] Although the legislature has not exempted wellness data from the secondary use framework, it envisaged that it could be part of the opt-out regime.[51] Furthermore, data subjects must consent to wellness data being sent to their EHR,[52] though questions still remain regarding the adequacy of the existing consent models in respecting the rights and interest of the individuals.

1.4.5 The place and role of individuals in secondary use

The existing variety of approaches regarding how health data for secondary use are governed can hardly be seen as surprising in light of the established power allocation between the EU and the member states. In light of the right to private life, health data privacy opens up various avenues to access data on the condition that certain requirements are met. These then historically have offered various rules, and preconditions in safeguards for different situations. While, for example, public health policy and health system administration have commonly been outside the control of the data subject, participation in research – as set out in the Biomedicine Convention – has often been subject to, at least, a patient's opt-out.[53] The European Commission in its proposal for an EHDS sought to transform this and put an equation mark between various electronic health data uses set out in the EHDS, disregarding the previous approach and reasons for different rules in different situations. In response, the European Parliament proposed a right to opt out of processing for secondary use.[54] Meanwhile, an opt-in mechanism was envisaged for secondary use of selected categories of health data, namely genetic data, data from wellness apps, and EHR data, whereby individuals would have to give consent.[55] Such an approach would increase data subjects' control over research participation but could also undermine the diversity of the datasets. It would embody genetic exceptionalism. The final text provides for an opt-out to secondary use and allows member states to introduce stricter measures and safeguards for specific categories of data.[56] The proposed opt-out mechanism is expected to be limited to opting out from purposes rather than specific categories of data. In addition, overrides of opt-outs reserved for public sector bodies and for important reasons of public interest introduce another set of restrictions on opt-out mechanisms. All in all, a successful roll-out of opt-out systems will be heavily dependent on various factors, including establishing an easy and accessible system in a transparent data processing ecosystem.

1.4.6 Access by Big Tech

Concern surrounding industry access to health data has loomed large in the negotiations and analyses of the EHDS. The fear has been that EU lawmakers are opening the floodgates and providing Big Tech and pharmaceutical companies with access to precious, personal data with insufficient safeguards and limited obligations to ensure that benefits reach the individuals providing the data.[57] In addition, concerns have been raised over adopting a market economy of sensitive health data, which may not align with broader social values.[58] This may expand the reach of Big Tech into healthcare contrary to patients' interests and benefit companies with copious resources compared to public bodies and researchers. Of particular relevance is the wide number of purposes for which health data could be requested through health data access bodies as well as the data that must be made available for secondary use. While the final text refines these elements, as discussed in parts II and III of this book, it remains to be seen whether these safeguards will prove sufficient.

1.4.7 Intellectual property rights and protection of trade secrets

A novel facet of the EHDS is that it not only facilitates access to data for public and private bodies but also imposes obligations on these actors, categorising them as health data holders that must share data with Health Data Access Bodies (HDABs). This created push back from actors like EUCOPE (European Confederation of Pharmaceutical Entrepreneurs) who argued for sufficient safeguards for intellectual property rights and protection of trade secrets.[59] The EHDS proposal had been light on details as to the scope of these rights and did not provide explicit means for protecting such rights. The EHDS now contains Article 52 on intellectual property rights and trade secrets. While such data shall be made available for secondary use, health data holders can communicate to the health data access bodies that the data is protected by intellectual property or trade secrets and also justify the basis for specific protection. It is for the health data access bodies to take the appropriate and proportionate measures to protect these rights based on their determination. Furthermore, access to data may be conditional, such as requiring contractual arrangements to protect the data. Access must be refused, should granting access incur a serious risk of infringing these rights. The extent to which such claims will prove successful remains to be seen and will require HDABs to build competencies in these fields.

1.4.8 Fragmentation of secondary use: to overcome or to avoid it? The case of ethics

In recent decades, scientific research has been subject to ethics reviews by institutional or national ethics committees that are in charge of reviewing research protocols prior to the commencement of projects. In its proposal, the European Commission acknowledged that member states could regulate ethics and thus indicated the necessity to ensure compliance with such requirements. However, it failed to lift ethics up to the EU level, in a way comparable to the Clinical Trials Regulation.[60] As national legal orders generally tend to require ethics review for scientific research, one incidental effect was the risk of subjecting scientific research – a domain, where the trust of individuals is commonly high – to higher requirements than product development driven by market actors – a domain, where trust levels might not be comparable to that in scientific research. The insufficient attention to ethics and ethical principles in general in the early drafts of the EHDS raised many concerns. In particular, it has been argued that the EHDS was adopting a rather narrow approach to respecting the rights of individuals and limiting that to the protections offered by the anonymisation of health data.[61] In response, the final text has explicitly included the importance of adherence to ethical principles in several places, including Article 54(e). However, it did not proceed with including ethical review as a mandatory requirement for (personal) electronic health data access. By introducing some strengthening of research ethics, nonetheless, the EHDS does not reiterate what those ethical principles should be but leaves it to the existing ethical traditions and norms and recognises the existing ethical safeguards for research.

1.4.9 Responsibility and liability

Sanctions generally serve as compliance enhancers for prescribed responsibilities. It has been common in the EU legal order to set out that sanctions need to be effective, proportionate, and dissuasive. A significant change was introduced by the GDPR, which set forth clear and considerable sanctions. To further compliance within the secondary- use framework, the proposal included various forms of sanctions directed at data holders and users. In terms of penalties, it reverted to the pre-GDPR approach of instructing member states that '[t]he penalties shall be effective, proportionate and dissuasive'[62] and fines 'shall be transparent and proportionate'.[63] This approach, while mindful to the member state competencies, risked compromising trust in the EHDS secondary use framework. The final form of the EHDS contains significant changes. Administrative fines have become part of the EHDS identity, and this could be argued to have somewhat comparable preconditions for effective compliance to those set out in the GDPR and AI Act, for example.[64]

1.5 EHDS timeline for accommodation

The battles, such as those highlighted above, also provide insight into some of the transformations that can already be clearly seen on the horizon. While some are considerable in light of EU competencies, as exercised until the entry into force of the EHDS, others are minimal or may not result in any changes. To adjust to the transformations and to fully realise the EHDS' ambitions, considerable implementation times are provided for. Generally, the EHDS will not be applied until two years after the entry into force save where otherwise prescribed.[65] Many of the EHDS provisions, however, will not apply until four to six years later. It could be said that this is an acknowledgement of the transformative nature of the EHDS and the requirements it imposes on member states, in particular those with limited digitisation of healthcare and that currently lack (adequate) infrastructure for sharing of health data for secondary use. It is also necessary to give industry time to develop technical solutions.

The EHDS, throughout the implementation period and thereafter, will remain an evolving legal framework. With the powers vested in the Commission for adopting delegated and implementing acts, several dimensions of the EHDS are subject to further specification or change. Thus, it can be said that not only is it difficult to fully appraise the EHDS at present, but it is also a living legal framework. It can be expected to require continuous changes to keep achieving the overall EHDS ambition, and thus also close monitoring from the concerned parties and readiness for further adaptions.

1.6 This book

1.6.1 The aim

The aim of this edited volume is to capture the EHDS in the making and examine the regulatory and administrative transformations that the new ecosystem proposes. The book analyses the various stages of the EHDS' legislative journey from proposal to final text. As such, book captures the legal and policy aspirations for electronic health data governance, and more generally, the scope of ambition of the European Commission for using electronic health data as a means to achieve the aspirations set out in the European Strategy for Data. Thus, in addition to analysing the proposed phenomenon in the making and contributing to preparing the health domain for the transition, it also offers an insight for the other data spaces.

1.6.2 The structure and contributions

This book offers an analysis capturing the central dimensions of the EHDS. The first part focuses on the primary-use mechanism and data subject control over health data in the wellness context. Katharina Ó Cathaoir dives into the topic of 'The EHDS and electronic health records: GDPR+ or transforming patients' rights?' and examines the extent to which the EHDS transforms the rights of patients. Thereafter, Andelka M. Phillips examines 'The right to insert and add information to my health record – does my doctor need to know this?' She pursues a critical discussion of the right to insert information in an EHR by using data from direct-to-consumer genetic testing as a case study. Finally, in the chapter 'European Health Data Space: A breakthrough in user control over health data in wellness apps?', Petra Holmberg takes a deep dive into wellness applications and looks at the role of the wellness application user in relation to the data collected through the use of the application.

The second part focuses on secondary use and captures the questions of legal basis, confidentiality, and commercial uses as main elements. Daniela Spajić opens the section with her contribution, 'Transforming the secondary use of patient data in the European Health Data Space: A challenge for the patient's right to medical confidentiality?' She scrutinises how the secondary-use mechanism challenges one of the most fundamental milestones of the doctor patient relationship: confidentiality. Thereafter, Eila El Asry, Juli Mansnérus, and Sandra Liede contribute with an analysis on 'Striking the Balance: Genomic Data, Consent and Altruism in the European Health Data Space'. Following this, Patricia Cervera de la Cruz and Mahsa Shabani scrutinise fairness in their contribution 'Fair enough? Exploring the role of fairness in secondary uses of health data in the European Health Data Space'. Finally, Enrique Santamaría Echeverría concludes the section with an analysis of 'The European Health Data Space: A New Paradigm for Secondary Uses of Health Data for Scientific Research?'

The third part focuses on data governance through health data access bodies and adequate safeguards. Tjasa Petročnik begins the section with a contribution on the 'Secondary use of health data, public interest and the role of HDABs', focusing on the role of the EHDS in realising the data sharing objectives. Thereafter, in 'Administrative tools for balancing societal and individual interests – data protection safeguards and administrative, procedural guarantees in secondary use in the European Health Data Space', Jane Reichel takes a deep dive into the administrative mechanisms needed for secondary use. It is a well-established tradition to use safeguards when dealing with personal data, including special categories of data, like federated networks. The governance of federated networks under the EHDS and GDPR is examined by Magdalena Kogut-Czarkowska and Mahsa Shabani in the chapter 'Federated networks and secondary uses of health data – challenges in ensuring appropriate safeguards for sharing health data under the GDPR and EHDS'. Thereafter, in the chapter 'EHDS: Transforming the role of technological platforms for health data analysis', Hrefna D. Gunnarsdóttir offers a case study on how such safeguards, which gained a prominent position in the GDPR research regulatory framework, play out in the context of the EHDS.

The book concludes with a chapter summarising the findings of each chapter focusing on the theme of the EHDS' transformation of the various aspects of primary and secondary uses by Mahsa Shabani, Santa Slokenberga, and Katharina Ó Cathaoir.

Acknowledgements

Santa Slokenberga's work has been supported by WASP HS 'AI and Automated Systems and the Right to Health – Revisiting Law Accounting for the Exploitation of Users Preferences and Values', 2021–2025 and PROMOT – the project has received funding from the Canadian Institutes of Health Research (CIHR), and in partnership with L'Agence Nationale de la Recherche (France), Health Research Board (Dublin, Ireland), Instituto de Salud Carlos III (Spain), IRSC – IG, Swedish Research Council (Sweden), and Swiss National Science Foundation (Switzerland) – partners of the EJP RD, under grant agreement No. 02424 – 000. The EJP RD initiative has received funding from the European Union's Horizon 2020 research and innovation programme under grant agreement No. 825575.

The origins of this volume lie in a symposium on the regulation of health and genetic data that the editors organised in June 2023. The symposium was organised under the auspices of Nordic PerMed Law – a network aimed at improving knowledge and awareness among Nordic lawyers and legal academics on the legal implications of new medical technologies. We are grateful to the participants of the symposium, many of whom went on to become contributors to the book. We appreciate the invaluable work of the symposium's discussants who read and commented on draft papers, which later became chapters in this volume in some cases. Thank you to Sandra Friberg, Anna-Sara Lind, Ana Nordberg, and Kyle McKibbin.

Notes

1 Council of the European Union, 'Proposal for a Regulation on the European Health Data Space- Analysis of the final compromise text with a view to agreement' 2022/0140(COD) (hereinafter EHDS [compromise text]), art 1(1).

2 EHDS art 1(2).

3 See in that regard David Fåhraeus, Jane Reichel, Santa Slokenberga, 'The European Health Data Space: Challenges and Opportunities' (SIEPS, 2024) https://sieps.se/en/publications/2024/the-european-health-data-space/ accessed on 30 May 2024.

4 The initial aspiration was to build at least nine data spaces, see European Commission, 'A European strategy for data' (Communication) (2020) 66 final. For further insights on the data spaces, see European Commission, 'on Common European Data Spaces' (Commission staff working document) SWD (2022) 45 final. As of 2024, already 14 data spaces are envisaged, see 'Common European Data Spaces | Shaping Europe's Digital Future' https://digital-strategy.ec.europa.eu/en/policies/data-spaces accessed 1 June 2024.

5 A European strategy for data (n 4).

6 For a thorough insight, see the explanatory memorandum of the Commission's proposal to the EHDS, European Commission, 'Proposal for a regulation – The European Health Data Space' COM(2022) 197 final.

7 See, for example, David Peloquin and others, 'Disruptive and Avoidable: GDPR Challenges to Secondary Research Uses of Data' (2020) 28(6) *European Journal of Human Genetics* 697. Ciara Staunton, Santa Slokenberga and Deborah Mascalzoni, 'The GDPR and the Research Exemption: Considerations on the Necessary Safeguards for Research Biobanks' (2019) 27 *European Journal of Human Genetics* 1159.

8 Decision (EU) 2022/2481 of the European Parliament and of the Council of 14 December 2022 establishing the Digital Decade Policy Programme 2030 (Text with EEA relevance) PE/50/2022/REV/1 [2022] OJ L 323/4.

9 See further Daniela Spajić 'Transforming the secondary use of patient data in the European Health Data Space: A challenge for the patient's right to medical confidentiality?' in this volume.

10 A European strategy for data (n 4).
11 A European strategy for data (n 4).
12 A European strategy for data (n 4).
13 One such highlight is the CJEU ruling in the case of C-307/22 F*T (Copies du dossier médical)*, clarifying the data subject's rights regarding free access to the copy of the medical records. See C-307/22 *FT v DW* ECLI:EU:C:2023:811. 'Overview of the National Laws on Electronic Health Records in the EU Member States and Their Interaction with the Provision of Cross-Border eHealth Services. Final Report and Recommendations' https://health.ec.europa.eu/document/download/3eb04ec0-b1c3-4e01-8ffb-46765744c049_en?filename=laws_report_recommendations_en.pdf accessed 1 June 2024.
14 See, for example, Council of Europe, Convention for the Protection of Human Rights and of the Human Being with regard to the Application of Biology and Medicine (Convention on Human Rights and Biomedicine or the Oviedo Convention) European Treaty Series 164.
15 See, for example, UNESCO international declaration about human genetic data, UNESCO 2004.
16 Consolidated text: Commission Implementing Decision 2019/1765 of 22 October 2019 providing the rules for the establishment, the management and the functioning of the network of national authorities responsible for eHealth, and repealing Implementing Decision 2011/890/EU (notified under document C(2019) 7460) (Text with EEA relevance)Text with EEA relevance, ELI: http://data.europa.eu/eli/dec_impl/2019/1765/2020-07-17 accessed 1 June 2024.
17 See EHDS proposal (n 6).
18 European Commission 'The European Health Union: Acting Together for People's Health' (Communication) (2024) 206 final.
19 European Commission, 'EU Global Health Strategy Better Health for All in a Changing World' (Communication) 675 final.
20 See Consolidated version of the Treaty on the Functioning of the European Union [2012]OJ C 326/47.
21 See, for example, EDPB-EDPS, Joint Opinion 03/2022 on the Proposal for a Regulation on the European Health Data Space, adopted on 12 July 2022, para 14.
22 Johan van de Gronden and Marc Veenbrink, 'EHDS and Free Movement of Patients: What EU Intervention Is Needed?' (2024) 1 European Journal of Health Law 1.
23 See Bruno de Witte, 'Non-Market Values in Internak Market Kegislation' in Niamh Nic Shuibhne (ed), *Regulating the Internal Market* (Edward Elgar Publishing 2006).
24 See, for example, C-380/03 *Federal Republic of Germany v. European Parliament and Council of the European Union* ECLI:EU:C:2006:772, para 37 and case C-491/01 *The Queen v. Secretary of State for Health, ex parte British American Tobacco (Investments) Ltd and Imperial Tobacco Ltd* ECLI:EU:C:2002:741 para 61. Santa Slokenberga, *European Legal Perspectives on Health-Related Direct-to-Consumer Genetic Testing* (Jure 2016) 176.
25 Kai P. Purnhagen and others, 'More Competences Than You Knew? The Web of Health Competence for European Union Action in Response to the COVID-19 Outbreak' (2020) 11 *European Journal of Risk Regulation* 297.
26 EHDS art 2(2)(a).
27 EHDS art 2(2)(b).
28 See C-604/22 *IAB Europe v Gegevensbeschermingsautoriteit*, ECLI:EU:C:2024:214.
29 EHDS art 1.
30 EHDS art 19(1).
31 See EHDS art 21(1).
32 EHDS art 27(1).

33 See EHDS art 47(1).
34 See EHDS art 72.
35 EHDS art 68.
36 EHDS art 68.
37 EHDS art 68.
38 See EHDS arts 92 and 94.
39 EHDS art 93.
40 EHDS art 95.
41 EHDS art 96.
42 Standing Committee of European Doctors (CPME), Position on the European Health Data Space (October 2022).
43 See EHDS proposal arts 3(6) and 4(4). See also David Fåhraeus, Jane Reichel, Santa Slokenberga (n 3).
44 See Consolidated text: Directive 2011/24/EU of the European Parliament and of the Council of 9 March 2011 on the application of patients' rights in cross-border healthcare, ELI: http://data.europa.eu/eli/dir/2011/24/2014-01-01 accessed 1 June 2024, art 3(d) as well as art 7(7).
45 EHDS proposal art 8 'Where a Member State accepts the provision of telemedicine services, it shall, under the same conditions, accept the provision of the services of the same type by healthcare providers located in other Member States.'.
46 See, for example, Standing Committee of European Doctors (n 41).
47 EHDS recital 28.
48 Stephen Gilbert and others, 'Citizen Data Sovereignty Is Key to Wearables and Wellness Data Reuse for the Common Good' (2024) 7 npj Digital Medicine 1.
49 See, for example, Digital Europe, 'European Health Data Space (EHDS): key issues to address in trilogues' (2024) https://www.digitaleurope.org/resources/european-health-data-space-ehds-key-issues-to-address-in-trilogues/ 1 June 2024.
50 For a comprehensive insight, see Petra Holmberg'European Health Data Space: A breakthrough in user control over health data in wellness apps?' in this volume.
51 See EHDS art 71.
52 See EHDS art 48(2).
53 See Biomedicine Convention, art 22. See also Explanatory Report to the Convention for the protection of Human Rights and Dignity of the Human Being with regard to the Application of Biology and Medicine: Convention on Human Rights and Biomedicine para 137.
54 European Parliament, 'Amendments Adopted by the European Parliament on 13 December 2023 on the Proposal for a Regulation of the European Parliament and of the Council on the European Health Data Space (COM(2022)0197–C9-0167/2022–2022/0140(COD))1' art 33(5).
55 European Parliament, 'Amendments Adopted by the European Parliament on 13 December 2023 on the Proposal for a Regulation of the European Parliament and of the Council on the European Health Data Space (COM(2022)0197–C9-0167/2022–2022/0140(COD))1' art 33(5a).
56 EHDS art 71 and art 51(4), respectively.
57 For example, European Digital Rights, 'Make the European Health Data Space Serve Patients and Research' (2023) https://edri.org/wp-content/uploads/2023/03/EHDS-EDRi-position-final.pdf accessed 31 May 2024.
58 Luca Marelli and others, 'The European Health Data Space: Too Big to Succeed?' (2023) 135 *Health Policy* 104861.
59 The European Health Data Space: Common statement on the Amendment proposals of the Council of the EU and the European Parliament (EUCOPE in partnership with Hogan Lovells LLP, December 2023).
60 See Santa Slokenberga, 'Scientific Research Regime 2.0? Transformations of the GDPR Research Regime That the Proposed EHDS Regulation Promises to Bring Along' [2022] *Tech Reg*.

61 Ciara Staunton and others, 'Ethical and Social Reflections on the Proposed European Health Data Space' (2024) 32 *European Journal of Human Genetics* 498.
62 EHDS proposal art 69.
63 EHDS proposal art 43(5).
64 For insight into challenges, see Jane Reichel 'Administrative tools for balancing societal and individual interests – data protection safeguards and administrative procedural guarantees in secondary use in the European Health Data Space' in this volume.
65 EHDS art 105.

List of sources

Treaties, legislative acts, conventions and declarations

Consolidated version of the Treaty on the Functioning of the European Union [2012] OJ C 326/47.
Consolidated text: Commission Implementing Decision 2019/1765 of 22 October 2019 providing the rules for the establishment, the management and the functioning of the network of national authorities responsible for eHealth, and repealing Implementing Decision 2011/890/EU (notified under document C(2019) 7460) (Text with EEA relevance) Text with EEA relevance, ELI: http://data.europa.eu/eli/dec_impl/2019/1765/2020-07-17 accessed 1 June 2024.
Consolidated text: Directive 2011/24/EU of the European Parliament and of the Council of 9 March 2011 on the application of patients' rights in cross-border healthcare, ELI: http://data.europa.eu/eli/dir/2011/24/2014-01-01 accessed 1 June 2024.
Council of Europe, Convention for the Protection of Human Rights and of the Human Being with regard to the Application of Biology and Medicine (Convention on Human Rights and Biomedicine or the Oviedo Convention) European Treaty Series 164.
Explanatory Report to the Convention for the protection of Human Rights and Dignity of the Human Being with regard to the Application of Biology and Medicine: Convention on Human Rights and Biomedicine.
Decision (EU) 2022/2481 of the European Parliament and of the Council of 14 December 2022 establishing the Digital Decade Policy Programme 2030 (Text with EEA relevance) PE/50/2022/REV/1 [2022] OJ L 323/ 4.
UNESCO international declaration about human genetic data, UNESCO 2004.

Official documents and other Policy Documents

Council of the European Union, 'Proposal for a Regulation on the European Health Data Space- Analysis of the final compromise text with a view to agreement' 2022/0140(COD).
European Commission, 'The European Health Union: Acting Together for People's Health' (Communication) (2024) 206 final.
European Commission, 'A European strategy for data' (Communication) (2020) 66 final.
European Commission, 'on Common European Data Spaces' (Commission staff working document) SWD(2022) 45 final.
European Commission, 'Proposal for a regulation – The European Health Data Space' COM(2022) 197 final.
European Commission, 'EU Global Health Strategy Better Health for All in a Changing World' (Communication) 675 final.
European Commission, 'Common European Data Spaces | Shaping Europe's Digital Future' https://digital-strategy.ec.europa.eu/en/policies/data-spaces accessed 1 June 2024

European Parliament, 'Amendments Adopted by the European Parliament on 13 December 2023 on the Proposal for a Regulation of the European Parliament and of the Council on the European Health Data Space (COM(2022)0197–C9-0167/2022–2022/0140(COD))1.'

EDPB-EDPS, Joint Opinion 03/2022 on the Proposal for a Regulation on the European Health Data Space, adopted on 12 July 2022.

Other secondary sources

de Witte B, 'Non-Market Values in Internak Market Kegislation' in Niamh Nic Shuibhne (ed), *Regulating the Internal Market* (Edward Elgar Publishing 2006).

Digital Europe, 'European Health Data Space (EHDS): Key issues to address in trilogues' (2024) https://www.digitaleurope.org/resources/european-health-data-space-ehds-key-issues-to-address-in-trilogues/ accessed 1 June 2024.

European Digital Rights, 'Make the European Health Data Space serve patients and research' (2023). https://edri.org/wp-content/uploads/2023/03/EHDS-EDRi-position-final.pdf accessed 31 May 2024.

Fåhraeus F, Reichel J, Slokenberga S, 'The European Health Data Space: Challenges and Opportunities' (SIEPS, 2024) https://sieps.se/en/publications/2024/the-european-health-data-space/ accessed 30 May 2024.

Gilbert S and others, 'Citizen Data Sovereignty Is Key to Wearables and Wellness Data Reuse for the Common Good' (2024) 7 *NPJ Digital Medicine* 1. DOI 10.1038/s41746-024-01004-z.

Marelli L and others, 'The European Health Data Space: Too Big to Succeed?' (2023) 135 *Health Policy* 104861. DOI 10.1016/j.healthpol.2023.104861.

Overview of the National Laws on Electronic Health Records in the EU Member States and Their Interaction with the Provision of Cross-Border eHealth Services. Final Report and Recommendations'. https://health.ec.europa.eu/document/download/3eb04ec0-b1c3-4e01-8ffb-46765744c049_en?filename=laws_report_recommendations_en.pdf accessed 1 June 2024.

Peloquin D and others, 'Disruptive and Avoidable: GDPR Challenges to Secondary Research Uses of Data' (2020) 28(6) *European Journal of Human Genetics* 697.

Purnhagen K P and others, 'More Competences than You Knew? The Web of Health Competence for European Union Action in Response to the COVID-19 Outbreak' (2020) 11 *European Journal of Risk Regulation* 297. DOI 10.1017/err.2020.35

Slokenberga S, *European Legal Perspectives on Health-Related Direct-to-Consumer Genetic Testing* (Jure 2016).

Slokenberga S, 'Scientific Research Regime 2.0? Transformations of the GDPR Research Regime That the Proposed EHDS Regulation Promises to Bring Along' (2022) *Tech Reg*. DOI 10.26116/techreg.2022.014.

Staunton C and others, 'Ethical and Social Reflections on the Proposed European Health Data Space' (2024) 32 *European Journal of Human Genetics* 498. DOI 10.1038/s41431-024-01543-9

Staunton C, Slokenberga S and Mascalzoni D, 'The GDPR and the Research Exemption: Considerations on the Necessary Safeguards for Research Biobanks' (2019) 27 *European Journal of Human Genetics* 1159. DOI 10.1038/s41431-019-0386-5

The European Health Data Space: Common statement on the Amendment proposals of the Council of the EU and the European Parliament (EUCOPE in partnership with Hogan Lovells LLP, December 2023).

van de Gronden J, Veenbrink M, 'EHDS and Free Movement of Patients: What EU Intervention Is Needed?' (2024) 1 European Journal of Health Law 1. DOI 10.1163/15718093-bja10125

Case Law

C-491/01 *The Queen v. Secretary of State for Health, ex parte British American Tobacco (Investments) Ltd and Imperial Tobacco Ltd* ECLI:EU:C:2002:741.
C-380/03 *Federal Republic of Germany v. European Parliament and Council of the European Union* ECLI:EU:C:2006:772.
C-307/22 *FT v DW* ECLI:EU:C:2023:811.
C-604/22 *IAB Europe v Gegevensbeschermingsautoriteit* ECLI:EU:C:2024:214.

2 The EHDS and Electronic Health Records

GDPR+ or Transforming Patients' Rights?

Katharina Ó Cathaoir

2.1 Introduction

Record keeping is an essential aspect of healthcare, which can serve multiple aims. It can support the provision of safe and efficient healthcare through facilitating communication between healthcare workers. For patients, records can enable them to understand and monitor their health. Effective use of health records avoids unnecessary duplication of examinations and tests, thereby saving resources and supporting patient well-being. As healthcare systems have become increasingly digitised, in some member states, electronic health records (EHRs) are now the norm. Under perfect conditions, healthcare records are no longer locked in cabinets and can be easily and safely accessed by healthcare workers and patients alike using secure digital platforms.

Chapter III of the General Data Protection Regulation (GDPR) provides for a catalogue of rights of relevance to EHR but assessments have shown that patients struggle to exercise these rights in the healthcare context,[1] as also described in the 2023 Court of Justice judgement, *FT v DW*.[2] Differences in how the GDPR has been implemented across the Union in healthcare have resulted in legal fragmentation in this sphere with implications for patients' rights over their data.[3] Progress is unevenly distributed among member states (MSs).[4] While in some MSs, patients can easily access their electronic health data (EHD), in others, healthcare data is not stored electronically nor is there an available platform that allows the citizen to safely access their information. National law often provides limited patient access to healthcare data, and exercising control over such data can be burdensome.[5] Furthermore, even where electronic infrastructure is in place, this is often not interoperable, even within member states. This means that EHD does not straightforwardly flow between providers inside and outside the state, inhibiting patient choice and slowing treatment.

In light of these barriers, the European Health Data Space (EHDS) aims to revolutionise individuals' access to and control over their EHD. The Regulation supports the European Commission's ambitious vision to grant all European Union (EU) residents access to their EHR by 2030.[6] It concretises the rights provided for under the GDPR and transforms the voluntary provisions in Article 14 of the Patients' Rights Directive[7] into binding obligations across the Union.

DOI: 10.4324/9781003544111-3

The aim of this chapter is to analyse the extent to which the EHDS transforms patients' rights, specifically their control over electronic health records. It focuses on Chapter II of the EHDS which provides for new rights and obligations related to access to and transmission of personal EHD for primary use. The chapter also draws on examples from Danish legislation to illustrate how the rights proposed in the EHDS may function in practice. The member state position is important as the relevant provisions of the EHDS will need to be implemented at the domestic level and, due to the differences among member states, will have varied implications. Denmark is used as a case study as a 2023 report prepared for the Commission on e-health indicators identified the country as a best practice example.[8] As will be highlighted, in Denmark, there is also an ongoing political backlash against documentation, which is used to nuance some of the praise surrounding its digitisation of health records. It is submitted that it will be helpful for member states to assess the relevance of such considerations for their implementation of EHR. Reference to other member states' legislation is included, though this analysis primarily relies on a report published in 2014 prepared for the Consumers, Health and Food Executive Agency (Chafea) under the mandate of the European Commission.[9] The report is, where possible, cross-referenced with the 2023 study.[10] Thus, the scope of this chapter is not to lay out member state law in detail but to provide reflections on key challenges for implementation based on selected past experiences.

The next section introduces electronic healthcare records, including the central challenges facing the Union and member states and the proposed exchange format. Following this, the duty to record health data electronically under the EHDS is explained. The subsequent section compares the rights included in the EHDS with the rights already provided for under the GDPR. Finally, the chapter concludes by assessing the transformative potential of the EHDS.

2.2 Electronic Health Records in EU: From Voluntary Measures to Binding Obligations

Prior to the EHDS, the legal position was that Directive 2011/24/EU on the application of patients' rights in cross-border healthcare placed an obligation on the Union to support and facilitate cooperation and exchange of information among member states within a voluntary network connecting authorities responsible for ehealth.[11] Subsequent to this provision, several member states took part in the eHealth Digital Services Infrastructure, which allows for cross-border exchange of eprescriptions.[12] The eHealth network has issued several guidelines on interoperability of certain categories of health data, such as the patient summary.[13]

Successive reports conclude that this voluntary approach has proven unsuccessful.[14] Currently, only nine member states use MyHealth@EU for cross-border healthcare, specifically for eprescriptions and patient summaries.[15] In a 2019 recommendation on a European Electronic Health Record exchange format, the Commission highlighted that EHR information systems used across the Union are incompatible.[16]

The EHDS marks a shift in the EU's strategy in the field of electronic health records from merely encouraging harmonisation to mandating it. The Commission is now under an obligation to establish MyHealth@EU as an interoperability platform for digital health.[17] The platform will provide services to support and facilitate the exchange of personal health data between national contact points for digital health. A national contact point will be designated by each member state, and these shall enable the exchange of EHD based on the now-mandatory European exchange format. Supplementary cross-border digital health services and infrastructures may be provided for by member states.[18]

Key to these obligations is how electronic health records are defined, as this has important ramifications for what data healthcare workers must record and to what information patients have a right of access. The EHDS describes EHR as 'a collection of electronic health data related to a natural person and collected in the health system, processed for the purpose of the provision of healthcare' (Article 2(2)(j)). Meanwhile, recital 7 further describes EHRs as 'typically contain[ing] a natural person's medical history, diagnoses and treatment, medications, allergies, and vaccinations, as well as radiology images and laboratory results, spread between different actors in the health system, such as general practitioners, hospitals, pharmacies or care services'. Note that there is somewhat of a disconnect between these two descriptors, with the former focused on the health system and provision of healthcare, while the latter is wider, stretching to entities like pharmacies and care services, which are not necessarily traditionally considered as part of the health system.

While the above descriptors mention a wide range of data, the EHDS does not currently create *obligations* on providers to record and grant access to *all* of these data types. Instead, certain categories of heath data should be prioritised. Mirroring the 2019 Commission Recommendation, the priority categories listed in Article 14(1) are patient summary, electronic prescription and dispensations, medical imaging studies and related imagining reports, medical test results, including laboratory and other diagnostic results and related reports, and hospital discharge reports. The characteristics of these categories are described in Annex I of the EHDS, which the Commission is empowered to amend subject to criteria specified in Article 14(2). Member states may provide for access and exchange of further categories of EHD under national law. The EHDS thereby seeks to establish a middle ground, designed to fit both the least and most digitised member states. This position however carries a risk of fragmentation.

Based on the e-health indicators study, some states do not provide access to even the priority categories at present. The study found that eprescription and edispensation data are the most widely accessible and frequently updated health data categories to which patients have access (75% of member states provide access). Meanwhile, most member states provided online access to personal information, dates of procedures and operations, and current and past medicines. The least accessible category was electronic results and reports.[19] Medical images were only available online in a quarter of member states.[20] This suggests that for many member states, the provisions, described in the coming sections of this chapter, will mark a significant transformation in terms of access to electronic healthcare data.

Central to the EHDS is that priority categories of EHD must be issued in the European electronic health record exchange format, the technical specifications of which the Commission must lay down (Article 15(1)). The format should be: 'commonly used, machine-readable and allow transmission ... between different software applications, devices and providers'. Chapter III sets out the requirements for EHR systems, such as the declaration of conformity, CE marking and documentation requirements. In summary, the EHDS seeks to ensure that member states and the Commission put conditions in place that allow for patient information to cross boundaries seamlessly. Interoperability is crucial for guaranteeing that the data subject can make effective use of their rights of access, portability, etc. As the voluntary approach has been unsuccessful, the Regulation will, in the future, place binding obligations on manufacturers and providers.

It is imperative in light of the EU and member states' human rights obligations that the proposed benefits of EHR are enjoyed equally. On the one hand, digitisation has the potential to support citizens in attaining the right to the highest attainable standard of health. Recital 9 EHDS recognises, for example, that paper records can inhibit access to timely care. Digital health records give patients the opportunity to check that they have correctly understood a conversation with a doctor and monitor their health, through for example reviewing how their blood pressure or blood tests change over time. For example, for people who are hearing or memory impaired, easy access to medical records can facilitate inclusion.

On the other hand, there are also risks that digital transformation leaves some groups behind. Electronic health systems must therefore be developed in an inclusive manner to ensure that they benefit all citizens. This is confirmed in Directive (EU) 2016/2102 (Web Accessibility Directive). The final text includes greater references to accessibility and persons with disabilities than the Proposal, which is welcomed. A concrete step is the inclusion of a provision requiring member states to promote and support digital literacy.[21] However, key concerns remain such as digital access.

2.3 The Duty to Register Health Data in an EHR and Patients' Rights

Article 13 of the EHDS imposes an obligation on member states to ensure that health professionals register at least priority categories of health data in electronic format in an EHR system. The obligation to record only relates to the provision of healthcare, not social care, for example. There is thereby a risk that parallel systems of health records will be in place, which could create extra burdens for healthcare workers, confusion and maintain data siloes.

It remains to be seen how member states will construct this obligation in national law. In some jurisdictions, medical records are understood as forming part of the healthcare worker's professional duties. For example, Danish legislation places authorised healthcare workers, such as doctors and nurses, under an obligation to keep patient records.[22] Information on investigations and treatments carried out on a patient must be recorded.[23] This includes notes on the patient's condition and planned or carried out treatments.[24] The stated aim of record keeping is to record information that is necessary for good quality and safe treatment.[25] EHR is further explained as a 'work tool' for healthcare workers that should be constructed in a manner that enables the healthcare worker to grasp the patient's condition and planned treatments.[26] This physician-oriented standard differs from member states that require that specific categories of information must be included.[27] This approach is found in inter alia Latvian law,[28] which is more akin to the approach chosen for the EHDS.

Where the healthcare record is part of the healthcare worker's professional obligations, it is the latter, not the patient, who determines the information that must be recorded. Under Danish law, the healthcare worker decides which information must be regarded as 'necessary' based on the concrete situation.[29] As will be discussed below, understanding patient records as a professional responsibility can place limitations on patients' rights to control the information contained therein. Furthermore, when patients gain automatic access to their records, healthcare professionals may adapt the type of information that they record.[30]

2.3.1 Opting Out of EHR Under the EHDS

During the negotiation of the EHDS, a question has been how the Regulation should construct the tension between self-determination and patient safety/professional interests. The position taken in the Proposal was that citizens could restrict access to their EHR but not refuse to take part in the infrastructure. In Denmark, healthcare information is generally not stored in the patient record based on patient consent but based on GDPR articles 6(1)(e) and 9(2)(h).[31] In this manner, the GDPR can be considered to place limitations on the citizen's right to private life which can be justified as necessary to ensure that adequate healthcare can be provided. A healthcare worker may consider that it is unsafe to treat a patient whose medical history they are not aware of. This position can be criticised for forcing patients to take part in digitisation, and thereby the processing of sensitive personal data when they can adequately recall such information. This can be of particular concern for citizens in countries like Denmark that allow for secondary use of healthcare data, including data in patient records, without the individual's consent or the ability to opt-out.[32] This scenario is contrary to the promises of control forged in the EHDS.

The final EHDS allows member states to adopt rules establishing a right for individuals to object to access to EHD by anyone except the original data controller. If the member state makes use of this legal basis and the patient in turn opts out, the patient will not be able to use the health data services and MyHealth@EU established under the EHDS. However, the patient's treatment will continue to be documented, and the provider will have access. This provision thereby represents an opt-out, not an opt-in. As of 2014, both models were found in EU member states, meaning that this will prompt changes in states like Germany.[33]

It is also for the member states to determine whether the right to object to registration of data should be absolute or subject to an emergency override. The question of how patients should be informed prior to the creation of an EHR also seems to have been left up to states to determine (following information requirements of the GDPR, they should be informed of the processing of their sensitive personal data in any event). Member states must also establish adequate safeguards should they provide for the right to object.

Recital 10 also mentions that member states can put restrictions in place on the initial registration of EHD, such as requiring consent to register genetic data. It can be questioned whether consent is the correct legal basis in this case (if this is what the recital is inferring) given that the citizen will suffer a detriment (i.e., not being able to use the EHR infrastructure) should they refuse consent. These provisions appear to have been necessary to reach an agreement but create a risk of fragmentation across the Union. Wellness applications are another area where patients can exercise control over their health record as such data can only be transmitted to the patient's EHR with their consent (Article 48(2)).

2.3.2 Risks to Patient Rights

It is furthermore important to reflect on not only the positive transformations that mandatory EHRs offer but also the negative implications for patient safety. For example, in Denmark, patients have been given the wrong medicine doses due to problems with the software, resulting in injuries and deaths.[34] The Danish Data Protection Authority has also seriously criticised a healthcare region for data breaches in its EHR system.[35] Thus, with even the most digitised member state in the Union struggling to bring an EHR system in line with the GDPR, concerns may be raised regarding the prospect of the EHDS to guarantee that patient data is stored safely.

Scholars have also noted that by making EHR mandatory, vital public functions become dependent on Big Tech and its infrastructure.[36] These systems can eat up substantial healthcare resources and may not be fit for purpose. In the Danish case, the leading US software for EHR, Epic, was installed in several healthcare regions. The system has been seriously criticised, including because it was developed with the US healthcare system in mind, based on billing and not a tax-financed public system.[37]

Generally, in Denmark, there has been significant backlash against documentation among healthcare workers and politicians. The arguments include that there is a lack of time to document, the systems are difficult to use, and that documentation takes time away from patient care and is arduous, especially for healthcare workers working in their non-native language.[38] Criticisms have led to populist initiatives by the government to 'reduce bureaucracy' and 'release' professionals from documentation requirements.[39] Furthermore, implementing new EHR systems can be time-consuming and challenging.[40] EHR can cause frustration among doctors.[41] It is vital that healthcare workers are provided with adequate training and assistance in digital transitions. For example, an audit ordered by the Danish state auditor found that the introduction of the new e-health platform in several healthcare regions was carried out without adequate training and testing.[42]

Reflecting on and developing mitigation strategies for these risks may be instructive for other less-digitised states when undertaking the transformation required by the EHDS. In this regard, it is positive that the final text includes obligations in relation to upskilling for health professionals that were not present in the Proposal. Following Article 83, states are under an obligation to develop and implement or provide access to training programmes for health professionals on their obligations to register health data.

Finally, the thorny question of language must be mentioned, namely in what language patient information across borders should be recorded. According to the Ehealth Network patient summary guidelines, the summary should be recorded in the local language and then translated to the language of the receiving country.[43] If healthcare providers are obligated to accept data from other member states, how can they guarantee that they adequately grasp the context and instructions? This raises questions regarding the importance of obtaining faithful translations to avoid risks to patient safety and whether AI is equipped to meet this need.

2.4 Rights Under the EHDS

Moving to the rights provided for in the EHDS, these build on and concretise rights contained in the GDPR. The EHDS rights are described in this section and, where relevant, compared to the protection already afforded to data subjects under the GDPR.

2.4.1 Rights of Access to Health Records

The EHDS includes a right of access to health records, which is not new to European law but instead supports Article 8 ECHR,[44] Article 15 GDPR and Article 9 of the Council of Europe Convention 108+ on Data Protection. The coming sections focus on Article 15 GDPR as it offers the most specificity.

2.4.1.1 Scope of Access Under EHDS and GDPR

The EHDS asserts a right of access to EHD without charge and in easily readable, 'consolidated and accessible format'.[45] Access should be provided immediately after registration, though the final text specifies 'respecting, technological practicability'. It remains to be seen whether some member states will interpret this room for manoeuvre in a manner that waters down the immediacy of the right. The right encompasses 'at least' priority categories of data. This open-ended phrasing means that the scope of the right may vary subject to member state law. Patients will furthermore have a right to download a free electronic copy of at least the priority categories of health data. This addition will hopefully improve information accessibility compared to the Proposal.

Meanwhile, Article 15 GDPR is wider in scope than the EHDS, comprising of three parts: confirmation of processing of personal data, access to personal data and access to information about the processing, including the presence of automated decision-making and profiling.[46] The controller is under an obligation to provide a copy of the personal data being processed, while any further copies may be subject to 'a reasonable fee based on administrative costs'. Meanwhile, it is not clear from the wording of the EHDS whether 'an electronic copy' should be understood as one copy or encompasses further copies. Following the GDPR, where the request is transmitted electronically, the information must be provided 'in a commonly used electronic form' (Article 15(3)). Access must be provided within one month of receipt of the request, though the period may be extended by two months where necessary (Article 12(3)). The EHDS thereby provides for faster access, and seemingly no charge may be levied for further copies. As outlined in recital 9 of the EHDS, Article 15 GDPR does not mandate electronic access unlike the EHDS. However, where a provider uses analogue records, the EHDS does not create obligations, meaning that patients would have to submit separate requests to gain access to all data relevant to their health, should paper records still be used alongside EHR.

Until the 2023 CJEU judgement *FT v DW*, the scope of Article 15 GDPR in the context of healthcare records was unclear.[47] The case relates to an individual who had requested access to their medical records related to dental care where they believed that errors had been made and wished to establish liability. The provider refused, arguing that the individual must cover the costs as provided for by the German Civil Code. The individual then initiated domestic proceedings against the provider. The patient's right of free access was upheld at first instance and on appeal. In the course of a further appeal, the German Federal Court of Justice referred several questions to the CJEU for a preliminary ruling on, inter alia, the charging system put in place by the member state prior to the entry into force of the GDPR and the scope of access to the patient's personal data.

The CJEU upheld that the first copy of the individual's personal data must be provided free of charge. A reasonable fee, attributable to administrative costs, may however be levied for further copies.[48] The Court recalled that the data subject does not have to give reasons for the data request. While the right to a first copy of one's records is not absolute and may be restricted following Article 15(4) and Article 23(1)(i),[49] the data provider cannot put in place a blanket fee requirement for the first copy merely to protect their economic interests.[50]

For our purposes, it is pertinent to note that the CJEU held that Article 15 includes access for patients to 'data concerning their health, for example the data in their medical records containing information such as diagnoses, examination results, assessments by treating physicians and any treatment or interventions provided'.[51] According to the CJEU, individuals should be 'given access to the data contained in their medical records as fully and precisely as possible, but also in a form which is intelligible'.[52] The Court continued that

> the provision of a simple summary or a compilation of those data by the medical practitioner, in order to present them in an aggregated form, could create the risk of some relevant data being omitted or incorrectly reproduced, or, in any event, of it being made harder for the patient to verify how accurate and exhaustive those data are and to understand those data.[53]

Thus, access to medical records following Article 15 must be 'a faithful and intelligible reproduction' of the data.

Based on the Court's judgement, depending on how access is framed in national law, the EHDS may not provide patients with access to more detailed health records than what is already provided for under this now-authoritative interpretation of the right to access under the GDPR. Where the EHDS is most significant therefore is by mandating that member states put in place infrastructure that enables patients to exercise their rights. This includes health data access services following Article 4 and a Digital Health Authority responsible for ensuring implementation of the rights and technical solutions following Article 19(2).

2.4.1.2 Proxy Services

Furthermore, the EHDS not only concerns access for the patient but also requires that member states put in place interoperable proxy services free of charge to enable guardians and other representatives to access the healthcare record of those they represent.[54] This will enable patients to provide a friend or relative with access to their record to support them in understanding their healthcare. For those without legal capacity, it could allow smoother access for those already supporting their healthcare in practice. The services must be easily accessible for persons with disabilities, vulnerable groups and persons with low digital literacy.

It is again up to member states to establish the contours of proxy services. This is sensible given the variations among the domestic laws of member states in relation to legal capacity and the age of consent. Access for representatives raises important questions regarding the balance between protection of patients with limited capacity from harm and patient privacy. Children have a right to private life under Article 8 of the European Convention on Human Rights and a right to privacy under Article 16 of the Convention on the Rights of the Child. It should be possible to restrict guardians' access to information if the patient's interest in protecting the confidentiality of such information outweighs the guardian's interest in accessing it, such as may be the case with information on abortion, sexual health or mental health. Likewise, adults with limited capacity or who require support in certain areas may wish to restrict access to certain types of information, and this must be possible. The author can also foresee situations where abusive partners/relatives may demand access as a form of coercive control, and it is therefore vital that access can be limited in a manner that does not alert the representative to the presence of confidential information.

2.4.1.3 Restrictions on the Right of Access

The right of access envisaged under the EHDS is subject to limitations. While the Proposal allowed for certain limitations, it did not refer to Article 23 GDPR, which is now mentioned in the final text. Following Article 23(1)(e), GDPR rights may be restricted by national law provided such restriction respects 'the essence of the fundamental rights and freedoms' and is a necessary and proportionate measure in a democratic society to safeguard, inter alia, other important objectives of general public interest, including public health, and the protection of the data subject or the rights and freedoms of others.

Following the EHDS, member states may restrict the scope of access to EHR 'in particular' when necessary for the protection of the natural person based on patient safety and ethics by delaying access for a limited time until a health professional can properly communicate and explain information that 'can have a significant impact' on the individual's health. Recital 10 EHDS describes how it could be unethical to inform a patient of an incurable diagnosis electronically and that it should therefore be possible to delay access to such data. As compared to the Proposal, the scope for restrictions of access is significantly widened through the addition of 'in particular' and reference to Article 23. Following Article 12(5) GDPR, requests may be refused where they are 'manifestly unfounded or excessive', which could fall under 'objectives of general public interest'. Yet again, the potential for fragmentation arises as the precise framing of possible restrictions is left to member states. Still, it seems wise that the scope of restrictions on rights of access now corresponds to the GDPR. Furthermore, what is judged as ethically acceptable likely differs among member states, and it may thereby be sensible to allow for differences to safeguard national medical norms.

The question therefore remains what the scope of such restrictions should be. The explanatory report to the Council of Europe Convention 108+ specifies that access to health data should be through a health professional 'when it is in the interest of the data subject, notably to help him/her understand the data or ensure that the data subject's psychological state is appropriately considered when imparting information – in line, of course, with deontological principles'.[55] The 1997 recommendation to the 1981 CoE Convention[56] recognised that access could be refused, limited or delayed if provided by law and subject to other specified criteria, including that the information is 'likely to cause serious harm to the data subject's health'.[57] It seems that several member states allow for access to health data to be restricted if the medical professional judges that access may cause harm.[58] For example, Latvian law allows for healthcare workers to not transmit information if they determine that it may threaten the life or health of the patient or other persons.[59] It is submitted that the scope of any permitted delays should be designed with patients' interests in mind, such as allowing the patient to determine whether they wish to access the information prior to seeing their healthcare professional. From a patients' rights perspective, it is positive that a paternalistic position on refusal of access has not been mandated.

In summary, while the right of access under the EHDS mirrors that which is provided for under the GDPR, it makes important advances in relation to cost (no provision is made for levying charges) and the immediacy of access. This is logical given that the EHDS will put in place the necessary infrastructure to facilitate immediate digital access. The scope of restrictions among member states is likely to vary based on traditions of domestic medical law, which may lead to fragmentation and hamper cross-border access. This again is to be expected due to the EU's limited competences within the field of healthcare.

2.4.2 Right to Rectification

Access and rectification are viewed as symbiotic in the EHDS, i.e., as per recital 13 access to electronic health records enables patients to identify incorrect data and request its correction. The EHDS requires that EHR services provide individuals with the ability to easily request rectification of their personal data online.

The Regulation now clearly specifies the duty bearers in response to a key criticism of the EDPB and EDPS that the EHDS proposal had failed to make clear who was under a duty to rectify patient data.[60] The final text also added that the service provider can check the validity of the rectification requested with a health professional. As the operative text does not specify an immediate obligation, it appears that the time limits provided for under the GDPR apply, i.e., without undue delay and within one month. However, recital 13 suggests that the obligation should be immediate and free of charge, as with the right of access. This, however, does not appear in the operative text, suggesting that it is aspirational.

As already described in the access section, all rights under the GDPR can be restricted following Article 23. In the case of health records, patient safety could be relied upon to justify restricting the right to rectification. For example, imagine a patient considered a description of their condition inaccurate while the treating healthcare worker found it to be valid. In such instances, it could be necessary and proportionate to refuse a request to rectify that involved deletion or supplementation of the information in order to safeguard the protection of the data subject.

A right of erasure, following Article 17(1) of the GPDR, is not envisaged in the EHDS. As of 2014, this was only a possibility in two member states, France and Austria.[61] Under Danish law, a healthcare worker can correct or add to the patient record but the original text must be retained.[62] Had the EHDS included a right to erasure, this would have been a significant step towards more control for patients over their records. At the same time, such a departure could also be questioned on grounds of patient safety. Permanently deleting healthcare information could limit patients' abilities to complain about sub-par care or receive compensation. Furthermore, it may be important to retain this information so that healthcare workers can get a full picture of the patient's treatment history.

Still, a middle ground could have been reached, whereby erasure would be provided for subject to restrictions. There may be scenarios where information in the EHR is no longer necessary nor proportionate as the patient's interest in having information deleted outweighs competing concerns. One could imagine cases of misdiagnoses that are not relevant to the patient's current and future health. This may be possible in some member states, depending how they interpret the right to rectification, i.e., whether it allows for editing in a way that deletes erroneous information. A further middle ground could be to archive some health information. This could be previous diagnoses or procedures that are no longer relevant but remain part of the patient's history, such as previous abortions or diagnoses of sexually transmitted diseases. This is envisaged by the right to restriction, explored further below.

2.4.3 Right to Insert

The EHDS provides for a further and significant possibility for advancing patients' rights in the context of EHR, namely the right of individuals to insert information. This right is considered in detail in Chapter 3. In the Proposal, Council and Parliament texts, the decision of whether patients may add data to their record was left to the member states. The compromise text instead marked a significant transformation for European patients as the right to insert is now established. The 2014 study found that few member states allowed patients to directly alter their medical record (only Germany and Portugal).[63] No member state allowed the patient to directly alter information inputted by a healthcare professional, which position is maintained by the EHDS. The regulation provides that information provided by the patient or their representative must be clearly distinguishable and that patients must not be able to directly alter the information entered by healthcare professionals. Recital 12 notes that the reason for rendering information entered by patients distinguishable is that it does not have the same clinical nor legal value as information added by health professionals. The EHDS thereby cements a hierarchy among professionals and patients. A lingering question is whether the health professional can alter information added by the patient or refuse to accept the insertion of observations that they find misleading or incorrect. It is left to member states to construct duties for the healthcare professional, such as a requirement to review and consider the information recorded by the patient.

The rights to rectification and insertion are also important as EHR data will be reprocessed for secondary-use pursuant to Chapter IV of the EHDS. Scholars have expressed concerns regarding the reliability of the data found in medical records.[64] Studies have identified racial and ethnic bias in records inputted by healthcare workers.[65] For example, one study in the US found that black patients had 2.54 times higher odds of being given a negative descriptor in their EHR than a white patient.[66] There is a risk that biased EHR data are then fed into algorithms which will in turn result in biased decisions on prioritisation or treatment. By enabling the patient to correct and contribute to their record, the patient may be able to facilitate more accurate data for secondary uses or counter such bias. However, this will not remedy all the risks of bias associated with EHR, such as access to healthcare.[67]

2.4.4 Right to Restriction

Article 11 EHDS provides healthcare workers with an entitlement to access 'relevant and necessary' personal EHD of persons under their treatment across the Union. However, such access is not absolute as Article 8 of the final text provides patients with a right to restrict access. This provision is an important means by which patients can control access to their data and thereby protect their right to private life.

As with the other rights provided for in the EHDS, the right to restriction is not necessarily absolute. Per recital 17, the scope of possible limitations is left up to member states. Article 3(9) of the Proposal specified that Article 6(1) (d) GDPR could be relied upon in emergency situations as it provides a legal basis for processing that is necessary in order to protect the vital interests of the data subject or of another natural person. The Council text added the example of restriction for purposes of public health in the case of highly contagious and hazardous disease (recital 13). These limitations have been removed, and it is now up to member states to decide whether and how to permit limitations on the right to restriction in line with the GDPR.

Examples where a patient's restriction of access may be legitimately overridden could be where a patient is unconscious and immediate healthcare decisions with implications for their survival need to be made. Imagine a patient who has previously restricted access to information on, for example, their use of prescription medications, who is brought to an emergency room in a confused state. In such a scenario, the healthcare workers' obligations to provide safe and effective treatment may conflict with the patient's right to private life. An autonomy-focused view could hold that the patient's autonomy should triumph, and they – as a rational individual – should be free to run this risk. A more paternalistic or protective standpoint suggests that the individual right can be restricted for the patient's 'own good'. The question of when the 'rights of others' could override the patient's wishes is more complex. Relevant

considerations could be diagnoses of communicable diseases or the presence of genetic variants that may inform a close contact or relative's care or risk profile. Here, a balance must be found between the patient's right to privacy and the third party's right to life and healthcare.

Returning to Danish practice, a right of restriction is already operationalised through 'private marking', whereby patients can mark health information in their electronic health record as private. For example, a patient could conceal that specific medicine has been prescribed to them from all healthcare workers, though not the one who prescribed the medicine. Patients can also restrict access to information about stays in hospital or appointments in specific treatment facilities or periods of time.[68] This promotes patients' control over their personal health information, though, as with the EHDS, the right is not absolute and can be overridden.

The right to restrict access to one's health information is important in increasingly digitised healthcare systems. The question of the scope of any possible limitations on such rights requires careful consideration. Should patients have an absolute right to restrict access even though it can impair the standard of care they receive or lead to worse health outcomes? It is left to the member states to determine the relative weight that should be afforded to patient autonomy versus protection/ paternalism, which seems in line with existing norms. The final text specifies that patients must be made aware that such restrictions may impact the quality of healthcare afforded to them, which is an important safeguard.

2.4.5 Information

A further right provided for following Article 9 is the right of the patient to obtain information on the healthcare providers and professionals that have accessed their EHD for healthcare purposes. Such a right should be 'without delay' (though no longer immediate as in the Proposal) and free of charge through EHD access services. This right is an important means by which patients can monitor and protect their privacy rights.

In Denmark, patients can see who has accessed their patient record and complain where they believe that their data has been accessed unlawfully. There have been numerous complaints to the Danish Healthcare Worker's disciplinary authority where acquaintances or former partners have unlawfully accessed a patient's record.[69] The right provides an important means by which patients can preserve their integrity and privacy.

At the same time, it is important that healthcare workers who are acting lawfully are protected and not subject to harassment or misuse of their personal data. Thus, it is welcomed that the EHDS allows member states to restrict this right in exceptional circumstances. While these circumstances are not defined, it could include instances where a healthcare worker is at risk of being targeted, such as where the patient has previously harassed or misused the personal data of a treating healthcare professional.

2.4.6 Right to Data Portability

Another significant innovation of the EHDS for patients' rights to control their health data is the right to data portability provided for under Article 7. This provision offers individuals a right to give access to or request a healthcare provider to transmit all or part of their EHD to another healthcare provider of their choice. This right should be immediate, free of charge and without hindrance. Furthermore, in the case of priority categories of data, other healthcare providers will be obligated to accept the transported data.

The right to data portability in the EHDS goes beyond the more limited right provided for in Article 20 GDPR. Notably, the EHDS includes inferred data (not just data provided by the data subject) and is not limited to data processed subject to specific legal bases.[70] However, as compared to the Proposal, the final text is more limited in relation to which providers are covered. The individual can only request that a *healthcare provider* transmit EHD to a *social security or reimbursement services sector provider*, not the other way round. Article 3(8) of the Proposal had applied to data holders from the health or social security sector, though the provision quickly seemed doomed given that the Council and Parliament texts sought to limit it to healthcare providers. It remains to be seen how a healthcare provider will be understood under domestic law. For example, does the right apply to healthcare provided to a resident of a social care institution by that institution, such as delivery of prescription medications or basic wound care? The 2023 e-health indicators report noted that geriatric nursing homes are the institutions least connected to domestic EHR infrastructures, which poses a barrier to these citizens enjoying their EHDS rights. Another example is treatment for alcoholism or addiction by a social care provider. It is recalled that the definition of primary health data in Article 2 of the EHDS includes social care. The right to access applies to data processed for the provision of healthcare, which appears to include the scenario mentioned above, while the use of the term 'provider' may be narrower. It seems counterintuitive and contrary to patients' rights that social care data may be shared for secondary use but not primary use.

The EDPB-EDPS joint opinion highlighted that the right does not establish a corresponding obligation to transmit the data.[71] For example, in member states where Article 9(2)(h) GDPR is relied upon as a processing ground, Article 9(3) specifies a professional secrecy obligation. The transmission of data gathered under this legal basis based on portability may violate such obligations. This may also require domestic legislation to be amended, and the question has not been resolved in the final text.

For the provision of cross-border care, portability is particularly crucial as it provides for a right to transmit data to a recipient in another member state and an obligation on the latter to read and accept this data. Per recital 33, this is particularly vital for those living in border regions given that the nearest provider may be across a border, not in the member state of residence.

It remains to be seen how providers will respond to these new obligations, which may require a cultural shift among providers who typically order new tests for new patients.

2.4.7 *Right to Complain*

Finally, rights can be toothless where rights holders are not provided with complaints' mechanisms. A question is therefore to whom patients can complain should their rights under Chapter II EHDS not be respected. The Proposal established the Digital Health Authority (DHA) as the complaints body in such cases. Meanwhile, the Council's proposal would have required the DHA to transmit the complaint to the supervisory authorities and consult and cooperate with them in dealing with the complaint, whereas the Commission's proposal merely required the DHA to inform the data protection authorities. The final text has resolved that complaints related to access, insertion, rectification, data portability, restriction and objection must be transmitted by the DHA to the relevant data protection authority. This appears to be an appropriate solution given that there is a risk that adding further complaints bodies would be of detriment to patients' rights instead of supporting them in enjoying their rights. At domestic level, member states are likely to already have established complaints mechanisms, and it is vital that the EHDS does not add to regulatory complexity. At the same time, data protection authorities are notoriously overburdened and under resourced. Thus, it is important that extra resources and training are provided for to enable them to fulfil these new obligations.

2.5 Conclusion

This chapter concludes by emphasising the transformative potential of the European Health Data Space in relation to patients' rights to control their EHR, particularly in the EU's least digitised member states. The relevant provisions necessitate profound changes, mandating legal frameworks that compel healthcare professionals to digitally document patient care. The chapter aligns with the European Data Protection Board (EDPB) and the European Data Protection Supervisor (EDPS) in recognising that the rights conferred by the EHDS to individuals concerning their personal data are essentially 'add-ons' to those established by the General Data Protection Regulation (GDPR).[72] However, these enhancements are anticipated to significantly boost patients' rights, granting them increased access to and control over their EHR, thereby reshaping patients' control of their data throughout the EU. Thus, Chapter II of EHDS can be considered to amount to both GDPR+ and a transformation for patients' rights.

The EHDS sets a foundation for improving patients' informational self-determination by facilitating access to health data without charge and promptly. In light of *FT v DW*, the EHDS does not significantly expand EU law in respect to the scope of access. However, the specificity of the EHDS may help to streamline and accelerate access to health data for patients. Access will be enabled through mandating member states to put in place the necessary infrastructure. Furthermore, through easier access, patients will be able to enjoy other rights, such as rectification. It remains to be seen to what extent rectification will encompass erasure, as this right is omitted from the EHDS. The EHDS also expands the rights to data portability and restriction, potentially enhancing patient choice and control. Additionally, it introduces the right to insert, enabling patients to actively contribute to their healthcare records. Through the right to object, patients have enhanced possibilities to opt-out of taking part in the EHDS, though in some member states, this position represents less control than the status quo.

The chapter questions, however, the exclusion of social care services from provisions of the text on primary use. The significance of healthcare data to patients is based on its relevance to their health rather than its location. The original ambition of the EHDS to include social security providers was scaled back in the final text, limiting its scope to primarily healthcare-related data. However, as is seen in other chapters of this volume, the EHDS is more ambitious when it comes to secondary use of care data.

The potential for transformation also comes with the caveat of likely fragmentation among member states, given the latitude provided in determining the extent of their rights. The Regulation's mix of prescriptive 'shall' and permissive 'may' renders continued fragmentation in EHR practices across the EU all but unavoidable. The lack of clarity on how these differences will be reconciled poses a potential obstacle to the full realisation of patients' rights. This challenge reflects the inherent complexity of harmonising aspects closely related to healthcare provision, considering the EU's limited healthcare competencies and variations among member states' healthcare systems.

Acknowledgements

The author acknowledges funding received from the Swedish Collegium for Advanced Studies and Riksbankens Jubileumsfond through the Pro Futura Scientia Fellowship programme. This chapter was prepared while on sabbatical at the Centre for Health, Law and Emerging Technologies (HeLEX), Faculty of Law, University of Oxford. Thank you to Miranda Mourby and Michael Morrison for helpful comments. All errors remain attributable to the author.

Notes

1 European Commission, 'Commission Staff Working Document, Impact Assessment Report accompanying the document Proposal for a Regulation of the European Parliament and of the Council on the European Health Data Space' (3 May 2022 Swd(2022) 131 Final Part 1/4) 18.

2 Case C-307/22 *FT v DW* (4 December 2023).

3 European Commission (n 1) 20.

4 Lucas Deimel and others, *Digital decade e-Health indicators development – Executive summary* (European Commission, Directorate-General for Communications Networks, Content and Technology, Publications Office of the European Union 2023) https://data.europa.eu/doi/10.2759/792901 accessed 29 April 2024.
5 European Commission (n 1) 18. See also Johan Hansen and others, *Assessment of the EU Member States' rules on health data in the light of GDPR* (European Commission, Consumers, Health, Agriculture and Food Executive Agency Publications Office 113, 2021) 85.
6 Deimel (n 4).
7 Directive 2011/24/EU of the European Parliament and of the Council of 9 March 2011 on the application of patients' rights in cross-border healthcare (2011) OJ L 88/165 (Patients' Rights Directive).
8 Lucas Deimel and others, *Digital Decade e-Health Indicators Development – Final Report* (Publications Office of the European Union 2023) 8.
9 Time.lex and Milieu, 'Overview of the National Laws on Electronic Health Records in the EU Member States and Their Interaction With the Provision of Cross-Border eHealth Services. Final Report and Recommendations' (2014) 45–47 https://health.ec.europa.eu/other-pages/basic-page/overview-national-laws-electronic-health-records-eu-member-states-2016_en accessed 29 April 2024.
10 Deimel and others (n 8).
11 Patients' Rights Directive, art 14.
12 Commission Recommendation (EU) 2019/243 of 6 February 2019 on a European Electronic Health Record exchange format, recital 16.
13 eHealth Network, 'Guideline on the Electronic Exchange of Health Data Under Cross-Border Directive 2011/24/EU Patient Summary Release 3.3', June 2023.
14 Commission (n 1) 21.
15 Commission (n 1) 18.
16 Commission (n 13) recital 8. See also, European Council, 'Health in the Digital Society', 8 December 2017 2017/C 440/05.
17 EHDS art 23.
18 EHDS art 24(1).
19 Deimel and others (n 8) 6.
20 Deimel and others (n 8) 8.
21 EHDS art 84.
22 *Bekendtgørelse af lov om autorisation af sundhedspersoner og om sundhedsfaglig virksomhed* (LBK no 122 of 24 January 2023) (Denmark) (Autorisationsloven) § 21.
23 Autorisationsloven § 22(1).
24 *Bekendtgørelse om autoriserede sundhedspersoners patientjournaler (journalføring, opbevaring, videregivelse, overdragelse m.v.)* (BEK no. 1225 of 8 June 2021) (Denmark) (Journalføringsbekendtgørelsen) § 2(1).
25 Autorisationslovens § 22(2).
26 Journalføringsbekendtgørelsen § 11(2).
27 Time.lex and Milieu (n 9) 24–25.
28 Procedures for Keeping Medical Documents, regulation no 265, 4 April 2006 (20 September 2011) issued pursuant to section 59 of the Medical Treatment Law (Republic of Latvia) https://likumi.lv/ta/en/en/id/132359 accessed 29 May 2024.
29 Journalføringsbekendtgørelsen § 13(1).
30 Tom Delbanco and others, 'Open Notes: Doctors and Patients Signing On' (2010) 153 *Ann Intern Med* 121.
31 Region Hovedstaden, 'Persondatapolitik for Region Hovedstaden' www.regionh.dk/om-region-hovedstaden/om-hjemmesiden/Sider/Persondatapolitik-for-Region-Hovedstaden.aspx accessed 29 April 2024.
32 Katharina Eva Ó Cathaoir, 'In Search of Solidarity: Personalised Medicine in Denmark' (2019) 21–22 *Nordisk socialrättslig tidskrift* 65.

33 Time.lex and Milieu (n 9) 33.
34 Line Gudnitz Rønø Baun and Marcel Mirzaei-Fard, 'Sundhedsplatformen skyld i fejlmedicinering: Første sag meldt til Patienterstatningen' *Danmarks Radio* (Copenhagen, 30 November 2018) www.dr.dk/nyheder/regionale/hovedstadsomraadet/sundhedsplatformen-skyld-i-fejlmedicinering-foerste-sag-meldt accessed 29 April 2024.
35 Datatilsynet, 'Alvorlig kritik, påbud og advarsel til Region Hovedstaden efter to sikkerhedsbrud' (18 February 2022) www.datatilsynet.dk/afgoerelser/afgoerelser/2022/feb/alvorlig-kritik-paabud-og-advarsel-til-region-hovedstaden-efter-to-sikkerhedsbrud- accessed 29 April 2024.
36 Petros Terzis and Enrique Santamaria Echeverria, 'Interoperability and Governance in the European Health Data Space Regulation' (2023) 23(4) *Medical Law International* 368.
37 Morten Hertzum, Gunnar Ellingsen and Åsa Cajander, 'Implementing Large-Scale Electronic Health Records: Experiences From Implementations of Epic in Denmark and Finland' (2022) 167 *International Journal of Medical Informatics* 104868.
38 These reflections are derived from a workshop held in connection with the DOCURA project funded by Queen Mary's Centre, University of Copenhagen.
39 See, for example, Finansministeriet, 'Færre regler og mindre bureaukrati' (Regeringen 2018) www.regeringen.dk/media/5633/faerre-regler-og-mindre-bureaukrati_web-2.pdf accessed 29 April 2024.
40 Aziz Sheikh and others, 'Implementation and Adoption of Nationwide Electronic Health Records in Secondary Care in England: Final Qualitative Results from Prospective National Evaluation in 'Early Adopter' Hospitals' (2011) 343 *BMJ* d6054.
41 Saif Khairat and others, 'Perceived Burden of EHRs on Physicians at Different Stages of Their Career' (2018) 9(2) *Applied Clinical Informatics* 336.
42 Rigsrevisionen, 'Extract from Rigsrevisionen's report on Sundhedsplatformen submitted to the Public Accounts Committee' (2017) https://uk.rigsrevisionen.dk/Media/7/7/17-2017.pdf accessed 29 April 2024.
43 eHealth Network (n 14).
44 *KH and others v Slovakia* App 32881/04 (ECHR, 28 April 2009) para 48.
45 EHDS art 3(1).
46 See further, EDPB, 'Guidelines 01/2022 on data subject rights – Right of access, version 2.0', 28 March 2023.
47 Case C-307/22 *FT v DW* ECLI:EU:C:2023:811.
48 *FT v DW* para 58.
49 *FT v DW* paras 59–62.
50 *FT v DW* para 68.
51 *FT v DW* para 63.
52 *FT v DW* para 77.
53 *FT v DW* para 78.
54 EHDS art 4.
55 Council of Europe, Convention for the Protection of Individuals with regard to the Automatic Processing of Personal Data, Explanatory Report, 18 May 2018 (Convention 108+) para 74.
56 Council of Europe, Convention for the Protection of Individuals with Regard to Automatic Processing of Personal Data CETS 108 (1981).
57 Recommendation No R (97)5 of the Committee of Ministers to Member States on the Protection of Medical Data (Committee of Ministers, 13 February 1997) principle 8.2.b.
58 Time.lex and Milieu (n 9) 42.
59 Procedures for record keeping of medical documents (n 29) § 4(7).
60 EDPB-EDPS, 'Joint Opinion 03/2022 on the Proposal for a Regulation on the European Health Data Space' (2022) 12 July 2022, para 54.
61 Time.lex and Milieu (n 9) 43.
62 Journalføringsbekendtgørelsen, § 20(1).

63 Time.lex and Milieu (n 9) 43.
64 Robert A Verheij and others, 'Possible Sources of Bias in Primary Care Electronic Health Record Data Use and Reuse Possible Sources of Bias in Primary Care Electronic Health Record Data Use and Reuse' (2018) 20(5) *Journal of Medical Internet Research* e185.
65 Lisa S Rotenstein and Jose F Figueroa, 'Uncovering Hidden Racial and Ethnic Bias through Electronic Health Record Logs' (2023) 6(10) *JAMA Network Open* e2336336.
66 Michael Sun and others, 'Negative Patient Descriptors: Documenting Racial Bias in the Electronic Health Record' (2022) 41(2) *Health Affairs* 203.
67 Milena A Gianfrancesco and Neal D Goldstein, 'A Narrative Review on the Validity of Electronic Health Record-Based Research in Epidemiology' (2021) 21 *BMC Medical Research Methodology* 234.
68 Sundhed, 'Privatmarkering og Spaerring' (23 June 2021) www.sundhed.dk/borger/service/kontakt/hjaelp-borger/teknisk-opsaetning/privatmarkering-og-spaerring/ accessed 29 April 2024.
69 Sundhedsvæsenets Disciplinærnævn, 'Uberettiget indhentning i bekendts journal' (23DNM89, 11 December 2023) https://stpk.dk/afgorelser-og-domme/afgorelser-fra-sundhedsvaesenets-disciplinaernaevn/23dnm89/ accessed 29 April 2024.
70 Wenkai Li and Paul Quinn, 'The European Health Data Space: An expanded right to data portability?' (2024) 52 *Computer Law & Security Review* 105913.
71 EDPB-EDPS (n 61) para 57.
72 EDPB-EDPS 3.

List of Sources

Treaties, Legislative Acts and Conventions

Council of Europe, Convention for the Protection of Individuals with Regard to Automatic Processing of Personal Data CETS 108 (1981).

Council of Europe, Convention for the Protection of Individuals with regard to the Automatic Processing of Personal Data, Explanatory Report, 18 May 2018 (Convention 108+).

Council of Europe, European Convention on Human Rights as amended by Protocols Nos. 11, 14 and 15, supplemented by Protocols Nos. 1, 4, 6, 7, 12, 13 and 16, 4 November 1950, CETS 5.

Directive 2011/24/EU of the European Parliament and of the Council of 9 March 2011 on the application of patients' rights in cross-border healthcare (2011) OJ L 88/165 (Patients' Rights Directive).

Directive (EU) 2016/2102 of the European Parliament and of the Council of 26 October 2016 on the accessibility of the websites and mobile applications of public sector bodies (Text with EEA relevance) OJ L 327/1.

United Nations, Convention on the rights of the child (1989) UNT no 27531, 1577/3.

Domestic Legislation

Bekendtgørelse af lov om autorisation af sundhedspersoner og om sundhedsfaglig virksomhed (LBK no 122 of 24 January 2023) (Denmark) (Autorisationsloven).

Bekendtgørelse om autoriserede sundhedspersoners patientjournaler (journalføring, opbevaring, videregivelse, overdragelse m.v.) (BEK no. 1225 of 8 June 2021) (Denmark) (Journalføringsbekendtgørelsen).

Procedures for Keeping Medical Documents, regulation no 265, 4 April 2006 (20 September 2011) issued pursuant to section 59 of the Medical Treatment Law (Republic of Latvia) https://likumi.lv/ta/en/en/id/132359

Official Documents and Other Policy Documents

Commission Recommendation (EU) 2019/243 of 6 February 2019 on a European Electronic Health Record exchange format.

Council of the European Union, 'Proposal for a Regulation on the European Health Data Space Analysis of the final compromise text with a view to agreement' 2022/0140(COD) (EHDS (compromise text)).

Deimel L and others, Digital decade e-Health indicators development – Executive summary (European Commission, Directorate-General for Communications Networks, Content and Technology, Publications Office of the European Union 2023a) https://data.europa.eu/doi/10.2759/792901

Deimel L and others, Digital decade e-Health indicators development – Final report (Publications Office of the European Union 2023b) https://data.europa.eu/doi/10.2759/530348

EDPB, 'Guidelines 01/2022 on data subject rights – Right of access, version 2.0', (2023) 28 March 2023.

EDPB-EDPS, 'Joint Opinion 03/2022 on the Proposal for a Regulation on the European Health Data Space' (2022) 12 July 2022.

eHealth Network, 'Guideline on the electronic exchange of health data under Cross-Border Directive 2011/24/EU Patient Summary Release 3.3', June 2023.

European Commission, 'Commission Staff Working Document, Impact Assessment Report accompanying the document Proposal for a Regulation of the European Parliament and of the Council on the European Health Data Space' (3 May 2022 Swd(2022) 131 Final Part 1/4).

European Council, Health in the Digital Society adopted on 8 December 2017 2017/C 440/05.

European Parliament, 'Amendments adopted by the European Parliament on 13 December 2023 on the proposal for a regulation of the European Parliament and of the Council on the European Health Data Space' (COM(2022)0197 – C9-0167/2022 – 2022/0140(COD))(1), T9-0462/2023 https://oeil.secure.europarl.europa.eu/oeil/popups/ficheprocedure.do?reference=2022/0140(COD)&l=en

Hansen J and others, Assessment of the EU Member States' rules on health data in the light of GDPR (European Commission, Consumers, Health, Agriculture and Food Executive Agency Publications Office 113, 2021) doi: 10.2818/546193

Recommendation No R (97)5 of the Committee of Ministers to Member States on the Protection of Medical Data (Committee of Ministers, 13 February 1997).

Rigsrevisionen, 'Extract from Rigsrevisionen's report on Sundhedsplatformen submitted to the Public Accounts Committee' (2017) https://uk.rigsrevisionen.dk/Media/7/7/17-2017.pdf

Time.lex and Milieu, 'Overview of the national laws on electronic health records in the EU Member States and their interaction with the provision of cross-border eHealth services. Final report and recommendations' (2014) 45–47 https://health.ec.europa.eu/other-pages/basic-page/overview-national-laws-electronic-health-records-eu-member-states-2016_en

Literature and Other Secondary Sources

Datatilsynet, 'Alvorlig kritik, påbud og advarsel til Region Hovedstaden efter to sikkerhedsbrud' (18 February 2022) www.datatilsynet.dk/afgoerelser/afgoerelser/2022/feb/alvorlig-kritik-paabud-og-advarsel-til-region-hovedstaden-efter-to-sikkerhedsbrud-

Delbanco T and others, 'Open notes: Doctors and patients signing on' (2010) 153 *Annals of Internal Medicine* 121–125. doi:10.7326/0003-4819-153-2-201007200-00008

Finansministeriet, 'Færre regler og mindre bureaukrati' *Regeringen* (2018) www.regeringen.dk/media/5633/faerre-regler-og-mindre-bureaukrati_web-2.pdf

Gianfrancesco MA and Goldstein ND, 'A narrative review on the validity of electronic health record-based research in epidemiology' (2021) 21 *BMC Medical Research Methodology* 234. doi:10.1186/s12874-021-01416-5.

Gudnitz Rønø Baun L and Mirzaei-Fard M, 'Sundhedsplatformen skyld i fejlmedicinering: Første sag meldt til Patienterstatningen' *Danmarks Radio* (Copenhagen, 30 November 2018) www.dr.dk/nyheder/regionale/hovedstadsomraadet/sundhedsplatformen-skyld-i-fejlmedicinering-foerste-sag-meldt

Hertzum M, Ellingsen G and Cajander Å, 'Implementing large-scale electronic health records: experiences from implementations of epic in Denmark and Finland' (2022) 167 *International Journal of Medical Informatics* 104868. doi: 10.1016/j.ijmedinf.2022.104868

Khairat S and others, 'Perceived burden of EHRs on physicians at different stages of their career' (2018) 9(2) *Applied Clinical Informatics* 336–347. doi: 10.1055/s-0038-1648222

ÓCathaoir KE, 'In search of solidarity: Personalised medicine in Denmark' (2019) 21–22 *Nordisk socialrättslig tidskrift* 65–95.

Region Hovedstaden, 'Persondatapolitik for Region Hovedstaden' www.regionh.dk/om-region-hovedstaden/om-hjemmesiden/Sider/Persondatapolitik-for-Region-Hovedstaden.aspx

Rotenstein LS and Figueroa JF, 'Uncovering hidden racial and ethnic bias through electronic health record logs' (2023) 6(10) *JAMA Network Open* e2336336. doi: 10.1001/jamanetworkopen.2023.36336

Sheikh A and others, 'Implementation and adoption of nationwide electronic health records in secondary care in England: Final qualitative results from prospective national evaluation in "early adopter" hospitals' (2011) 343 *BMJ* d6054. doi: 10.1136/bmj.d6054

Sun M and others, 'Negative patient descriptors: Documenting racial bias in the electronic health record' (2022) 41(2) *Health Affairs* 203–211. doi: 10.1377/hlthaff.2021.01423

Sundhed, 'Privatmarkering og Spaerring' (23 June 2021) www.sundhed.dk/borger/service/kontakt/hjaelp-borger/teknisk-opsaetning/privatmarkering-og-spaerring/

Sundhedsvæsenets Disciplinærnævn, 'Uberettiget indhentning i bekendts journal 23DNM89, 11 December 2023) https://stpk.dk/afgorelser-og-domme/afgorelser-fra-sundhedsvaesenets-disciplinaernaevn/23dnm89/

Terzis P and Santamaria Echeverria E, 'Interoperability and governance in the European Health Data Space regulation' (2023) 23(4) *Medical Law International* 368–376. doi: 10.1177/09685332231165692

Verheij RA and others, 'Possible sources of bias in primary care electronic health record data use and reuse possible sources of bias in primary care electronic health record data use and reuse' (2018) 20(5) *Journal of Medical Internet Research* e185. doi: 10.2196/jmir.9134

Wenkai Li and Quinn P, 'The European Health Data Space: An expanded right to data portability?' (2024) 52 *Computer Law and Security Review* 105913. doi: 10.1016/j.clsr.2023.105913

Case Law

Case C-307/22 *FT v DW* ECLI:EU:C:2023:811.

KH and others v Slovakia App 32881/04 (ECtHR, 28 April 2009).

3 The right to insert and add information to my health record – does my doctor need to know this?

A critical discussion of the right to insert information in an EHR using the example of data from direct-to-consumer genetic testing

Andelka M. Phillips

3.1 Introduction

A right to insert information into an electronic health record (EHR) is included in the Regulation establishing the European Health Data Space[1] (EHDS Regulation)[2] alongside other rights that patients can exercise in relation to their electronic health data, as set out in Chapter II, 'Primary Use' of the Regulation[3]. Contemporary society is experiencing rapid technological changes, which are impacting the way people live and work. Together with engaging with more traditional healthcare providers, individuals are now utilising a wide range of technologies to track aspects of their health and well-being (this ranges from DNA tests to wearable technology and Femtech[4]). Unfortunately, although many services and products may offer potential benefits to individuals, not all of them adhere to the same standards or oversight mechanisms as more established tests and devices. Furthermore, as more of these services and products are offered online and rely on collecting information from individuals, this also increases the likelihood that individuals may experience data breaches. Several of these new industries also operate internationally and have presented significant challenges in their regulation and governance. This is exemplified by the direct-to-consumer genetic testing industry (DTC or personal genomics), which has created a market for genetic tests as consumer services, taking them outside traditional governance mechanisms for DNA testing in a medical setting.[5] The right to insert will allow individuals and their representatives to add information to their EHRs from all of these sources.

This chapter provides a critical analysis of the right to insert information into an EHR, as set out in Chapter 2.[6] The discussion focuses on how people will utilise this right in the context of primary healthcare by adding information to their EHRs. The right to insert is a novel right and sits alongside rights to rectification and portability, which build upon their previous conceptualisation in the General Data Protection Regulation (GDPR).[7] Unlike the rights to rectification and portability, the right to insert allows individuals

DOI: 10.4324/9781003544111-4

and their representatives to add information to their EHRs, which does enhance their control over their information. The author has suggested in other work that a consumer data right could be utilised in the context of the DTC industry to enhance consumers' rights in relation to their genetic data.[8] However, the potential for patients to add a wide variety of data to their EHRs from commercial sources could cause other problems for medical practice. These relate to both the variety of information – people might wish to insert, as well as the range of technologies, such as mobile devices that they might use to do this.

Although this right could help to empower patients, there are several challenges in how it will be realised and exercised by patients. It should be emphasised in line with Fåhraeu et al.'s policy analysis that the premise of the EHDS relies significantly on patients being digitally literate and having access to sufficient resources to exercise the rights provided for by the Regulation.[9] In order for a patient to make use of the right to insert specifically, they will need either a sufficient level of digital literacy or resources to help them in exercising this.

One problem that should be emphasised is that individuals and their representatives may have different perceptions of the value and quality of information that they insert. These perceptions may differ significantly from the views of medical professionals who are provided with this inserted information. Especially in the context of DTC tests provided for health purposes, studies have demonstrated that individuals may not necessarily understand the import and limitations of test results.[10]

Furthermore, it is clear that much of the impetus behind the DTC industry's engagement in medical research is the desire to develop pharmaceutical and diagnostic products, in relation to which they can protect their intellectual property rights.[11] While this might be unsurprising, one problem here is that although the industry aims to create these products, it is more focused on doing this through secondary research on consumers' data than on the quality and benefits, which tests provide for individual consumers. This is especially concerning in relation to tests provided for health purposes, as it is reasonable that a consumer might believe that the tests are reliable and something that they should insert into their EHR. As will be discussed, companies' contractual terms may in fact indicate that the tests are not provided for diagnostic purposes and also limit a person's ability to insert this information.

This chapter is structured as follows. Section 3.2 first introduces the right as framed in the Regulation linking it to the rights of rectification and portability. Section 3.3 then discusses the right and problems with its conceptualisation, highlighting challenges relating to interoperability and cyber security in light of recent data breaches, specifically the 23andMe breach. Section 3.4 then provides a case study of the DTC industry as an example of a source of data, which people may wish to insert into their EHR. This industry is considered in order to illuminate the problems of the diverse variety of information, which could be inserted. The section draws upon previous work examining the online contracts of companies that market DTC tests for health purposes and highlights key problems. Finally, Section 3.5 makes concluding remarks, highlighting the need for further consultation among stakeholders and recommending the development of guidelines, best practices and codes of conduct in relation to the exercise of this right.

3.2 The right to insert information in EHR

The right to insert is included in Chapter II of the Regulation. For the sake of accuracy, given its novelty, the text used for the purposes of the analysis in this chapter is provided below.

> Right of natural persons to insert information in their own EHR Natural persons or their representatives as referred to in Article 8G(2) shall have the right to insert information in their own EHR through electronic health data access services or applications linked to these services as referred to in Article 8G. That information shall in such cases be clearly distinguishable as inserted by the natural person or by his or her representative. Natural persons shall not have the possibility to directly alter the electronic health data and related information inserted by health professionals.[12]

As this right is framed, it is limited in application to 'natural persons' and their 'representatives.' This right should give individuals more of a voice in their EHR, but as will be seen, more consultation will be needed in order to assist people with the implementation of this right and to assist the healthcare sector in understanding their responsibilities in this context. The article links to another on proxies, which allows people to permit individuals and also 'legal representatives of patients' to access their EHRs and insert electronic health data on their behalf. Chapter II also makes requirements for member states to establish rules relating to the establishment of such proxies, which also need to ensure that such services 'shall be easily accessible for persons with disabilities, vulnerable groups and persons with low digital literacy.' This is important and is something that member states should pay careful attention to if the right to insert is to be implemented in a way that caters for all people's interests, especially the most vulnerable.

This right has also been described as a right to add or a right to upload.[13] It is submitted herein that it is most helpful to refer to it using the phrasing used in the Regulation. This is because as it is currently framed, it is not limited in relation to the types of data that could be added and goes beyond a right to upload. For instance, as well as uploading test results from a DTC test or data from a Femtech application, an individual may simply want to insert a comment that may or may not directly relate to their health.

As the right is framed, it includes an important qualification, which was not present in the original Proposal. This is that it does not allow for individuals or their representatives to make alterations to their 'electronic health data' or other information that has been 'inserted by a health professional.' This is a helpful limitation. However, as will be seen in the example of DTC genetic test results, it is possible that in exercising this right, patients may believe that by adding information from a DTC test or other information, they are in fact making corrections to their records.

Recital 12 is also relevant to the right to insert and how information inserted by individuals is to be treated. It provides that information 'inserted ... may not be as reliable as electronic health data entered and verified by health professionals.' This can be related to the example of results inserted from the DTC industry, which are discussed below, as concerns have been raised about the reliability and clinical utility of such tests.[14] It should be noted though that where one family member inserts information from a DTC test into their EHR, it is possible that this will impact the privacy of their relatives and that in some contexts health practitioners or researchers may wish to access this data. Guidelines should therefore be developed to assist health practitioners in making it clear where responsibilities and liabilities lie.

Two other rights should be noted here. These are the rights to rectification and data portability, both of which are also set out in Chapter 2. The article on rectification allows for 'natural persons to easily request online the rectification of their personal data' under the GDPR. This right essentially allows people to request the correction of errors in their EHRs. It is likely that issues could arise with rectification and the right to insert if an individual believes that the information they insert has the same validity or is more accurate than other types of test results that are included in their EHR. It is also unclear what responsibilities health professionals have in relation to inserted data; and this is something that will need to be considered by stakeholders, and it is hoped that it will be addressed in implementing acts.

Meanwhile, the right to data portability allows patients to request the transfer of their data, which will include having data transferred to an entity in another member state. In other work, the author has suggested that a consumer data right could be utilised in the context of the DTC industry to enhance consumers' rights in relation to their genetic data.[15] However, it is suggested herein that in order to fully achieve the implementation of the right to insert, this will have implications for the right to data portability in the sense that provision will have to be made for ensuring that data inserted by individuals or their representatives into their EHR is also able to be transferred. This is mentioned, because in relation to some datasets that an individual might wish to insert (such as genetic data or genetic test results), this may require additional technical infrastructure to support this.[16]

3.3 Discussion of the right to insert and problems with conceptualising this right

The right to insert can be viewed as building upon the rights to portability and rectification, by allowing a patient to have more of a voice in what is included in their EHR. While the right to data portability allows people to make choices about providers and to transfer their data to another entity, the right to rectification essentially allows people to have errors in their records corrected. The right to insert represents a novel development though in a healthcare setting, as it allows people to add any type of information to their record, some of which may not be health related. While the right to insert data holds the promise of allowing patients to add information they believe is important, it poses several problems in its implementation.

As noted by Fåhraeu et al., there are two particular challenges in terms of the implications of this right for medical practice here. These are that the Regulation lacks measures requiring that the information added to the EHR 'relates to health' and that although there is a requirement for the information so inserted to be clearly marked as inserted, there are no requirements set in relation to the quality of the information inserted.[17] Meanwhile, as Marelli et al. note, 'it is not clear how health professionals should take responsibility for this data, given that health professionals cannot control the data they receive, its language, or format.'[18] Thus, the right itself may offer benefits to patients in allowing them to tell their health professionals about information they consider important, but if there is no clarity on what health professionals are to do with this information, it is likely to create problems in practice. A further problem may be that some patients may choose to insert significant amounts of diverse information, such as a large variety of DNA test results together with information from wearable technology, and it is not clear what the responsibilities are for health practitioners in relation to handling this data. In some member states, the exercise of this right may prove particularly challenging in terms of already overstretched resources.

In considering the right to insert, it is also necessary to consider issues related to cyber security.

Cyber security is growing in importance, and the risk of identity theft and a variety of types of fraud are growing, as more organisations are suffering data breaches. No industry is immune from this, and while it is not possible for an organisation to say it is completely secure against all possible attacks, much more attention needs to be paid to the security of systems that handle health data. The health sector globally has experienced significant growth in cyberattacks and data breaches, and the European Union (EU) is no exception.[19] A report by ENISA in 2023 found that the 'European health sector experienced a significant number of incidents, with healthcare providers accounting for 53% of the total incidents.'[20] Unfortunately, according to this report, the most popular mode of attack is ransomware, and the report mentions: 'According to a recent study by ENISA, only 27% of organisations surveyed in the health sector have a dedicated ransomware defence programme and 40% of the organisations have no security awareness programme for non-IT staff.'[21]

The lack of awareness noted above is extremely problematic, and in light of this, there are two positive developments to note in the Regulation. These are concerned with promotion of digital literacy and training related to cyber security. Requirements relating to these matters can be found in Chapter V, which addresses 'Additional Actions,' as well as recitals. Article 83 sets requirements for member states to develop training programmes for health professionals and also for digital literacy of patients. It specifies that 'training programmes and information shall be accessible to and affordable systems all health professionals, without prejudice to the organisation of healthcare at national level.' It is noted that this could prove a challenge for healthcare resourcing in some member states. Recital 89 stresses that improving digital literacy both for patients and healthcare providers will be fundamental to the success of the Regulation and the EHDS. This requires that member states should allow for their health professionals to take digital literacy courses, which will enable these professionals to be better prepared to 'ensure cybersecurity and ethical management of health data.'

While data breaches can have significant consequences for individuals and their families, security threats to hospitals can also cause physical safety risks to patients. One example to highlight the risks here is that of the US Federal Drug Administration's (FDA's) alert about the Hospira drug pump, as it had been found that it was possible to alter the dosage of the drug pump remotely so that it could in fact administer a lethal dose.[22]

Given that the next section considers the example of the DTC industry in relation to the types of data an individual might want to insert into their EHR, it seems timely to briefly consider the recent 23andMe data breach. This breach has meant that almost half of 23andMe's customers are left vulnerable (this amounts to nearly seven million people).[23] In the wake of the breach, more than 40 class actions were filed against 23andMe in the USA and one in Canada, the US class actions have been settled, but the Canadian action is ongoing.[24] This data breach unfortunately was enabled through the use of credential stuffing, which means that attackers were able to use passwords and usernames stolen from other sites to login into 23andMe customer accounts as though they were the actual customers.[25] This type of attack was made possible by 23andMe allowing consumers to create accounts by linking to other accounts, such as Apple or Google. While allowing consumers to create accounts on websites by linking to existing accounts saves them time, it is very problematic in the context of sensitive services and products and is a practice which ought to be discontinued in the context of specific industries, such as DTC. Most problematically here was the range of types of data, which hackers were able to access, as this included data related to genetic heritage, photographs, full names, dates of birth and home addresses, which will pose serious ongoing risks for the privacy and physical safety of the consumers who were impacted and their families.[26]

Some of the background to the EHDS can be found in a desire to increase the accessibility of data for medical research.[27] The EHDS is premised on the ideas of interoperability and security, but also the idea that as far as possible health data will be open. This is mentioned in Recital 3, which notes that the COVID-19 pandemic, as well as anchoring 'the work of the eHealth Network,' has highlighted the need for sharing electronic health data that are findable, accessible, interoperable and reusable ('FAIR principles') while also ensuring that data are 'as open as possible, while respecting the principle of data minimisation.' Together with this is the idea that more data will be made available to researchers and other entities in the EHDS in an anonymised form. It should be noted that making data as open as possible will not always be in a patient's best interests, especially in relation to maintaining their privacy. It is also a difficult feat to achieve while also preserving privacy in relation to some forms of more sensitive data, such as genetic data. The aims mentioned in the recital above are in some ways contradictory.

Likewise, actual anonymisation of several types of health data, including genetic data, can be difficult to achieve.[28] Relating this back to the right to insert, where patients choose to insert genetic data from DTC companies, it is possible that this could create privacy risks for them, and it is not clear whether this data might be made available for further research. More work will be needed to establish guidance on how inserted information is to be protected, especially when it is highly sensitive in nature. As Terzis and Santamaria Echeverria note in relation to future research uses of data in the EHDS and intellectual property rights of data users, citing the work of Keller and Tarkowski, there is a 'paradox of open' here.[29] This stems from the possibility that 'opening up informational resources means exposing them to the power structures governing the networked information ecosystem.'[30] This paradox should not be underestimated given the growing interests of Big Tech in the health technology space.

Although the EHDS aims to empower patients through a range of rights, trying to facilitate patients' ability to implement the right to insert is going to require significant collaboration. Additionally, the fact that this right allows for the insertion of potentially a wide variety of data by people located across the European Union with differing levels of access to the Internet and resources may pose further cyber security risks. While the goal of the EHDS is to streamline access through interoperability, the right to insert introduces further complexity, as people will be accessing these systems using a wide range of devices that may have security vulnerabilities, and individuals may also experience vulnerability in relation to digital literacy, but also interpreting and understanding results from DTC companies. This challenge will be heightened in relation to specific types of data, such as genetic test results or raw genomic data uploaded by an individual who has undergone a DTC test. The recent 23andMe data breach also highlights that commercial providers do not necessarily have high levels of cyber security in practice. Finally, interoperability is something that many systems strive to achieve, but which can prove challenging.[31] It becomes more difficult to achieve in practice, when numerous entities are involved. This is likely to be challenging given the range of member states included in the European Union and making such diverse systems and devices interoperable can create security risks. There is also the possibility that security vulnerabilities in this context could lead to significant data breaches, which could potentially involve citizens of multiple or all member states, if the proposed networks are compromised.

In relation to interoperability of the EHDS, there are challenges[32] going forward. This is primarily due to the often uneasy relationship, which interoperability has with preserving privacy and security. As Terzis and Santamaria Echeverria note, 'interoperability brings efficiency and inter-organisational alignment, but usually comes with privacy compromises.'[33] They highlight a useful example of how interoperability can be achieved while protecting privacy. This is the work that 'the Dp-3T team demonstrated during the Covid-19 pandemic that one can build an interoperable infectious disease exposure system without necessarily compromising people's privacy.'[34] They also note problems with the way the earlier version of the regulation on EHDS addressed privacy in relation to interoperability[35]. The author agrees with the criticism in relation to Article 23 and Annex III of the Proposal, and unfortunately, the final version of the text may still not fully capture these issues. It is hoped that the implementing acts will be able to improve and foster a data protection by design approach but also, as Terzis and Santamaria Echeverria point out, given the importance of protecting privacy and security in 'data-intensive projects,' including more of the technical standards in the actual Regulation would have been preferable to deferring this to implementing acts.[36]

Another point to note here relates to the provisions in Chapter II relating to setting technical standards. Article 15 addresses the European electronic health record exchange format. Article 15 also refers back to Article 14, as this format is to relate 'to priority categories of personal electronic health data' and contemplates a series of implementing acts to assist with setting these technical standards, this is going to require much thought and collaboration. In the Regulation, Article 15(1) states: 'Such format shall be commonly used, machine-readable and allow transmission of personal electronic health data between different software applications, devices and healthcare providers.'

As Article 15(1) makes it clear that interoperability requirements are likely to encompass a wide range of devices, it needs to be understood that this may lead to security vulnerabilities. Furthermore, it is not entirely clear from the current wording of Article 14(1) in relation to these 'priority categories,' whether any of them might in fact incorporate information that a person or their representative has inserted into their EHR. At present, it is unclear whether inserted information is a priority category. It is conceivable that such data might be included under either the category set out in Article 14(1)(a) 'patient summaries' or 14(1)(e) 'medical test results, including laboratory and other diagnostic results and related reports.' This is mentioned, because if a patient inserts results from a genetic test provided by a DTC company, for example, a test for breast cancer risk, it is possible that either the patient or their healthcare professional may wish to transmit this information to another provider.

It needs to be emphasised that while interoperability has benefits, it can also pose security risks.[37] In the context of the right to insert, it is possible that an individual might wish to add a wide variety of data from a range of devices, and this could also contribute to further vulnerabilities, especially where accounts are linked.

3.4 Types of data a patient might insert – case study – genetic data from direct-to-consumer genetic test

The DTC testing industry[38] provides a case study of a source of data, which an individual may wish to insert into an EHR. This industry has created a market for genetic tests as consumer services. Some prominent companies in this space include 23andMe, AncestryDNA, MyHeritage, FamilyTreeDNA and Living DNA. The industry operates online and allows people to buy DNA tests internationally online with the consumer completing the purchase on a website and the company sending a kit in the mail. The consumer will then typically collect a sample of either saliva or a cheek swab and send it back to the company. This is the main way that many people can access their genetic data outside of the healthcare system, and companies have marketed their services using a rhetoric of consumer empowerment and democratising research.[39] However, regardless of the marketing of the industry, the focus has not been on benefiting individual consumers, but instead on amassing data[40] and from entering into partnerships and mergers with other entities. While the market for ancestry tests and health tests has grown, the industry is diverse, and companies offer a wide range of other types of tests, which can be very dubious (e.g., tests for child talent and infidelity).[41] Many of the health tests offered focus on disease susceptibility or predisposition, which is 'intended to provide an indication of the absolute lifetime risk and/or relative risk of an individual developing a condition.'[42] DTC companies may also provide consumers with raw genetic data. Consequently, it is possible that an individual might want to insert either genetic test results with disease susceptibility estimates, as well as raw data to their EHR. It is also conceivable that some individuals may wish to add in their genetic ancestry results in the hopes that it may be useful for their medical treatment.

In the context of the proposed right to insert information in an EHR, this section examines key issues, which the industry has raised, focusing on privacy together with the reliability, utility of tests offered and their limitations. While the author supports the enhancement of patients' rights, especially in relation to control over information and data portability, there are risks here in relation to uploading data from a DTC company's service, and much more oversight is needed of the way this industry operates. It should be emphasised that this is only one example of information that people may wish to insert. Wearable devices are another likely source of information, which people may wish to insert, and as they track a wide variety of data, some of which may relate to health and some of which may not, this widens the potential for non-health-related information to be directly inserted. However, given that studies have shown that some devices have vulnerabilities that allow attackers to tamper with the record and both insert and delete data,[43] this could cause further problems with the right to insert in relation to data quality, and much more oversight will be needed.

As the industry provides tests as consumer services, although it should comply with applicable data protection and consumer protection law, it has been largely unregulated to date.[44] Furthermore, as this is an industry, which operates internationally with several market leaders based in the USA,[45] it is possible that a European consumer's genetic data may be processed and stored in the USA or another country outside the EU.

Certain aspects of genetic and genomic data mean that it warrants greater protection. When an individual undergoes a genetic test whether that is in a clinical setting or through a DTC company, their physical genetic sample will be processed and analysed, and the process of genetic sequencing will generate genetic data in digital form. This genetic data is sensitive information, which can potentially be stored forever. Genetic data is also to a large extent inherently identifiable, and studies have demonstrated that it is very difficult to de-identify genetic data. As it can also serve as a unique identifier for the individual, but as people also share a lot of DNA with their family, this can pose privacy risks on an ongoing basis that will not decrease over time.[46] Given these characteristics, genetic data is also afforded special protection in the GDPR, and there are stronger requirements for consent.[47] It should be noted, however, that in general the industry may not be meeting the requirements of the GDPR, as it is still possible for websites to deem consent through use of the website or service. It is also often possible for a consumer to get through to the payment screen on a DTC website without being forced to view their contract or privacy policy.[48]

This industry has relied on the use of online contracts to govern relationships with its consumers. Previous work reviewed the contracts of 71 DTC companies that marketed tests for health purposes. This review identified several terms commonly included in these contracts, which could be challenged on the basis of unfairness in the UK and also in the EU. It is likely these could also be challenged on this basis in New Zealand and Australia, as these countries have very similar legislative control on unfair terms in consumer contracts.[49] As with other industries operating online, there is a significant problem here in relation to consumer engagement and understanding of these contracts,[50] as well as privacy policies. In relation to the right to insert, certain clauses in DTC companies' contracts may in fact limit their consumers' rights in relation to their genetic data, which in turn has an impact on their ability to exercise the right to insert by adding their genetic test results or raw data to their EHR. As one example, the current version of 23andMe's 'Terms of Service' for the EU includes a broad indemnity clause. This purports to bind the consumer to indemnify the company and 'its employees, contractors, successors, and assignees' '...from any liability arising out of the use or disclosure of any information obtained from analysing your sample and/or analysing your information.' This specifically includes indemnification where a person discloses information to 'third parties for diagnostic or other purposes.' [51] Unfortunately, indemnity clauses are common across this industry with the aforementioned review finding that 44 percent of the contracts considered included an indemnity clause.[52]

The previous review also found that companies often allow for sharing with affiliates.[53] This may mean that an individual's genetic data will be shared without their knowledge. Companies also commonly included clauses providing for broad powers to alter their terms, making it likely that even where a company states that it will not share certain data in a privacy policy, that may change over time.[54] If individuals are going to insert data from this industry in their EHR, then there is a real need for more attention to be paid to the regulation of this industry at the EU level, as well as the content of the industry's contracts and privacy policies. This is necessary, because some of the terms included in these contracts may in fact limit an individual's ability to access or share their data.[55]

Building upon the previous review of DTC contracts, the author has forthcoming work that compares some case-study examples of intellectual property licence clauses included in the contracts of DTC companies together with providers of wearable technology and online dating. The aim of this work was to explore the types of intellectual property rights that companies are acquiring in very sensitive forms of data.[56] Unfortunately, this new study found that there were significant similarities in the scope and language of licence clauses used across the three industries, and some of the rights obtained seem to breach both the GDPR and applicable consumer protection legislation. While this study was conducted in New Zealand, and New Zealand, Australian and American versions of documents were considered, future work will explore a larger sample of these and consider these in the EU context. For present purposes, in order to determine whether there may be problems with how these businesses operate in the EU, the author also accessed the EU 'Terms of Service' of Fitbit and 23andMe. Both companies' contracts contain these problematic clauses, including a clause in Fitbit's contract that allows for a non-exclusive licence to use a person's name and likeness.[57] These types of licences conflict with the protection of privacy and the rights of individuals in their personal data, which the GDPR provides and which the EHDS Regulation builds upon. Where companies acquire licences in their users' data and content, this may lead to problems with affording protection to the rights of EU and other citizens in their personal data. It may specifically cause problems with implementing the right to insert, as well as the right to data portability in the context of data collected from DTC companies, wearable devices and applications, where the company has acquired a licence in such data (which they may be able to transfer or sub-license) or where the company purports to limit their consumers' other rights, such as through the inclusion of an indemnity clause.

In the EU, while some tests provided by DTC companies should be captured by the Regulation on In Vitro Diagnostics (IVD Regulation),[58] much of the industry still operates outside the Regulation's remit. Specifically, the IVD Regulation Article 4 sets out requirements for all genetic tests used in a healthcare context, including that genetic counselling should be made available to all individuals undergoing testing. Furthermore, Recital 10 of the Regulation states 'that all tests that provide information on the predisposition to a medical condition or a disease, such as genetic tests, … are in vitro diagnostic medical devices.'

The provisions of the IVD Regulation seem applicable to DTC companies that provide tests for health purposes, as many do provide estimates related to disease predisposition. However, it is perhaps Article 4's use of the phrase 'in the context of healthcare' that may be a loophole at present, as DTC companies may be able to argue that their tests are not provided in this context. Currently, it seems that much of the DTC industry providing tests for health purposes may not in fact be compliant with this Regulation. A further problem here is that DTC companies commonly include terms purporting to limit the purposes of their testing specifying that tests are provided for 'informational' or 'educational purposes.' Thus, they may argue that they are not providing tests in the context of healthcare. For example, 23andMe's EU 'Terms of Service' specifies: 'Services are not intended to be used by the customer for any diagnostic purpose...'[59]

It should also be understood that most companies do not restrict themselves to offering tests of just one type[60] and may be performing secondary research for a variety of purposes. Unfortunately, DTC companies that provide ancestry tests and tests for other purposes may not be caught by the IVD Regulation. Genetic and genomic data can be used for a variety of secondary purposes, including medical research, but also other purposes, such as finding a suspect by law enforcement (this is often referred to as forensic investigative genetic genealogy).[61]

Concerns have been raised over the reliability and clinical utility of DNA tests offered by DTC companies.[62] A very significant issue in this context is that the industry itself has primarily focused on amassing data from their consumers that companies can use for secondary research purposes, rather than focusing on the quality of test results and value for individual consumers. Thus, in relation to the right to insert, much of this information may have very limited utility in a health context at present. Studies have demonstrated that in the context of DNA tests provided for health purposes, different DTC companies will be interested in different things and will even frame their populations differently, so that it is possible to get contradictory results from different companies.[63] This means that an individual seeking to find out about their risk of a particular type of cancer may receive different estimates from different companies about their level of risk for the same disease. Consequently, the information received may not be something that the individual or their clinician can rely upon to make a healthcare decision. Furthermore, concerns have been raised previously about the clinical utility of such testing, and there is a serious question regarding whether such tests should be offered on a direct-to-consumer basis. It is also true that currently most DTC companies do not provide their customers with whole genome sequence, but often focus instead on portions of an individual's genome, often focusing on specific single-nucleotide polymorphisms (SNPs).[64] This further limits the personal utility of test results, as certain SNPs have been found to be more common in some population groups and studies have demonstrated that companies may offer tests for only a limited number of SNPs that may in fact only be relevant for specific ethnic groups and be far less useful for the general population.[65] A study which considered the clinical utility of 23andMe's BReast CAncer Gene (BRCA) testing found that it 'misses almost 90 percent of BRCA mutation carriers, both in those with and those without a personal or family history of cancer,' and this study suggested that individuals would need follow-up tests to confirm both positive and negative results.[66] Meanwhile, it is likely that some people who undergo DTC tests will want to visit their doctor in order to help them to understand test results.[67]

There is a challenge here in that patients may want to add results or raw data from DTC companies to their EHR, but simultaneously many physicians may not be prepared to deal with these results.[68] It is unclear what responsibilities they should have in relation to inserted information. Recital 12 noted above indicates that information that is inserted does not have the same validation as other medical information. Given the concerns about the reliability of DTC tests, combined with the reality that even where DNA tests are carried out in a clinical setting, there is potential for misdiagnosis and misinterpretation,[69] and in a research context, the association of specific genetic variants with disease may be disputed,[70] an influx of this type of data could prove problematic for medical practice. As work on the EHDS progresses, guidelines, best practices and codes of conduct should be developed in consultation with physicians, other health professionals (e.g., genetic counsellors) and all stakeholders.

An individual's perception here is also an issue, as where a person has received DTC test results without the assistance of a genetic counsellor or physician, they may misunderstand the results or perceive them in a different way than they might with further informational resources.[71] The ability of an individual to correctly understand their results may also have a link to educational levels.[72] However, as the costs of tests have significantly dropped, this has widened the availability of DTC to a broader range of people, who may experience vulnerability and may be unnecessarily worried by their results or falsely reassured.

A further issue in relation to DTC tests is that results may include false positives[73] or false negatives. Consequently, even where an individual correctly understands their results, the results themselves may be incorrect or of limited value. This would normally require follow-up testing in order to establish, as with the BRCA study mentioned above. This in turn has an impact on the quality of data, which an individual may insert, and if it was relied upon without follow-up testing, this could also lead to unnecessary procedures, ranging from additional DNA testing to surgery, such as a mastectomy.[74] There are also liability issues that will need to be considered in relation to health practitioners' responsibilities, but as noted above, DTC companies often attempt to broadly limit their liability, which is likely in breach of EU data protection and consumer protection legislation.

Finally, as Terzis and Santamaria Echeverria also highlight, there is a need to give further attention to the possible roles of Big Tech in the EHDS, and this is very important in the context of services offered in the consumer realm.

They highlight the growing interest of Big Tech in the health sector and critique the way that the earlier drafting of the EHDS Regulation addressed intellectual property rights. This author echoes those concerns in relation to Article 52 of the Regulation.[75] Together with the examples they mention,[76] there has been significant investment by Big Tech in both the DTC and wearable tech industries. Google has invested in 23andMe[77] and has collaborated with AncestryDNA,[78] as well as acquiring Fitbit.[79] The DTC industry has also been characterised by partnerships and mergers,[80] widening the potential for consumers' data to be used for a variety of secondary research purposes, which they may not anticipate. If privacy rights are to be protected, not only in the EU, but in other countries outside the EU, such as New Zealand and Australia, there is a need for more oversight of Big Tech's interests in the health and health technology space. It is hoped that the recently launched proceedings against Meta's Facebook in the EU, together with the recent fining of Google in France, may lead to improvements in how these companies operate,[81] although their history so far does not bode well.[82]

3.5 Conclusion

This chapter has provided a critical examination of the right to insert data into the EHR, as it is framed in the EHDS Regulation. It has sought to highlight some of the issues that implementing such a right is likely to raise. In doing so, it has considered the specific example of the DTC genetic testing industry and potential risks, which stem from an individual's engagement with that industry and desire to add genetic data to their EHR. While the EHDS has many positive aspirations, it is suggested herein that the path ahead will be very challenging, especially as it relates to the right to insert. The DTC industry is an illuminating example, because it is the main way that many people can now access their genetic information. This industry is problematic, because it lacks harmonised standards and also provides both information that is health related and information that is not health related. Furthermore, while the industry does engage in medical research, it often seeks to limit the purposes of even its health tests, meaning that more work is needed to improve governance of this industry both in the EU and globally. An individual may wish to directly add all of this information to their EHR, and while the issues raised here are not entirely unique, given the rise in popularity of ancestry testing, if large numbers of people begin to add this information to their EHRs, this is likely to place a strain on the healthcare systems of individual member states. It is recommended that further consultation is conducted regarding the implementation of this right, and it would be ideal if together with educational initiatives for patients, guidelines, best practices and codes of conduct were developed to assist health professionals in dealing with information that is inserted by their patients and their representatives. It is hoped that this will serve to encourage further discussion around the implementation of this right and the cyber security and privacy risks, which it may entail.

Notes

1 European Commission, 'Commission welcomes political agreement on European Health Data Space' Press Release (15 March 2024) https://ec.europa.eu/commission/presscorner/detail/en/ip_24_1346 accessed 31 May 2024.
2 G Fortuna, 'EU Policy. Deal on landmark health data space clinched in the eleventh hour' *Euro News Health* (15 March 2024) https://www.euronews.com/health/2024/03/15/deal-on-landmark-health-data-space-clinched-in-the-eleventh-hour accessed 31 May 2024.
3 The Compromise Text is now available here Proposal for a Regulation on the European Health Data Space- Analysis of the final Compromise Text with a view to agreement https://www.consilium.europa.eu/media/70909/st07553-en24.pdf accessed 31 May 2024; see also Proposal for a REGULATION OF THE EUROPEAN PARLIAMENT AND OF THE COUNCIL on the European Health Data Space COM/2022/197 final.
4 L Rosencrance, 'Femtech' *TechTarget* (last updated 22 April 2022) https://www.techtarget.com/whatis/definition/femtech accessed 31 May 2024; J Scott, 'What Is Femtech, and How Is It Evolving in Healthcare?' *HealthTech* (14 September 2022) https://healthtechmagazine.net/article/2022/09/what-is-femtech-how-is-it-evolving-perfcon.
5 AM Phillips, *Buying Your Self on the Internet: Wrap Contracts and Personal Genomics* (EUP 2019) https://www.jstor.org/stable/10.3366/j.ctvnjbgvb; AM Phillips, 'Reading the Fine Print When Buying Your Genetic Self Online: Direct-to-Consumer Genetic Testing Terms and Conditions' (2017) 36(3) *New Genetics and Society* 273–295. Doi: 10.1080/14636778.2017.1352468; SI Becher and AM Phillips, 'Data Rights and Consumer Contracts: The Case of Personal Genomic Services' in D Clifford, KH Lau, and J Paterson, *Data Rights and Private Law* (Hart Publishing 2023) 84–101; AM Phillips and J Charbonneau also have forthcoming work detailing findings from the GenePri 2022 public survey.
6 EHDS art 3.
7 Regulation (EU) 2016/679 of the European Parliament and of the Council of 27 April 2016 on the protection of natural persons with regard to the processing of personal data and on the free movement of such data, and repealing Directive 95/46/EC (General Data Protection Regulation) [2016] OJ 2 119/1.
8 Becher and Phillips, 'Data Rights…' (n 5) 84–101.
9 D Fåhraeus, J Reichel, and S Slokenberga, 'The European Health Data Space: Challenges and Opportunities' *Sieps* (February 2024). https://www.sieps.se/globalassets/publikationer/2024/2024_2epa.pdf accessed 31 May 2024.
10 J Charbonneau et al., 'Public Reactions to Direct-to-Consumer Genetic Health Tests: A Comparison Across the US, UK, Japan and Australia' (2019) *European Journal of Human Genetics* 28 339; and J Charbonneau and D Nicol, 'Pathways, Processes and Protections: Australia's Clinical and Direct-To-Consumer Genetic Testing Spaces' (2021) 28(2) *Journal of Law and Medicine* 370–388; JW Leighton, K Valverde, and BA Bernhardt, 'The General Public's Understanding and Perception of Direct-To-Consumer Genetic Test Results' (2012) 15(1) *Public Health Genomics* 11–21; and JE Ostergren et al, 'PGen Study Group. How Well Do Customers of Direct-to-Consumer Personal Genomic Testing Services Comprehend Genetic Test Results? Findings from the Impact of Personal Genomics Study' (2015) 18(4) *Public Health Genomics* 216–224.
11 S Sterckx et al, 'Trust Is Not Something You Can Reclaim Easily': Patenting in the Field of Direct-To-Consumer Genetic Testing' (2013) 15(5) *Genetics in Medicine* 382–387; and also forthcoming AM Phillips, 'Owning Me, Owning You – How Private Companies Acquire Rights in Our Most Intimate Data' in forthcoming

volume G Reynolds, A Mogyoros, and T Dagne (Eds), *IP's Futures* (University of Ottawa Press 2024); 23andMe, *23ANDME HOLDING CO. ANNUAL REPORT FISCAL 2023* (25 May 2023) at 7 https://investors.23andme.com/static-files/f539b943-c01b-4baf-a071-b4fbc809083b accessed 31 May 2024.

12 EHDS art 3.

13 L Marelli et al, 'The European Health Data Space: Too Big to Succeed?' (2023) 135 *Health Policy* 104861.

14 J Karow, '23andMe DTC Breast and Ovarian Cancer Risk Test Misses Almost 90 Percent of BRCA Mutation Carriers' *GenomeWeb* (5 April 2019) https://www.genomeweb.com/molecular-diagnostics/23andme-dtc-breast-and-ovarian-cancer-risk-test-missesalmost-90-percent-brca#.XKfbrS1L1PU accessed 31 May 2024 citing E Esplin et al, 'Limitations of HBOC Direct-To-Consumer Genetic Screening: False Positives, False Negatives and Everything in Between' Abstract 27 presented at the ACMG Annual Clinical Genetics Meeting, 4 April 2019, Washington State Convention Center https://aacrjournals.org/cancerres/article/79/4_Supplement/P4-03-06/639589/Abstract-P4-03-06-Limitations-of-direct-to accessed 12 March 2024; R Collier, 'Genetic Tests for Athletic Ability: Science or Snake Oil?' (2012) 184(1) *Canadian Medical Association Journal* E43–E45.

15 Becher and Phillips, 'Data Rights…' (n 5) 84–101.

16 AB Carter et al, 'Electronic Health Records and Genomics: Perspectives from the Association for Molecular Pathology Electronic Health Record (EHR) Interoperability for Clinical Genomics Data Working Group' (2022) 24(1) *The Journal of Molecular Diagnostics* 1–17.

17 Fåhraeus et al (n 9) 8.

18 Marelli et al (n 13).

19 N Huber, 'Cyber Attacks Are One of the Biggest Threats Facing Healthcare Systems' *Financial Times* (16 January 2024) https://www.ft.com/content/77d54679-0915-4ce2-a42f-0c2b844da7ef?signupConfirmation=success accessed 12 March 2024.

20 ENISA, 'Checking-Up on Health: Ransomware Accounts for 54% of Cybersecurity Threats' Press Release (5 July 2023) https://www.enisa.europa.eu/news/checking-up-on-health-ransomware-accounts-for-54-of-cybersecurity-threats ; and see the report, ENISA, *ENISA Threat Landscape: Health Sector (January 2021 to March 2023)* (ENISA July 2023) https://www.enisa.europa.eu/publications/health-threat-landscape accessed 31 May 2024.

21 ENISA, *ENISA Threat* (n 20) 4.

22 FDA, 'Cybersecurity vulnerabilities of Hospira Symbiq Infusion System' (FDA Safety Communication, 31 July 2015) https://www.fda.gov/medicaldevices/digitalhealth/ucm373213.htm – archived content available at http://wayback.archive-it.org/7993/20170722144742 / https://www.fda.gov/MedicalDevices/Safety/AlertsandNotices/ucm446809.htm accessed 31 May 2024.

23 AM Phillips, 'Hacking Your DNA? Some Things to Consider Before Buying a DNA Test Online' *Health Law Blog Sweden* (2 March 2024) https://healthlawsweden.blogg.lu.se/2024/03/02/hacking-your-dna-some-things-to-consider-before-buying-a-dna-test-online/ accessed 31 May 2024.

24 Phillips, 'Hacking Your DNA…' ; and J Dworetzky, 'Hackers Target Jewish and Chinese 23andMe Customers; Class Action Lawsuit Filed Against South City DNA Data Company' *The Daily Journal* (13 March 2024). https://www.smdailyjournal.com/news/local/hackers-target-jewish-and-chinese-23andme-customers-class-action-lawsuit-filed-against-south-city-dna/article_22e9c192-e0e7-11ee-92c1-2bec18317904.html accessed 31 May 2024.; S Alder, '23andMe Settles Data Breach Lawsuit for $30 Million' The HIPAA Journal (16 September 2024) https://www.hipaajournal.com/23andme-class-action-data-breach-settlement/.

25 J McKeon, 'What the 23andMe Data Breach Reveals About Credential Stuffing' TechTarget Health IT Security (7 December 2023) https://healthitsecurity.com/features/what-the-23andme-data-breach-reveals-about-credential-stuffing accessed 31 May 2024; N Mueller, 'Credential Stuffing' *OWASP* https://owasp.org/www.community/attacks/Credential_stuffing accessed 12 March 2024.
26 See Filing – Motion to Appoint Interim Leadership – *David Melvin and J.L v 23andMe Inc Case No.* 24-cv-00487-SK – hearing date set at 4th March 2024 https://fingfx.thomsonreuters.com/gfx/legaldocs/gkvlddmwnvb/frankel-23andMedatabreach–Edelsonleadcounsel.pdf accessed 12 March 2024.
27 MH Shahin et al, 'Open Data Revolution in Clinical Research: Opportunities and Challenges' (2020) 13(4) *Clinical and Translational Science* 665–674. doi: 10.1111/cts.12756; European Parliament, 'EU Health Data Space to Support Patients and Research' (Press Release, 15 March 2024) https://www.europarl.europa.eu/news/en/press-room/20240304IPR18765/eu-health-data-space-to-support-patients-and-research accessed 12 March 2024.
28 C McCluskey, S Jounus and G Scott, 'Shaping the Future: the European Health Data Space' *Goodwin Privacy and Cyber Security Insights* (12 February 2024) https://www.goodwinprivacyblog.com/2024/02/12/shaping-the-future-the-european-health-dataspace/#:~:text=The%20problem%20is%20it%27s%20difficult,space%20have%20been%20embracing%20pseudonymisatio accessed 12 March 2024; J Taylor, 'Medibank v the hackers: how the health insurer fell to a mass data theft' *The Guardian* (London, 11 November 2022) https://www.theguardian.com/australia-news/2022/nov/12/medibank-v-the-hackers-how-the-health-insurer-fell-to-a-mass-data-theft accessed 12 March 2024.
29 P Terzis and OE Santamaria Echeverria, 'Interoperability and Governance in the European Health Data Space Regulation' (2023) 23(4) *Medical Law International* 368–376, 373.
30 Terzis and Santamaria Echeverria, 'Interoperability and Governance in the European Health Data Space Regulation', 373 citing P Keller and A Tarkowski, 'The Paradox of Open' (Open Future), https://paradox.openfuture.eu/ (accessed 7 February 2023).
31 For example, LT Martin et al, 'The Issues of Interoperability and Data Connectedness for Public Health' (2022) 10(S1) *Big Data* S19–S24. doi: 10.1089/big.2022.0207; M Edmunds et al, 'Ten Reasons Why Interoperability Is Difficult' in C Weaver et al (eds), *Healthcare Information Management Systems* (Health Informatics Springer, 2016).
32 Trasys International, *Study on an Infrastructure and Data Ecosystem Supporting the Impact Assessment of the European Health Data Space – Executive Summary* (Directorate-General for Health and Food safety European Commission 29 April 2022)https://health.ec.europa.eu/system/files/2022-05/ehealth.ehds_ia_infrastructure-dataecosystem_en_1.pdf accessed 31 May 2024.; Digitaleurope, 'Digitaleurope's Recommendations for the European Health Data Space' (3 February 2021) https://www.digitaleurope.org/resources/digitaleuropes-recommendations-for-the-european-health-data-space/#_ftn3 accessed 31 May 2024.
33 Terzis and Santamaria Echeverria (n 29) 370.
34 Terzis and OE Santamaria Echeverria, 'Interoperability and Governance in the European Health Data Space Regulation', 370.
35 Terzis and OE Santamaria Echeverria, 'Interoperability and Governance in the European Health Data Space Regulation' 370–7, see (n 7).
36 Terzis and OE Santamaria Echeverria, 'Interoperability and Governance in the European Health Data Space Regulation' 374.
37 C Robbins, 'Security and Interoperability – A Conflict' *NEXOR* https://www.nexor.com/blog/security-and-interoperability-a-conflict accessed 31 May 2024; AS

Fernando, 'Chapter 4 – Interoperability Risks and Health Informatics' in DC Klonoff, D Kerr, and ER Weitzman (eds), *Diabetes Digital Health and Telehealth* (Academic Press 2022) 43–50; S Poremba, 'Health Care Interoperability: What Are the Security Considerations?' *Security Intelligence* (20 September 2021) https://securityintelligence.com/articles/health-care-interoperability-security-considerations/ accessed 12 March 2024; L Barrett, 'Data Security Remains a Challenge as Interoperability Moves Closer to Reality' *Chief Healthcare Executive* (19 June 2022) https://www.chiefhealthcareexecutive.com/view/data-security-remains-a-challenge-as-interoperability-moves-closer-to-reality accessed 12 March 2024.

38 House of Commons Science and Technology Committee, *Direct-to-Consumer Genomic Testing* (First Report of Session 2021–22, House of Commons 2021) https://committees.parliament.uk/publications/6347/documents/69832/default/ accessed 12 March 2024; S Hogarth and P Saukko, 'A Market in the Making: The Past, Present and Future of Direct-To-Consumer Genomics' (2017) 36(3) *New Genetics and Society* 197–208, 197.

39 A Nordgren, 'Neither as Harmful as Feared by Critics nor as Empowering as Promised by Providers: Risk Information Offered Direct to Consumer by Personal Genomics Companies' (2014) 5(1) *Journal of Community Genetics* 59; A Demopoulos, 'There Are No Serious Safeguards': Can 23andMe Be Trusted With Our DNA?' *The Guardian* (17 February 2024) https://www.theguardian.com/technology/2024/feb/17/23andme-dna-data-security-finance accessed 12 March 2024.

40 LI Laestadius, JR Rich, and PL Auer, 'All Your Data (Effectively) Belong to Us: Data Practices Among Direct-To-Consumer Genetic Testing Firms' (2016) 19 *Genetics in Medicine* 513–520. doi:10.1038/gim.2016.136.

41 AM Phillips, 'Only a Click Away – DTC Genetics for Ancestry, Health, Love… and More: A View of the Business and Regulatory Landscape' (2016) 8 *Applied & Translational Genomics* 16–22; and AM Phillips and S Becher, 'At-Home DNA Tests Just Aren't That Reliable – And the Risks May Outweigh the Benefits' *The Conversation* (29 November 2022) https://theconversation.com/at-home-dna-tests-just-arent-that-reliable-and-the-risks-may-outweigh-the-benefits-194349 accessed 31 May 2024.

42 Human Genetics Commission, *A Common Framework of Principles for Direct-To-Consumer Genetic Testing Services* (Department of Health, 2010) 2–3, Table 1. https://ukgtn.nhs.uk/resources/library/article/human-genetics-commission-a-common-framework-of-principles-for-direct-toconsumer-genetic-testing-services-70/ accessed 31 May 2024.

43 A Hilts, C Parsons and J Knockel, *Every Step You Fake: A Comparative Analysis of Fitness Tracker Privacy and Security* (Open Effect Report 2016) https://openeffect.ca/reports/Every_Step_You_Fake.pdf accessed 8 April 2024; and Norwegian Consumer Council, #WatchOut Analysis of smartwatches for children (October 2017) https://storage02.forbrukerradet.no/media/2017/10/watchout-rapport-october-2017.pdf accessed 8 April 2024.

44 See Phillips, *Buying Your…* (n 5) chs 1 and 6; and Phillips, 'Reading the…' (n 5); Becher and Phillips, 'Data Rights…' (n 5).

45 23andMe, AncestryDNA and FamilyTreeDNA are all based in the USA, as well as several other prominent companies.

46 E Ayday et al, 'Whole Genome Sequencing: Revolutionary Medicine or Privacy Nightmare?' (2015) 48(2) *Computer* 58–66 doi: 10.1109/MC.2015.59; see also M Gymrek et al, 'Identifying Personal Genomes by Surname Inference' (2013) 339(6117) *Science* 321–324; CY Johnson, 'Even If You've Never Taken a DNA Test, a Distant Relative's Could Reveal Your Identity' *The Washington Post* (Washington, 11 October 2018) https://www.washingtonpost.com/science/2018/10/11/even-if-youve-never-taken-dna-test-distant-relatives-could-reveal-your-identity/.

– citing Y Erlich et al, 'Identity Inference of Genomic Data Using Long-Range Familial Searches' (2018) *Science* 362, 690–694; also T Woodage, 'Relative Futility: Limits to Genetic Privacy Protection Because of the Inability to Prevent Disclosure of Genetic Information by Relatives' (2010) 95 *Minnesota Law Review* 682–713.

47 See GDPR art 9.

48 Becher and Phillips, 'Data Rights…' (n 5).

49 There are strong similarities in the legislation providing for control of unfair terms in consumer contracts in all these jurisdictions. See Council Directive 93/13/EEC of 5 April 1993 on unfair terms in consumer contracts [1993] OJ L95/36/29; in the UK, see the Consumer Rights Act 2015; in New Zealand, see Fair Trading Act 1986 and Fair Trading Amendment Act 2021; in Australia, the relevant legislation can be found in the Australian Consumer Law, which is included in Schedule 2 to the Competition and Consumer Act 2010 (Cth) (CCA).

50 U Benoliel and SI Becher, 'The Duty to Read the Unreadable' (January 11, 2019) 60 *Boston College Law Review* 2255 https://ssrn.com/abstract=3313837 accessed 31 May 2024.

51 23andMe, 'Terms of Service' EU Version (last updated 8 June 2022) https://www.23andme.com/en-eu/legal/terms-of-service/full-version/ accessed 9 April 2024.

52 Phillips, *Buying Your…* (n 5) 193; and Becher and Phillips, 'Data Rights…' (n 5) 93.

53 Phillips, *Buying Your…* (n 5) ch 5.

54 Becher and Phillips, 'Data Rights…' (n 5) 182-186.

55 Phillips, 'Owning me…' (n 11).

56 Phillips, 'Owning me…' (n 11).

57 Fitbit, 'Terms of Service' EU Version (last updated 2 February 2024) https://www.fitbit.com/global/ie/legal/terms-of-service accessed 9 April 2024; 23andMe, 'Terms of Service' (n 51).

58 Council Regulation (EU) 2017/746 of 5 April 2017 on in vitro diagnostic medical devices and repealing Directive 98/79/EC and Commission Decision 2010/227/EU [2017] OJ L 117/176; and L Kalokairinou et al, 'Legislation of Direct-To-Consumer Genetic Testing in Europe: A Fragmented Regulatory Landscape' (2018) 9(2) *Journal of Community Genetics* 117–32, 118.

59 23andMe, 'Terms of Service' (n 51).

60 Phillips, 'Only a Click…'; and Phillips, *Buying Your…*(n 5) ch 3.

61 J Lynch, 'Forensic Genetic Genealogy Searches: What Defense Attorneys & Policy Makers Need to Know' *Electronic Frontier Foundation* (26 July 2023) https://www.eff.org/wp/forensic-genetic-genealogy-searches-what-defense-attorneys-need-know accessed 31 May 2024.

62 Karow; Collier (n 14).

63 US Government Accountability Office, (GAO) Direct-To-Consumer Genetic Tests: Misleading Test Results Are Further Complicated by Deceptive Marketing and Other Questionable Practice (GAO-10-847T, 2010) Testimony before the Subcommittee on Oversight and Investigations, Committee on Energy and Commerce, House of Representatives 1–8 http://www.gao.gov/assets/130/125079.pdf accessed 31 May 2024; Collier.

64 L Jostins and JC Barrett, 'Genetic Risk Prediction in Complex Disease' (2011) 20 *Human Molecular Genetics* R182–R188. https://doi.org/10.1093/hmg/ddr378; KS Panacer, 'Ethical Issues Associated With Direct-to-Consumer Genetic Testing' (2023) 15(6) *Cureus* e39918.

65 NV Desai et al, 'Retrospective Cohort Study on the Limitations of Direct-to-Consumer Genetic Screening in Hereditary Breast and Ovarian Cancer' (2023)7 *JCO Precision Oncology* e2200695. doi: 10.1200/PO.22.00695; MF Martins et al, 'Direct-To-Consumer Genetic Testing: An Updated Systematic Review of Healthcare Professionals' Knowledge and Views, and Ethical and Legal Concerns' (2022) 30 *European Journal of Human Genetics* 1331–1343.

66 Esplin et al, 'Limitations of …' (n 14) and Desai et al (n 65); see also National Cancer Institute, 'BRCA Gene Changes: Cancer Risk and Genetic Testing' (Reviewed 19 July 2024 https://www.cancer.gov/about-cancer/causes-prevention/genetics/brca-fact-sheet#:~:text=affect%20cancer%20treatment%3F-,What%20are%20BRCA1%20and%20BRCA2%3F,copy%20inherited%20from%20each%20parent.
67 Charbonneau et al, 'Public Reactions…' (n 10); and Charbonneau and Nicol, 'Pathways, Processes and Protections…' (n 10); AL McGuire et al, 'Social Networkers' Attitudes Toward Direct-To-Consumer Personal Genome Testing' (2009) 9 (6–7) *American Journal of Bioethics* 3–10. doi: 10.1080/15265160902928209; and R Horton et al, 'Direct-to-Consumer Genetic Testing' (2019) 367 *BMJ* l5688. doi: 10.1136/bmj.l5688; J Lenzer and S Brownlee, 'Knowing Me, Knowing You' (2008) 336(7649) *BMJ* 858–860.
68 KP Powell et al, 'Educational Needs of Primary Care Physicians Regarding Direct-To-Consumer Genetic Testing' (2012) 21(3) *Journal of Genetic Counselling* 469–478; KP Powell et al, 'Primary Care Physicians' Awareness, Experience and Opinions of Direct-To-Consumer Genetic Testing' (2012) 21(1) *Journal of Genetic Counselling* 113–126. https://www.researchgate.net/profile/Karen_Powell8/publication/51502589_Primary_Care_Physicians%27_Awareness_Experience_and_Opinions_of_Direct-to-Consumer_Genetic_Testing/links/547487340cf2778985abe54c.pdf accessed 31 May 2024; A Gerdes et al, 'Direct to Consumer Genetic Testing in Denmark – Public Knowledge, Use, and Attitudes' (2021) 29 *European Journal of Human Genetics* 851–860.
69 T Shaw et al, 'Missed Diagnosis or Misdiagnosis: Common Pitfalls in Genetic Testing' (2023) 64(1) *Singapore Medical Journal* 67–73.
70 Heidi L Rehm et al, 'ClinGen The Clinical Genome Resource' (2015) 372(23) *New England Journal of Medicine* 2235–2242. doi:10.1056/NEJMsr1406261.
71 Charbonneau et al, 'Public Reactions…' (n 10).
72 Ostergren et al, 'PGen Study …' (n 10).
73 S Tandy-Connor et al, 'False-Positive Results Released by Direct-To-Consumer Genetic Tests Highlight the Importance of Clinical Confirmation Testing for Appropriate Patient Care' (2018) 20 *Genetics in Medicine* 1515–1521.
74 Panacer, 'Ethical Issues Associated…' (n 64); C Farr, 'Why the FDA Is Targeting Google-Backed 23andMe: Unnecessary MRIs, Mastectomies' *VentureBeat* (26 November 2013) https://venturebeat.com/business/warning-letter-to-23andme-could-be-a-landmark-case-for-health-care/ accessed 8 April 2024.
75 Also note recital 40c Regulation.
76 Terzis and Santamaria Echeverria (n 29) 371–372.
77 D Spiegel, 'One of Google's Earliest Genetic Experiments, 23andMe, Paid Off – Here's What Will Make or Break Its Future' *CNBC* (25 January 2022) https://www.cnbc.com/2022/01/25/how-one-of-googles-earliest-genetic-experiments-23andme-paid-off.html accessed 12 March 2024.
78 E Brodwin, 'A Collaboration Between Google's Secretive Life-Extension Spinoff and Popular Genetics Company Ancestry Has Quietly Ended' *Business Insider* (1 August 2018) http://uk.businessinsider.com/google-calico-ancestry-dna-genetics-aging-partnershipended-2018-7?r=US&IR=T accessed 31 May 2024.
79 R Osterloh, 'Google Completes Fitbit Acquisition' (*Google*, 14 January 2021) https://blog.google/products/devices-services/fitbit-acquisition/ accessed 31 May 2024; Spirion, 'Is Google's Purchase of Fitbit a Data Privacy Risk?' (2019) https://www.spirion.com/blog/google-fitbit-acquisition-data-privacy-risk accessed 12 March 2024.
80 M Sullivan, '23andMe Has Signed 12 Other Genetic Data Partnerships Beyond Pfizer and Genentech' *VentureBeat* (14 January 2015) https://venturebeat.com/2015/01/14/23andme-has-signed-12-other-genetic-data-partnerships-beyond-pfizerand-genentech/ accessed 12 March 2024; Virgin, '23andMe and Virgin Group's VG Acquisition Corp. Successfully Close Business Combination' (Press Release 16 June 2021) https://www.virgin.com/about-virgin/virgin-group/news/23andme-and-virgin-groups-vg-acquisition-corp-successfully-close-business accessed 12 March 2024.

81 BEUC, 'Commission Digital Markets Act Enforcement Against Tech Giants a Boost for Consumers' Press Release (25 March 2024) https://www.beuc.eu/press-releases/commission-digital-markets-act-enforcement-against-tech-giants-boost-consumers accessed 15 April 2024; BEUC, 'Consumer Groups Launch Complaints Against Meta's Massive, Illegal Data Processing Behind Its Pay-Or-Consent Smokescreen' (29 February 2024) https://www.beuc.eu/press-releases/consumer-groups-launch-complaints-against-metas-massive-illegal-data-processing accessed 31 May 2024; a summary of the complaint is available here 'How Meta Is Breaching Consumers' Fundamental Rights' (February 2024) https://www.beuc.eu/sites/default/files/publications/BEUC-X-2024-020_How_Meta_is_breaching_consumers_fundamental_rights.pdf accessed 31 May 2024 ; N Lomas and R Dillet, 'Google Hit With $270M Fine in France as Authority Finds News Publishers' Data Was Used for Gemini' *TechCrunch* (21 March 2024) https://techcrunch.com/2024/03/20/google-hit-with-270m-fine-in-france-as-authority-finds-news-publishers-data-was-used-for-gemini/ accessed 31 May 2024.

82 T Revell, 'Google DeepMind's NHS Data Deal 'Failed to Comply' With Law' *New Scientist* (3 July 2017) https://www.newscientist.com/article/2139395-google-deepminds-nhs-data-deal-failed-to-comply-with-law/ accessed 31 May 2024.

List of sources

Legislation

Council Regulation (EU) 2017/746 of 5 April 2017 on in vitro diagnostic medical devices and repealing Directive 98/79/EC and Commission Decision 2010/227/EU [2017] OJ L 117/76.

Regulation (EU) 2016/679 of the European Parliament and of the Council of 27 April 2016 on the protection of natural persons with regard to the processing of personal data and on the free movement of such data, and repealing Directive 95/46/EC (General Data Protection Regulation) [2016] OJ 2 119/1.

Policy documents

Council of the European Union, 'Proposal for a Regulation on the European Health Data Space – Analysis of the final compromise text with a view to agreement' 2022/0140(COD).

European Commission, 'Proposal for a regulation – The European Health Data Space' COM(2022) 197 final.

House of Commons Science and Technology Committee, *Direct-to-consumer genomic testing* (First Report of Session 2021–22, House of Commons 2021) https://committees.parliament.uk/publications/6347/documents/69832/default/

New South Wales Police, 'Forensic Investigative Genetic Genealogy'. https://www.police.nsw.gov.au/about_us/information_of_interest_to_the_community/forensic_investigative_genetic_genealogy#:~:text=FIGG%20combines%20new%20DNA%20analysis,built%20to%20identify%20potential%20candidates

Norwegian Consumer Council, #WatchOut Analysis of smartwatches for children (October 2017) https://storage02.forbrukerradet.no/media/2017/10/watchout-rapport-october-2017.pdf

Literature and other secondary resources

Ayday E et al, 'Whole Genome Sequencing: Revolutionary Medicine or Privacy Nightmare?' (2015) 48(2) *Computer* 58–66. doi: 10.1109/MC.2015.59

Bakos Y et al, 'Does Anyone Read the Fine Print? Consumer Attention to Standard-Form Contracts' (2014) 43(1) *The Journal of Legal Studies* 1–35. doi: 10.1086/674424

Becher SI and Phillips AM, 'Data Rights and Consumer Contracts: The Case of Personal Genomic Services' in D Clifford, KH Lau, and J Paterson (eds), *Data Rights and Private Law* (Hart Publishing 2023) 84–101.

Benoliel U and Becher SI, 'The Duty to Read the Unreadable' (January 11, 2019) 60 *Boston College Law Review* 2255 https://ssrn.com/abstract=3313837

Brothers KB and Knapp EE, 'How Should Primary Care Physicians Respond to Direct-to-Consumer Genetic Test Results?' (2018) 20(9) *AMA Journal of Ethics* E812–818. doi: 10.1001/amajethics.2018.812

Conklin K and Hyde R, 'If Small Print "Terms and Conditions" Require a PhD to Read, Should They Be Legally Binding?' *The Conversation* (10 May 2018) https://theconversation.com/if-small-print-terms-and-conditions-require-a-phd-to-read-should-they-be-legally-binding-75101

Fåhraeus D, Reichel J and Slokenberga S, 'The European Health Data Space: Challenges and Opportunities' *Sieps* (February 2024). https://www.sieps.se/globalassets/publikationer/2024/2024_2epa.pdf

Majumder MA et al, 'Direct-to-Consumer Genetic Testing: Value and Risk' (2021) 72 *Annual Review of Medicine* 151–166. doi: 10.1146/annurev-med-070119-114727

Martins MF et al, 'Direct-to-Consumer Genetic Testing: An Updated Systematic Review of Healthcare Professionals' Knowledge and Views, and Ethical and Legal Concerns' (2022) 30 *European Journal of Human Genetics* 1331–1343. doi: 10.1038/s41431-022-01205-8

McGrath SP et al, 'Are Providers Prepared for Genomic Medicine: Interpretation of Direct-To-Consumer Genetic Testing (DTC-GT) Results and Genetic Self-Efficacy by Medical Professionals' (2019) 19 *BMC Health Services Research* 844. doi: 10.1186/s12913-019-4679-8

Nordgren A, 'Neither as Harmful as Feared by Critics nor as Empowering as Promised by Providers: Risk Information Offered Direct to Consumer by Personal Genomics Companies' (2014) 5(1) *Journal of Community Genetics* 59.

Phillips AM, 'Genomic Privacy and Direct-to-Consumer Genetics: Big Consumer Genetic Data -- What's in that Contract?' (2015) *IEEE Security and Privacy Workshops*, San Jose, CA, USA, 2015, 60–64. doi: 10.1109/SPW.2015.19

Phillips AM, 'Reading the Fine Print When Buying Your Genetic Self Online: Direct-to-Consumer Genetic Testing Terms and Conditions' (2017) *New Genetics and Society* 36(3) 273–295. doi: 10.1080/14636778.2017.1352468

Phillips AM, *Buying Your Self on the Internet: Wrap Contracts and Personal Genomics* (Edinburgh University Press 2019) https://www.jstor.org/stable/10.3366/j.ctvnjbgvb

Phillips AM, 'The Age of Personalised Medicine – From Patients to Consumers: The Digital Environment, Clickwrap Contracts, and Implications for Autonomy' in AM Phillips, TC de Campos, and J Herring (eds), *Philosophical Foundations of Medical Law* (Oxford University Press 2019) doi: 10.1093/oso/9780198796558.003.0023

Phillips AM, and Charbonneau J, 'From the Lab to the Market' (2015) 28(3) *GeneWatch* 7–10. https://issuu.com/genewatchmagazine/docs/genewatch_28-3

Spiegel D, 'One of Google's Earliest Genetic Experiments, 23andMe, Paid Off – Here's What Will Make or Break Its Future' *CNBC* (25 January 2022) https://www.cnbc.com/2022/01/25/how-one-of-googles-earliest-genetic-experiments-23andme-paid-off.html

Tandy-Connor S et al, 'False-Positive Results Released by Direct-To-Consumer Genetic Tests Highlight the Importance of Clinical Confirmation Testing for Appropriate Patient Care' (2018) *Genetics in Medicine*. doi: 10.1038/gim.2018.38

Te Aka Matua o te Ture New Zealand Law Commission, *The Use of DNA in Criminal Investigations | Te Whakamahi i te Ira Tangata i ngā Mātai Taihara (NZLC R144)*. https://www.lawcom.govt.nz/our-work/the-use-of-dna-in-criminal-investigations/tab/report

4 European Health Data Space

A breakthrough in user control over health data in wellness apps?

Petra Holmberg

4.1 Introduction

In 2020, the application market concerning health services was bursting at the seams, with 250 apps being added daily.[1] The applications covered a wide range of health services, from monitoring the patient's physiological parameters through diagnosis to providing psychological support and physical activity measurement. Depending on their functions, the type of data collected and the binding nature of the provided recommendations also varied. Currently, between 22% and 41% of European citizens use at least one health app.[2] Today, these apps represent a market of approximately 370,000 apps.[3] In 2020, a survey in the UK showed that 62% of respondents were willing to incorporate mobile health (mHealth) apps;[4] by 2022, these percentages had already increased.[5]

The applications that process users' health data, commonly known as mobile health apps, medical apps, or wellness apps, have attracted considerable attention in EU policy documents for over a decade. However, the lack of clear definitions for the relevant terms in European legislation appears to be a challenge. This situation is now undergoing a transformation with the introduction of the European Health Data Space (EHDS). For the first time, the EHDS has provided a definition for a wellness application and included it as a source of health data for the electrionic health record (EHR). This development is a significant stride towards bringing regulatory clarity. In view of this development, this chapter focuses on wellness applications.

Notably, the pandemic's impact on patient's access to treatment led to a willingness to accept the terms of wellness apps and pay fees to ensure healthcare availability while ignoring possible risks. Despite the surge in wellness app adoption during the COVID-19 pandemic, there is a current trend towards a cautious approach due to potential issues with app usability, functionality and security features.[6] With the pandemic fading and with the newly adopted EHDS, it is essential to shift the focus to how and if at all wellness app users can realistically control their health data processed by these apps.

In connection with the use of health data from wellness applications, the question arises whether these data should be used at all. It is not always easy to verify whether the data were obtained based on valid consent and also

DOI: 10.4324/9781003544111-5

the data can be highly inaccurate. A recent study has confirmed that some applications can have up to 30% data inaccuracy in the long term.[7] Even if the accuracy increases in the short term, they show measurement errors due to, for example, darker skin tones and higher BMI.[8] While sensors improve applications' accuracy, less than 40% of apps use sensors at all, and most are based on the user's personal records.[9] This means they are subjective, inaccurate and often incomplete because users forget to write them down. The inaccuracy of application data can significantly affect the further use of data for the patient or secondary use. This risk was also recognised by the rapporteurs of the European Parliament's report on the EHDS. They state that the data on wellness applications would provide data of lower quality for secondary use and may not cover the entire population. It may still be of relevance but exclusively combined with other data.[10]

Already in 2013, the Article 29 Working Party (WP29) recognised significant risks in personal data protection associated with the operation of these applications. Its 'Opinion on apps on smart devices'[11] emphasises that the most critical risks were the lack of clarity and transparency, poor security measures and invalid consent defined at the time by the Data Protection Directive.[12] Wellness apps often do not provide trustworthy instruments to execute these rights, and when provided, they do not guarantee a complete execution according to the General Data Protection Regulation (GDPR).[13] In turn, the EHDS is intended to facilitate citizens' control over their personal health data in all EU member states and promote the secondary uses of citizens' health data for allowed purposes, including scientific research. The EHDS considers wellness applications as products that process electronic health data that can be interoperable with EHR.[14] Given the possibility of integrating citizens' electronic health data from wellness applications into their EHR, addressing the issues of secure and legal obtaining and processing of citizens' electronic health data by apps is crucial. Therefore, the chapter sets out to answer the following research question: To what extent does EHDS transform the control of wellness app users over their health data while using these apps? Subsequently, it will investigate whether the provisions in the EHDS guarantee that users can fully exercise their rights when using labelled wellness applications interoperable with EHRs.

4.2 What is a wellness application?

The European Commission (Commission) used the term 'wellness apps' in 2014 in a 'Mobile Health Green Paper'.[15] The same document also uses the terms 'wellbeing apps' and 'mHealth application' without clearly distinguishing these three terms. According to the usage in the text, it is evident that the terms wellness and well-being are used synonymously. Although the Commission does not provide a clear definition, it describes well-being applications as '[an application] that may connect to medical devices or sensors (e.g. bracelets or watches), personal guidance systems, health information and medication reminders provided by SMS and telemedicine provided wirelessly'.[16]

This document also provides an overview of the number of wellness and mHealth apps. When describing the market for mHealth apps, the Commission mentions a Deloitte study which states that 70% of these apps are created by wellness and fitness users. The remaining 30% of apps are aimed at medical professionals.[17] From this description, it can be inferred that mHealth apps comprise wellness applications and those that target medical applications.

Medical applications have a more specific position. The term medical application is associated with a medical device based on the literature. According to some authors, whether there is a legal definition of this term is not essential because these apps are mainly used in medical devices.[18] Medical devices are regulated by the Medical Device Regulation[19], which provides a higher level of health protection for users.[20] Can a wellness app also be a medical device? According to the Court of Justice of the European Union (CJEU), the applications should be distinguished based on whether they have a medical purpose. The CJEU decided in the Brain Products GMBH case that '[…] the concept of "medical device" covers an object conceived by its manufacturer to be used for human beings for the purpose of investigation of a physiological process only if it is intended for a medical purpose'.[21]

The CJEU's decision summarises that a medical app must have a medical purpose, an element which is not required for a wellness app. The app's manufacturer must declare whether it has one. Although it is legally obligatory to certify the applications for medical purposes as medical devices, some manufacturers are circumventing the law. They do not want to subject the app to stricter standards based on the Medical Device Regulation; it will be declared a wellness app. Therefore, we can find applications with a medical purpose within wellness applications. Thus, the definition of a wellness app in the framework of the EHDS can stop the circumvention of the mandatory certification of medical apps as wellness apps.

Hence, it is significant that the Commission's proposal for the EHDS Regulation included a definition of wellness apps. Article 2(2)(o) defined wellness apps as 'Any appliance or software intended by the manufacturer to be used by a natural person for processing electronic health data for other purposes than healthcare, such as well-being and pursuing healthy life-styles'.[22]

The proposed definition excluded all applications used to provide health care, which will be most medical applications. Furthermore, the definition is very vague and broad. According to the GDPR, all data relating to the mental or physical health of the natural person is included in the definition of health data, demonstrating the breadth of the Commission's definition.[23] If we try to define wellness apps by the term 'healthy life-style', some authors define these apps more medically as apps designed for disease prevention.[24] Others see these apps only as a product that helps users to develop healthy habits.[25] The Commission apparently did not realise that such a broad definition would create confusion about which applications were specifically concerned.

From the beginning, it's evident that even among legislators, there's no consensus on what should be considered a wellness application and how user security should be ensured. The Council maintains the Commission's definition, while the Parliamentary definition narrows the scope to applications related to specific health data processing actions. This definition is crucial for creating certainty about which types of mHealth applications will be regulated. The terminological problem may seem irrelevant to data protection in applications included in the EHDS. Still, it reveals the confusion among legislators about which applications should provide data to a patient's EHR. This lack of clarity complicates the regulation's implementation and allows Member States to approach the same applications differently. Certainty and transparency are crucial, as the EHDS Regulation emphasises that member states are free to regulate all other aspects of the wellness application, apart from those explicitly designed by the Regulation, as long as they comply with EU law.

The final version of the EHDS Regulation largely contains in Article 2 (2) (ab), the definition:

> *'wellness application' means any software, or any combination of hardware and software, intended by the manufacturer to be used by a natural person, for the processing of electronic health data, specifically for providing information on the health of natural persons, or the delivery of care for purposes other than the provision of healthcare.*[26]

The provided definition avoids using vague terms such as lifestyle and well-being and uses a similar style to describe the purpose of the wellness application as the medical device definition. In addition, the definition no longer excludes the provision of care as one of its purposes. Although the definition does not fully clarify the position of wellness applications within the large group of mHealth applications and can be criticised for lack of precision, it provides a basis for determining the applicable laws for processing health data through such applications.

4.3 Processing of the user's health data within wellness applications

To answer the research question of this chapter, we first need to address the question, to what extent does EU law currently provide a framework that enables data subjects to control the processing of their health data by wellness applications?

Since wellness apps generate, process and store large amounts of personal data, they are subject to GDPR, and most specifically, Article 6 of the GDPR. Moreover, because they include the user's health status, they are subject to stricter regulation specified in Article 9 of the GDPR. Most wellness apps process user data according to Article 6(1) based on the data subject's consent for one or more specific purposes. Based on an exception in Article 9(2)(a), it is lawful to process health data based on the data subject's consent for any purpose except where a Member State or the EU provides that the prohibition on processing cannot be lifted by consent. Consequently, consent is the main tool by which users can exercise control over their data processed by wellness apps. The GDPR guarantees that data subjects can control their data by defining the validity of the data subject's consent. This means that if a wellness application receives valid consent as defined in the GDPR, it most likely provides the user with sufficient control over the processing of their data.

The question of consent is crucial because users' willingness to share their personal data with wellness applications is relatively high, and the risk of using these apps is moderate to high. A study shows that of 82 respondents, as many as 41% indicated a high willingness to share data using an app, and another 43% expressed potential consent.[27] At the same time, 40% of apps pose a high risk to user privacy, 32% pose a moderate to high risk, and 28% pose a low to moderate risk.[28] Users are often unaware of how the service may collect and process their data.[29] Other authors interpret this issue as a lack of user education.[30] Their answer lies in raising awareness and educating users of their rights, considering the grant of valid consent.

To guarantee the validity of the user's consent, it must meet the requirements defined under Article 7 of the GDPR, which describes the basic principles, including that this should be freely given, specific and informed. Although Article 7 does not explicitly use the phrase 'informed consumer', it describes this obligation as making the subject aware of the circumstances of the data processing as well as the possibility of withdrawing the consent given. Article 4 of the GDPR points out in the definition of consent that information is a condition of valid consent when the subject, by a statement or by an explicit affirmative action, signifies specific and unambiguous agreement to the processing of their personal data.

4.4 Primary conditions of users' consent

The first principle of valid consent – 'freely given consent' – requires the user to be able to change or withdraw their consent at any time.[31] The CJEU, in its decision in the case *Orange România*, also underlined the need for an active role for the data subject linked with the principle of unambiguity of the consent: 'Silence, pre-ticked boxes or inactivity should not, therefore, constitute consent'.[32] The application manufacturer cannot assume what the users want. The duty is to give the users a choice. An example of a wellness app that may violate this regulation is the 'Amaha: anxiety self-care' app.[33] This app offers only three options after downloading: to log in with a Google account, to log in with a Facebook account or to create a profile. None of the login methods provides the possibility to familiarise users with the terms of use and privacy policy of the application. A small letter informs users that they automatically agree to the 'Terms & Conditions' and 'Privacy Policy' by logging in. With this approach, the manufacturer assumes users' silent consent. Such practices contradict the principle of unambiguity of the consent.

Article 7(4) of the GDPR states that inappropriate pressure on the user, which prevents them from exercising their free will, renders the consent invalid. Guidelines 05/2020 issued by the European Data Protection Board (EDPB) provide an example of invalid consent for an application requiring uploading data unrelated to the content when it is impossible to use the application without uploading this data.[34]

The last requirement associated with free consent defined by Recital 43 GDPR is often referred to as an 'imbalance of power'. It focuses on the unequal position between the data subject and the data controller. The consent is considered invalid if expressing consent to each type of processed data separately is impossible. It points to the opinion of Article 29 Working Party that if the data subject cannot exercise a real choice without the risk of deception or significant negative consequences, then the consent is considered invalid.

In their review of privacy in mobile health systems, Katusiime and Pinkwart note that users must often consent to data sharing to access wellness applications.[35] Users criticise that they download an app when already feeling low, to realise that the support they need is only available under conditions where one must share data unrelated to the app's purpose. The data controllers exploit their vulnerabilities, and this consent cannot be considered freely given.[36] However, researchers point out that fulfilling the principles set out in Recitals 42 and 43 GDPR concerning power imbalances can be difficult.[37]

The second principle consists of granting consent for one or more specific purposes as set out in Article 9(2) (a) of the GDPR. The so-called granularity of consent is vital. This means that in the case of data processing for several purposes, the subject must consent to each purpose separately. Closely linked to this element is the possibility for the subject to withdraw consent at any time for any purpose. An essential condition in Article 7(3) of the GDPR stipulates that withdrawing consent must be as simple as giving it. According to a study by Haque and Rubya, users of mental health apps often complain about the lack of transparency regarding the ability to withdraw consent.[38]

The last principle is the informed data subject because only a data subject with objective information regarding personal data processing can provide informed consent. Although the GDPR does not define how informed consent should look, the General Advocate's interpretation of the case *Orange România* lists the data that the subject must know to give informed consent.[39] The CJEU decision confirms the Advocate General's opinion and adds that the controller should also inform whether the answers are mandatory or voluntary. Wellness apps usually contain all this information in the sections appearing after downloading the app, such as 'Terms & Conditions' and 'Privacy Policy'. However, the EDPB underlines that the information relevant to informed consent must not be generally hidden under 'Terms & Conditions'.[40] The study from 2017 shows that 91% of users do not read the terms of use and only confirm them.[41] Research shows that users of apps emphasise that it does not matter whether they read them or not if they need the application.[42]

Another reason not to read the terms of use is their complexity and use of legal or technical language. Recital 42 specifies the wording of the consent if it is predefined by the data controller: '[consent] should be provided in an intelligible and easily accessible form, using clear and plain language…'.[43] The EDPB specifies that controllers cannot use long privacy policies that are difficult to understand. Otherwise, the consent is invalid.[44] Yet, Sunyaev describes that most of the mHealth application privacy policies studied were found to be roughly the length of an academic journal article and readable at the university level.[45] This fact makes the app's terms of use inaccessible to a large percentage of users.[46] The authors of the 2017 study note that even educated users, aware that agreeing to an app's terms of use constituted a binding contract, did not read the terms.[47] Unfortunately, neither the EU nor the member states have the capacity to control the conformity of all wellness apps with the GDPR. For this reason, manufacturers often can abuse their position vis-à-vis users to benefit from their data. The literature is consistent that the mHealth applications industry is not sufficiently compliant in providing users with relevant privacy policies or terms of service.[48] A 2021 cross-sectional study of 20,000 apps demonstrated severe privacy problems.[49]

In conclusion, the GDPR provides a detailed framework for the possibilities for processing personal data, notably in Articles 6 and 7. Users' health data is subject to enhanced protection under Article 9. Although there may be criticism of the GDPR for the lack of specification of the conditions of informed and freely given consent, this issue is dealt with in the case law of the CJEU. In addition to the CJEU, the EDPB provided further guidelines on the subject.[50] However, research shows that wellness apps fail to respect their obligations, and enforcement is insufficient. A 2018 study shows that of 79 apps certified as clinically safe and trustworthy by the UK National Health Service, 89% were found to transmit information online, 66% of which were not encrypted.[51] In addition to the lack of security in data transfer, wellness apps often do not comply with consent requirements. A study of mental health applications indicates that some applications take advantage of the user's weaker position. So, under pressure from the application, users agree to the processing of certain types of data that they would not usually agree to be processed.[52] Given the well-established principles in EU law, arguably, the legislative protection appears sufficient, but not its enforceability. Thus, the users' rights to control their data are often only theoretical and not applicable in practice.

4.4.1 Potential risks connected with the labelling of wellness applications in the framework of EHDS

To provide a comprehensive view of the EHDS Regulation's evolution, this section outlines the modifications within the four key documents: the Commission's Proposal,[53] the Proposal adopted by the plenary of the European Parliament (Parliament proposal)[54], the Council of EU mandate for negotiations with the European Parliament (Council's Position)[55] and the final agreed text (Final text).[56] It is important to note that according to the EHDS, wellness applications should serve as a source of health data both for patient and secondary purposes. For this reason, it introduces specific rules for the interoperability of these applications with EHR systems. It follows that it is necessary to ensure both the security of data transmission and the rights of patients to control their health data throughout the process.

The EHDS adopts mandatory labelling of wellness apps claiming interoperability with EHR, where the Commission has the opportunity to guarantee users' choice of a wellness application that allows them to fully apply their rights regarding the processing of their electronic health data.[57] The Commission should focus on two phases of data processing in assessing the wellness application considering user privacy: firstly, if the app acquires data based on valid user consent and verifies if the user wants to share health data with the EHR; second, whether the secure retrieval of data within the application and subsequent secure sharing of data from the application to the EHR are ensured. If the application meets such requirements, the app can be deemed safe for user privacy because it provides them with control over the processing of their data.

According to Article 47:

> Where a manufacturer of a wellness application software claims interoperability with an EHR system in relation to the harmonised components of EHR systems and therefore compliance with the common specifications referred to in Article 36 and essential requirements laid down in Annex II, such wellness application shall be accompanied by a label, clearly indicating its compliance with those specifications and requirements. The label shall be issued by the manufacturer of the wellness application.[58]

It should be noted that legislators have been divided during the legislative process on the voluntary or mandatory nature of the labelling. The Commission proposed voluntary labelling probably based on a consideration that the labelling will give manufacturers a competitive advantage in the market, and they will voluntarily agree to it. Likewise, the Council supported the system's voluntariness by arguing that given the large number of apps and the fact that they do not play a primary role in providing health data for EHR, mandatory labelling will not be practical.[59] In contrast, the Parliament insisted on mandatory labelling, arguing that while mandatory certification, including the testing, would cause some complications, mandatory labelling does not cause them because it does not include the testing. Therefore, it will provide users with some explicit guarantee for control over their data and will not be so demanding for the manufacturers.

Another concern is related to the labelling process itself. The wellness application should comply with the essential requirements in Annex II and common specifications in Article 36. However, the manufacturer only claims that the application meets all the requirements by registering it in the EU publicly available database and does not need to prove it. This is, for example, against the recommendation of the International Organization for Standardization, which requires that applications should be certified, not based on manufacturer claims but based on evidence of a good application design process, which should be supported by empirical evidence of user-friendliness – ideally from independent evaluations conducted by experts.[60] While the EHR manufacturer has to report, among other things, the results of the testing environment, the manufacturers of wellness applications do not have this obligation.[61] While market surveillance authorities should control the compliance of applications with the requirements in Annex II, there are two limitations associated with this control.[62] Firstly, while the app manufacturer is required to register the app before introducing it to the market, the Final text does not state that the app cannot be put into service before market surveillance authorities control it.[63] This loophole seems insignificant, but if even 1% of these applications are registered (around 3500), they can be used for a long time without verification because of the limited capacity of market surveillance authorities. Secondly, the market surveillance authorities are only responsible for verifying compliance with Annex II, so compliance with the general specifications in Article 36 is not part of any verification. From the point of view of the user's control over their health data, Article 36 is significant because it states requirements and principles related to security, confidentiality, patient safety and protection of electronic health data.[64]

The more severe shortcoming is the lack of user protection, as represented by the common specifications in Article 36 and the essential requirements in Annex II for obtaining this label. Fontaine and Clinck underline that Annex II sets out, in general terms, the requirements for performance, interoperability and safety, and as such, it does not specify any requirements for user consent.[65] The processed health data is subject only to a general condition of security and safety. This condition can arguably be interpreted as an obligation to comply with the measures defined in GDPR.

Recital 49 specifically points out that the labelling is to inform users about the compliance of these applications with interoperability and security requirements, focusing on data transfer between wellness applications and EHRs. However, the lack of adequate awareness among users can lead to them believing that the labelling indicates that these applications are privacy compliant and secure and consequently not scrutinising them sufficiently on their own.[66]

To sum up, Article 47 and Annex II do not alter the power imbalance between the user and the manufacturer, nor do they address the lack of enforceability of existing measures for users to control their health data. Monitoring the compliance of the apps carried out by the market surveillance authorities should be extended to verify the validity of the user's consent and elements such as the granularity of consent, comprehensible terms of use and the simple possibility of withdrawing consent for any of the purposes at any time. By verifying these requirements of valid consent, the EHDS could contribute to protecting the health data of the wellness app users.

4.4.2 The potential of EHDS to change the power imbalance between manufacturers and users of wellness applications

Arguably, the Commission's proposal and the Council's position maintain the status quo. They describe, in particular, the need for interoperability and technical specifications of the applications for interfacing with the EHR and address very marginally the need to protect personal data. They do not pay enough attention to the effective enforcement of good practice and CJEU jurisprudence on user consent for data processing. Thus, the Final text does not sufficiently reflect the reality of wellness applications. However, the regulation of the labelling introduced in the EHDS allows the Commission to refute the power imbalance between the manufacturer and the user, thanks to enshrining the Commission's power to adopt delegated and implementing acts.

Based on Parliament's proposal, the Final text shifted the focus to 'privacy by design'. Privacy by design should be the default setting of every wellness application to ensure the highest level of data protection. Cavoukian maps fundamental principles that should be respected when applying privacy by design.[67] The first principle is based on proactive rather than reactive application. In the framework of the EHDS, it would have been recommended to enshrine the precise protective measures, such as gathering health data based on users' valid consent to obtain labelling, rather than leaving this obligation as an option for future regulation by the Commission. Even if the proactivity principle is not met, the EHDS can still significantly increase users' control over their health data based on Article 47(3) of the Final text, allowing the Commission to determine the label's form and content through the implementing act.

The second principle is 'Privacy by default'. The highest possible data protection is based on lawful data processing, specific purpose and limitation of further data processing. In the framework of the EHDS, users' control can be achieved exclusively if the applications respect the consent's granularity. Therefore, the granularity of consent should be a specific requirement in the Commission's implementing act. This does not happen in practice. It is not clear whether the Commission does not have sufficient data or whether there is another reason why this serious malpractice is not being addressed. After all, the Final text requires the app manufacturers to obtain consent to share data from a wellness app with an EHR. In doing so, the legislator has clearly expressed how vital the granularity of consent is in this regard. The article further underlined this by stating:

> The manufacturers of wellness applications claiming interoperability with an EHR system shall ensure that the natural person concerned is able to choose which categories of health data from the wellness application are to be inserted in the EHR system and the and the circumstances for the sharing or transmission of those categories of data.[68]

One can argue that the most straightforward and functional solution to meet the requirement of granular consent is the so-called 'pop-up notification', which alerts users that an application wants to access their data outside its primary purpose.[69] Thus, users would be obligated to confirm or withdraw their consent and pay close attention to each purpose and change in their data processing.

The third principle, 'Privacy Embedded Into Design', states that health technology's impact on privacy must be minimised and not easily broken. This principle is perhaps most reflected in the EHDS and guarantees users' complete protection. A significant part of Annex II is devoted to the system's interoperability and data protection integration. From the point of view of the user's control over the data, the user must have sufficient information about the transfer and, therefore, confidence that their data will not be leaked. The Final text contains a provision that directly states that the user of wellness applications shall be duly informed about interoperability and its effects.[70] From this point of view, this principle is fulfilled in the EHDS framework.

The fourth principle concerns ensuring that the full functionality focuses on the user's outcome without forcing a trade-off between the user's wellness and privacy. Consequently, the purposes for which health information is disclosed and who discloses it should be authorised by the users' choice.[71] In the Commission's proposal, it is assumed that within the framework of the user's consent regulated by GDPR, the users have the right to decide for what purpose the application will process their data. It has to be underlined that this possibility is often only theoretical. If users want to use the application, they must frequently confirm the purposes for which they disagree, which is considered the main challenge of introducing these applications into EHR. In this context, an unresolved issue remains the sharing of anonymised user data for secondary use, such as scientific research. The user does not have the right to decide on anonymised data because it is impossible to identify the user directly or indirectly from them. However, in principle, the user has the right to consent to processing their data before it is anonymised. Hence, the EHDS should also address whether the data were obtained based on valid consent before being anonymised to ensure users control how their data is used for secondary purposes.

The last relevant principles are visibility and transparency. Accountability requires that all technologies are transparent and visible so that users can check privacy compliance at every step of the process. Recital 51 EHDS points out that creating an EU database for wellness applications aims to increase overall transparency and facilitate the flow of information. At the same time, users complain about the lack of transparency of terms of use within wellness applications.[72] The EHDS did not sufficiently reflect on this fact and did not introduce any special requirement that would increase accountability, even if it is possible to incorporate these common requirements in Article 36 EHDS or special ones in Annex II. This deficiency can be corrected in several ways. Firstly, Article 49(4) EHDS empowers the Commission to adopt a delegated act specifying the list of required data from manufacturers that they will have to supply for registration in the EU wellness app database as part of the labelling process. The second possibility is the powers of the Digital Health Authority. One of the roles of these authorities is to contribute at the Union level to developing common specifications for wellness applications that address security, safety or fundamental rights issues by Article 36 EHDS.[73]

To sum up, the concerns over the users' privacy and diminishing their control over their health data in the context the wellness applications are significant. Similarly, the rapporteurs of the Parliament's report underlined privacy concerns regarding sharing health data under such applications. Although the report expressed that these concerns must be addressed through enforcement by the responsible authorities under the GDPR, research shows that applying the GDPR is insufficient.[74] The EHDS provides an opportunity to refine the power imbalance between app manufacturers and users. Although the Commission's proposal was not precisely user-centric, the Final text suggests a transformation towards greater user control over data. By using the privacy by design principles, the tendency of the EHDS to enshrine the granularity of consent, comprehensible terms of use and the simple possibility of withdrawing consent have been shown. Together with mandatory labelling, this provides a reasonable basis for better user control over their health data. The outstanding challenge is ensuring that only those apps that have initially acquired user data based on valid consent and meet all the requirements of the GDPR will become the labelled wellness apps. This challenge can be solved within the framework of the EHDS. Based on Article 47 EHDS, the Commission can determine the form and content of the labels using an implementing act. Article 49(4) EHDS empowers the Commission to adopt a delegated act setting out the list of data that must be added to the labelling registration. Last but not least, there is the crucial role of the Digital Health Authorities, which can propose specific requirements for user safety. Combining these allows the user to reinstall the control of the user over their data in the wellness application. Therefore, it is up to the Commission to use its powers to introduce the requirement to check for valid consent when obtaining wellness app data.

4.5 Conclusion

The chapter discusses concerns related to user control over health data in wellness applications within the framework of European law. Firstly, it examines the adequacy of EU legislation, particularly the GDPR, in defining requirements for valid consent. While the data protection legislation provides clear guidelines, the application of user rights remains inadequate, with wellness app manufacturers often circumventing obtaining valid consent. This prompts a following question regarding the EHDS's potential to transform user control over data. The EHDS faces challenges such as vague definitions, unclear labelling processes and insufficient oversight. While the EHDS improves user control by requiring specific consent for data sharing with EHR, it falls short of addressing the power imbalance between manufacturers and users, particularly in enforcing valid consent for data acquisition by wellness apps. Recommendations include embedding the requirement of valid consent for initial data acquisition by wellness applications as a fundamental change and enhancing transparency in the labelling process.

Notes

1 *'Digital Health Trends'* (*IQVIA Institute*, July 2021) Biblio-iqvia-institute-digital-health-trends-2021.pdf (cens.cl) accessed 22 April 2024, pp. 6.
2 Katharina Buchholz, 'Where Health App Usage Is Most Common' (*Statista*, 9 October 2020) Chart: Where Health App Usage Is Most Common | Statista accessed 22 April 2024.
3 'ORCHA's Digital Health Insights Featured in National Newspapers' (*ORCHA*, 28 May 2021) ORCHA's digital health insights featured in national newspapers – ORCHA (orchahealth.com) accessed 22 April 2024.
4 Conor Stewart, 'Share of Health App Users in Selected Countries as of 2022' (*Statista*, 22 December 2022) Health app users by country 2022 | Statista accessed 22 April 2024.
5 Stewart, 'Share of Health App Users in Selected Countries as of 2022' (*Statista*, 22 December 2022) Health app users by country 2022 | Statista accessed 22 April 2024.
6 Swathikan Chidambaram and others, 'Observational Study of UK Mobile Health Apps for COVID-19' (2020) 8 *Lancet Digital Health* (2).
7 Filippo Piccinini and Giovanni Martinelli and Antonella Carbonaro, 'Accuracy of Mobile Applications versus Wearable Devices in Long-Term Step Measurements' (2020) 20 *Sensors* (21).
8 Anna Shcherbina and others, 'Accuracy in Wrist-Worn, Sensor-Based Measurements of Heart Rate and Energy Expenditure in a Diverse Cohort' (2017) 24 *Journal of Personality* (7).
9 Ben Joseph Philip and others, 'Data Collection Mechanisms in Health and Wellness Apps: Review and Analysis' (2022) 9 *JMIR Mhealth* (10).
10 European Parliament, 'Report on the Proposal for a Regulation of the European Parliament and of the Council on the European Health Data Space' COM (2022) 0197.
11 'Opinion on Apps on Mobile Devices' (*Article 29 Working Party*, 27 February 2013) WP29 opinion on apps on mobile devices (europa.eu) accessed 22 April 2024.
12 Directive 95/46/EC on the protection of individuals with regard to the processing of personal data and on the free movement of such data [2003] OJ L 281/31.
13 Tomás Robles and others, 'Enabling Trustworthy Personal Data Protection in eHealth and Well-Being Services Through Privacy-By-Design' (2020) 16 *International Journal of Distributed Sensor Networks* (5).
14 EHDS, art 2(2)(ab) and (ab) EHDS.
15 European Commission, 'Green Paper on Mobile Health ("mHealth")' COM (2014) 219 final.
16 European Commission, 'Green Paper on Mobile Health ("mHealth")' COM 15, p. 3.
17 'mHealth in an mWorld – How Mobile Technology Is Transforming Health Care' (*Deloitte*, 2012) 1375 Katrina mHealth (deloitte.com) accessed 23 April 2024.
18 'Draft Code of Conduct on Privacy for Mobile Health Applications' *(European Commission*, 2016) https://digital-strategy.ec.europa.eu/en/library/code-conduct-privacy-mhealth-apps-has-been-finalised accessed 23 April 2024.
19 Regulation (EU) 2017/745 on medical devices, amending Directive 2001/83/EC, Regulation (EC) No 178/2002 and Regulation (EC) No 1223/2009 and repealing Council Directives 90/385/EEC and 93/42/EEC [2017] OJ L 117.
20 Juhamatti Huusko and Ulla-Mari Kinnunen and Kaija Saranto, 'Medical Device Regulation (MDR) in Health Technology Enterprises – Perspectives of Managers and Regulatory Professionals' (2023) 23 *BMC Health Services Research* (310).
21 Case C-219/11 *Brain Products GmbH v BioSemi VOF e.a* [2012] ECJ 2012/11 [34].
22 Commission, 'Proposal for a Regulation of the European Parliament and of the Council on the European Health Data Space' COM/2022/197 final.

23 GDPR Article 4(15).
24 Habiba Shabir and others, 'The Barriers and Facilitators to the Use of Lifestyle Apps: A Systematic Review of Qualitative Studies' (2022) 12 *European Journal of Investigation in Health, Psychology and EducationEur J Investig Health Psychol Educ* (2).
25 'How to Create Outstanding Healthy Lifestyle Apps With Best Examples' (*AHT Tech*, 2022) https://blog.arrowhitech.com/how-to-create-healthy-lifestyle-apps/ accessed 23 April 2024.
26 Article 2(2)(ab) EHDS.
27 Daniel Di Matteo and others, 'Patient Willingness to Consent to Mobile Phone Data Collection for Mental Health Apps: Structured Questionnaire' (2018) 5 *JMIR Mental Health* (3).
28 Achilleas Papageorgiou and others, 'Security and Privacy Analysis of Mobile Health Applications: The Alarming State of Practice' [(2018)] *IEEE Access* (6). DOI: 10.1109/ACCESS.2018.2799522.
29 Alexander Mense and others, 'Analyzing Privacy Risks of mHealth Applications' [(2016)] *Studies in Health Technology and InformaticsStud Health Technol Inform* (221).
30 L Fernandez-Luque and P Staccini, 'All that Glitters Is not Gold: Consumer Health Informatics and Education in the Era of Social Media and Health Apps. Findings from the Yearbook 2016 Section on Consumer Health Informatics' [(2016)] Yearbook of Medical Informatics. (1); Amanda Edwards-Stewart and others, 'Mobile Applications for Client Use: Ethical and Legal Considerations' (2016) 16 *Psychological Services* (2).
31 Recitals 42 and 43 GDPR.
32 C-61/19 *Orange Romania SA v Autoritatea Naţională de Supraveghere a Prelucrării Datelor cu Caracter Personal* [2020] ERC 2020/901 [8].
33 More information about the application: https://play.google.com/store/apps/details?id=com.theinnerhour.b2b&hl=en_US&pli=1.
34 'Guidelines 05/2020 on Consent under Regulation 2016/679' (*European Data Protection Board*, 2020) https://edpb.europa.eu/sites/default/files/files/file1/edpb_guidelines_202005_consent_en.pdf accessed 23 April 2024, pp. 8.
35 Jane Katusiime and Niels Pinkwart, 'A Review of Privacy and Usability Issues in Mobile Health Systems: Role of External Factors' (2017) 25 *Health Informatics* (3).
36 Md Romael Haque sand Sabirat Rubya, '"For an App Supposed to Make Its Users Feel Better, It Sure is a Joke" – An Analysis of User Reviews of Mobile Mental Health Applications' (2022) 6 *Proceedings of the ACM Conference on Human-Computer Interaction* (2).
37 Mary Kirwan and others, 'What GDPR and the Health Research Regulations (HRRs) Mean for Ireland: "Explicit Consent"—A Legal Analysis' (2021) 190 Irish Journal of Medical Science (2).
38 Kirwan and others, 'What GDPR and the Health Research Regulations (HRRs) Mean for Ireland: "Explicit Consent"—A Legal Analysis' (2021) 36.
39 Opinion of Advocate General, C-61/19 *Orange Romania SA v Autoritatea Naţională de Supraveghere a Prelucrării Datelor cu Caracter Personal* [2020] ERC 2020/901 [46][47].
40 'Guidelines 05/2020 on Consent under Regulation 2016/679' (*European Data Protection Board*, 2020) https://edpb.europa.eu/sites/default/files/files/file1/edpb_guidelines_202005_consent_en.pdf accessed 23 April 2024, pp. 16.
41 'Global Mobile Consumer Survey: US Edition' (*Deloitte*, 2017) 246075 GMCS executive summary (deloitte.com) accessed 23 April 2024.
42 Yue Liu, 'User Control of Personal Information Concerning Mobile-App: Notice and Consent?' (2014) 30 *Computer Law & Security Review* (5).

43 Recital 42 GDPR.
44 'Guidelines 05/2020 on Consent under Regulation 2016/679' (*European Data Protection Board*, 2020) https://edpb.europa.eu/sites/default/files/files/file1/edpb_guidelines_202005_consent_en.pdf accessed 23 April 2024, pp. 35.
45 Ali Sunyaev and others, 'Availability and Quality of Mobile Health App Privacy Policies' (2015) 22 *Journal of the American Medical Informatics Association* (1).
46 Hannah K Galvin and Paul R DeMuro, 'Developments in Privacy and Data Ownership in Mobile Health Technologies' (2020) 29 *Yearbook of Medical Informatics* (01).
47 Kirsten Ostherr and others, 'Trust and Privacy in the Context of User-Generated Health Data' (2017) 4 *Big Data and Society* (01).
48 Ostherr and others, 'Trust and Privacy in the Context of User-Generated Health Data' (2017) 42.
49 Gioacchino Tangari and others, 'Mobile Health and Privacy: Cross Sectional Study' (2021) 373 *BMJ* (1248).
50 Tangari and others, 'Mobile Health and Privacy: Cross Sectional Study' (2021) 34.
51 John Torous and others, 'Clinical Review of User Engagement With Mental Health Smartphone Apps: Evidence, Theory and Improvements' (2018) 21 *Evidence- Based Mental Health* (03).
52 Torous and others, 'Clinical Review of User Engagement With Mental Health Smartphone Apps: Evidence, Theory and Improvements' (2018) 36.
53 Torous and others, 'Clinical Review of User Engagement With Mental Health Smartphone Apps: Evidence, Theory and Improvements'(2018) 22.
54 European Parliament, 'Amendments Adopted By the on 13 December 2023 on the Proposal for a Regulation of the European Parliament and of the Council on the European Health Data Space' COM (2022) 0197.
55 General Secretariat of the Council, 'Proposal for a Regulation on the European Health Data Space- Mandate for negotiations with the European Parliament' 2022/0140(COD).
56 Corrigendum to the position of the European Parliament adopted at first reading on 24 April 2024 with a view to the adoption of Regulation (EU) 2024/... of the European Parliament and of the Council on the European Health Data Space', (COM(2022)0197 – C9-0167/2022 – 2022/0140(COD)), 27 November 2024.
57 Recitals 49 and 50 EHDS.
58 Article 47 (1) EHDS.
59 Recital 35, General Secretariat of the Council, 'Proposal for a Regulation on the European Health Data Space- Mandate for negotiations with the European Parliament' 2022/0140(COD).
60 David Neal and others, 'Limitations of the New ISO Standard for Health and Wellness Apps' (2022) 4 *The Lancet Digital Health* (2).
61 Article 40 EHDS.
62 Article 47(7) EHDS.
63 Article 49(2) EHDS.
64 Article 36(3)(e) EHDS.
65 Quentin Fontaine and Jan Clinck, 'The European Health Data Space Proposal: A First Look at the Newest Piece of the EU Data Sharing Puzzle' (2022) 6 *EHPL* (2).
66 Fontaine and Jan Clinck, 'The European Health Data Space Proposal: A First Look at the Newest Piece of the EU Data Sharing Puzzle (2022) 30.
67 Ann Cavoukian, '*Privacy by Design: The 7 Foundational Principles: Implementation and Mapping of Fair Information Practices*' (2010) Information & Privacy Commissioner of Ontario: Toronto, ON, Canada.
68 Article 48 (2) EHDS.

69 Yue Liu, 'User Control of Personal Information Concerning Mobile-App: Notice and Consent?' (2014) 30 *Computer Law & Security Review* (5).
70 Article 48 (1) EHDS.
71 Ann Cavoukian and others, 'Remote Home Health Care Technologies: How to Ensure Privacy? Build It in: Privacy by Design' [(2010)] *Identity Inf. Soc.* (3).
72 Cavoukian and others, 'Remote Home Health Care Technologies: How to Ensure Privacy? Build It in: Privacy by Design' [(2010)] 24.
73 Article 19(2)(h) EHDS.
74 Ben Joseph Philip and others, 'Data Collection Mechanisms in Health and Wellness Apps: Review and Analysis' (2022) 9 *JMIR Mhealth* (10).

List of sources

Treaties, legislation and conventions

Directive 95/46/EC of the European Parliament and of the Council of 24 October 1995 on the protection of individuals with regard to the processing of personal data and on the free movement of such data [2003] OJ L 281/31.
Regulation (EU) 2016/679 of the European Parliament and of the Council of 27 April 2016 on the protection of natural persons with regard to the processing of personal data and on the free movement of such data, and repealing Directive 95/46/EC [2016] OJ L 119/1.
Regulation (EU) 2017/745 of the European Parliament and of the Council of 5 April 2017 on medical devices, amending Directive 2001/83/EC, Regulation (EC) No 178/2002 and Regulation (EC) No 1223/2009 and repealing Council Directives 90/385/EEC and 93/42/EEC [2017] OJ L 117/1.

Official publications and policy documents:

Amendments adopted by the European Parliament on 13 December 2023 on the proposal for a regulation of the European Parliament and of the Council on the European Health Data Space (COM(2022)0197 – C9-0167/2022 – 2022/0140(COD)
Article 29 Working Party, 'Opinion on Apps on Mobile Devices' (27 February 2013). https://ec.europa.eu/justice/article-29/documentation/opinion-recommendation/files/2013/wp202_en.pdf
European Commission, 'Green Paper on Mobile Health ("mHealth")' COM (2014) 219 final.
European Commission, 'Draft Code of Conduct on Privacy for Mobile Health Applications' (2016) https://digital-strategy.ec.europa.eu/en/library/code-conduct-privacy-mhealth-apps-has-been-finalised
European Data Protection Board, 'Guidelines 05/2020 on Consent under Regulation 2016/679' (2020). https://edpb.europa.eu/sites/default/files/files/file1/edpb_guidelines_202005_consent_en.pdf
European Parliament, 'Report on the proposal for a regulation of the European Parliament and of the Council on the European Health Data Space' COM (2022) 0197.
European Parliament, 'The European Health Data Space' (December 2022). www.europarl.europa.eu/RegData/etudes/STUD/2022/740054/IPOL_STU(2022)740054_EN.pdf
Proposal for a Regulation of the European Parliament and of the Council on the European Health Data Space (2022) COM/2022/197 final.

Corrigendum to the position of the European Parliament adopted at first reading on 24 April 2024 with a view to the adoption of Regulation (EU) 2024/... of the European Parliament and of the Council on the European Health Data Space', (COM(2022)0197 – C9-0167/2022 – 2022/0140(COD)), 27 November 2024.

Proposal for a Regulation on the European Health Data Space- Mandate for negotiations with the European Parliament (2023) https://data.consilium.europa.eu/doc/document/ST-16048-2023-REV-1/en/pdf

Literature and other secondary sources

AHT Tech, 'How to Create Outstanding Healthy Lifestyle Apps With Best Examples' (2022) https://blog.arrowhitech.com/how-to-create-healthy-lifestyle-apps/

Buchholz K, 'Where Health App Usage Is Most Common' (*Statista*, 9 October 2020). Chart: Where Health App Usage Is Most Common | Statista. https://www.statista.com/chart/23161/health-app-usage-country-comparison/

Cavoukian A, *Privacy by Design: The 7 Foundational Principles: Implementation and Mapping of Fair Information Practices* (2010) Information & Privacy Commissioner of Ontario: Toronto, ON, Canada.

Cavoukian A,'Understanding How to Implement Privacy by Design, One Step at a Time' (2020) 9 *IEEE Consumer Electronics Magazine* (2) DOI: 10.1109/MCE.2019.2953739

Cavoukian A, Fisher A, Killen S and Hoff D A, 'Remote Home Health Care Technologies: How to Ensure Privacy? Build It In: Privacy by Design' (2010) *Identity in the Information Society* (3). DOI: 10.1007/s12394-010-0054-y

Chidambaram S, Erridge S, Kinross J and Purkayastha S, 'Observational Study of UK Mobile Health Apps for COVID-19' (2020) 8 *Lancet Digital Health* (2). DOI: 10.1016/S2589-7500(20)30144-8

Deloitte, 'Global Mobile Consumer Survey: US Edition' (2017). 246075 GMCS executive summary (deloitte.com). https://www2.deloitte.com/content/dam/Deloitte/us/Documents/technology-media-telecommunications/us-tmt-2017-global-mobile-consumer-survey-executive-summary.pdf

Deloitte, 'mHealth in a mWorld – How Mobile Technology Is Transforming Health Care' (2012) 1375 Katrina mHealth (deloitte.com). https://www2.deloitte.com/content/dam/Deloitte/us/Documents/life-sciences-health-care/us-lhsc-mhealth-in-an-mworld-103014.pdf

Di Matteo D, Fine A, Fotinos K, Rose J and Katzman M, 'Patient Willingness to Consent to Mobile Phone Data Collection for Mental Health Apps: Structured Questionnaire' (2018) 5 *JMIR Mental Health* (3). DOI: 10.2196/mental.9539

Edwards-Stewart A, Alexander C, Armstrong C M, Hoyt and O'Donohue W, 'Mobile Applications for Client Use: Ethical and Legal Considerations' (2016) 16 *Psychological Services* (2) DOI: 10.1037/ser0000321

Fernandez-Luque L and Staccini P, 'All That Glitters Is not Gold: Consumer Health Informatics and Education in the Era of Social Media and Health Apps. Findings From the Yearbook 2016 Section on Consumer Health Informatics' (2016) *Yearbook of Medical Informatics* (1) DOI: 10.15265/IY-2016-045

Fontaine Q and Clinck J, 'The European Health Data Space Proposal: A First Look at the Newest Piece of the EU Data Sharing Puzzle' (2022) 6 *EHPL* (2). DOI: 10.21552/ehpl/2022/2/8

Galvin H K and DeMuro P R, 'Developments in Privacy and Data Ownership in Mobile Health Technologies' (2020) 29 *Yearbook of Medical Informatics* (01). DOI: 10.1055/s-0040-1701987

Huusko J and Kinnunen U M and Saranto K, 'Medical Device Regulation (MDR) in Health Technology Enterprises – Perspectives of Managers and Regulatory Professionals' (2023) 23 *BMC Health Services Research* (310). DOI: 10.1186/s12913-023-09316-8

Haque R and Rubya S, '"For an App Supposed to Make Its Users Feel Better, It Sure is a Joke" – An Analysis of User Reviews of Mobile Mental Health Applications' (2022) 6 *Proceedings of the ACM Conference on Human-Computer Interaction* (2) DOI: 10.1145/3555146

IMS Institute for Healthcare Informatics, 'Patients Apps for Improved Healthcare, From Novelty to Mainstream' (October 2013). iihi_patient_apps_report_editora_39_2_1.pdf (ignacioriesgo.es).

IQVIA Institute. *Digital Health Trends.* (2021). Biblio-iqvia-institute-digital-health-trends-2021.pdf (cens.cl).

Katusiime J and Pinkwart N, 'A Review of Privacy and Usability Issues in Mobile Health Systems: Role of External Factors' (2017) 25 *Healthcare Informatics* (3) DOI: 10.1177/1460458217733121

Kirwan M, Mee B, Clarke N, Tanaka A, Manaloto L, Halpin E, Gibbons U, Cullen A, McGarrigle S, Connolly E M, Bennett K, Gaffney E, Flanagan C, Tier L, Flavin R, and McElvaney N G, 'What GDPR and the Health Research Regulations (HRRs) Mean for Ireland: "Explicit Consent"—A Legal Analysis' (2021) 190 *Irish Journal of Medical Science* (2). DOI: 10.1007/s11845-020-02331-2

Mense A, Steger S, Sulek M, Jukicsunaric D and Mészáros A, 'Analyzing Privacy Risks of mHealth Applications' (2016) 221 *Studies in Health Technology and Informatics.* DOI: 10.3233/978-1-61499-633-0-41

Neal D, Engelsma T, Tan J, Craven M P, Marcilly R, Peute L, Dening T, Jaspers M and Dröes R-M, 'Limitations of the New ISO Standard for Health and Wellness Apps' (2022) 4 *The Lancet Digital Health* (2). DOI: 10.1016/S2589-7500(21)00273-9

ORCHA, '*ORCHA's Digital Health Insights Featured in National Newspapers*'. (28 May 2021). https://orchahealth.com/orchas-digital-health-insights-featured-in-national-newspapers/ORCHA's digital health insights featured in national newspapers – ORCHA (orchahealth.com).

ORCHA, 'Digital Health in The UK National Attitudes and Behaviour Research' (2022). https://25077478.fs1.hubspotusercontent-eu1.net/hubfs/25077478/2022%20OnePoll%20Report/Digital%20Health%20in%20the%20UK%20National%20Attitudes%20and%20Behaviour%20Research%202022.pdf?__hstc=14005480.caa8c01bf84b245538008b442.13156e.1676023643446.1681333676437.1682608155946.15&__hssc=14005480.2.1682608155946&__hsfp=3839259116 Digital Health in the UK National Attitudes and Behaviour Research 2022.pdf (hubspotusercontent-eu1.net).

Ostherr K, Borodina S, Bracken R C, Lotterman C, Storer E and Williams B, 'Trust and Privacy in the Context of User-Generated Health Data' (2017) 4 *Big Data & Society* (01). DOI: 10.1177/2053951717704673

Papageorgiou A, Strigkos M, Politou E, Alepis E, Solanas A and Patsakis C, 'Security and Privacy Analysis of Mobile Health Applications: The Alarming State of Practice' (2018) 6 *IEEE Access.* DOI: 10.1109/ACCESS.2018.2799522

Philip B J, Abdelrazek M, Bonti A, Barnett S and Grundy J, 'Data Collection Mechanisms in Health and Wellness Apps: Review and Analysis' (2022) 9 *JMIR Mhealth* (10). DOI: 10.2196/30468

Piccinini F, Martinelli G and Carbonaro A, 'Accuracy of Mobile Applications versus Wearable Devices in Long-Term Step Measurements' (2020) 20 *Sensors* (21). DOI: 10.3390/s20216293

Robles T, Bordel B, Alcarria R and Sánchez-de-Rivera D, 'Enabling Trustworthy Personal Data Protection in eHealth and Well-Being Services Through Privacy-By-Design' (2020) 16 *International Journal of Distributed Sensor Networks* (5). DOI: 10.1177/1550147720912110

Shabir H, D'Costa M, Mohiaddin Z, Moti Z, Rashid H, Sadowska D, Alam B and Cox B, 'The Barriers and Facilitators to the Use of Lifestyle Apps: A Systematic Review of Qualitative Studies' (2022) 12 *European Journal of Investigation in Health, Psychology and Education* (2). DOI: 10.3390/ejihpe12020012

Shcherbina A, Mattsson M, Waggott D, Salisbury H, Christle J, Hastie T, Wheeler M and Ashley E, 'Accuracy in Wrist-Worn, Sensor-Based Measurements of Heart Rate and Energy Expenditure in a Diverse Cohort' (2017) 24 *Journal of Personality* (7). DOI: 10.3390/jpm7020003

Stewart C, 'Share of Health App Users in Selected Countries as of 2022' (*Statista*, 22 December 2022). https://www.statista.com/forecasts/1181436/share-of-health-app-users-by-countryHealth app users by country 2022 | Statista.

Sunyaev A, Dehling T, Taylor P L and Mandl K D, 'Availability and Quality of Mobile Health App Privacy Policies' (2015) 22 *Journal of the American Medical Informatics Association* (1). DOI: 10.1136/amiajnl-2013-002605

Tangari G, Ikram M, Ijaz K, Kaafar M A and Berkovsky S, 'Mobile Health and Privacy: Cross Sectional Study' (2021) 373 *BMJ* (1248). DOI: 10.1136/bmj.n1248

Torous J, Nicholas J, Larsen M-E, Firth J and Christensen H, 'Clinical Review of User Engagement With Mental Health Smartphone Apps: Evidence, Theory and Improvements' (2018) 21 *Evidence-Based Mental Health* (03) DOI: 10.1136/eb-2018-102891

Yue Liu, 'User Control of Personal Information Concerning Mobile-App: Notice and Consent?' (2014) 30 *Computer Law and Security Review* (5). DOI: 10.1016/j.clsr.2014.07.008

Case law

Case C-219/115 *Brain Products GmbH v BioSemi VOF e.a* [2012] ECJ 2012/11.

C-61/19 *Orange Romania SA v Autoritatea Națională de Supraveghere a Prelucrării Datelor cu Caracter Personal* [2020] ERC 2020/901.

Part II

Secondary use: Legal basis, confidentiality and commercial uses

5 Transforming the secondary use of patient data in the European Health Data Space

A challenge for the patient's right to medical confidentiality?

Daniela Spajić

5.1 Introduction

Health data collected during healthcare provision is essential for advancing medical research and public health.[1] In particular, it is crucial for developing new medicines and improving personalised treatment.[2] Yet, this data – collected in a patient's medical records – contains sensitive information about the individual's health.

Historically, and also under modern human rights frameworks, patients' medical information has been subject to medical confidentiality. At the core of this principle is the unique relationship of trust between the patient and the medical professional, which encompasses an ethical dimension. It allows medical professionals to share data with others without patient consent exceptionally for reasons that are, for instance, in the public interest or serve patient safety.[3] The healthcare professional's duty of confidentiality ensures that the use of such data is restricted to the limitations of the treatment contract between patients and healthcare providers.[4]

In the EU, exceptions to patient confidentiality are laid down at multiple levels. The General Data Protection Regulation (GDPR) balances an individual's right to data protection and privacy with the collective interest in the (re-) use of personal data. Currently however, the specifics of access to patient data for different purposes are largely regulated at the national level. Regarding the sharing of patient data, some domestic legal frameworks reflect the balance between maintaining an individual's right to privacy and the objective of providing quality care by differentiating between sharing information with other care professionals to ensure quality care and the disclosure to other third-party actors.[5] The Council of Europe Recommendation also integrates such a differentiation. It urges that controllers and processors who are not health professionals should only process health-related data according to rules of confidentiality and security measures that ensure a level of protection equivalent to the one imposed on health professionals.[6]

The recently adopted European Health Data Space Regulation[7] (EHDS) seeks to transform the health data sharing regime as it implements rules that facilitate the secondary use of electronic health record data, which includes

DOI: 10.4324/9781003544111-7

patient data concerning health and genetic data in an electronic form, for various purposes. By providing specific rules for the use of such data at European Union (EU) level, the EU legislature shifts the focus from national to EU law, thereby transforming the legislative landscape to enable the sharing of patient data within and across member states.

Existing analyses have given little attention to the implications of the European Health Data Space for the physician's obligation to confidentiality. Understanding the balance between confidentiality and data protection law is an essential cornerstone of the protection of patient data, since sensitive pieces of information can provide pivotal insights into a person's health status.

The objective of this chapter is to scrutinise the rules of the EHDS concerning the secondary use of patients' electronic health record data (EHRD) from the perspective of medical confidentiality. The chapter first introduces the concept of medical confidentiality to illustrate its overarching significance in healthcare. Next, pertinent jurisprudence decided by the European Court of Human Rights (ECtHR) on the confidentiality of health data will be discussed. Afterwards, the author analyses selected provisions of the GDPR and the EHDS which relate to the secondary use of electronic health record data and confidentiality. This chapter argues that further specification within the legislative text through the EU legislature would have been needed to offer adequate protection to patients without diminishing their right to medical confidentiality.

5.2 The concept of medical confidentiality

Medical confidentiality is a keystone in medical ethics. The duty of medical professionals to maintain confidentiality guarantees the protection of patient information collected by and shared with medical professionals in the course of the patient's treatment, even after the patient's death.[8] Patients ought to speak freely about their mental and physical condition with their doctor, which in turn ought to enable healthcare professionals to make correct diagnoses and identify adequate treatments for their patients.

Although it can also extend to other healthcare professionals, the duty to preserve medical confidentiality is grounded in the Hippocratic Oath, which is historically binding on physicians. Confidentiality is sometimes enshrined in domestic law (for example, in general[9] or healthcare-related[10] frameworks). If breached without justification, this can result in disciplinary proceedings or sanctions under penal or civil law.[11]

The European Regional Office of the World Health Organisation published a notable set of principles regarding the rights of patients in Europe in 1994, including an articulation of what confidentiality and privacy ought to constitute.[12] Specifically, Article 4 of the declaration states that all 'information about a patient's health status, medical condition, diagnosis, prognosis and treatment and all other information of a personal kind must be kept confidential, even after death'. Such confidential information may 'only be disclosed if the patient gives explicit consent or if the law expressly provides for this'. The Oviedo Convention, which aims to protect the dignity and identity of human beings with regard to the application of biology and medicine, incorporates the right to respect for private life, hence confidentiality, concerning information about one's health.[13] As similar formulations have found their way into domestic texts codifying patient rights,[14] it becomes evident that the physician's obligation to maintain patient confidentiality constitutes not only a duty of physicians and other care professionals but also a right of patients.[15] Even the sharing of patient data among medical professionals can be subject to limitations, which vary among member states.[16]

The way that patient information is managed has changed over the past decades. Patient information is not merely about what the doctor knows. It is stored in various locations such as medical records or registries, facilitating potential disclosure through access to these files.

5.3 Confidentiality and its interaction with data protection law regarding the secondary use of health data in healthcare

In this section, relevant case law of the European Court of Human Rights will be presented and elaborated upon in order to demonstrate the jurisprudential and doctrinal development of confidentiality of health data. The section then discusses patient confidentiality under the GDPR. The analysis builds the basis for the later investigation of the secondary use of health data in the EHDS.

5.3.1 Confidentiality as per the European Court of Human Rights: a vital principle, but not an absolute right

At the European regional level, Article 8 of the European Convention on Human Rights (ECHR),[17] guaranteeing the right to respect for private and family life, home and correspondence, protects the right to confidentiality of medical data. While the right to respect for one's private life is broader in scope, confidentiality forms part thereof, imposing limitations on the disclosure of information.[18] However, medical confidentiality is not an absolute right, and the patient's interest in confidentiality can be overruled where it conflicts with a competing interest, such as the re-use of patient data for public health purposes. As per Article 8(2) ECHR, there shall be no interference by a public authority with the exercise of this right unless in accordance with the law and necessary in a democratic society, taking into account the interests listed in Article 8(2) of the Convention.

5.3.1.1 Confidentiality as an aspect of the right to respect for private life

The ECtHR has assessed the relevance of the confidentiality of health data in various cases. In particular, *Z v Finland*[19] delivers a significant decision where the Court assessed the applicant's objection to the use of her medical data (encompassing information about the applicant's HIV infection) during the proceedings of a criminal court.

The Court determined that respecting the confidentiality of health data is a 'vital principle' in light of this fundamental right and thus must be respected by all contracting parties to the Convention.[20] The importance of the case is that it presents the twofold objective of medical confidentiality. Maintaining confidentiality of patient data addresses privacy concerns that arise for the patient through the disclosure of such sensitive information about their health. Furthermore, protecting patients' privacy enables patients to control who can access their data and maintains their trust and confidence in the medical profession and the provision of healthcare.[21]

Diminished confidence in the healthcare system bears various risks. Individuals could be reluctant to visit their physician, which would adversely impact their health. Also, this carries further-reaching implications that can harm community interests in preventing the spread of community diseases or a pandemic. Consequently, the Court concluded that maintaining trust in confidentiality will 'weigh heavily' in the balancing exercise. The ECtHR shows special consideration for the protection of the confidentiality of health data such as information about an individual's HIV infection, requiring 'careful scrutiny' by the court and 'the safeguards designed to secure an effective protection'. Thus, it is pivotal that domestic law safeguards patient confidentiality and discourages any disclosure of personal data to the public unless a public interest is present.[22]

5.3.1.2 *Interference in accordance with the law and necessary in a democratic society*

According to the jurisprudence of the European Court of Human Rights, the storing and using of personal data can already constitute an interference[23] with an individual's right to respect for private life as per Article 8(1) of the Convention. Nonetheless, such an interference can be justified according to paragraph two, provided the interference is in accordance with the law and necessary in a democratic society for one of the reasons enumerated in Article 8(2) of the Convention.

According to the majority view of the European Court of Human Rights, information about a person's medical history and treatment may be disclosed to the public under certain circumstances if the law justifies it.[24] Notably, some voices have questioned the relationship between the duty of medical confidentiality and data protection law, in particular, whether data protection legislation can take precedence over the duties of the medical professional to safeguard confidentiality and, hence, exempt the professional from the prohibition to share data concerning health without the patient's consent.[25] Similarly, according to the partly dissenting opinion of Judge de Mayer in *Z v Finland*,[26] medical confidentiality is not merely a matter of national discretion, but a human right that does not embed a margin of appreciation, and is thus to be respected by all member states. Furthermore, the dissenting opinion suggests that disclosing patient data must be subject to high standards, which not every public interest fulfils.

Even if domestic law allows access to and collection of medical data by public authorities, *LH v Latvia*[27] illustrates that it is not sufficient if the competence of the public authority is described in a general manner. In the case, a national body inspected and evaluated the medical treatment that the applicant received in a public hospital based on the applicant's medical files obtained from three different institutions. For conducting this inquiry, the national law transposed a legal basis.

The European Court of Human Rights indicated that the law must be formulated with sufficient precision and provide adequate safeguards against arbitrariness in order to be compatible with the rule of law.[28] In the case at hand, the domestic law did not limit the scope of the data that could be collected by the public authorities, which led the public authority to collect medical data about the applicant for seven years without assessing whether the data was 'potentially decisive', 'relevant' or 'important'[29] for achieving the aim of the public authority. As the inquiry by the public authority commenced seven years after the applicant's sterilisation, it was doubted whether the data was even 'necessary for purposes of medical treatment [or] provision or administration of health care services' in accordance with the national law. In light of these considerations, it became less relevant for the court whether the staff of the public authority itself had a legal duty to maintain confidentiality.[30] Consequently, the court held that the domestic law was not sufficiently precisely formulated. Furthermore, the scope of discretion by the public authority and the manner of its exercise were not sufficiently specified.[31]

As indicated above, Article 8(2) of the European Convention on Human Rights lists concrete interests that can be balanced against an individual's interest in his or her right to private life, namely interests of national security, public safety or the economic well-being of the country, the prevention of disorder or crime, the protection of health or morals, or the protection of the rights and freedoms of others. Interestingly, however, the Oviedo Convention[32] did not consider all exceptions listed in Article 8(2) of the European Convention on Human Rights as relevant. The reason being was that it did not appear desirable to make the protection of a person's rights in the health sphere subject to defending the economic well-being of the country,[33] public order or morals, and national security.[34]

Finally, unavoidable interference should be limited to the extent that it is strictly necessary in a democratic society.[35] According to the European Court of Human Rights, the notion of necessity within the meaning of Article 8 of the Convention implies the existence of a 'pressing social need' and, in particular, that the measure is proportionate to the legitimate aim.[36] Thus, the notion of 'public interest' has to meet the high threshold of a 'pressing social need' which could encompass for instance travel restrictions as a potential public health measure where a risk of the spread of highly contagious diseases exists.[37] What constitutes a 'pressing social need' and how the principle of confidentiality is to be applied is, according to the Court, a decision that remains with the contracting countries as it is in their 'margin of appreciation'.[38]

5.3.2 The concept of medical confidentiality under the GDPR

Moving to the GDPR, the Regulation seeks to balance the (re-)use of patient data for the improvement of healthcare, research and public health with the patient's right to data protection and (medical) privacy.[39] Consequently, for data holders to share personal electronic healthcare record data (EHRD) with health data access bodies as foreseen by the EHDS, they need to comply with the rules of the GDPR in addition to those set out in the EHDS.

According to the GDPR, the processing of data concerning health and genetic data as a special category of personal data is generally prohibited as per Article 9(1) GDPR. In contrast, Article 9(2) GDPR exempts this prohibition, thereby legitimising the processing of data concerning health in conjunction with an adequate legal basis laid down in Article 6 GDPR. Data controllers must choose an adequate legal basis for the processing of these data types, whereby none of the legal grounds receives precedence over the other.

The GDPR uses the notion of professional secrecy where the medical confidentiality of patient data is concerned. For healthcare purposes, the GDPR incorporates a provision with Article 9(2)(h) GDPR that is tailored to the need for processing patient data. Specifically, it enables processing of special categories of personal data such as data concerning health and genetic data for purposes of preventive or occupational medicine, medical diagnosis, or the provision of health or social care more generally on the basis of Union or national law or pursuant to contract with health professionals and subject to the conditions and safeguards as per Article 9(3) GDPR.[40] The latter in particular requires that special categories of personal data are processed by or under the responsibility of a professional who is subject to the obligation of professional secrecy. Other persons may also process personal data as long as they are subject to an obligation of secrecy.[41] From this provision, it becomes evident that the GDPR uses the notion of professional secrecy where the medical confidentiality of patient data is concerned.

Additionally, although it does not provide a specific definition for the term, the GDPR has also embedded the concept of 'confidentiality' as one of its principles applicable to the processing of personal data, namely the principle of integrity and confidentiality.[42] This principle requires data controllers and processors to process personal data in a manner 'that ensures appropriate security of personal data'. This includes the obligation to implement appropriate technical and organisational safeguards for protection against unauthorised or unlawful processing, accidental loss, destruction or damage, using technical or organisational measures.[43] By doing so, the GDPR positions the term 'confidentiality' mainly in relation to the security of the processing operations.[44] It also does so in terms of other relevant provisions of the GDPR, such as in Articles 28[45] and 32 GDPR.[46] Similarly, the European Data Protection Board (EDPB) specifies the role of the principle of integrity and confidentiality, considering it as a means to avoid data breaches and to ensure compliance with the rules and principles concerning data processing under the GDPR, thereby also assuring compliance with the data protection by design and by default principles.[47] Implementing security is, as the EDPB stresses, an ongoing process that requires continuous assessment of the measures in place and their appropriateness to address technical threats or weaknesses.[48]

The deployment of appropriate technical and organisational measures is pivotal, particularly for protecting the rights and freedoms of natural persons, as Recital 78 GDPR highlights. In addition to putting adequate information systems in place (such as the technical means to manage access control and enable secure data transfers),[49] against that background, the principle of data minimisation[50] can be considered another component or facilitator for securing data confidentiality by limiting personal data collection and data usage to the absolute minimum.[51] The process of pseudonymising[52] or anonymising personal data can be a safeguard that maintains data confidentiality and secures the data subject's identity. Anonymisation as such is a further processing of personal data and, thus, must fulfil the compatibility clause as per Article 5(1)(b) GDPR taking account of the circumstances of said further processing.[53] Yet, note should be taken that the compatibility clause may not be applicable where data concerning health is collected during the provision of healthcare for research purposes if national law does not account for both purposes.[54]

5.4 Patient data under the secondary use framework of the European Health Data Space

The EHDS transposes a framework for secondary use that is defined as the processing of electronic health data (EHD) for purposes (set out in Chapter IV of the Regulation) other than the initial purposes for which they were collected or produced.[55]

EHRD will be collected by default, whereby individuals have the right to opt-out from the processing of their data for secondary use at any time.[56] Member states shall transpose mechanisms to implement the right to opt-out at the national level. The right to opt-out will be limited as member states may establish rules in national law transposing exceptions for certain purposes,[57] namely for the public interest in the area of public and occupational health (Articles 71(4)(a)(i) and 53(1)(a) EHDS), policy making and regulatory activities (Articles 71(4)(a)(i) and 53(1)(b) EHDS), statistics (Articles 71(4)(a)(i) and 53(1)(c) EHDS), and, finally, scientific research for important reasons of public interest (Article 71(4)(a)(ii) EHDS).[58] Access to data for these purposes shall be reserved for public sector and Union bodies, as well as third parties who carry out a task on their behalf.[59]

While EU member states may transpose further categories of EHD for secondary use,[60] Article 51 EHDS enumerates the minimum categories of EHD, which includes data from electronic health records (EHRs).[61] Nonetheless, other data categories that are listed in Article 51 EHDS may also be collected during the patient's treatment such as data on factors impacting on health (for example, socio-economic, environmental, and behavioural factors), automatically generated personal EHD through medical devices, or human genetic, epigenomic and genomic data.[62] All these categories of data are typically collected in the healthcare system, which is an environment significantly shaped by trust and confidentiality,[63] which the EHDS fails to consider.

The reuse of the enumerated categories will be possible for an array of purposes. Chapter IV of the EHDS provides a list of grounds based on which it should be possible to process EHD for secondary use, including purposes such as public interest in the area of public and occupational health,[64] education or teaching activities in the health or care sector at the level of vocational or higher education,[65] or scientific research related to health or care sectors, contributing to public health or health technology assessment or ensuring high levels of quality and safety of health care, of medicinal products or medical devices.[66] These have been embedded in the EHDS (presumably) in accordance with the corresponding legal grounds laid down in the GDPR (i.e., Articles 9(2)(g, h, i and j) GDPR).[67] The challenges that may arise from the interaction between the EHDS and the GDPR – particularly with a view to these provisions – will be elaborated later in this chapter.

Article 54 stipulates that health data users shall process EHD for secondary use only in compliance with the data permit and data request as per Articles 68 and 69 EHDS, respectively. Considering the sensitivity of EHD, and in particular EHRs, the EU legislature integrated a list of prohibited secondary uses of EHD, including a prohibition for advertising or marketing activities or for taking decisions detrimental to a natural person or a group of natural persons based on their EHD or in relation to a job offer.[68]

To foster access to health data for secondary use, the EHDS foresees the establishment of so-called health data access bodies, which will be responsible for granting access to EHD and which are further discussed in Chapters 9 and 10.[69] Data holders will have to make various categories of EHD available to health data access bodies, as the framework establishes a duty in the sense of Article 6(1)(c) GDPR for them to share EHD with health data access bodies[70] for secondary use.[71] While the original proposal put forward by the Commission considered such a duty for 'data holders',[72] the compromise text speaks of '*health* data holders'.[73] Although the amendment to the concept of health data holder and its corresponding definition suggests a clearer delineation as to whom the obligation to share health data applies, it still encompasses a wide range of stakeholders. This is because, according to the EHDS, a health data holder is a natural and legal person, public authority, agency or other body in the healthcare or the care sector as well as any natural or legal person developing products or services intended for the health, healthcare or care sectors, developing or manufacturing wellness applications, performing research in relation to healthcare or care sectors, or acting as a mortality registry as well as Union institutions, body, office or agency.[74]

Following a successful permit request for data access, health data access bodies will issue a permit in a subsequent step and offer access to EHD in an anonymised format to data users.[75] Similar to the definition of the health data holder, the final text speaks now of 'health data users' while still providing a broad definition for this concept, covering a natural or legal person that has been granted lawful access to EHD for secondary use pursuant to a data permit, data request or an access approval by an authorised participant in HealthData@EU.[76] Notably, the text of the EHDS did not adopt the suggestion put forward by the European Parliament to restrict data access to health data applicants who have a demonstratable professional link to the areas of health care, public health or medical research and that submit an application for health data.[77] By neglecting to do so, the final text again expands its scope of application to all kinds of data users with and without a professional link to the medical field, including commercial players, raising potential challenges for the patient's right to confidentiality (see further in Chapter 8).

Though health data users should primarily be granted access to anonymised data, the EHDS does not entirely exclude the sharing of personal data. Access to pseudonymous data,[78] hence personal data, can be granted where the data user cannot fulfil the anticipated purpose with anonymised data.[79] In such cases, data users will have to demonstrate how the data processing complies with the GDPR, in particular regarding the legal basis as per Article 6(1) GDPR on which they rely for the secondary use of EHD as part of the data access application.[80] Thereby, the compromise text fails to create harmonisation with the secondary use of personal EHD under the EHDS, especially as the identification of a legal basis as per GDPR is required.

5.5 Potential challenges arising between the EHDS, ECtHR case law and GDPR with regard to the secondary use of patient data

The above overview of relevant jurisprudence of the European Court of Human Rights and provisions of the GDPR and EHDS provided insights into the legal requirements of (patient) confidentiality, and how certain public interests can outweigh a patient's interest in confidentiality. The following analysis will elaborate on these perspectives in relation to the secondary use framework under the European Health Data Space.

The Regulation foresees that health data holders should be able to rely on the legal grounds of Article 6(1) GDPR, i.e., a (consent), c (compliance with a legal obligation), e (public interest) or f (legitimate interest), in conjunction with Article 9(2) GDPR, i.e., g (substantial public interest), h (preventive or occupational medicine), i (public interest in the area of public health) or j (archiving purposes in the public interest, scientific research or statistical purposes), when sharing personal health data with health data access bodies.[81] The following section thus investigates the challenges that the new framework carries for patient confidentiality, namely the need for legal specification of the patient's right to confidentiality and the need to improve the delineation of the purposes laid down in Article 53 EHDS with regard to Article 9 GDPR.

5.5.1 Article 9(2)(h) in conjunction with Article 9(3) GDPR

Neither the Proposal nor the latest EHDS text have specified how the grounds set out in the GDPR and the EHDS are compatible.[82] This question persists in particular concerning Article 9(2)(h), as it integrates an exception to the prohibition tailored to the processing of data concerning health for the provision of care. This provision enables the use of patient data for various types of medical care such as diagnosis or health prevention. Further processing that is not necessary for the provision and management of healthcare services, such as medical research, is not covered by the provision.[83]

Article 9(2)(h) has to be read in conjunction with Article 9(3) GDPR, and therefore, the latter's conditions must also be fulfilled in order for the exception of paragraph (h) to apply. Article 9(3) GDPR requires that special categories of personal data can be

> "processed by or under the responsibility of a professional subject to the obligation of professional secrecy under Union or Member State law or rules established by national competent bodies or by another person also subject to an obligation of secrecy under Union or Member State law or rules established by national competent bodies."

Given that such obligations of professional secrecy are usually embedded in national legislation, the fulfilment of the requirements of Article 9(3) GDPR – and consequently also the fulfilment of the conditions laid down in Article 9(2)(h) GDPR – will depend on domestic legislation.[84]

In relation to Article 8(3) of the EU Data Protection Directive,[85] which constitutes the preceding equivalent to what is now Article 9(2)(h) GDPR, the Article 29 Data Protection Working Party (hereafter WP29) concluded that all patients may 'reasonably expect that confidentiality and protection of their personal information will be rigorously upheld by all healthcare professionals', also 'as regards electronic health record (EHR) systems'.[86] Data collected under Article 8(3) Data Protection Directive had thus to be interpreted in a restrictive way. Subsequently, Article 8(3) could only serve as a legal ground to the extent that such data were processed strictly for medical and healthcare purposes and were required to be processed by a health professional.[87]

Given the restricted scope of Article 9(3) GDPR, the obligations established under data protection law appear to collide with the obligation to share data with health data access bodies. This constitutes an issue for healthcare professionals, since, as the WP29 pointed out, the obligation of professional secrecy must be established by law or by professional bodies through binding rules at national level.[88] In other words, does Article 9(2)(h) GDPR constitute an adequate legal basis for healthcare professionals when providing care to their patients while having to share the data further with health data access bodies as foreseen under the EHDS, or will this provision become obsolete once the EHDS is transposed? The question persists as the EDPB held in its opinion from 2021 that the presumption of compatibility as per Article 5(1)(b) GDPR cannot be upheld in terms of the further sharing of patient data for scientific research purposes unless national legislation stipulates otherwise.[89]

Certain categories of health data holders, namely natural persons, individual researchers and legal persons that are micro-enterprises, should be exempted from the obligations on the secondary use as per Article 50 EHDS. However, member states may provide that the obligations apply to them under national legislation.[90] Also, health data intermediation entities may support health data holders to fulfil their duties if domestic law provides for it,[91] although the relationship between healthcare professionals and health data intermediation entities may require further clarification.[92]

This prompts the subsequent question of whether healthcare providers will need to rely on explicit consent in order to respect their legal obligation to share data with health data access bodies. The European Parliament originally required that the patient's explicit consent (opt-in) should be requested for the secondary use of certain sensitive data, such as genetic data.[93] The EHDS transposes instead a right to opt-out, which member states ought to facilitate, leaving it within their competence to offer an absolute right to object to access related to specific categories of personal EHD, such as genetic data (see further in Chapter 7).[94]

Meanwhile, the so-called data altruism consent established under the Data Governance Act (DGA) may be a useful tool in addressing this concern (see further in Chapter 6). The EHDS foresees fostering altruistic data sharing based on the data altruism consent. However, legal uncertainty is created through the lack of clarity regarding the interplay between the EHDS, the GDPR and the DGA.[95] The latter has established particular rules to foster data sharing for the public good through the data altruism consent form. Data altruism encompasses objectives of general interest as provided for in national law,[96] such as (but not limited to) healthcare.[97] By doing so, the data altruism consent established under the DGA gives the impression that this form of consent is broader in scope compared to the 'common' GDPR consent which orients itself more strictly after the purpose limitation principle. Legal uncertainties remain given that as per Recital 50 DGA, data altruism consent will rely on the meaning of consent as established under the GDPR. Thus, the lack of alignment between the provisions of the GDPR and the DGA is carried into the scope of the EHDS. Furthermore, the vague definition of data altruism potentially extends access to protected patient data a little further by including stakeholders who do not demonstrate a professional link to healthcare.

The adaptations which had been suggested by the European Parliament in December 2023 appeared to address this issue to the extent that access would have been restricted to 'health data applicants', who are 'any natural or legal person with a demonstratable professional link to the areas of health care, public health or medical research and that submits an application for health data'.[98] However, this definition has not been integrated into the final text. Instead, considerations regarding the need to respect professional duties such as confidentiality duties have been integrated into the recitals. More specifically, according to Recital 55 of the EHDS, health data holders (such as healthcare providers) should make different categories of EHD available for secondary use 'provided that such effort is always made through effective and secured processes, with due respect for professional duties, such as confidentiality duties'. Although recitals represent the legislature's will and are hence needed for the interpretation of the law, they are not directly binding. Thus, also considering the case law of the European Court of Human Rights requiring the implementation of safeguards and legal specificity, a provision dedicated to professional duties and patient confidentiality should have been adopted.[99]

Besides, Recital 55 addresses only the sharing of health data through health data holders while the need to address confidentiality concerns with regard to health data *users*, who are not subject to such professional duties, persists. Even though the EHDS focuses on the sharing of anonymous data, this concern exists as the sharing of anonymous EHD facilitated through the European Health Data Space bears the risk to lead to centralised data silos carrying with them privacy and security concerns.[100]

Eliminating the risk of re-identification has proven to be difficult in practice, particularly in the context of healthcare.[101] Especially in terms of genetic data, which should also be integrated into the European health data space as a data category,[102] anonymisation seems to be unattainable according to the current technological state of the art.[103] Certain categories of health data, such as health data collected from patients with rare diseases, which occur in not more than five in ten thousand persons, carry a risk for individuals to be re-identified even when state-of-the-art anonymisation techniques have been applied, as the combination of information or vastly evolving technological developments can reveal sensitive information. The legislature acknowledges that a risk of re-identification remains regarding such data types. According to Recital 92 EHDS, this falls within the criteria of Article 5(13) DGA, which allows the European Commission to adopt delegated acts to lay down requirements for data transfer to third countries.[104] As the provision focuses on data transfers to third countries, interestingly, the legislature seems to suggest that a risk of re-identification for such data types does not exist within the European Union.[105]

5.5.2 Articles 9(2)(i) and (j) GDPR

While the purposes for secondary use were much broader defined in the Proposal, the European Parliament suggested narrowing the scope of application of secondary use. In particular, secondary use in, for instance, the labour market or financial services was to be banned, given that the data shared for research purposes should foster the improvement of medicine and healthcare services and products.[106] This certainly aligns better with the notions of public interest in the area of public health and scientific research as per Articles 9(2)(i) and (j) GDPR, respectively.

According to the EHDS, individuals will be able to exercise the opt-out mechanism without having to provide any reason for their decision. However, patients will not be able to opt-out for purposes that have a strong link to the public interest.[107] Recital 54 EHDS exemplifies some purposes which constitute a strong link to the public interest, such as activities for protection against serious cross-border threats to health or scientific research for important reasons of public interest, including, for instance, research addressing medical needs (such as rare diseases or emerging health threats). These purposes align in parts with the case law illustrated earlier in this chapter.

However, what can constitute a reason that is in the public interest and is necessary to pursue, meaning fulfilling a 'pressing social need',[108] and how the principle of confidentiality is to be applied is, returning to the jurisprudence of the European Court of Human Rights, a decision that remains with the contracting countries as it is within their 'margin of appreciation'.[109] Exceptions to the healthcare provider's duty of confidentiality can, thus, be found in national laws. The transposition of these laws can deviate between countries. For instance, some countries enable the use of EHR data for secondary purposes based on data protection legislation, while others implement specific legislation for it,[110] or they may transpose provisions supporting data transfer to specific registries.[111]

While acknowledging that some of these notions comprise altruistic purposes,[112] meaning purposes which serve broader societal interests such as the improvement of healthcare services, they have created legal uncertainty due to a deficient definition.[113] This may be partly due to the fact that member states conceptualise the notion of public interest or scientific research differently, leading to fragmented approaches to research and public health interests among EU member states.

For instance, if interpreted in the strict sense, the public interest may encompass purely public purposes such as public health, thereby excluding the full or partial involvement of commercial companies.[114] In such circumstances, sharing health data with the latter could lead to a violation of patient confidentiality, which the Proposal did not seem to consider sufficiently.[115] In contrast, the EHDS, as mentioned earlier, reserves explicitly the use of EHD for public interest to public sector bodies. However, it does again not account for professional secrecy although Article 9(2)(i) GDPR explicitly requires the implementation of suitable and specific measures to safeguard the rights and freedoms of individuals, in particular in relation to professional secrecy.

Furthermore, a clearer alignment by the legislature of the purposes listed in Article 53 EHDS by delineating still ambiguous notions, such as scientific research (Article 9(2)(j) GDPR), would have been needed to safeguard patient confidentiality. This is because the concept of scientific research can be associated with two different legal grounds in the EHDS, i.e., 'public interest' (Article 53(1)(a) EHDS) and 'scientific research related to health and care' (Article 53(1)(e) EHDS). Especially regarding the former, scientific research may constitute a 'public interest' as per Article 53(1)(a) EHDS if conducted for an important reason in the public interest according to Recital 54 EHDS. However, it is yet to be seen how both legal grounds (i.e., paragraphs a) and e)) will be applied. A possibility to address this issue can be to link the purposes more explicitly to the exceptions laid out in Article 9(2) GDPR[116] given that Article 9(2)(i) GDPR specifies that it applies to the protection 'against serious cross-border threats to health or ensuring high standards of quality and safety of health care and of medicinal products or medical devices'.

Finally, while complete datasets may be admirable to achieve, the unlimited collection and storage of personal EHD for the secondary use should be avoided in light of ECtHR case law. In particular, the collection and sharing of medical data should be assessed in terms of its 'relevance' or 'importance' to understand whether the data is (still) necessary for the purpose for which it was collected in order to ensure compatibility with the rule of law.

5.5.3 Article 9(4) GDPR

The question of the legality of the processing of sensitive patient data in the European Health Data Space with a view to the physician's duty of medical confidentiality remains, especially also in light of Article 9(4) GDPR. This provision allows member states to introduce further requirements, including limitations on the processing of data concerning health, biometric data and genetic data. These have led to varying levels of digitalisation of health data depending on data categories.[117] While the legislature constructs the EHDS as an EU law that addresses the fragmented implementation created by Article 9(4) GDPR,[118] it remains somewhat unclear how the EHDS plans to conform with this provision.[119] Notably, the EHDS explains that member states may no longer make use of paragraph 4 to transpose further conditions, including limitations and specific provisions requesting consent of individuals, regarding secondary use, except as referred to in Article 51(4) EHDS.[120] This has prompted the question of if and how the margin of appreciation per Article 9(4) GDPR can be sustained.

5.6 Conclusion

The analysis in this chapter shows that the EHDS is not fully harmonised with the existing rules of the GDPR. Above all, the forthcoming legislative changes initiated to foster the secondary use of health data appear to challenge patient confidentiality.

Deontological rules of confidentiality primarily concern healthcare professionals and their obligations rather than those who seek to process patient data. Breach of such duty would thus primarily concern healthcare professionals if punishable under domestic law. More importantly, however, these rules exist for the protection of the patient, making the duty of medical professionals a patients' right. The European Parliament's propositions following their reading in December 2023 considered this concern to a certain degree and thus would have gone in the right direction. Integrating the duty to patient confidentiality into the provisions, not only with a view to data holders but also with a view to data users, contributes to avoiding potential disharmony with the patient's right to confidentiality.

Finally, it should be considered that healthcare is primarily a matter of national competence, which complicates the re-use of patient data and does not seem to be taken sufficiently into consideration by the EHDS. This may lead to a collision between the patient's interest in medical confidentiality and the EHDS's interest in fostering the availability of EHR data. Also, attention must be paid to the fact that the patient–doctor relationship is characterised by a special bond of trust, creating high standards for the potential re-use and sharing of sensitive data. Otherwise, this could impede patients from receiving suitable healthcare. To this end, the jurisprudence by the European Court of Human Rights provides some guidance that could shape the implementation of the European health data space and its Regulation.

Acknowledgement

The research for this chapter was in part performed in a project that received funding from the European Union's Horizon Europe research and innovation programme under Grant Agreement No 101095717. Views and opinions expressed are however those of the author(s) only and do not necessarily reflect those of the European Union or the Health and Digital Executive Agency. Neither the European Union nor the granting authority can be held responsible for them.

Notes

1 Commission, 'A European strategy for data' (Communication) COM/2020/66 final.
2 Data Saves Lives, 'Why is health data important?' www.datasaveslives.eu/why-is-health-data-important accessed 28 April 2024; MedTech Europe, 'Unlocking the full benefits of health data. Recommendations from MedTech Europe' (2021) position paper 16 June 2021 www.medtecheurope.org/wp-content/uploads/2021/06/mte_160621_positionpaper_health-data.pdf accessed 28 April 2024.
3 Henriette Roscam Abbing, 'Medical Confidentiality and Patient Safety: Reporting Procedures' (2014) 21(3) *European Journal of Health Law* 245.
4 Article 29 Working Party (WP29), 'Working Document on the processing of personal data relating to health in electronic health records (EHR)' (WP 131, 15 February 2007) 10.
5 See Mette Hartlev, 'Forwards or backwards? New directions in Danish patients' Rights Legislation' (2011) 18(4) *European Journal of Health Law* 365, 371, according to which such differentiation can be found in the Danish Health Act (see Chapter 9 of the Danish Health Act (*Sundhedsloven LBK nr 247 of 12 March 2024* (Denmark)); another example is § 9 of the (Model-)Professional Code for Physicians in Germany (*(Muster-) Berufsordnung für die in Deutschland tätigen Ärztinnen und Ärzte MBO-Ä 1997*) (Germany).
6 Council of Europe, 'Protection of health-related data' Recommendation CM/Rec(2019)2, 2 March 2019. See Article 9.4, which stipulates similar obligations for the communication of health-related data to an authorised recipient for purposes other than providing and administering health care.

7 European Parliament, 'CORRIGENDUM to the position of the European Parliament adopted at first reading on 24 April 2024 with a view to the adoption of Regulation (EU) 2024/... of the European Parliament and of the Council on the European Health Data Space' P9_TA(2024)0331 (COM(2022)0197 – C9-0167/2022 – 2022/0140(COD)), 27.11.2024 (hereafter EHDS).

8 See, for instance, World Medical Association (WMA), 'Declaration of Lisbon on the rights of the patient' (1981) www.wma.net/policies-post/wma-declaration-of-lisbon-on-the-rights-of-the-patient/ accessed 28 April 2024, art 8(a).

9 See, for instance, Public Access to Information and Secrecy Act (*Offentlighets- och sekretesslag* (2009:400)) (Sweden).

10 See, for instance, (Model-)Professional Code for Physicians in Germany (n 5). The duty of confidentiality may be specified in soft law (see, for instance: Medical Council, 'Guide to Professional Conduct and Ethics for Registered Medical Practitioners (Amended)' (2016) last updated 2019, 25 (Ireland) www.medicalcouncil.ie/news-and-publications/reports/guide-to-professional-conduct-ethics-8th-edition.html accessed 28 April 2024).

11 For instance, Germany regulates the penalties for the breach of medical secrecy in section 203 of the German Criminal Code (*Strafgesetzbuch*) in conjunction with the (Model-)Professional Code for Physicians in Germany (n 5).

12 Abbing (n 3); The duty is also embedded in other instruments at international level, in particular in the Declaration of Geneva which is considered to be the 'modern Hippocratic oath' (see WMA, 'Declaration of Geneva' (1948) www.wma.net/policies-post/wma-declaration-of-geneva/ accessed 28 April 2024; or WMA, 'Declaration of Geneva, The 'Modern Hippocratic Oath' www.wma.net/what-we-do/medical-ethics/declaration-of-geneva/ accessed 28 April 2024; Other international instruments are, for instance: WMA, 'Declaration of Lisbon on the rights of the patient' www.wma.net/policies-post/wma-declaration-of-lisbon-on-the-rights-of-the-patient/ accessed 28 April 2024, or 'WMA International Code of Medical Ethics' www.wma.net/policies-post/wma-international-code-of-medical-ethics/ accessed 28 April 2024.

13 Council of Europe, Convention for the protection of Human Rights and dignity of the human being with regard to the application of biology and medicine: Convention on Human Rights and Biomedicine CETS no 164 (Oviedo Convention) art 10; see also: Council of Europe, Explanatory report to the Convention on Human Rights and Biomedicine, para 63, 10, www.coe.int/en/web/bioethics/oviedo-convention accessed 28 April 2024.

14 See, for example, § 9 of (Model-)Professional Code for Physicians in Germany (n 5); or § 54 of Federal Physicians Act (*Bundesgesetz über die Ausübung des ärztlichen Berufes und die Standesvertretung der Ärzte (Ärztegesetz 1998 – ÄrzteG 1998*), StF: Federal Law Gazette I Nr. 169/1998 (Austria).

15 Abbing (n 3).

16 See legislation (n 9-10).

17 Council of Europe, European Convention for the Protection of Human Rights and Fundamental Freedoms (as amended by Protocols no 11, 14 and 15, supplemented by Protocols no 1, 4, 6, 7, 12, 13 and 16) 4 November 1950, ETS 5 (hereinafter also referred to as the Convention/ECHR).

18 Maria Sokalska, 'Medical confidentiality – Quo Vadis?' (2004) 11(1) *European Journal of Health Law* 35; Oviedo Convention, art 10 (n 13). The right has been reiterated in Council of Europe, Convention for the Protection of Individuals with regard to the Automatic Processing of Personal Data CETS No 108 (2018) (Convention 108+)); also, the Council of Europe's recommendation on the protection of health-related data (see above (n 6)) takes account of the concept of patient confidentiality.

19 *Z v Finland* App no 22009/93 (ECtHR, 25 February 1997).

20 *Z v Finland* (n 19) para 94.

21 *Z v Finland* (n 19) para 95.
22 *Armonas v Lithuania* App no 36919/02 (ECtHR, 25 November 2008) para 40; *Biriuk v Lithuania* App no 23373/03 (ECtHR, 25 November 2008) paras 43-44; *Z v Finland* (n 19) para 95.
23 See *Leander v Sweden* App no 9248/81 (ECtHR, 26 March 1987) para 48; *S and Marper v the United Kingdom* App nos 30562/04 and 30566/04 (ECtHR, 4 December 2008); *Rotaru v Romania* App no 28341/95 (ECtHR, 4 May 2000).
24 See, for instance, *Panteleyenko v Ukraine* App no 11901/02 (ECtHR, 29 June 2006).
25 See Christian Katzenmeier, 'Berufsgeheimnis und Dokumentation' in Adolf Laufs, Christian Katzenmeier and Volker Lipp (eds), *Arztrecht* (Verlag CH Beck oHG 2021) para 79.
26 *Z v Finland* (n 19).
27 *LH v Latvia* App no 52019/07 (ECtHR, 29 April 2014).
28 *LH v Latvia (n 27)* para 47.
29 See *LH v Latvia (n 27)* para 58, referring to *LL v France* App no 7508/02 (ECtHR, 10 October 2006) para 46, and *MS v Sweden* App no 20837/92 (ECtHR, 27 August 1997) paras 38, 42 and 43.
30 *LH v Latvia* (n 27) para 58.
31 *LH v Latvia (n 27)* para 59.
32 Oviedo Convention (n 13).
33 The economic aspect is taken into account insofar as Article 3 of the Convention refers to 'available resources'. This, however, should not be a reason for allowing exceptions to the rights established under the Convention (see Explanatory Report (n 13) paras 157 and 159, at 22; Abbing (n 3) 248–249).
34 See Explanatory Report (n 13) para 156, at 22; Article 26 of the Oviedo Convention covers interests of public safety, prevention of crime, protection of public health, protection of rights and freedoms of others as possible exceptions to medical confidentiality; see Abbing (n 3) 248–249.
35 See, for instance, *LL v France* (n 29) para 43.
36 See *Biržietis v Lithuania* App no. 49304/09 (ECtHR, 14 June 2016).
37 See *Handyside v the United Kingdom* App no 5493/72 (ECtHR, 07 December 1976); *Kiyutin v Russia* App no 2700/10 (ECtHR, 10 March 2011).
38 *Z v Finland* (n 19).
39 See, for instance, Edward S Dove, 'Confidentiality, public interest, and the human right to science: when can confidential information be used for the benefit of the wider community?' (2023) 10(1) *J Law Biosci Journal of Law and the Bioscience* lsad013.
40 See GDPR art 9(2)(h).
41 GDPR art 9(3).
42 GDPR art 5(1)(f).
43 GDPR art 5(1)(f).
44 Sometimes, the GDPR connects confidentiality to the role of a person (see art 38(5) GDPR).
45 See art 28(3)(b) GDPR which refers to confidentiality related to (un-)authorised access.
46 See art 32(1)(b) GDPR which refers to the security of processing.
47 EDPB, 'Guidelines 4/2019 on Article 25 Data Protection by Design and by Default. Version 2.0' (2019) 20 *October* 2020, 26.
48 EDPB, 'Guidelines 4/2019 on Article 25 Data Protection by Design and by Default. Version 2.0' (2019) 20 *October* 2020.
49 EDPB, 'Guidelines 4/2019 on Article 25 Data Protection by Design and by Default. Version 2.0' (2019) 20 *October* 2020, 26–27.
50 See GDPR art 5(1)(c).
51 See GDPR rec 78.
52 See GDPR rec 78, art 4(5).

53 WP29, 'Opinion 05/2014 on Anonymisation Techniques' (WP 216, 10 April 2014).
54 EDPB, 'EDPB Document on response to the request from the European Commission for clarifications on the consistent application of the GDPR, focusing on health research' (2021) 2 February 2021, 6–7.
55 EHDS art 2(2)(e).
56 EHDS rec 54, art 71.
57 EHDS art 71(4)(a).
58 See also: EHDS rec 54.
59 EHDS arts 53(2), 71(4)(a).
60 EHDS art 51(2).
61 EHDS arts 51(1)(a), 2(2)(j).
62 EHDS art 51(1)(b), (f) and (h).
63 Santa Slokenberga, 'Scientific research regime 2.0? Transformations of the research regime and the protection of the data subject that the proposed EHDS regulation promises to bring along' (2022) Technology and Regulation 135, 142.
64 EHDS art 53(1)(a).
65 EHDS art 53(1)(d).
66 EHDS art 53(1)(e).
67 See: EHDS rec 52, art 2(2)(a).
68 EHDS art 54(a-c).
69 EHDS art 55.
70 EHDS art 57.
71 See EDPB-EDPS, 'Joint Opinion 03/2022 on the Proposal for a Regulation on the European Health Data Space' (2022) 12 July 2022, para 22.
72 See Commission, 'Proposal for a Regulation of the European Parliament and of the Council on the European Health Data Space' COM/2022/197 final (EHDS (proposal)) art 2(2)(y).
73 EHDS art 2(2)(t). Emphasis added.
74 EHDS art 2(2)(t).
75 EHDS rec 53, art 66(2).
76 EHDS art 2(2)(u).
77 See European Parliament, 'Amendments adopted by the European Parliament on 13 December 2023 on the proposal for a regulation of the European Parliament and of the Council on the European Health Data Space' (COM(2022)0197 – C9-0167/2022 – 2022/0140(COD))(1), T9-0462/2023, Amendment 105, art 2 – paragraph 2 – point z a (new).
78 See GDPR art 4(5).
79 EHDS arts 66(3), 67(2)(e), 67(4).
80 EHDS rec 52, art 67(4).
81 EHDS rec 52.
82 EDPB-EDPS (n 71) para 89-90.
83 WP29 (n 4) 10.
84 Georgieva Ludmila, Christopher Kuner, 'Article 9 Processing of special categories of personal data' in Christopher Kuner and others (eds), *The EU General Data Protection Regulation (GDPR): A Commentary* (Oxford Academic, online edn 2020).
85 Directive 95/46/EC of the European Parliament and of the Council of 24 October 1995 on the protection of individuals with regard to the processing of personal data and on the free movement of such data, OJ 1995 L 281/31.
86 WP29 (n 4) 21.
87 WP29 (n 4) 11.
88 WP29 (n 4) 11.
89 EDPB (n 54) 7, para. 22.
90 EHDS art 50(1 and 2).

91 EHDS art 50(3).
92 Standing Committee of European Doctors (CPME), 'European doctors call for more ambition on professional secrecy and patient confidentiality in European Health Data Space', 8 February 2024, https://www.cpme.eu/news/european-doctors-call-for-more-ambition-on-professional-secrecy-and-patient-confidentiality-in-european-health-data-space accessed 28 April 2024.
93 European Parliament, 'EP supports creating EU Health Data Space to boost access to data and research' (press release, 13 December 2023) www.europarl.europa.eu/news/en/press-room/20231208IPR15783/ep-supports-creating-eu-health-data-space-to-boost-access-to-data-and-research accessed 28 April 2024; see also: European Parliament (n 77) amendment 39, recital 39 a (new).
94 EHDS rec 18; see also EHDS rec 11.
95 Regulation (EU) 2022/868 of the European Parliament and of the Council of 30 May 2022 on European data governance and amending Regulation (EU) 2018/1724 (Data Governance Act) PE/85/2021/REV/, OJ L 152 [hereinafter also referred to as 'DGA']).
96 See DGA art 2(16).
97 See DGA art 2(16) for all examples constituting 'objectives of general interest'.
98 European Parliament (n 77) amendment 105, Article 2, paragraph 2, point z a (new).
99 Standing Committee of European Doctors (CPME) (n 92).
100 René Raab and others, 'Federated electronic health records for the European Health Data Space' (2023) 5(11) *Lancet Digital Health* e840.
101 See WP29 (n 53) 22, 33-34.
102 EHDS art 51(1)(f).
103 See Harald Schmidt and Shawneequa Callier, 'How anonymous is "anonymous'anonymous"? Some suggestions towards a coherent universal coding system for genetic samples' (2012) 38(5) *Journal of Medical Ethics* 304.
104 EHDS rec 92. see also DGA arts 5(13) and 32.
105 David Fåhraeus, Jane Reichel and Santa Slokenberga, 'The European Health Data Space: Challenges and Opportunities' (European Policy Analysis, Sieps – Swedish Institute for European Policy Studies, February 2024) 9–10.
106 European Parliament, 'EP supports creating EU Health Data Space to boost access to data and research' (2023) press release, 13 December 2023 www.europarl.europa.eu/news/en/press-room/20231208IPR15783/ep-supports-creating-eu-health-data-space-to-boost-access-to-data-and-research accessed 28 April 2024.
107 EHDS rec 54; EHDS 71(4).
108 See *Biržietis v Lithuania* (n 36); *Handyside v the United Kingdom* (n 37); *Kiyutin v Russia* (n 37).
109 *Z v Finland* (n 19).
110 See Time.lex and Milieu, 'Overview of the national laws on electronic health records in the EU Member States and their interaction with the provision of cross-border eHealth services. Final report and recommendations' (2014) 45–47 https://health.ec.europa.eu/other-pages/basic-page/overview-national-laws-electronic-health-records-eu-member-states-2016_en accessed 28 April 2024.
111 For instance, see: Der Bundesbeauftragte für den Datenschutz und die Informationsfreiheit (BfDI), 'Register im Gesundheitsbereich' www.bfdi.bund.de/DE/Buerger/Inhalte/GesundheitSoziales/Allgemein/RegisterimGesundheitsbereich.html accessed 28 April 2024.
112 Anton Vedder and Daniela Spajic, 'Moral autonomy of patients and legal barriers to a possible duty of health related data sharing' (2023) 25 *Ethics and Information Technology* 23.
113 For instance, the EDPS stresses that not every research activity can fulfil the criteria for *scientific* research (see EDPS, 'A Preliminary Opinion on data protection

and scientific research' (2020) 11–12). Also, uncertainties remain as to what public interest can be considered as *substantial* public interest as per Article 9(2)(g) GDPR (see Daniela Spajic, 'Patient data sharing for the improvement of healthcare and medical research: Towards a moral duty of patients to share health-related data?' (PhD Dissertation, KU Leuven 2023)).

114 John Mark Michael Rumbold and Barbara Pierscionek, 'The Effect of the General Data Protection Regulation on Medical Research' (2017) 19(2) *Journal of Medical Internet Research* e47, 2.

115 See EHDS (proposal) (n 72) art 2(1)(z), according to which data user is broadly defined as 'a natural or legal person who has lawful access to personal or non-personal electronic health data for secondary use'.

116 Veronique Cimina, 'The Proposal for a European Health Data Space: between pursued objectives and data protection challenges' (2023) 24 ERA Forum 343, referring to EDPB-EDPS (n 71) paras 82 to 99.

117 EHDS rec 27.

118 EHDS (proposal) (n 72) explanatory memorandum. Notably, the EHDS still considers a potential fragmentation as valid when it comes to international transfers of personal electronic health data (see EHDS art 90).

119 EDPB-EDPS (n 71) paras 57, 89.

120 See EHDS rec 52.

List of sources

Treaties, legislation and conventions

Council of Europe, Convention for the protection of Human Rights and dignity of the human being with regard to the application of biology and medicine: Convention on Human Rights and Biomedicine, CETS No. 164 (Oviedo Convention).

Council of Europe, Convention for the Protection of Individuals with Regard to the Automatic Processing of Individual Data, 28 January 1981, CETS 108.

Council of Europe, Convention for the Protection of Individuals with regard to the Automatic Processing of Personal Data, 18 May 2018 (Convention 108+).

Council of Europe, European Convention on Human Rights as amended by Protocols Nos. 11, 14 and 15, supplemented by Protocols Nos. 1, 4, 6, 7, 12, 13 and 16, 4 November 1950, CETS 5.

Directive 95/46/EC of the European Parliament and of the Council of 24 October 1995 on the protection of individuals with regard to the processing of personal data and on the free movement of such data, OJ 1995 L 281/31.

European Parliament, 'CORRIGENDUM to the position of the European Parliament adopted at first reading on 24 April 2024 with a view to the adoption of Regulation (EU) 2024/... of the European Parliament and of the Council on the European Health Data Space' P9_TA(2024)0331 (COM(2022)0197 – C9-0167/2022 – 2022/0140(COD)), 27.11.2024 (European Health Data Space Regulation - EHDS).

Proposal for a Regulation of the European Parliament and of The Council on the European Health Data Space (EHDS proposal) COM/2022/197 final.

Proposal for a Regulation of The European Parliament and of The Council on European data governance (Data Governance Act, DGA) COM/2020/767 final.

Regulation (EU) 2016/679 of the European Parliament and of the Council of 27 April 2016 on the protection of natural persons with regard to the processing of personal data and on the free movement of such data, and repealing Directive 95/46/EC (General Data Protection Regulation, GDPR) OJ L 119/1.

Regulation (EU) 2022/868 of the European Parliament and of the Council of 30 May 2022 on European data governance and amending Regulation (EU) 2018/1724 (Data Governance Act) PE/85/2021/REV/, OJ L 152/1.

Domestic legislation

Criminal Code in the version published on 13 November 1998 (Federal Law Gazette I, p. 3322), as last amended by Article 2 of the Act of 22 November 2021 (Federal Law Gazette I, p. 4906) (*Strafgesetzbuch*) (Germany).

Federal Physicians Act (*Bundesgesetz über die Ausübung des ärztlichen Berufes und die Standesvertretung der Ärzte (Ärztegesetz 1998 – ÄrzteG 1998)*, StF: Federal Law Gazette I Nr. 169/1998 (Austria).

Health Act (consolidated) (*Sundhedsloven LBK nr 247 of 12 March 2024*) (Denmark).

Medical Council, 'Guide to Professional Conduct and Ethics for Registered Medical Practitioners (Amended)' (2016) last updated 2019 (Ireland). www.medicalcouncil.ie/news-and-publications/reports/guide-to-professional-conduct-ethics-8th-edition.html accessed 26 March 2024).

(Model-)Professional Code for Physicians in Germany (*(Muster-)Berufsordnung für die in Deutschland tätigen Ärztinnen und Ärzte MBO-Ä 1997*) (Germany). www.aerzteblatt.de/archiv/198641/(Muster-)Berufsordnung-fuer-die-in-Deutschland-taetigen-Aerztinnenund-Aerzte-in-der-Fassung-der-Beschluesse-des-121-Deutschen-Aerztetages-2018-in-Erfurt

Public Access to Information and Secrecy Act (*Offentlighets- och sekretesslag (2009:400)*) (Sweden).

Policy documents

Article 29 Data Protection Working Party (WP29),—— 'Working Document on the processing of personal data relation to health in electronic health records (EHR)' (2007) 15 February 2007, WP 131.

Article 29 Data Protection Working Party (WP29), 'Opinion 05/2014 on Anonymisation Techniques' (2014) 10 April 2014, WP216.

Council of Europe,—— 'Protection of health-related data' Recommendation CM/Rec(2019)2 (2019). https://edoc.coe.int/en/international-law/7969-protection-of-health-related-date-recommendation-cmrec20192.html

Council of Europe, Oviedo Convention, Explanatory report. https://www.coe.int/en/web/bioethics/oviedo-convention

Council of the European Union, 'Proposal for a Regulation on the European Health Data Space Analysis of the final compromise text with a view to agreement' (2022) 2022/0140(COD) (EHDS (compromise text).

EDPB-EDPS, 'Joint Opinion 03/2022 on the Proposal for a Regulation on the European Health Data Space' (2022) 12 July 2022.

European Commission, Communication from the Commission to the European Parliament, The Council, The European Economic and Social Committee and The Committee of The Regions, 'A European strategy for data' (2020) COM/2020/66 final.

European Data Protection Board (EDPB), 'Guidelines 4/2019 on Article 25 Data Protection by Design and by Default. Version 2.0' (2019) 20 October 2020.

European Data Protection Board (EDPB), 'EDPB Document on response to the request from the European Commission for clarifications on the consistent application of the GDPR, focusing on health research' (2021) 2 February 2021.

European Parliament, 'Amendments adopted by the European Parliament on 13 December 2023 on the proposal for a regulation of the European Parliament and of the Council on the European Health Data Space' (2023) (COM(2022)0197 – C9-0167/2022 – 2022/0140(COD))(1), T9-0462/2023. https://oeil.secure.europarl.europa.eu/oeil/popups/ficheprocedure.do?reference=2022/0140(COD)&l=en

MedTech Europe, 'Unlocking the full benefits of health data. Recommendations from MedTech Europe' (2021) position paper, 16 June 2021. https://www.medtecheurope.org/wp-content/uploads/2021/06/mte_160621_positionpaper_health-data.pdf

The European Data Protection Supervisor (EDPS), 'A preliminary opinion on data protection and scientific research' (2020) 6 January 2020.

World Medical Association (WMA), Declaration of Geneva, 1948. https://www.wma.net/policies-post/wma-declaration-of-geneva/

World Medical Association (WMA),—— Declaration of Geneva, the 'Modern Hippocratic Oath'. (n.d.). https://www.wma.net/what-we-do/medical-ethics/declaration-of-geneva/

World Medical Association (WMA),—— Declaration of Lisbon on the rights of the patient. https://www.wma.net/policies-post/wma-declaration-of-lisbon-on-the-rights-of-the-patient/

World Medical Association (WMA),—— WMA International Code of Medical Ethics. https://www.wma.net/policies-post/wma-international-code-of-medical-ethics/

Literature and other secondary sources

Abbing HR, 'Medical confidentiality and patient safety: Reporting procedures' (2014) 21(3) *European Journal of Health Law* 245–259. https://doi.org/10.1163/15718093-12341319

Cimina V, 'The proposal for a European Health Data Space: Between pursued objectives and data protection challenges' (2023) 24 *ERA-Forum* 343–359. https://doi.org/10.1007/s12027-023-00764-7

Data Saves Lives, 'Why is health data important?' (n.d.). www.datasaveslives.eu/why-is-health-data-important

Der Bundesbeauftragte für den Datenschutz und die Informationsfreiheit (BfDI), 'Register im Gesundheitsbereich'. (n.d.). www.bfdi.bund.de/DE/Buerger/Inhalte/GesundheitSoziales/Allgemein/RegisterimGesundheitsbereich.html

Dove ES, 'Confidentiality, public interest, and the human right to science: when can confidential information be used for the benefit of the wider community?' (2023) 10(1) *Journal of Law and the Biosciences* lsad013. https://doi.org/10.1093/jlb/lsad013

European Parliament, 'EP supports creating EU Health Data Space to boost access to data and research' (2023) press release, 13 December 2023. www.europarl.europa.eu/news/en/press-room/20231208IPR15783/ep-supports-creating-eu-health-data-space-to-boost-access-to-data-and-research

Fåhraeus D, Reichel J and Slokenberga S, 'The European Health Data Space: Challenges and Opportunities' (2024) European Policy Analysis, Sieps – Swedish Institute for European Policy Studies, February 2024. www.sieps.se/en/publications/2024/the-european-health-data-space/

Hartlev M, 'Forwards or backwards? New directions in Danish patients' rights legislation' (2011) *European Journal of Health Law* 18(4), 365–374. https://doi.org/10.1163/157180911X575758

Katzenmeier C, 'Berufsgeheimnis und Dokumentation' in Laufs A, Katzenmeier C and Lipp V, Arztrecht. Verlag C.H. Beck oHG (2021).

Ludmila G and Kuner C, 'Article 9 Processing of special categories of personal data', in Kuner C and others (eds), *The EU General Data Protection Regulation (GDPR): A Commentary* (2020) online edn, Oxford Academic, 365–384. https://doi.org/10.1093/oso/9780198826491.003.0038

Raab R and others, 'Federated electronic health records for the European Health Data Space' (2023) 5 *Lancet Digit Health* e840–e847. https://doi.org/10.1016/S2589-7500(23)00156-5

Rumbold JMM and Pierscionek B, 'The effect of the general data protection regulation on medical research' (2017) 19(2) *Journal of Medical Internet Research* e47. https://doi.org/10.2196/jmir.7108

Schmidt H and Callier S, 'How anonymous is "anonymous"? Some suggestions towards a coherent universal coding system for genetic samples' (2012) 38(5) *Journal of Medical Ethics* 304–309. https://doi.org/10.1136/medethics-2011-100181

Slokenberga S, 'Scientific research regime 2.0? Transformations of the research regime and the protection of the data subject that the proposed EHDS regulation promises to bring along' (2022) *Technology and Regulation* 135–147. https://doi.org/10.26116/techreg.2022.014
Sokalska, M, 'Medical confidentiality – Quo Vadis?' (2004) 11(1) *European Journal of Health Law* 35–43. https://doi.org/10.1163/1571809043230423 26
Spajic D, 'Patient data sharing for the improvement of healthcare and medical research: Towards a moral duty of patients to share health-related data?' (2023) (PhD Dissertation, KU Leuven 2023).
Standing Committee of European Doctors (CPME), 'European doctors call for more ambition on professional secrecy and patient confidentiality in European Health Data Space', 8 February 2024. https://www.cpme.eu/news/european-doctors-call-for-more-ambition-on-professional-secrecy-and-patient-confidentiality-in-european-health-data-space
Time.lex, Milieu, 'Overview of the national laws on electronic health records in the EU Member States and their interaction with the provision of cross-border eHealth services. Final report and recommendations' (2014) 23 July 2024. https://health.ec.europa.eu/other-pages/basic-page/overview-national-laws-electronic-health-records-eu-member-states-2016_en
Vedder A and Spajic D, 'Moral autonomy of patients and legal barriers to a possible duty of health related data sharing' (2023) 25 *Ethics and Information Technology* 23. https://doi.org/10.1007/s10676-023-09697-8

Case law

Armonas v Lithuania App no. 36919/02 (ECtHR, 25 November 2008).
Biriuk v Lithuania App no 23373/03 (ECtHR, 25 November 2008).
Biržietis v Lithuania App no. 49304/09 (ECtHR, 14 June 2016).
Handyside v the United Kingdom App no. 5493/72 (ECtHR, 07 December 1976).
Kiyutin v Russia no. 2700/10 (ECtHR, 10 March 2011).
LH v Latvia App no 52019/07 (ECtHR, 29 April 2014).
Leander v Sweden App no 9248/81 (ECtHR, 26 March 1987).
Panteleyenko v Ukraine App no 11901/02 (ECtHR, 29 June 2006).
Rotaru v Romania App no 28341/95 (ECtHR, 4 May 2000).
S and Marper v the United Kingdom App nos 30562/04 and 30566/04 (ECtHR, 4 December 2008).
Z v Finland App no 22009/93 (ECtHR, 25 February 1997).

6 Striking the Balance

Genomic Data, Consent and Altruism in the European Health Data Space

Eila El Asry, Juli Mansnérus and Sandra Liede[*]

6.1 Introduction

The Data Governance Act (the DGA) establishes a legal framework for the concept of data altruism, which involves the sharing of data for the common good without expecting any form of compensation. Data altruism is motivated by a desire to contribute to the greater good or general interest, such as supporting scientific research or enhancing public services. It signifies a willingness to share data for the betterment of society, even when there is no direct personal benefit or financial gain involved.[1] Within the context of data altruism, obtaining the consent of the data subject is a fundamental requirement. This consent is a voluntary expression of a commitment to furthering altruistic objectives without any expectation of individual rewards or compensation. By incorporating the concept of data altruism into the DGA, the legislation aims to cultivate a culture of responsible data sharing[2] and encourage individuals and organisations to share their data for the benefit of society, particularly in the field of personalised medicine.[3] The legislation emphasises the significance of consent[4] in facilitating such initiatives.

Simultaneously, the Regulation on the European Health Data Space (the EHDS) sets a further example of responsible data sharing as one of its objectives is to ensure a consistent and efficient harmonised data governance framework for the secondary use of electronic health data for the purposes of, inter alia, research, innovation and regulatory activities, thus at least partly sharing common goals with the concept of data altruism. Scaling up the activities of the EHDS could bring wide-ranging benefits to healthcare-related activities in the EU, provided that the associated risks are appropriately eliminated or sufficiently mitigated. Yet, the EHDS is not entirely aligned with the concept of data altruism. A fundamental distinction lies in the nature of data sharing. The DGA sees data altruism as a purely voluntary and consensual activity, rooted in the willingness of individuals and organisations to contribute to the common good without expecting personal gain. It embodies the spirit of altruism, driven by consent and a sense of collective responsibility.

* Eila El Asry and Juli Mansnérus have jointly contributed to all parts of this publication. Sandra Liede has provided valuable insights as a commentator of the article.

DOI: 10.4324/9781003544111-8

Conversely, the EHDS, while promoting data sharing for noble purposes, introduces an element of obligation for data holders to share electronic health data sets for a great variety of purposes for secondary use that are not all entirely altruistic ones.[5] This obligation was combined with legal and technical requirements aimed at securing the rights and freedoms of individuals. This mandatory aspect departs from the pure essence of altruism, as it lacks the key element of voluntary consent.[6] However, in return, the EHDS promises to safeguard sensitive data sets with a strong regulatory and technical data governance framework. In essence, while the EHDS appears wrapped in the ideals of data altruism,[7] it is not synonymous with it, given the inherent obligation associated with health data sharing. In this light, the EHDS should ensure that the provisions permitting the processing of personal electronic health data[8] for secondary purposes factually constitute a necessary and proportionate legislative measure to ensure the rights and freedom of others.

A consent-based approach in health embodies patient empowerment, recognises patients as active participants in their healthcare and enables them to contribute to the responsible and ethical use of data in the pursuit of improved healthcare outcomes. Yet, the EHDS is not built on this type of foundation. The secondary use of health data under the EHDS is planned to be based on a data holder's legal obligation, rather than an individual's consent. This aims to extend the wide use of sensitive and confidential personal electronic health data. It can thus be considered to limit fundamental rights of protection of private life and personal data[9] and demands that the requirements for necessity and proportionality are appropriately addressed. The EHDS and the DGA do not amend existing data protection legislation, especially the General Data Protection Regulation (the GDPR).[10] The EHDS and the DGA both have many interdependencies with the GDPR, and they often need to be applied in conjunction with data protection legislation. There are however some uncertainties on how these different legal frameworks should be interpreted in parallel with each other.

The purpose of this chapter is to assess the compatibility of and relation between the data subject consent requirements with both the DGA on the one hand and the EHDS on the other hand. These new legal instruments and especially their respective approaches to a data subject's consent are addressed in Sections 6.2 and 6.3 of this chapter. Furthermore, this chapter aims in Section 6.4 to assess whether consent can be an adequate basis for sharing genomic data, and if not, what alternatives are available to enable the secondary use of genomic data.[11] In this context, the Finnish approach is also discussed, as Finland has since 2019 had legislation on the secondary use of health and social data, and specific questions related to the use of genomic data have also been debated nationally in connection with the proposal for the establishment of a national genomic centre. It is arguable whether an individual may give consent to process his/her genomic data for secondary purposes – for altruistic or other purposes, as such consent may compromise the very core of the privacy of the individual or their relative who could be identified from the same set of genomic data. In the meantime, the advanced utilisation of genomic data holds vast potential for innovative biomedical research, advanced analytics and the provision of personalised healthcare services.[12] Could altruistic objectives be met in the EHDS data governance framework and be developed even further to secure the rights of present and future generations?

6.2 Data Altruism – An Ambiguous Legal Concept

6.2.1 Data Altruism as Introduced in the DGA

In the context of the DGA, data altruism aligns with the principle of promoting the use of data for general interest purposes, such as scientific research and improving public services.[13] By definition, the consent of the data subject is required if personal data is shared within the context of data altruism, whereas if personal data is not involved, then the permission of the data holder is needed.[14] Chapter IV of the DGA sets forth the framework for data altruism organisations, including the registration of and requirements for data altruism organisations that may collect and process altruistically shared data and, where relevant, further make it available for third parties to be processed for permitted objectives of general interest. The DGA provides examples for general interest purposes, including healthcare, combating climate change, improving mobility, facilitating the development, production and dissemination of official statistics, improving the provision of public services, public policy making and scientific research purposes in the general interest, in any case as provided for in national law.[15]

The objective of creating the mechanisms for data altruism in the DGA was to create an enabling data governance framework,[16] not to impose an obligation of data sharing. Data altruism is driven by a sense of contributing to the general interest and embodies a willingness to share data for the betterment of society, even when there is no direct personal benefit or financial gain involved. The concept of data altruism thus represents a contrast to mandatory data sharing rules as well as to practices where data would be treated as a commodity to be protected or monetised. Instead, data altruism recognises the potential value that data can hold for broader societal advancements, and it fosters a culture of data sharing by encouraging individuals and organisations to voluntarily contribute their data.[17]

Data altruism is neither a new term nor an altogether novel concept; however, through the DGA, it is for the first time defined at the statutory level in the EU.[18] Prior to the definition provided in the DGA, it seems that no common understanding of the legal meaning of the term existed. The legislative process for the development and definition of data altruism can be traced to the European Commission Strategy for Data in 2020. In February 2020, the Commission issued a communication for the data strategy, mentioning data altruism as one of the issues to be addressed by an enabling legislative framework, which is the first priority for setting up a cross-sectoral governance framework for data access and use. In the communication, data altruism is referred to as the concept of individuals allowing the use of the data that they generate for the public good, if they wish so, in compliance with the GDPR.[19] In a report produced within the framework of the EU Health Programme 2014–2020, data altruism was defined as a 'system to allow patients to make data available for research without reference to a particular research project'.[20]

In parallel with the term data altruism, somewhat similar notions of 'data solidarity' and 'data donation' have been used as complementing the concept of data altruism. Data donation has even in some instances been used as a synonym for data altruism. However, in the legislative process for the DGA, its use was discussed and rejected, as 'data donation' would presuppose property rights to the data, and it could have suggested an irreversible transfer of data, whereas the data subject should always be able to withdraw consent, also in this context.[21] Furthermore, the use of the term 'donation' could be interpreted to imply an ownership transfer, while the fundamental right to protection of personal data cannot be agreed away.[22] Between data solidarity and data altruism, there seems to be only a subtle distinction. With solidarity, doing some good for others may empower and bring something good to the giver as well, whereas the term altruism assumes that an act is pursued only in the interest of others, and there is no reward for the giver, even at a later stage.[23]

It seems that prior to the DGA, few member states had a data altruism system (in the sense of the DGA) in place. In some, certain partly similar concepts and tools for data altruism existed.[24] It is thus notable that even if the concept of data altruism may not be completely novel, for many member states, its statutory definition and modalities were introduced for the first time through the DGA. It can also be argued that the DGA does not establish the definition of data altruism but somewhat formalises or codifies its meaning.[25]

Although the DGA's definition of data altruism includes a non-exhaustive list of examples of what could be considered as objectives of general interest, the DGA leaves room for national interpretations and consequently for possible discrepancies among the member states. Within the definition of data altruism, the 'objectives of general interests' are to be interpreted in the light of the applicable national law.[26] Whereas the legal cultures among the different member states may be considered somewhat similar at a larger scale, it is possible or even probable that there are differences in the interpretation on what are considered as objectives of general interest if interpreted in accordance with national law, and not in accordance solely with the Union law nor with predefined objectives of general interest.

One of the listed examples for objectives of general interest under the DGA is 'scientific research purposes in the general interest'. The wording of the DGA leaves it uncertain whether and to what extent the general interest should be assessed in light of the proposed research agenda, funding sources and/or planned distribution of research results.[27] According to GDPR Recital 159, also privately funded research is to be considered as a scientific research purpose. It is however questionable whether privately funded research may fall under a scientific research purpose in the general interest within the context of the DGA. In the case of privately funded research, especially for-profit privately funded research, there appears to be a need to determine the general interest to be primarily against commercial and private interests.[28] All in all, the exact scope of data altruistic purposes is not clear based on the text of the DGA and may in practice vary from one member state to another. Eventually, it will be the Court of Justice of the European Union that will through its jurisprudence shed light on the definition of those terms and the scope of the altruistic purposes in the sense of the DGA.

It is to be noted that the definition of data altruism excludes situations in which data is made available for an objective of general interest, but which would, even as a side effect, result in some sort of reward to the party sharing the data. Only costs that the data holder or data subject incurs when making the data available may be compensated. The concept of data altruism reflects a growing recognition of the potential benefits that can be derived from open and collaborative data practices, ultimately aiming to contribute to advancements in research, innovation and the delivery of healthcare services. It relies on the data holders' and data subjects' voluntary consent to engage in such data sharing.

6.2.2 Consent in the DGA

As discussed above, the definition of data altruism emphasises the importance of obtaining consent from data subjects for processing their personal data. It is specified in the DGA that the term consent is used in the same meaning as defined in the GDPR,[29] and thus it could be concluded that the DGA does not establish a new type of consent. Furthermore, the DGA does not create a legal basis for the processing of personal data, and it is not intended to affect any of the rights and obligations set out in the GDPR. In case of conflict, the GDPR takes precedence over the DGA.[30] Consequently, as the term consent as used in the DGA makes reference to the GDPR, all the requirements set forth in the GDPR for a lawful consent and how it should be obtained, as well as how it should be possible to withdraw the consent, are to be duly considered in the context of data altruism.

Overall, the data subject's consent is given significant importance in the context of data altruism. DGA recitals mention that data subject consent will typically be relied on as the legal basis for processing of personal data for altruistic purposes.[31] The DGA does not however explicitly exclude the possibility of a data altruism organisation relying on another legal basis for processing of personal data. In the context of the GDPR, the data subject's consent is only one of the six possible legal bases for lawful processing of personal data under Article 6 of the GDPR. Although the spirit of data altruism emphasises the voluntary aspect of such data sharing, and thus the consent-centric approach seems to be an informed choice of a lawmaker, other legal bases for processing seem to remain possible.[32]

The DGA does not impose an obligation but rather sets objectives and ambitions for the member states for the promotion of data altruism. According to Article 6 of the DGA, the member states may have in place organisational or technical arrangements, or both, to facilitate data altruism. Based on the recitals, such organisational or technical arrangements could include, for instance, the availability of tools to be used for the purpose of data subjects or data holders giving consent or permission for the use of their data for altruistic purposes. Furthermore, the DGA provides that the Commission will adopt implementing acts establishing and developing a data altruism consent form, which would be modular and could be customised to different circumstances.[33] The consent form will be adopted in order to serve as a tool facilitating the collection of data; the consent form as such will not necessarily serve as a legal basis.[34]

In their joint opinion on the DGA proposal, the European Data Protection Board (EDPB) and the European Data Protection Supervisor (EDPS) considered that the definition of data altruism should provide an exhaustive list of clearly defined purposes of general interest, instead of an open-ended non-exhaustive list of potential purposes of general interest. Based on their opinion, a lack of clear definition may lead to legal uncertainty. Furthermore, it may actually lower the level of protection of personal data in the EU.[35] In accordance with the GDPR, consent should be freely given, specific, informed and unambiguously indicate the data subject's agreement to the processing of his/her personal data.[36] It has been acknowledged in the GDPR recitals that in the scientific research context, it is often not possible at the time of data collection to fully identify the purposes of processing, and consequently, a data subject could give his/her consent to certain areas of scientific research when in compliance with recognised ethical standards for scientific research.[37] The EDPB and the EDPS highlight that it is not allowed under the GDPR to grant such broad consent to purposes of general interest, where such purposes are not clearly defined but only a non-exhaustive list of examples is proposed, and given that such purposes may include a different and/or broader scope than scientific research.[38] The final wording of the DGA did not however take this critique into account.

The DGA specifies that the consent form shall ensure that data subjects are able to give consent to and withdraw consent from a *specific data processing operation*. This differs from the wording of the GDPR under which the data subject may give consent to the processing of his/her data for *one or more specific purposes*. A data processing operation and a purpose of processing are not the same; several processing operations may be performed for the same purpose, and one data processing operation may in some cases serve for several purposes of processing.[39] This ambiguity remains in the final version of the DGA, and it can even be interpreted to tighten the requirements for a consent compared to what is set forth under the GDPR.[40]

The DGA provides that the processing of collected data could be done by data altruism organisations for purposes for which they establish, or, if relevant, by third parties for those purposes.[41] The applications of a data altruism organisation for registration will need to include, for example, the objectives of general interest it intends to promote when collecting data.[42] This seems however too general for defining the purposes of processing in accordance with the principle of purpose limitation under the GDPR. According to the GDPR, personal data should be collected for *specified* and *explicit* purposes, and the consent given by a data subject is to be specific and informed.[43] As it is presumable that data altruism organisations will rely on the consent form provided by the Commission, it is hoped that the final form will live up to the expectations of facilitating the granting of necessary, GDPR-compliant consent.

The DGA underscores the significance of obtaining consent from data subjects for processing their personal data. It aligns with the GDPR on the definition of consent, emphasising that all GDPR consent conditions should be considered in the context of data altruism. While the DGA highlights the importance of data subject consent, it does not explicitly rule out other legal bases for data processing. The Commission will develop a data altruism consent form as a tool for data collection. While the DGA encourages data altruism, there are legal and practical concerns that need to be addressed to ensure GDPR compliance and protect data subjects' rights in the context of data sharing for general interest purposes, for instance, the concerns relating to the open-ended definition of objectives of general interest included in the definition of data altruism. Furthermore, it remains to be seen whether and to what extent the voluntary framework will accelerate data sharing.

6.3 Secondary Use of Health Data and the Relevance of a Consent

6.3.1 Diverse Approaches to Secondary Use of Health Data Across EU Countries

Prior to the EHDS, there has not been an EU-wide approach to the secondary use of health data. This may be partly due to the fact that during the years leading up to the preparation of the EHDS, Europe was learning to interpret the GDPR, and many countries had not yet arrived at a conclusion as to what would be the best approach regarding the secondary use of health data. There are currently variations among EU member states on whether the secondary use of health data is allowed and, if affirmative, under which conditions. The differences in national approaches are understandable especially given the room that the GDPR leaves for the member states to implement further conditions and limitations regarding the use of health data. The EHDS seeks to address the issue by setting forth directly applicable rules in all EU member states.

The processing of health data is, as a main rule, prohibited under Article 9(1) of the GDPR. The GDPR includes a ten-point list of conditions based on which processing of health data and other prohibited data types would exceptionally be allowed. With respect to health data, it is further stated under Article 9(4) of the GDPR that the member states may maintain or introduce further conditions or restrictions to processing of such data types. Although it is noted in the GDPR recitals that the aforementioned should not hamper the free flow of personal data within the Union in cross-border situations,[44] the reality is that legislations of different member states have developed in different directions with respect to the use of genomic and other health data.[45]

Under Article 9(2) of the GDPR, one of the exceptions to the general prohibition of processing of health data is the so-called 'research exemption', included in sub-section (j). Based on Article 9(2)(j) of the GDPR, the prohibition on processing health data does not apply in case the processing is necessary, for instance, for scientific research purposes, and is based on EU or national law. The said subsection as well as Article 89 of the GDPR set forth further preconditions relating to such processing, for instance with respect to additional safeguards for the data subject's fundamental rights.[46] Article 89 of the GDPR further allows under certain conditions derogations based on a national or Union law from some of the data subject's rights generally set forth in the GDPR, such as the right of access by the data subject under Article 15 of the GDPR and the right to rectification of inaccurate personal data concerning the data subject provided under Article 16 of the GDPR.

Especially given the discretion granted to the member states under Articles 9 and 89 of the GDPR, national legislation with respect to secondary use of health data may look very different from one member state to another.[47] Based on an assessment of the EU member states' rules on health data, it was found that 18 member states had adopted sectoral legislation or authoritative guidance further specifying the application of Article 89 of the GDPR on suitable safeguards in the context of health research based on Article 9(2)(j) of the GDPR. It was also found that there were variances in such safeguards.[48]

A factor that adds to the possible regulatory discrepancy is the term 'scientific research', which is not precisely defined in the GDPR. Instead, Recital 159 of the GDPR states that 'the processing of personal data for scientific research purposes should be interpreted in a broad manner including for example technological development and demonstration, fundamental research, applied research and privately funded research'.[49] The variation in the approach towards the secondary use of health data among EU member states may consequently also result from different interpretations and readings of the GDPR, especially with the meaning of the term 'scientific research', in addition to national regulation applied on top of the GDPR.[50]

Furthermore, one of the legal grounds under the GDPR permitting the processing of health data is the data subject's explicit consent as specified in Article 9(2)(a) of the GDPR. There may be differences in the way the member states have interpreted the requirements for a consent to be explicit, which is likely to cause disruptions in data sharing especially in cross-border situations.[51] In addition, based on Article 9(2)(a) of the GDPR, explicit consent may not be relied upon as grounds for processing in case Union or national law provides that the prohibition to process such data may not be lifted by the data subject. This may be the case under some EU member states' national laws.

According to case studies conducted by TEHDAS, a joint action carried out by 25 European countries and co-ordinated by the Finnish Innovation Fund Sitra, issues such as discrepancies in national legislations applied in addition to the GDPR as well as differences in interpretation have made it difficult to use certain data types, such as genomic data for secondary purposes. It is further noted that the controllers have generally an over-reliance on consent as a legal basis for processing of personal data for secondary purposes, even when it is not required by the GDPR.[52] This may also be due to the influence of bioethical principles and especially the difficulties in some instances to differentiate between bioethical consent and consent as meant in the GDPR. The differences in the implementation and interpretation of the GDPR by EU member states as well as the resulting legal uncertainty have also been highlighted by the EU Commission as reasons and objectives for the EHDS,[53] which includes harmonising a common EU approach to the secondary use of electronic health data as one of its objectives.

All in all, the regulatory landscape of secondary use of health data across EU countries prior to the EHDS has been marked by significant diversity and variations. The GDPR allows member states some flexibility in introducing their own conditions and limitations, leading to differences in national approaches. In particular, the GDPR's research exemption under Article 9(2)(j) has played a crucial role in permitting the processing of health data for scientific research, but its implementation varies across member states. Additionally, the interpretation of the term 'scientific research' and the requirements for explicit consent have not been standardised, causing disruptions in cross-border data sharing. The EHDS aims to address the challenges arising from legislative discrepancies and the overreliance on consent as a legal basis for data processing[54] by introducing directly applicable rules to harmonise the EU's approach to secondary health data use.

6.3.2 Consent in the EHDS

It is important to note that the processing of personal electronic health data for secondary purposes under the EHDS, will not, in principle, be based on a data subject's consent. The EHDS as such establishes a legal obligation in the sense of Article 6(1)(c) of the GDPR for data holders to provide certain data to the health data access body. Furthermore, it sets the legal basis and establishes the safeguards for processing as required under Article 9(2)(g)-(j) of the GDPR when processing health data for instance based on a substantial public interest, healthcare provision and management, and public interest in the area of public health and research. At the same time, a data applicant should demonstrate a legal basis under Articles 6(1) and 9(2) of the GDPR in order to receive access to other than anonymised electronic health data for secondary use.[55] The EHDS defines on the one hand the purposes of processing for which a data applicant may be provided access to the data for secondary use, as well as on the other hand the prohibited purposes of secondary use. Whilst there are several available legal bases for processing of health data for secondary use in accordance with the EHDS, a shift towards public interest as a basis for processing could be observed in the Commission's Proposal.[56]

> During the legislative process it seemed that the Parliament aimed to restrict this. In the Parliament's version of 13 December 2023 it was provided that health data access bodies should provide access to electronic health data only to a health data user where the processing of the data by the data user is, in addition to the processing being necessary for one of the purposes listed in the EHDS, in accordance with Article 6(1)(c) of the GDPR, meaning that the data user would thus need to have a legal obligation for such processing.[57]

During the EHDS legislative process, one of the interesting topics was the question of how the EHDS would erase the potential discrepancies between EU member states' national law approaches relating to the secondary use of health or other special data types, as discussed above in Section 6.3.1. The original Commission Proposal included in Article 33(5) the following rather ambiguous provision regarding the relation of the proposed regulation with any national-level consent requirements: 'Where the consent of the natural person is required by national law, health data access bodies shall rely on the obligations laid down in this Chapter to provide access to electronic health data'. It was unclear whether the provision suggested that health data access bodies could disregard national-level consent requirements if they were incompatible with the obligations set forth by the EHDS regarding the secondary use of electronic health data. Another way to read the provision would have been that the consent requirements should be respected alongside the obligations set forth in the EHDS. In practice, this second alternative reading would have likely meant that only anonymised data could have been within the scope of the secondary use of data where consent was required under national law and not received from the data subject. This reading would have been more in line with the objective of empowerment of individuals, as the ultimate decision and control on whether the data would have been further used and for which purposes and under which circumstances would have lied with the data subject if so provided by the national law.

The ambiguity of the provision in Article 33(5) of the proposed EHDS was initially pointed out by the EDPB and EDPS in their joint opinion. In particular, the EDPB and EDPS underlined the lack of clarity concerning at which step, in the proposed procedure, the health data access bodies could have disregarded such consent requirements set out in national law.[58]

In their texts, the European Parliament and the Council of the European Union amended the said article substantially. The Council took an approach compatible with the first interpretation option discussed above, meaning that the national law consent requirements could be disregarded by the health data access body when the electronic health data would have been made available under the conditions set forth in the EHDS:

> Notwithstanding national laws requesting the data subject's consent pursuant to Article 9(4) of Regulation (EU) 2016/679, health data access bodies shall rely on the obligations laid down in this Chapter, when requesting and processing personal electronic health data from the health data holder and provide access to pseudonymised electronic health data to the health data user.[59]

Despite the rather strict approach enabling health data access bodies to disregard national law consent requirements that are based on Article 9(4) of the GDPR, the Council at the same time proposed to include a possibility for the member states to provide for an opt-out for natural persons regarding the secondary use of their electronic health data under the EHDS. It also proposed a possibility for the member states to introduce stricter measures at national level with respect to data holders' obligation to make genetic data and other human molecular data available for secondary use. By leaving more room for member state discretion, these proposals would have been likely to lead to further discrepancies in national legislations.[60]

The European Parliament took a different view as it removed the above-quoted part regarding national law consent requirements and replaced it with an overall, automatic opt-out mechanism for all natural persons regarding their electronic health data for secondary use under the EHDS. Furthermore, the secondary use of certain health data types, including for instance genetic data, data from wellness applications and biobank data, should have only been made available for secondary use after obtaining the consent of the natural person, meaning that those types of electronic health data would have only been available based on the individual's choice to opt-in.[61]

Elements from the above-discussed versions from the European Parliament and the Council of the EU were implemented in the final EHDS text. The original ambiguous wording on the relation between national law consent requirements and the obligations laid down by the EHDS for secondary use was removed. Article 51(4) of the EHDS provides that member states may, with a notification to the Commission, introduce stricter measures and additional safeguards at national level aimed at safeguarding the sensitivity and value of for instance genomic and other human molecular data, data from wellness applications and health data from biobanks and associated databases. It is further specified in Recital 52 that apart from the above, member states may no longer maintain or introduce under Article 9(4) of the GDPR further conditions, consent requirements included, for the processing of health data for secondary use under the EHDS. This approach maintains the diversity among national legislations regarding further requirements for certain health data types, but there should in principle be less discrepancies in the member states' national legislations regarding secondary use. Furthermore, the EHDS imposes an obligation on member states to provide for an accessible and easily understandable opt-out mechanism for all natural persons to opt-out regardless of the category of health data, which was not included in the original EHDS proposal.

6.3.3 The Interplay of the DGA and EHDS

The interplay between altruistic data sharing as set forth in the DGA and the secondary use of electronic health data as regulated under the EHDS is also interesting. If a data altruism organisation, which has received health data from data subjects based on their consent, qualifies as a data holder under the EHDS, it will have an obligation to make such data available to a health data access body, which will further provide data to data applicants in accordance with the EHDS.[62] The legal basis for the initial processing, most likely consent in case of data altruism in the sense of the DGA, remains intact, but the EHDS would create a legal obligation for the data altruism organisation in the sense of Article 6(1)(c) of the GDPR to disclose the data as a data holder to a health data access body. The data altruism organisation is however bound by any specifications of, limitations to and/or withdrawals of consent by a data subject, in accordance with the GDPR.

In conclusion, the EHDS represents a significant shift in the processing of electronic health data for secondary purposes. During the EHDS legislative process, the individual's opt-in and opt-out possibilities as well as whether this should be a direct right deriving from the EHDS or something that would require further national-level legislation created discussion between the co-legislatures. Furthermore, the relation of the EHDS with national consent requirements was unclear in the Commission's original proposal but has been made clearer in the final EHDS text. In essence, the EHDS seems to allow certain discrepancies among the member states with respect to certain categories of health data, but for the rest, further requirements under national laws for secondary use are not allowed. Additionally, the interaction between the EHDS and data sharing governed by the DGA raises interesting questions. Data altruism organisations, which rely on data subject consent, may become data holders under the EHDS, creating legal obligations to disclose data. The GDPR's provisions on consent and data subject rights still apply, even within the EHDS framework. Thus, challenges remain in aligning the EHDS with diverse national requirements and ensuring consistency.

6.4 Genomic Data: Possibilities and Challenges for Use

6.4.1 The Potentials and Possibilities of Harnessing Genomic Data for Advancements in Personalised Healthcare

The advent of artificial intelligence, along with advancements in data collection, access and sharing, and computational efficiency, has the power to revolutionise disease discovery and outbreak prevention. There is especially vast potential in the advanced use of genomic data. By harnessing the power of genomics, researchers can identify new therapies and make clinical studies more effective by pinpointing relevant patient populations. In addition, health economics research has already demonstrated the positive impact of genomics on the effectiveness and optimal delivery of healthcare.[63] Genomic information holds significant promise;[64] among other things potentially enhancing the relevance, efficiency and cost-effectiveness of treatments, as well as accelerating the speed, value and cost-effectiveness of research recruitment processes. In addition, one of the remarkable applications of genomic data is the ability to calculate polygenic risk scores (PRS) based on individuals' genetic variants. These scores can help predict the risk of common diseases, enabling various preventive measures, improving early diagnostics and facilitating tailored therapies and scientific research.[65] Genomic data can also play a crucial role in pharmacogenomics, optimising drug response based on genetic factors and ensuring vaccine safety.[66] However, the calculation of PRS and health risks requires a substantial amount of population-level genomic data to establish robust and accurate risk assessments.[67]

6.4.2 Challenges Related to Anonymisation of Genomic Data and to Its Consent-Based Use

The GDPR does not apply to anonymous data, meaning data that does not relate to an identified or identifiable individual, or personal data that has been anonymised in a manner that prevents the identification of the data subject.[68] When it comes to genomic data, the concept of anonymisation poses unique challenges. The complex and identifiable nature of genomic data makes complete anonymisation while preserving research utility difficult to achieve. Genome variation data, which reveals only sequence differences between individuals or populations, may not always allow for the identification of a specific person.[69] Nonetheless, it may be possible to identify an individual if multiple types of genome variation data are examined together, particularly in cases where there are several atypical variations.[70] These challenges highlight the complexity of anonymising genomic data effectively. While genome variation data alone may not immediately identify an individual, the combination of various genomic data types could potentially reveal their identity.[71] This necessitates careful consideration and robust anonymisation techniques to ensure the privacy and protection of individuals when handling genomic data. Whether genomic data allows the identification of a natural person also depends on the possibility to associate the genomic data with other available data. While the genomic data itself would remain unchanged, if in time more advanced linking techniques to other data become available, this could have an effect on the identifiability of the individual.[72] Furthermore, genetic information can be shared among relatives (parents, children and so on) and relates to more than only one person. Thus, in some cases, processing of even small parts of genomic data, such as genomic variations, may provide information or enable the identification of these other individuals, if identifiability cannot be reliably excluded.[73]

If genomic data cannot be effectively anonymised, its use would require a legal basis under the GDPR. This question has been discussed in Finland in connection with steps taken to regulate genomic data through an initiative to establish a national genome centre.[74] The centre was envisioned to serve as a specialist authority, responsible for the development of a national genomic database and providing support for its advanced use. During the legislative process regarding the intention to establish the national genomic database, the Finnish legislature concluded that consent would not in general be deemed an appropriate legal basis for processing genomic data due to its unique nature and the potential identification of individuals distant from the data subject. The legislature also emphasised the confinement of genomic data processing to secure operating environments meeting supervisory authorities' requirements, ensuring stringent security measures and personalised data protection. The law on the national genome centre has not yet entered into force.

Similar questions were also debated in Finland during the parliamentary deliberation regarding the Finnish Act on Secondary Use of Social and Health Data (Act of 552/2019).[75] The Finnish Constitutional Law Committee[76] made a distinction between scientific research and commercial development and innovation activities, denying the classification of commercial development and innovation as an activity in the public interest. The Constitutional Law Committee highlighted the challenges of using consent as a legal basis for processing sensitive health data for development and innovation purposes and underlined that fundamental rights cannot only be protected by the consent of the person concerned.[77] The Constitutional Law Committee has considered that consent may, in itself, have significance in the constitutional assessment. However, the Committee has, in practice, found such a regulatory approach problematic and has emphasised restraint in using consent as a justification for limiting fundamental rights. According to the Committee, this kind of regulatory approach is not easily reconciled with the requirement, enshrined in Section 2(3) of the Finnish Constitution, that the exercise of public authority must be based on law. Moreover, the authority to interfere with an individual's fundamental rights must always be defined by a sufficiently precise and specific law.[78]

The Committee has made it clear in another context that the protection of fundamental rights cannot, as a legal matter, be made solely dependent on the consent of the person concerned. In this regard, the Committee has considered what can be regarded as legally valid consent in a specific situation and has required, among other things, precision and specificity in legislation that interferes with fundamental rights, rules on the manner of giving and withdrawing consent, verification of the authenticity and voluntary nature of consent, as well as the necessity of the measure.[79] The Constitutional Law Committee suggested securing privacy in these cases by using anonymisation and detailing the requirements for anonymisation strictly in legislation.

Applying the view of the Constitutional Law Committee in the context of genomic data may become more complex as genomic data encompasses sensitive information not only about the individual but their relatives as well. Given the profound implications of genomic data on an individual's privacy, it raises concerns about the adequacy of consent as the sole instrument for data control, especially for commercial use purposes. The Finnish Constitutional Law Committee's viewpoint suggests that in the context of genomic data, relying solely on consent may not be an appropriate mechanism for individuals to relinquish their rights, and thus anonymisation should be considered as a safeguard as well. This is because genomic data resides within the core area of privacy, and individuals should not be required to waive their rights through a consent-based approach. However, the balancing requirement of using anonymisation raises another set of challenges as it has also been suggested, as discussed above, that genomic data cannot be completely anonymised. It is important to strike a balance between protecting individuals' rights and privacy and enabling the potential benefits that genomic data can bring to scientific research and healthcare. This requires careful consideration of legal frameworks, ethical guidelines and technical solutions to ensure the responsible use of genomic data while upholding individuals' rights and autonomy.

Striking a balance between the potential benefits of genomic research and the protection of individuals' rights and autonomy is of utmost importance.[80] Efforts should be made to ensure that the potential benefits of genomic research, such as personalised medicine, are realised while upholding ethical principles and legal obligations. Given the special nature of genomic data, its processing is particularly challenging from a data protection perspective as both the anonymisation of genomic data as well as the processing of genomic data based on a consent prove to have notable flaws. Processing based on a legal basis other than consent under Articles 6 and 9 of the GDPR seems to be the most viable and legally solid option but leaves an open question as to whether the potential benefits of advanced use of genomic data may, under such circumstances, be achieved.

6.4.3 Balancing Genetic Data, Privacy and Patient Empowerment in Health Rights

Notwithstanding the limitations addressed above, it is worth noting that in the context of consumerisation of healthcare,[81] a consent-based system has been seen to play a significant role in patient empowerment and serving as a fundamental principle for data protection and privacy. Giving individuals control over their personal information and allowing them to make informed decisions about how their data is used and what they want to know about their genetic data are also embedded in the Biomedicine Convention.[82]

Health rights as human rights recognise the entitlement of individuals to access healthcare and enjoy good health.[83] Patient autonomy, which includes the role of consent in decision-making, is an essential aspect of health rights. By upholding patient autonomy through informed consent, healthcare providers respect individuals' rights to self-determination and active participation in their own healthcare decision-making.[84] Likewise, it could be argued that by implementing a consent-based system in data sharing, patients are granted the power to determine the extent to which their data is shared and used for various purposes. This could empower patients by recognising their autonomy and granting them the ability to exercise control over their personal information. Yet, genetic data is a particular case, as various types of genomic data and associated factors can introduce privacy and security risks when shared, and it is crucial to evaluate and address these risks in a responsible manner.[85] Furthermore, empirical evidence suggests that the environment in which informed consent process takes place in clinical genomics may in some cases fall short in terms of respecting participants' values and preferences, and it may not adequately facilitate informed decision-making.[86]

A relevant question is whether the opt-out mechanism under the EHDS is an adequate safeguard for individuals to exercise their self-determination rights in respect of sharing of their health data. During the legislative process, the major branch organisations lobbied in the stakeholder hearings quite heavily against incorporation of opt-out and especially opt-in mechanisms in the EHDS framework. Their point of view is understandable: data bias could be inherent in the EHDS from the outset, potentially compromising its actual usability for secondary research purposes, should an opt-out or opt-in mechanism be included.[87] Beyond purely legal considerations, other questions have been raised – should people have an ethical obligation to share their health information?[88]

Respecting the privacy and autonomy of individuals while enabling the responsible use of genomic data requires a comprehensive approach. Legal frameworks must be carefully designed to ensure that the use of genomic data adheres to strict privacy protections and ethical guidelines. It becomes essential to establish robust regulations that safeguard individuals' rights, prevent unauthorised access and provide clear guidelines for data handling and storage. Additionally, technical solutions can play a significant role in upholding privacy and security in the context of genomic data. Anonymisation techniques are crucial to protecting the privacy of individuals in genomic data handling.[89] Furthermore, secure data operating environments provide enhanced protection for human genomic data, demonstrating a strong commitment to personal data security[90] and offering a competitive advantage. Employing advanced encryption methods, secure storage systems and data anonymisation techniques can help mitigate the risks associated with data breaches and unauthorised access.[91] These technological measures,[92] combined with rigorous policies and procedures,[93] can enhance the protection of individuals' genomic data and confidence in data sharing initiatives.

The use of genetic data presents a significant challenge to traditional notions of privacy rooted in fundamental rights, highlighting the need for a human-rights-based approach. While a consent-based system has played a vital role in patient empowerment and data protection, it faces limitations in the clinical genomics context. Genetic data, given its complexity, introduces privacy and security risks that demand responsible handling. The path forward requires a meticulous evaluation of these concerns, striving to maintain the delicate balance between individual rights, privacy, patient empowerment and valuable research and healthcare advancement. The EHDS leaves room for the member states to do this assessment, as it allows member states, in addition to what is provided in the EHDS, to introduce stricter measures and additional safeguards for the secondary use of genomic data. It is left to be seen how these concerns will be handled at national level in different member states and whether the EHDS will have a harmonising effect on the secondary use of genomic data within the EU.

6.5 Conclusions

The EHDS and the DGA represent two partly diverse paradigms in the realm of data sharing, each with its own set of principles and objectives. While the DGA places voluntary sharing through individual consent as central to the concept of data altruism, the EHDS adopts a different approach. Although the EHDS appears to be wrapped in the ideals of data altruism, it is not synonymous with it, as in the EHDS, consent is not the primary mechanism for data sharing, marking a fundamental distinction in the regulatory frameworks. These disparate approaches hold far-reaching implications for data sharing practices and the protection of individuals' rights within the emerging European health data landscape, necessitating further evaluation and discussion.

Data altruism under the DGA envisions individuals actively consenting to share their genomic and health data. It stems from a sense of social responsibility and a desire to advance medical knowledge and healthcare outcomes for the greater good. This altruistic approach transcends individual consent and emphasises the collective impact of data contributions to research and patient care. It enables patients to actively shape healthcare advancements and outcomes by contributing their data, reflecting their empowerment. On the other hand, the DGA's consent-based system ensures that patients have the autonomy to decide whether to share their data and under what conditions. The central question arises: Can relying solely on a consent-based system, without exploring other potential legal bases for data processing, effectively support the goals of data altruism? While consent is integral to patient empowerment, data protection and privacy, it may not in practice fully align with the spirit of collective contribution and collaboration that data altruism embodies. On the other hand, stretching the boundaries of data-altruism by abandoning its incremental element of voluntary consent could risk diluting its essence.

To enhance the compatibility between the consent-based data sharing under the DGA and the EHDS framework, transparency, trust and meaningful patient engagement are essential. Patients must be empowered through education, clear communication and involvement in decision-making processes related to data sharing. Robust data governance frameworks that uphold ethical principles, data protection regulations and responsible data stewardship should be implemented. This includes mechanisms for individuals to have control over their data, understand its use and selectively share data based on preferences. Educating patients about the benefits of data sharing is vital to highlight the value of data altruism and encourage altruistic contributions.

The EHDS seems to closely follow the model of the Finnish approach, with Finland having served as a trailblazer through the Act on Secondary Uses of Social and Health Data. This Act was enacted during the period when national implementation of the GDPR was underway, albeit with some degree of interpretational ambiguity. It was during this phase the concept of consent alone proved insufficient in safeguarding individuals in the context of large-scale data processing. Consequently, the decision was made to employ legislation as a processing ground, thereby assigning significant weight to the GDPR's methods for the protection of individuals, including the requirement for adequate technical and other protective measures. Regrettably, the discourse on individual rights was somewhat eclipsed, remaining largely in the shadows throughout the application of the Act on Secondary Uses of Social and Health Data. The EHDS, in its pursuit of aligning with this paradigm, sought to better emphasise the rights of individuals. This led to the emergence of another conceptual framework, namely data altruism, a concept derived from the DGA. Thus, EHDS can be seen to represent a fusion of these two approaches and could be described as something of a conceptual amalgamation. It is advisable to consider a re-evaluation of this approach and to ensure that interpretations, particularly within the Finnish context, have been in the right direction in respect of the rights of the data subjects.

Genomic data presents unique challenges due to its sensitive nature. It encompasses personal health details and can potentially affect not only the individual but also their relatives. The right of future generations to decide on the use of their data must be ensured. The consent-based system may be inadequate to address these privacy (and in some jurisdictions constitutional law) concerns effectively. Achieving the right balance between safeguarding individual rights and harnessing the potential benefits of genomic data for research and healthcare is essential. It might have to be accepted that the tools to find the right balance do not yet exist, and thus, there is a need to maintain a sense of flexibility for the improvement and development of technology. Meanwhile within the EHDS, anonymising data presents specific challenges, especially for genomic data. Genomic data's inherent identifiability makes effective anonymisation difficult, potentially limiting its usability for research, product development or other innovation purposes, such as developing algorithms to help advance medicine and healthcare provision. Alternative approaches, such as pseudonymisation, may be necessary to ensure the use of genomic data for secondary purposes. The fragmented landscape of data sharing practices as well as different approaches to secondary use of health data among EU Member States underscores the importance of addressing the role of national law consent or other technical safeguard requirements in the EHDS's framework.

The interplay between consent-based data sharing, data altruism and the EHDS represents a complex and evolving landscape. The contrasting approaches of the EHDS and the DGA necessitate a delicate balance between individual consent and collective collaboration. Transparent patient engagement, responsible data governance and innovative approaches to sensitive data, such as genomic information, are essential. The journey towards harmonising the European take on secondary health data use requires continued dialogue and a thoughtful consideration of the legal, ethical and practical dimensions of data sharing. Data altruism should not end up as a 'declarative' legal concept but rather serve as a driving force for advancing healthcare and medical knowledge.

Notes

1 See Teodora Lalova-Spinks, Janos Meszaros and Isabelle Huys, 'The application of data altruism in clinical research through empirical and legal analysis lenses' (2023) 10 *Frontiers in Medicine* 1.
2 See James Brian Byrd and others, 'Responsible, practical genomic data sharing that accelerates research' (2020) 21 *Nature Reviews Genetics* 615.
3 Personalised medicine, also known as precision medicine, refers to an innovative approach to medical treatment and healthcare that takes into account individual variability in patients' genes, environments, and lifestyles. It aims to tailor medical decisions, practices and interventions to the specific characteristics of each patient.
4 See Sirpa Soini, 'Geenitestaus ja lakien henki: tutkimus geenitestien sääntelystä, Genetic testing and the spirit of the laws: a study of the regulation of genetic tests' (Doctoral Dissertation, University Helsinki 2020) 35.
5 EHDS text art 53 (1).
6 During the legislative process, an opt-out mechanism for natural persons regarding the secondary use of their health data was however introduced in the EHDS. See section below 6.2 for more details.
7 See for instance Towards European Health Data Space (TEHDAS), 'TEHDAS' proposals for promoting data altruism in the EHDS' (29 September 2023) https://tehdas.eu/results/tehdas-proposals-for-promoting-data-altruism-in-the-ehds/ accessed 25 March 2023.
8 'Personal electronic health data' is a term introduced in the EHDS referring to health data as defined in the GDPR processed in an electronic form.
9 Charter of Fundamental Rights of the European Union [2012] OJ C 326/391, arts 7 and 8.
10 See, for example, EHDS art 1(4): 'This Regulation shall be without prejudice to … requirements related to the processing of data in relation to electronic health data, in particular Regulations (EU) 2016/679" and Recital 4 of the EHDS: 'The processing of personal electronic health data is subject to the provisions of Regulation (EU) 2016/679 of the European Parliament and of the Council'.
11 It has been argued that in the context of the donation of tissue samples containing genetic data consent is not always sufficient to address the full scope of the donor's rights and legal position. See Laura Walin, 'Kun suostumus ei riitä – kudosnäytteen ja alkion luovuttajan oikeusaseman tarkastelua' (2008) 5 Lakimies 773.
12 Mubashir Hassan and others, 'Innovations in Genomics and Big Data Analytics for Personalized Medicine and Health Care: A Review' (2022) 23(9) International Journal of Molecular Sciences 4645.

13 See, for example, Heiko Richter, 'Looking at the Data Governance Act and Beyond: How to Better Integrate Data Intermediaries in the Market Order for Data Sharing' (2023) 72(5) GRUR International 458.
14 Regulation (EU) 2022/868 of the European Parliament and of the Council of 30 May 2022 on European data governance and amending Regulation (EU) 2018/1724 (Data Governance Act) (Text with EEA relevance) [2022] *OJ L 152/1* (hereinafter DGA) art 2(16).
15 DGA art 2(10).
16 Proposal for Regulation of the European Parliament and of the Council on European data governance (Data Governance Act) COM(2020) 767 final. See in particular Explanatory Memorandum – Legal Basis, Subsidiarity and Proportionality – Proportionality.
17 Mahsa Shabani, 'The Data Governance Act and the EU's move towards facilitating data sharing' (2021) 17(3) *Molecular Systems Biology* e10229.
18 Lalova-Spinks, Meszaros and Huys (n 1).
19 Commission, 'A European strategy for data' (Communication) COM (2020) 66 final.
20 Johan Hansen and others, *Assessment of the EU Member States' rules on health data in the light of GDPR* (European Commission, Consumers, Health, Agriculture and Food Executive Agency Publications Office, 2021) 113.
21 Commission, 'Impact Assessment Report Accompanying the DGA Proposal' (Staff Working Document 2020 295 final).
22 Hansen and others (n 20).
23 Barbara Prainsack and others, 'White Paper on Data Solidarity' (2022) https://www.governinghealthfutures2030.org/wp-content/uploads/2022/12/DataSolidarity.pdf accessed 26 March 2024.
24 Hansen and others (n 20) 114.
25 EDPB-EDPS, 'Joint Opinion 03/2021on the Proposal for a regulation of the European Parliament and of the Council on European data governance (Data Governance Act)' (2021) 10 March 2021, 39.
26 In Finland these general interests were codified in 2019 in the act on secondary use of social and health data, please see for more detail in section 6.4.2 below.
27 Mahsa Shabani, 'Will the European Health Data Space change data sharing rules?' (2022) 375(6587) *Science* 1357.
28 Mahsa Shabani, 'Will the European Health Data Space change data sharing rules?'.
29 DGA art 2(5).
30 DGA art 1(3): 'In the event of a conflict between this Regulation and Union law on the protection of personal data or national law adopted in accordance with such Union law, the relevant Union or national law on the protection of personal data shall prevail'.
31 DGA Recital 50.
32 Kristina Schreiber, Patrick Pommerening and Philipp Schoel, *New Data Governance Act, a Practitioner's Guide* (1st edn, Bloomsbury Publishing 2023) 81.
33 DGA art 25.
34 TEHDAS, 'Deliverable 8.2, Report on lessons learned to be applied and recommendations for data altruism practices in the implementation of construction of national and European health data spaces (including broad consent)' (29 September 2023) https://tehdas.eu/app/uploads/2023/09/tehdas-recommendations-for-data-altruism-practices.pdf accessed 26 March 2024.
35 EDPB-EDPS Joint Opinion on the Proposal for a regulation of the European Parliament and of the Council on European data governance (Data Governance Act) (2021) 41.
36 GDPR Recital 32.

37 GDPR Recital 33.
38 EDPB-EDPS (n 35) 41.
39 Lalova-Spinks, Meszaros and Huys (n 1).
40 Schreiber, Pommerening and Schoel (n 32).
41 DGA Recital 50.
42 DGA art 19(4)(h).
43 See, for example, GDPR art 4(11) and art 5(1).
44 GDPR Recital 53.
45 Kärt Pormeister, 'Genetic data and the research exemption: is the GDPR going too far?' (2017) 7 International Data Privacy Law 137; See also Ciara Staunton, Santa Slokenberga and Deborah Mascalzoni, 'The GDPR and the research exemption: considerations on the necessary safeguards for research biobanks' (2019) 27 *European Journal of Human Genetics* 1159.
46 The EHDS would need to fulfil the requirements under the 89 GDPR as it may apply to processing for archiving purposes in the public interest, scientific or historical research purposes or statistical purposes.
47 Edward SD and Jiahong Chen, 'Should consent for data processing be privileged in health research? A comparative legal analysis' (2020) 10(2) *International Data Privacy Law* 117; Mahsa Shabani, 'Will the European Health Data Space change data sharing rules?' (2022) 375(6587) *Science* 1357.
48 Hansen and others (n 20) 60.
49 Pormeister (n 45).
50 TEHDAS, 'Deliverable 5.1, Report on secondary use of health data through European case studies' (28 February 2022). https://tehdas.eu/app/uploads/2022/08/tehdas-report-on-secondary-use-of-health-data-through-european-case-studies-.pdf accessed 26 March 2024.
51 TEHDAS, 'Deliverable 5.1, Report on secondary use of health data through European case studies'.
52 TEHDAS, 'Deliverable 5.1, Report on secondary use of health data through European case studies'. See also Pormeister (n 45).
53 Commission, 'Proposal for a Regulation of the European Parliament and of the Council on the European Health Data Space' COM (2022) 197 final, explanatory memorandum 1.
54 TEHDAS (n 50).
55 In more detail, see the recitals 52 and 73 of the EHDS compromise text.
56 TEHDAS (n 34).
57 European Parliament, 'Amendments adopted by the European Parliament on 13 December 2023 on the proposal for a regulation of the European Parliament and of the Council on the European Health Data Space (COM(2022)0197 – C9-0167/2022 – 2022/0140(COD)).
58 EDPB-EDPS (n 25) 23.
59 Council of the European Union, 'Proposal for a Regulation on the European Health Data Space, mandate for negotiations with the European Parliament' 2022/0140(COD), the discussed provision is moved to Article 37(5) in the said version.
60 Council of the European Union, 'Proposal for a Regulation on the European Health Data Space, mandate for negotiations with the European Parliament' 2022/0140(COD) arts 33(1), 33(5) and 35F.
61 European Parliament (n 60) arts 33(5), 33(5)a and 33(1), see also Recital 39a.
62 TEHDAS (n 34).
63 Muin J Khoury and Kathryn E Holt, 'The impact of genomics on precision public health: beyond the pandemic' (2021) 13 *Genome Medicine* 67.
64 Noura S. Abul-Husn and others, 'Implementing genomic screening in diverse populations' (2021) 13 *Genome Medicine* 17; Muin J Khoury and others, 'The intersection of genomics and big data with public health: opportunities for precision public

health' (2020) 17(10) *PLoS Medicine*; Muin J Khoury and others, 'Beyond base pairs to bedside: a population perspective on how genomics can improve health' (2012) 120(1) *American Journal of Public Health* 34.
65 Cathryn M Lewis and Evangelos Vassos, 'Polygenic risk scores: from research tools to clinical instruments' (2020) 12(1) *Genome Medicine 44*.
66 Adam Lavertu and others, 'Pharmacogenomics and big genomic data: from lab to clinic and back again' (2018) 27(R1) *Human Molecular Genetics* 72.
67 Iftikhar J Kullo and others, 'Polygenic scores in biomedical research' (2022) 23 *Nature Reviews Genetics* 524.
68 GDPR Recital 26.
69 John E Pool and others, 'Population genetic inference from genomic sequence variation' (2010) 20(3) *Genome Research* 291.
70 Legislative proposal 110/2022 for a Finnish Genome Centre 11.
71 Kaya Akyüz and others, 'Post-identifiability in changing sociotechnological genomic data environments' (2023) *BioSocieties* 1–28. Advance online publication available at: https://doi.org/10.1057/s41292-023-00299-7.
72 Minna Paltiel, Mark Taylor and Ainsley Newson, 'Protection of genomic data and the Australian Privacy Act: when are genomic data "personal information"?' (2023) 13(1) *International Data Privacy Law* 47.
73 Shuang Wang and others, 'Genome privacy: challenges, technical approaches to mitigate risk, and ethical considerations in the United States' (2017) 1387(1) *Annals of the New York Academy of Sciences* 73.
74 Legislative proposal 110/2022 for a Finnish Genome Centre.
75 Statement of the Finnish Constitutional Law Committee (PeVL 1/2018 vp, HE 159/2017 vp) available at: https://www.eduskunta.fi/FI/vaski/Lausunto/Sivut/PeVL_1+2018.aspx.
76 In accordance with Article 74 of the Constitution of Finland (731/1999, as amended), the principal function of the Finnish Constitutional Law Committee is to issue statements on the constitutionality of legislative proposals and other matters brought for its consideration, as well as on their relation to international human rights treaties.
77 Statement of the Finnish Constitutional Law Committee (PeVL 1/2018 vp, HE 159/2017 vp) available at: https://www.eduskunta.fi/FI/vaski/Lausunto/Sivut/PeVL_1+2018.aspx; reference is made to the Statement of the Finnish Constitutional Law Committee PeVL 30/2010 vp, 6/II.
78 Statement of the Constitutional Law Committee (PeVL 30/2010 vp, 6/II).
79 Statements of the Constitutional Law Committee (PeVL 19/2000 vp, p. 3/II, PeVL 27/1998 vp, 2/II, and PeVL 19/2000 vp, 3/II).
80 Mats G Hansson, 'Striking a Balance Between Personalized Genetics and Privacy Protection from the Perspective of GDPR' in Santa Slokenberga, Olga Tzortzatou and Jane Reichel (eds), *GDPR and Biobanking. Law, Governance, and Technology Series* (volume 43, Springer Cham 2021).
81 For an overview on consumerisation of healthcare see for instance Tamara K Hervey and Jean V McHale, *European Union Health Law: Themes and Implications* (Cambridge University Press 2015) 98–126.
82 In accordance with the Convention for the Protection of Human Rights and Dignity of the Human Being with regard to the Application of Biology and Medicine: Convention on Human Rights and Biomedicine (ETS No 164), an individual has the right to know or not to know health-related information, and their informed consent is required for the test to be conducted.
83 See for instance Hervey and McHale (n 81) 156–183.
84 Christine S Cocanour, 'Informed consent – It's more than a signature on a piece of paper' (2017) 214(6) *The American Journal of Surgery* 993.
85 James Brian Byrd and others, 'Responsible, practical genomic data sharing that accelerates research' (2020) 21 *Nature Reviews Genetics* 615.

86 Matthew Norstad and others, 'The difficulties of broad data sharing in genomic medicine: Empirical evidence from diverse participants in prenatal and pediatric clinical genomics research' (2022) 24(2) *Genetics Medicine* 410.
87 See for instance: 'Enabling effective secondary use of health data in Europe: Specific recommendations for a potential optout mechanism for the EHDS' https://www.eucope.org/wp-content/uploads/2023/06/ehds-statement-multistakeholder-group-6-june-2023.pdf (European Confederation of Pharmaceutical Entrepreneurs (EUCOPE), June 2023) accessed 28 March 2024.
88 Minakshi Raj and others, 'Do people have an ethical obligation to share their health information? Comparing narratives of altruism and health information sharing in a nationally representative sample' (2020) 15(12) *PLoS One*., e0244767.
89 Luca Bonomi, Yingxiang Huang and Lucila Ohno-Machado, 'Privacy challenges and research opportunities for genomic data sharing' (2020) 52(7) *Nature Genetics* 646.
90 See for instance Haixu Tang and others, 'Protecting genomic data analytics in the cloud: state of the art and opportunities' (2016) 9(1) *BMC Medical Genomics 63*; Tsung-Ting Kuo and others, 'The evolving privacy and security concerns for genomic data analysis and sharing as observed from the iDASH competition' (2022) 29(12) *Journal of the American Medical Informatics Association* 2182-2190.
91 See for instance Md Momin Al Aziz and others, 'Privacy-preserving techniques of genomic data-a survey' (2019) 20(3) *Briefings in Bioinformatics* 887.
92 See for instance Bonnie Berger and Hyunghoon Cho, 'Emerging technologies towards enhancing privacy in genomic data sharing' (2019) 20(1) *Genome Biology* 128.
93 Sobia Raza and Alison Hall, 'Genomic medicine and data sharing' (2017) 123(1) *British Medical Bulletin* 35.

List of Sources

Treaties, Legislation and Conventions

Charter of Fundamental Rights of the European Union [2012] OJ C 326/391.

European Parliament, 'Amendments adopted by the European Parliament on 13 December 2023 on the proposal for a regulation of the European Parliament and of the Council on the European Health Data Space (COM(2022)0197 – C9-0167/2022 – 2022/0140(COD)).

Council of the European Union, 'Proposal for a Regulation on the European Health Data Space, mandate for negotiations with the European Parliament' 2022/0140(COD).

Convention for the Protection of Human Rights and Dignity of the Human Being with regard to the Application of Biology and Medicine: Convention on Human Rights and Biomedicine (ETS No 164).

Commission, 'Proposal for a Regulation of the European Parliament and of the Council on the European Health Data Space' COM (2022) 197 final.

Proposal for Regulation of the European Parliament and of the Council on European data governance (Data Governance Act) COM(2020) 767 final.

European Parliament and the Council Regulation 2016/679 of 27 April 2016 on the Protection of Natural Persons with Regard to the Processing of Personal Data and on the Free Movement of such Data (General Data Protection Regulation) [2016] OJ L 119/1.

Regulation (EU) 2022/868 of the European Parliament and of the Council of 30 May 2022 on European data governance and amending Regulation (EU) 2018/1724 (Data Governance Act) (Text with EEA relevance) [2022] *OJ L 152/1.*

Domestic Law

Constitution of Finland (731/1999, as amended).
Legislative proposal 110/2022 for a Finnish Genome Centre.
Statement of the Constitutional Law Committee (PeVL 30/2010 vp, p. 6/II).
Statement of the Finnish Constitutional Law Committee (PeVL 1/2018 vp, HE 159/2017 vp) available at: https://www.eduskunta.fi/FI/vaski/Lausunto/Sivut/PeVL_1+2018.aspx
Statements of the Constitutional Law Committee (PeVL 19/2000 vp, p. 3/II, PeVL 27/1998 vp, p. 2/II, and PeVL 19/2000 vp, p. 3/II).

Policy Reports

Commission 'A European strategy for data' (Communication) COM (2020) 66 final.
Commission 'Impact assessment report accompanying the DGA proposal' (Staff Working Document) (2020) 295 final.
EDPB-EDPS Joint Opinion on the Proposal for a regulation of the European Parliament and of the Council on European data governance (Data Governance Act) (2021).
EDPB-EDPS Joint Opinion 03/2022 on the Proposal for a Regulation on the European Health Data Space (2022).
European Observatory on Health Systems and Policies 'Regulating the unknown, A guide to regulating genomics for health policy-makers' (Policy brief) available at: https://iris.who.int/bitstream/handle/10665/338975/Policy-brief-38-1997-8073-eng.pdf, accessed 28 March 2024.
Hansen J, Wilson P, Verhoeve E, Korneman M, Kirwan M,Verheij R, van Veen EB, 'Assessment of the EU Member States' rules on health data in the light of GDPR' (2021) Publications Office https://doi.org/10.2818/546193
TEHDAS 'Deliverable 5.1, Report on secondary use of health data through European case studies' (28 February 2022) https://tehdas.eu/app/uploads/2022/08/tehdas-report-on-secondary-use-of-health-data-through-european-case-studies-.pdf accessed 26 March 2024.
TEHDAS 'Deliverable 8.2, Report on lessons learned to be applied and recommendations for data altruism practices in the implementation of construction of national and European health data spaces (including broad consent)' (29 September 2023) https://tehdas.eu/app/uploads/2023/09/tehdas-recommendations-for-data-altruism-practices.pdf accessed 26 March 2024.
TEHDAS' proposals for promoting data altruism in the EHDS' (29 September 2023) https://tehdas.eu/results/tehdas-proposals-for-promoting-data-altruism-in-the-ehds/ accessed 26 March 2023.

Literature and Other Secondary Sources

Abul-Husn NS, Soper ER, Braganza GT, Rodriguez JE, Zeid N, Cullina S, Bobo D, Moscati A, Merkelson A, Loos RJF, Cho JH, Belbin GM, Suckiel SA, Kenny EE, 'Implementing genomic screening in diverse populations' (2021) 13 *Genome Medicine* 17. https://doi.org/10.1186/s13073-021-00832-y
Akyüz K, Goisauf M, Chassang G, Kozera L, Mežinska S, Tzortzatou-Nanopoulou O, Mayrhofer MTh 'Post-identifiability in changing sociotechnological genomic data environments' (2023) *BioSocieties*. https://doi.org/10.1057/s41292-023-00299-7
Al Aziz MM, Sadat MN, Alhadidi D, Wang S, Jiang X, Brown CL, Mohammed N, 'Privacy-preserving techniques of genomic data—A survey' (2019) 20(3) *Briefings in Bioinformatics*. https://doi.org/10.1093/bib/bbx139
Berger B, Cho H, 'Emerging technologies towards enhancing privacy in genomic data sharing' (2019) 20(1) *Genome Biology*. https://doi.org/10.1186/s13059-019-1741-0

Bonomi L, Huang Y, Ohno-Machado L 'Privacy challenges and research opportunities for genomic data sharing' (2020) 52(7) *Nature Genetics*. https://doi.org/10.1038/s41588-020-0651-0

Byrd JB, Greene AC, Prasad DV, Jiang X, Greene CS, 'Responsible, practical genomic data sharing that accelerates research' (2020) 21 *Nature Reviews Genetics* 615. https://doi.org/10.1038/s41576-020-0257-5

Cocanour CS, Informed consent – It's more than a signature on a piece of paper (2017) 214(6) *The American Journal of Surgery*. https://doi.org/10.1016/j.amjsurg.2017.09.015

Dove ES, Chen J, 'Should consent for data processing be privileged in health research? A comparative legal analysis' (2020) 10(2) *International Data Privacy Law* 117. https://doi.org/10.1093/idpl/ipz023

Hansson MG, 'Striking a balance between personalized genetics and privacy protection from the perspective of GDPR' in: Slokenberga S, Tzortzatou O, Reichel J (Ed), *GDPR and Biobanking. Law, Governance, and Technology Series* (vol 43. Springer 2021). https://doi.org/10.1007/978-3-030-49388-2_3

Hassan M, Awan FM, Naz A, deAndrés-Galiana EJ, Alvarez O, Cernea A, Fernández-Brillet L, Fernández-Martínez JL and Kloczkowski A, 'Innovations in genomics and big data analytics for personalized medicine and health care: A review' (2022) 23(9) *International Journal of Molecular Sciences* https://doi.org/10.3390/ijms23094645

Hervey TK and McHale JV, *European Union Health Law: Themes and Implications* (Cambridge University Press 2015).

Khoury MJ, Armstrong GL, Bunnell RL, Cyril J, Iademarco D, 'The intersection of genomics and big data with public health: Opportunities for precision public health' (2020) 17(10) *PLoS Medicine*. https://doi.org/10.1371/journal.pmed

Khoury MJ, Gwinn M, Bowen MS, Dotson WD 'Beyond base pairs to bedside: A population perspective on how genomics can improve health' (2012) 120(1) *American Journal of Public Health*. https://doi.org/10.2105/AJPH.2011.300299

Khoury MJ, Holt KE, 'The impact of genomics on precision public health: Beyond the pandemic' (2021) 13 *Genome Medicine* 67. https://doi.org/10.1186/s13073-021-00886-y

Kullo IJ, Lewis CM, Inouye M, Martin AR, Ripatti S, Chatterjee N 'Polygenic scores in biomedical research' (2022) 23 *Nature Reviews Genetics*. https://doi.org/10.1038/s41576-022-00470-z

Kuo TT, Jiang X, Tang H, Wang XF, Harmanci A, Kim M, Post K, Bu D, Bath T, Kim J, Liu W, Chen H, Ohno-Machado L, 'The evolving privacy and security concerns for genomic data analysis and sharing as observed from the iDASH competition' (2022) 29(12) *Journal of the American Medical Informatics Association*. https://doi.org/10.1093/jamia/ocac165

Lalova-Spinks T, Meszaros J, Huys I, 'The application of data altruism in clinical research through empirical and legal analysis lenses' (2023) 10 *Frontiers in Medicine*. https://doi.org/10.3389/fmed.2023.1141685

Lavertu A, McInnes G, Daneshjou R, Whirl-Carrillo M, Klein TE, Altman RB 'Pharmacogenomics and big genomic data: From lab to clinic and back again' (2018) 27(R1) *Human Molecular Genetics*. https://doi.org/10.1093/hmg/ddy116

Lewis CM, Vassos E 'Polygenic risk scores: From research tools to clinical instruments' (2020) 12(1) *Genome Medicine*. https://doi.org/10.1186/s13073-020-00742-5

Norstad M, Outram S, Brown JEH, Zamora AN, Koenig BA, Risch N, Norton ME, Slavotinek A, Ackerman SL, 'The difficulties of broad data sharing in genomic medicine: Empirical evidence from diverse participants in prenatal and pediatric clinical genomics research' (2022) 24(2) *Genetics in Medicine*. https://doi.org/10.1016/j.gim.2021.09.021

Paltiel M, Taylor M, Newson A, 'Protection of genomic data and the Australian Privacy Act: When are genomic data "personal information"?' (2023) 13(1) *International Data Privacy Law*. https://doi.org/10.1093/idpl/ipad002

Pool JE, Hellmann I, Jensen JD, Nielsen R, 'Population genetic inference from genomic sequence variation' (2010) 20(3) *Genome Research*. https://doi.org/10.1101/gr.079509.108

Pormeister, K, 'Genetic data and the research exemption: Is the GDPR going too far?' (2017) 7 *International Data Privacy Law*. https://doi.org/10.1093/IDPL/IPX006

Prainsack B, El-Sayed S, Forgó N, Szoszkiewicz L, Baumer P, 'White paper on data solidarity', (2022). https://www.governinghealthfutures2030.org/wp-content/uploads/2022/12/DataSolidarity.pdf

Raj M, De Vries R, Nong P, Kardia SLR, Platt JE, 'Do people have an ethical obligation to share their health information? Comparing narratives of altruism and health information sharing in a nationally representative sample' (2020) 15(12) *PLoS One*. https://doi.org/10.1371/journal.pone.0244767

Raza S, Hall A, 'Genomic medicine and data sharing' (2017) 123(1) *British Medical Bulletin*. https://doi.org/10.1093/bmb/ldx024

Richter H, 'Looking at the data governance act and beyond: How to better integrate data intermediaries in the market order for data sharing' (2023) 72(5) *GRUR International*. https://doi.org/10.1093/grurint/ikad014

Schreiber K, Pommerening P, Schoel P, *New Data Governance Act, a Practitioner's Guide* (1st edn, Bloomsbury Publishing 2023).

Shabani M, 'The Data Governance Act and the EU's move towards facilitating data sharing' (2021) 17(3) *Molecular Systems Biology*. https://doi.org/10.15252/msb.202110229

Shabani M, 'Will the European Health Data Space change data sharing rules?' (2022) 375(6587) *Science*. https://doi.org/10.1126/science.abn4874

Soini S, 'Geenitestaus ja lakien henki: Tutkimus geenitestien sääntelystä, Genetic testing and the spirit of the laws: A study of the regulation of genetic tests' (University Helsinki Doctoral Dissertation 2020) http://hdl.handle.net/10138/317694

Staunton C, Slokenberga S, Mascalzoni D, 'The GDPR and the research exemption: Considerations on the necessary safeguards for research biobanks' (2019) 27 *European Journal of Human Genetics*. https://doi.org/10.1038/s41431-019-0386-5

Tang H, Jiang X, Wang X, Sofia H, Fox D, Lauter K, Malin B, Telenti A, Xiong L, Ohno-Machado L, 'Protecting genomic data analytics in the cloud: State of the art and opportunities' (2016) 9(1) *BMC Medical Genomics*. https://doi.org/10.1186/s12920-016-0224-3

Walin L, 'Kun suostumus ei riitä – kudosnäytteen ja alkion luovuttajan oikeusaseman tarkastelua' (2008) 5 *Lakimies* 773.

Wang S, Jiang X, Singh S, Marmor R, Bonomi L, Fox D, Do M, Ohno-Marchado L, 'Genome privacy: Challenges, technical approaches to mitigate risk, and ethical considerations in the United States' (2017) 1387(1) *Annals of the New York Academy of Sciences*. https://doi.org/10.1111/nyas.13259

7 Fair enough?

Exploring the role of fairness in secondary uses of health data in the European Health Data Space

Patricia Cervera de la Cruz and Mahsa Shabani

7.1 Introduction

In an ageing society where healthcare systems are under sustained pressure, re-using health data to improve healthcare outcomes in different population groups is becoming more important.[1] The secondary use of health data generally involves re-using existing data collected in biobanks, epidemiological registries, electronic health records and so on for other purposes, such as research. Examples include the reuse of electronic health records to improve risk assessment tools for specific diseases[2] or the linkage of health data from epidemiological cohorts and genetic information for infectious disease forecasting.[3] The emergence of data-driven tools, particularly those using artificial intelligence (AI), marks a significant step towards unlocking the full potential of health data. Analysing health data from diverse sources such as electronic health records, genetic data, biobank data or behavioural data from wearable devices or smartphones allows these advanced tools to unveil novel associations between diseases, offering, for example, nuanced estimations of persons' individualised risk of developing chronic diseases.

Despite its clear potential to improve healthcare, the secondary use of health data faces some challenges such as interoperability[4] and standardisation.[5] For example, the lack of standardised anonymisation techniques has led to great discrepancies between health data sets held in different repositories,[6] and stakeholders believe low levels of interoperability between health record systems across member states (MS) to be one of the main barriers to sharing health data.[7] At a regulatory level, the fragmented application of the General Data Protection Regulation (GDPR) rules on health data between MS poses a significant barrier for the reuse of health data.[8] The situation stems from the provisions under the GDPR, which afford MS the discretion to interpret the rules regarding the research exemption (Article 89(1)) differently, leading to a 'divergent and fragmented regulatory landscape',[9] which hinders cross-border research.[10]

Recognising these challenges, in May 2022, the European Commission introduced a proposal for a European Health Data Space Regulation (EHDS) with the aim of facilitating both primary and secondary uses of health data

DOI: 10.4324/9781003544111-9

across the Union. Notably, in addressing the issues of harmonisation, the rules set out by the EHDS on the secondary use of health data have important implications for individuals' rights and interests. In particular, the extent to which the secondary use of health data will be *fair* to individuals is unclear. The principle of fairness, enshrined in Article 8.2 of the Charter of the Fundamental Rights of the European Union and in Article 5(1)(a) GDPR, seems vital to harness trust, seen by the European Commission as a 'fundamental enabler for the success of the EHDS'.[11] Given the lack of consensus in the academic literature over the meaning of fairness,[12] in our previous work, we sought to conceptualise fairness in the context of secondary use of health data for research. Our findings revealed that balancing individual and public interests, reducing power asymmetries, setting conditions for commercial involvement and implementing benefit sharing were essential to guarantee fair secondary use of health data for research purposes.[13]

In this chapter, we seek to explore the extent to which these fairness concerns are addressed in the EHDS, by critically analysing (1) the use of public interest as both a legal and ethical basis, (2) the level of control afforded to individuals, (3) the involvement of commercial actors and (4) the sharing of benefits resulting from secondary use. This comprehensive analysis aims to provide insights into the EHDS's adherence to fairness in governing the secondary use of health data.

7.2 Public interest

According to Recital 52 of the EHDS, the Regulation provides a legal basis for the secondary use of health data for health or social care purposes GDPR article 9(2)(h); for public health reasons (GDPR article 9(2)(i)); and for archiving purposes in the public interest and for scientific research purposes (GDPR article 9(2)(j)). Furthermore, the Regulation 'also assigns tasks in the public interest in the sense of Article 6(1)(e) of Regulation (EU) 2016/679 to the health data access bodies, and meets the requirements of Article 9(2)(g), (h), (i), (j) of the Regulation (EU) 2016/679'.

The approach of the Regulation to the legal basis for such secondary uses of health data and its compatibility with the GDPR and other relevant national regulations have already sparked discussions among legal scholars. Indeed, some have criticised the appropriateness of approaching the public interest as a 'legal test', arguing that 'this narrow notion of what purports to be in the public interest is wholly disconnected from the views of actual publics, and lacks social legitimacy'.[14] Others have criticised the use of public interest as a legal basis to override consent to health data use, arguing:

> [W]hile demonstrating a common interest in health research might provide a pro tanto reason to will the means to its achievement, it does not follow that unfettered access to personal data for health research purposes is in the public interest.[15]

The Proposal specifically sets out that it aims to improve access to health data for 'purposes that would benefit the society',[16] making it clear that the secondary use of health data should be in the public interest. This approach has been adopted in some countries, such as Finland and Estonia, which 'have explicitly stated in their national laws that scientific research conducted with health data in the absence of the data subject's consent must be in the public interest'.[17] However, in countries like Germany, the reliance on public interest as a legal basis, stemming from the GDPR, has been found to 'conflict with incompatible Member State rules',[18] since German national law requires consent for the processing of personal data for any clinical research. Given these national divergences, the EHDS seeks to set common EU rules and standards and to harmonise the reliance on public interest for secondary use of health data.

As such, the EHDS regulation does not offer a definition of what is understood to be in the public interest. The list of permitted purposes which the Regulation includes for secondary use of health data[19] may serve as a proxy for understanding what uses are considered to be in the public interest, such as activities for protection against serious cross-border threats to health or scientific research 'related to health or care sectors, that contributes to public health or health technology assessments, or ensures high levels of quality and safety of health care, of medicinal products or of medical devices, with the aim of benefiting end-users',[20] providing some examples.

That said, still greater clarity in the use of the term seems necessary, particularly when considering the interplay of the EHDS with other data sharing regulations, such as the Data Governance Act (DGA), which instead uses the term 'general interest' when setting out the conditions for the reuse of data for the purpose of data altruism, a concept that enables the voluntary sharing of data on the basis of the consent of data subjects for altruistic objectives, such as for healthcare or combating climate change.[21] Consequently, this can leave room for wide interpretations that may differ between health data access bodies (HDABs), potentially leading to an uneven cross-border application of the Regulation (which is the very issue the EHDS set out to resolve). HDABs are considered in more detail in Chapters 9 and 10.

Notably, the discussion on the use of public interest has broader implications. From social and ethical perspectives, it is crucial to first have a clear understanding of what constitutes secondary use for public interest and ensure that the public's views have been adequately represented when implementing such secondary use regime. Otherwise, a lack of public acceptance will jeopardise establishing and implementing such secondary use infrastructures.

A review of the broader ethical discussions on appropriateness of public interest as a legal basis for secondary uses of health data shows sometimes opposing views. While on the one hand some argue in favour of greater sharing of health data under the justification that this serves the public interest,[22] others see that as putting individual interests such as those relating to personal data protection against larger societal interests, such as improving public health.

For example, some claim that health data should be considered as public goods because they have been generated through public healthcare systems, while the truth is that individuals contribute to their financing by paying their taxes[23] and the definition of personal data in the GDPR does not allow for this kind of interpretation. The general sentiment is that 'individuals favour data sharing and use if benefits are clear', as concluded by the TEHDAS project.[24] That said, engaging with individuals to understand what secondary uses they deem to be within the public interest would help to better frame the boundaries of this term. Another way to put this is that data users should always pursue their research policies 'with a mandate from society'.[25] The use of citizen juries and other similar engagement activities have proven to be successful in this context.[26]

In this way, in order to ensure that secondary use is fair, it seems crucial to introduce a 'practicable but meaningful test capable of discerning whether research processing is "in the public interest"'.[27] Some tools seeking to do this have been introduced, such as the Public Value Assessment Tool (PLUTO)[28] or the checklist provided by Involve, Carnegie UK Trust and Understanding Patient Data,[29] which identifies five criteria to determine the public benefit of a data sharing activity including that it benefits individuals' wellbeing, provides benefits for wider society, respects individuals and their privacy, represents an effective use of public resources and produces tangible benefits. Therefore, in making the claim that the secondary use of health data will be in the public interest, the EHDS needs to demonstrate the benefits that this brings for all individuals.

While the Regulation does not foresee such a requirement, it may be reasonably expected for the oversight bodies to carry out this task, requesting evidence of the benefits resulting from the reuse of health data for the public. As further explained in Chapter 9, the HDABs, as relevant oversight bodies, play a crucial role in managing access to health data for secondary uses. Broadly understood, and as indicated in Article 57, the HDABs will be tasked with reviewing data access applications, issuing data access permits with conditions for secondary use (or rejecting applications), requesting health data from data holders and providing access to health data in an anonymised (or pseudonymised) format through a secure processing environment. The cooperation of patient representatives and advocacy groups with HDABs would be a step in the right direction towards further engagement and open debate over the public interest question. As per the EHDS, it remains the sole task of HDABs to assess an application and make the decision to issue a data permit or not,[30] although Article 55(4) stipulates that they 'shall actively cooperate with relevant stakeholders' representatives, especially with representatives of patients, health data holders and health data users'. Similarly, digital health authorities, which will be responsible 'for the planning and implementation standards for access to and transmission of electronic health data of and the enforcement of the rights of natural persons and health professionals',[31] are also tasked with cooperating and consulting with relevant stakeholders' representatives, including patients' representatives.[32] How this cooperation will happen in both HDABs and digital health authorities and the extent to which patient representatives will be involved in data access applications remains to be seen. It seems that if appeals to public interest are to have social legitimacy, engaging with patient and citizen representatives in cases where the public interest of a data use seems unclear or may be called into question will be critically important.

A suggestion put forward by a multistakeholder group for engaging individuals in the EHDS has been to introduce steering groups within the EHDS made up of patient groups and representatives.[33] This has been incorporated into the text of the EHDS in the form of a stakeholder forum, which will support the EHDS Board by 'facilitating the exchange of information and promoting cooperation among stakeholders in relation to the implementation of this Regulation'.[34] As stipulated in paragraph 4, the forum 'may establish standing or temporary subgroups, as appropriate, for the purpose of examining specific questions related to the objectives of this Regulation'.[35] These subgroups, which could be composed of patient and citizen representatives, could reasonably be tasked with commissioning guidelines for determining public interest in health data access requests.

7.3 Control over health data

The EHDS significantly changes the control that individuals have over their health data. Control by individuals is an important feature in the reuse of health data, with a number of empirical studies highlighting that individuals expect to know, and in some cases decide, who uses their health data and for what purposes.[36] Our previous work highlighted the importance of control to ensure fairness in the secondary use of health data.[37]

Consent has traditionally been presented as *the* way to exert control over health data. In scientific research, regulations and guidelines such as the World Medical Association Declaration of Helsinki[38] or the Council for International Organizations of Medical Sciences guidelines[39] have long-established consent as 'a fundamental normative core'.[40] It should be noted that in the context of research, two types of consent may be required. One is an 'informed consent', which is an ethical requirement for any research with human subjects to respect their autonomy and right to self-determination. The second one will arise as a legal requirement for processing personal data, and in respect to privacy rights and as a data protection instrument.

Despite its historical convention, the appropriateness of consent as a control mechanism has been largely called into question. Indeed, data protection authorities have reiterated that there are other available legal bases under the GDPR that may be more appropriate for such data processing.[41] Moreover, Recital 43 of the GDPR stresses that consent may not be an appropriate legal basis where there are significant power asymmetries between data subjects and controllers. This point has also previously been raised concerning the interplay between the GDPR and clinical trials regulation, where consent has been deemed inappropriate when there is concern over power asymmetry.[42]

Notwithstanding the limitations of consent in secondary health data use, the possibility under Article 9(4) GDPR for MS to 'maintain or introduce further conditions, including limitations, with regard to the processing of genetic data, biometric data or data concerning health', has meant that some countries have chosen to impose consent requirements for the re-use of health data. This was highlighted in a report from the Commission, which assessed MS rules on health data in light of the GDPR.[43] For instance, the report mentions that Ireland has applied a blanket requirement of explicit consent under GDPR as a requirement for both primary and secondary research. Legal scholars have also observed that consent has strongly been privileged in some MS.[44] Therefore, while the GDPR allows (and possibly encourages) data users to rely on legal bases other than consent, the reality shows that consent as a legal basis is still applied.

Therefore, the EHDS's approach to not use consent as a legal basis for secondary uses of health data represents a significant shift in many MS' approach to regulating data processing. This was justified under the explanatory memorandum of the EHDS proposal as necessary to enable greater access to data 'at lower costs than relying on consent'.[45] Moreover, the Proposal initially withdrew existing consent requirements for health data use, noting: '[W]here the consent of the natural person is required by national law, health data access bodies shall rely on the obligations laid down in this Chapter to provide access to electronic health data'.[46]

This loss of control would have important implications for the fairness principle, since maintaining a certain level of control may be necessary to hold data users accountable. In response to the lack of a consent model in the proposed regulation, the introduction of an opt-out mechanism was put forward in the European Parliament amendments[47] and later incorporated in the EHDS, suggesting that consent is still considered to be an important model for individual control. Such an opt-out will allow individuals to decide not to share their health data for secondary use purposes. Opt-outs have previously been introduced for secondary health data use. In Denmark, for example, an opt-out for identification by researchers of Danish research participants through their civil registration number was introduced and later revoked, on the basis that it had negative impacts for the representativeness of research.[48] More recently, a national data opt-out in England allowing people to prevent the use of their health data for purposes other than direct care saw a large increase in the number of opt-outs in response to a government-led initiative to create a centralised pseudonymised database comprised of the coded primary care records of patients.[49]

In light of these examples, there are concerns about practically implementing an opt-out in the EHDS. For instance, it seems important that, if individuals decide to opt-out from sharing their health data for secondary use purposes, this process is simple and frictionless. In the case of Finland, the Finnish Health Data Authority website informing individuals about how to object to the secondary use of their health data explains: 'Finland does not have a centralised system through which the secondary use of data can be banned once and for all in a way that is binding on all parties'.[50] This means that individuals need to individually submit objection requests to each of the more than ten actors that control their health and social data. In the event that an opt-out is introduced in the EHDS, regulators should make a great effort to avoid this situation and instead introduce a 'one-stop shop' solution. Acknowledging these concerns, the EHDS notes:

> Member States shall provide for an accessible and easily understandable opt-out mechanism to exercise the right, whereby natural persons may explicitly state that they do not wish to have their personal electronic health data processed for secondary use.[51]

Another concern surrounding an opt-out approach in the EHDS was whether there would only be an opportunity to opt-out at the start, without an option to reconsider. Representatives of the European University Hospital Alliance (EUHA) have claimed that this would reduce the administrative and financial burden associated with setting up an opt-out.[52] However, it is important to recognise that offering an opt-out to individuals at a single moment in time may fail to respect individuals' rights. As Nordfalk and Hoeyer argue, 'a person might think opt-out sounds appealing at the age of 20 and feel differently when confronted with cancer at the age of 55'.[53] However, the Regulation clarifies this issue by stipulating that individuals 'shall have the right to opt-out at any time, and without providing any reason'[54] and that 'this right shall be reversible'.[55]

Furthermore, it is important to note that the opt-out has been restricted for health data uses which have 'a strong link to the public interest'.[56] This means that, for cases in which health data uses are determined to be more obviously in the public interest, MS will be able to override individual opt-outs for secondary use. However, the Regulation does require health data users to 'justify that the use of the override is necessary for an individual access application or data request'.[57] Nevertheless, some in the digital industry have anticipated that this derogation will cause implementation problems, especially in public-private research projects.[58]

In combination with the opt-out approach, Recital 39(a) of the EP amendments also included the introduction of an opt-in for sensitive kinds of data such as genetic data, arguing that 'it is appropriate to provide that the secondary use of such data can only occur following the consent of the natural person concerned in accordance with Article 4(11) of the Regulation (EU) 2016/679'. In the final text, MS are afforded the ability to implement consent or other safeguards for the secondary use of specific categories of personal electronic health data, such as genetic data.[59] This means that the decision to have an opt-in, or consent, for sensitive kinds of data like genetic data will be decided on a national level.

The suggestion to introduce an opt-in for sensitive types of data including genetic data was welcomed by some as a way to place stricter protections on health data that presents a higher risk of becoming identifiable or which holds particularly sensitive information about individuals and their biological relatives. However, other groups, such as the European Society of Human Genetics (ESHG), have communicated their concerns regarding this approach, arguing that it would 'substantially hinder progress in the field of human genetics within Europe' and instead suggested putting in place safeguards against misuse and re-identification to address any concerns about genetic privacy. Indeed, academic literature has argued that genetic exceptionalism is not justified because other types of non-genetic health data can be equally sensitive or even more so. This distinction complicates consent forms, and empirical evidence suggests that the public does not generally support genetic exceptionalism.[60]

Aside from the chosen opt-out model, other consent models have been suggested as potential solutions to the control issue in the secondary use of health data. One of these is the use of dynamic consent, which offers individuals opportunities to consent to health data sharing in a dynamic way, by offering ongoing information about the use of data and providing opportunities to change detailed preferences for health data sharing. The philosophy behind this concept is: '(A) single consent form cannot bear the burden of what must be a much fuller, ongoing engagement'.[61] Concerns remain over the appropriateness of dynamic consent as a consent model under the GDPR, especially in light of the fact that 'the implementation of a platform that contains sensitive consent information but must also be easily accessible to patients inevitably entails additional data safety and security risks'.[62] However, others argue that legal systems need to evolve with technological innovations.[63] In Germany, the Federal Council advocated for the Health Data Use Act to operate dynamic consent for the sharing of citizen-generated data.[64] Moreover, as suggested by Biasiotto et al., dynamic consent could be incorporated with the opt-out approach, allowing individuals to actively express their individual preferences to different data uses through an opt-out.[65] Up until now, calls to integrate dynamic consent models have been unsuccessful because of concerns over the technical feasibility of building such a platform[66] and because of worries that it will lead to consent fatigue.[67] New technological proposals that would facilitate the implementation of dynamic consent could be considered within the EHDS to allow individuals an opportunity for greater engagement with the secondary use of their health data.

Furthermore, there is also a need to find a balance between individuals' control over their data and the necessity for data users to share and access diverse datasets. In fact, while giving individuals greater control over their health data is useful,[68] it might introduce additional bias in the data and hamper future data-driven developments in healthcare, for example.[69] A leading concern has been that an opt-out by groups of individuals could lead to their underrepresentation in health data, undermining the potential benefits for everyone. This could be especially harmful in communities that typically mistrust healthcare providers due to 'historical exploitation and unethical practices in healthcare'.[70] Nevertheless, we should also acknowledge that not providing an opt-out (or any other consent model) because of fear of the negative consequences of such an approach would probably fail to respect the nature of individuals as autonomous agent-makers and constitutes a big shift from the traditional approach.[71] If the public benefits of health research were made abundantly clear to individuals, they could make a better informed and unbiased decision regarding their participation in the sharing of their health data in the EHDS. Furthermore, to reinforce the fairness principle, individuals will be reassured if they see that there is a clear data governance model in place to ensure that their data are sufficiently protected.[72] In the EHDS, this should mean clear information campaigns for citizens, so they understand that their data always remains in a secure processing environment with limited and controlled data users. In this respect, the budgetary commitment of 1.6 million euros for the 'Communication and Information Activities for the Proposed European Health Data Space' by the Commission[73] seems insufficient given the scale of the task, which involves adequately informing citizens in all 27 member states.

7.4 Commercial involvement and commercial uses

The EHDS allowing commercial actors to use health data for secondary purposes also raises some concerns. Commercial actors are important for developing the EU's data economy and innovative solutions in healthcare. The pharmaceutical industry, for example, is crucial for finding new and effective healthcare solutions, as demonstrated by its contribution in the development of COVID-19 vaccines during the pandemic.

At the same time, given the sensitivity of health data and the associated risks to privacy and data protection, giving commercial actors access to this data creates serious concerns of potential misuses and objectionable uses from a citizen's perspective. For example, in the UK, the contract between the NHS and Palantir, a US-based data analytics group, to develop a new patient data platform has caused major outcry because of the company's poor reputation and past experiences, which include the use of Palantir data in the US to locate and prosecute parents of immigrant children.[74] Moreover, an investigation revealed that the UK Biobank shared health data with insurance firms, despite pledging not to.[75] In particular, Big Tech companies' track record of data protection infringements[76] has arguably made them the leading source of individuals' mistrust in sharing health data with commercial actors. Indeed, recent surveys have found respondents to be least willing to share their health data with digital technology companies.[77] This type of commercial involvement has previously led to large opt-outs in health data sharing schemes,[78] which offers confirmation of individuals' mistrust. This lack of trust towards commercial involvement in healthcare could in part be explained by individuals' general lack of knowledge of the large role that industry plays in publicly financed healthcare systems.[79] Acknowledging these concerns, legislators in the EHDS have set out a list of prohibited purposes for the secondary use of health data, such as advertising, increasing insurance premiums or developing harmful products.[80]

Even if it would not be fair to see commercial actors as 'the bad guys',[81] it seems obvious that these data users need to be reliable and have a good data protection track record; otherwise, confidence and fairness in sharing health data with them may be severely undermined. As argued by Davis, while addressing issues in digital health such as access to health data in the EHDS is a legitimate concern, there is a risk that 'the issue could itself become a trojan horse … that legitimises sweeping access to health data for private actors'.[82] On the other hand, knowing that the harm of health data misuses for individuals can be irreversible and the financial benefits for data users massive, it cannot be expected that the penalties under Article 99 EHDS will be sufficiently dissuasive. During the legislative process, patient groups made calls to strengthen these sanctions, arguing: '(F)ines must be transparent, proportionate, and harmonised between Member States to ensure the same level of protection for all patients across the EU'.[83] The establishment of various general conditions for the imposition of administrative fines by HDABs[84] represents a significant step towards achieving proportionate and harmonised sanctions across MS. While individuals have the right to lodge complaints with digital health authorities,[85] their protection against health data misuses appears to be fairly limited, especially given that individuals will likely remain unaware of how their health data is used. Moreover, some have criticised that the sanctions against data users do not adequately emulate the sensitivity of the data, especially given that other enforcement frameworks offer more severe sanctions, such as the 6% on the worldwide annual turnover in the Digital Services Act (DSA)[86] as opposed to the 4% introduced by the EHDS.[87] Therefore, it seems that commercial actors will need to gain the trust of individuals through evidence of good practices of secondary use of health data in the EHDS.

Furthermore, with the involvement of commercial actors in secondary use of health data, the question of demonstrating public interest, which as we have already established is a key element for achieving fairness, is all the more important. In fact, the GDPR's explicit mention that sensitive data use for scientific research purposes must offer '*substantial* public interest'[88] may suggest that uses with a primary commercial motivation do not meet the conditions under the research exemption.[89] Moreover, the European Data Protection Supervisor's Preliminary Opinion on data protection and scientific research[90] highlights the importance of the public interest intention, citing European case law that infers that public interest implies 'a "pressing social need", as opposed to largely private or commercial advantages'. Prominent research organisations, such as BBMRI-ERIC, have also supported this interpretation of the GDPR, arguing that the research exemption should be restricted to public interest research.[91] Therefore, while the GDPR does not prohibit commercial research, the importance of the public interest condition seems to significantly limit the types of commercial health data use. Chapter 8 discusses public interest and the role of industry and private enterprises in greater detail.

Notably, under the EHDS proposal, the interpretation of public interest was extended beyond that of the GDPR to include innovation purposes and

AI training and testing, which are less clearly in the public interest. To address this legal inconsistency, the '(i) development and innovation activities for products or services and (ii) training, testing and evaluating of algorithms, including in medical devices, in vitro diagnostic medical devices, AI systems and digital health applications'[92] have now been included under the scientific research umbrella in the text of the regulation.

7.5 Benefit sharing

A fair secondary use of health data should entail a certain level of reciprocity or benefit sharing for individuals who share their data and for society at large. The requirement in the EHDS for health data access bodies to publicly share a summary of the results obtained through electronic health data uses contributes, as acknowledged in the regulation, 'to ensuring fair and transparent processing'.[93] A sound application of the fairness principle probably requires going further. For example, findings that are actionable and relevant for individuals or target groups should be properly communicated,[94] something which was not initially required in the proposal. The final text instead specifically stipulates that 'health data users shall inform the health data access body of any significant finding related to the health of the natural person whose data are included in the dataset'.[95] An important and welcome provision in the regulation also foresees a way to determine when these findings are significant, stipulating the EHDS Board shall create:

> In consultation and cooperation with relevant stakeholders, including representatives of patients, health professionals and researchers, guidelines in order to help health data users to fulfil their duties under Article 61(5), and in particular to determine whether their findings are clinically significant.[96]

Nevertheless, the EHDS does not mandate that the outcomes of this research be made directly available to the individuals whose data were used or to the target group of the research, when, in all logic, they should be the first to benefit from these outcomes in a proactive way. As claimed by Barbara Prainsack, '(R)ight now, commercial profits are being made with data, but communities are not receiving a fair share of the benefits'.[97] Under the EHDS, this may mean that persons trying to access the outcomes of health data research may face financial or other restrictions, in spite of their health data being used to develop the treatment. As argued by Cohen and others, '[A]s a matter of fairness, those who contribute the most to developing a model, including patients who contribute their data, should proportionally enjoy its benefits'.[98] We should seek to avoid perpetuating situations of unfair access, such as in the COVID-19 pandemic where access to vaccines was largely dominated by wealthier countries.[99] Perpetuating disparities in access to vital preventive healthcare interventions could occur, if those individuals, who stand to benefit the most from the outcomes of secondary use research, face unfair access restrictions. In failing to ensure that benefits are equitably shared with individuals, the EHDS could stand to face similar criticisms emerging from the WHO Pandemic Treaty negotiations, where wealthy states are failing to commit to demands for benefit sharing with poorer states.[100] In addressing these concerns, Recital 61 of the EHDS notes the importance of setting fair prices and enhancing access to the outcomes of secondary uses of health data:

> In particular, the secondary use of health data for research and development purposes should contribute to benefiting to society in the form of new medicines, medical devices and health care products and services at affordable and fair prices for Union citizens, as well as to enhancing access to and the availability of such products and services in all Member States.

Another important aspect to ensure benefit sharing in secondary use of health data is to ensure that secondary use does not disadvantage certain groups. In particular, the use of AI technologies, which have been found to embed biases against often-marginalised groups,[101] highlights the need to ensure that the secondary use of health data does not lead to worse outcomes for the individuals involved. Key to addressing any resulting biases from the secondary use of health data is the need for greater transparency and explainability. For instance, if a person's health data has been used to assign them a label or a profile, they should be informed about this and given an opportunity to challenge this or seek redress.[102] This seems important to ensure benefit sharing, especially in welfare states, where all individuals contribute to financing the healthcare system and are therefore entitled to equitable treatment. Furthermore, there seems to be an opportunity to use data-driven tools like AI to increase benefit sharing, by assisting data users with their responsibilities. For example, AI technologies could be helpful in communicating the results or outcomes of secondary data uses to individuals.

The involvement of commercial actors in the EHDS, while raising some concerns about the distribution of benefits, may however, in some ways, meet the principle of benefit sharing. This is because the Regulation makes all health data available for secondary use, regardless of whether this is from a public or private healthcare provider, organisation or other entity.[103] Therefore, health data from commercial actors that have traditionally been out of reach for academic institutions, for example, will now be available for secondary use. In this way, the EHDS seems to make health data use fairer by allowing access to all health data, ultimately making health data research more equitable and representative. However, it remains to be seen how the issues surrounding intellectual property (IP) rights held by many commercial actors will be addressed by the responsible HDABs.

Throughout the legislative process, industry players, such as pharmaceutical companies, lobbied for greater protections over their health data, including the possibility to challenge (and at times refuse) access to health data in order to protect their IP rights.[104] Given that patents and intellectual property rights are less commonly obtained in academia in comparison to industry,[105] this scenario would likely create an asymmetrical relationship in which industry players are able to access health data from public research institutions, whereas researchers will be met with data access rejections on the basis of IP rights and trade secrets protection. In the spirit of fairness, it seems that if one asks people to surrender control over their health data, the beneficiaries of this data should also to a large extent surrender their IP rights. Indeed, the Regulation notes, '[I]n order to fully exploit the benefits of secondary use, *all* health data holders should contribute to this effort'.[106] Recognising the importance of widening access to all available health data, the EHDS sets conditions for accessing and using health data protected by IP rights and trade secrets. Only when granting access to health data 'entails a serious risk'[107] is the access body allowed to refuse access to the health data user. In this sense, all other measures to protect IP rights and trade secrets should be explored before refusing access. However, given that the HDABs will likely 'not have the technical, scientific, commercial, or economic expertise to evaluate whether data constitutes a trade secret',[108] determining when access to health data incurs a serious risk and when it does not will likely be subject to large discrepancies across HDABs.

Moreover, while the return of benefits to individuals is not foreseen, it is important to recognise that the EHDS seems to bring about benefits that can be returned on a societal level.[109] For example, the secondary use of health data may generate new knowledge of diseases in ways that do not benefit individuals but that may be said to bring about the social benefit of expanding scientific knowledge.

7.6 Conclusion

Much of the discussion surrounding the secondary use of health data has often referred to the need for fair data processing. However, how this fairness can be ensured in practice through regulation has often been lacking from the discussion. This chapter helps to understand how the EHDS Regulation addresses some of the fairness-related concerns in the secondary use of health data. We discussed how the lack of clarity regarding what is understood to be in the public interest is concerning, especially having considered the key role that public interest holds as a legal and ethical basis for the secondary use of health data in the EHDS. There is room for including patient and citizen representatives in the oversight of the data access decisions, including those related to public interest. This would help oversight bodies like the HDABs to ensure that access requests made in the name of the public interest are legitimate and appropriately accommodate the views of the public themselves.

The discussion on the use of opt-out as a potential solution to concerns over control of health data by individuals seems to address some of the fairness-related concerns. However, the compromise arrived at in the regulation, which introduces the possibility for MS to introduce exceptions to opt-out for reasons of public interest (Recital 54), may bring about important divergences in how this limitation is applied across countries, especially given the lack of a common understanding of what is in the public interest. Moreover, while the importance of making the opt-out process understandable and accessible has been highlighted, it remains to be seen how this will be implemented in practice. How will individuals be notified of their right to opt-out? What will this notification include? Will individuals have a single access point to opt-out of secondary use of heath data, or will this have to be notified to each of the HDABs independently? These are just a few of the questions that will need to be addressed in the implementation phase.

Concerns about use of health data by commercial actors were also discussed. Importantly, when it comes to secondary uses for scientific research, EHDS is agnostic to the commercial versus public nature of data use which seems to fail to adequately address concerns about the expansion of commercial or private actors into healthcare. That said, provisions under Recital 54 regarding overrides on individuals' right to opt-out from such secondary uses of health data seem to limit the scope of those rights by stipulating:

> Such overrides should only be available to health data users that are public sector bodies, or relevant Union institutions, bodies, offices, or agencies, entrusted with the performance of tasks in the area of public health, or to another entity entrusted with the performance of public tasks in the area of public health or acting on behalf of or commissioned by a public authority, and only where the data cannot be obtained by alternative means in a timely and effective manner.

Furthermore, in order to ensure that access is fair for all data users, commercial data holders should not exploit their claims over IP rights and trade secrets in order to obstruct access to their datasets. A fair secondary use of health data under the EHDS requires that all data is made available, not only those which are held by the public sector. The Regulation's efforts in making all health data accessible, even when this is protected by IP rights and trade secrets, serves as a reassurance of its commitment to the fairness principle.

Finally, a discussion of benefit sharing is largely missing from the EHDS. While the EHDS introduces new obligations for HDABs to return findings to individuals, we argue that benefit sharing requires going further, by setting conditions for the benefits of secondary uses to be tangibly returned to society. Once again, here HDABs and citizens could jointly develop follow-up procedures to assess the impacts of health data uses, including the resulting benefits. Moreover, as stipulated in the Regulation, measures should be taken to address any intellectual property and trade secret claims that have the potential to increase disparities between industry and academia in data access. To uphold fairness, a balance must be struck between protecting these interests and ensuring equitable data access.

All in all, it is important not to view fairness as a simple check-box exercise and acknowledge that 'being "fair" and "ethical" are not fixed elements granted to a subject with certification-based procedures and compliance exercises'.[110] It is important to view fairness as an evolving concept, 'subject to a periodic re-evaluation',[111] where engaged and continuous discussion with individuals is essential. Being fair is an ethical commitment that needs to be actionable, operationalised, monitored and part of the standard procedures. If we want to guarantee that the EHDS is a fair data-sharing ecosystem for individuals, we must take action to ensure that appeals to fairness are not just empty words.

Acknowledgement

This work was supported by the Special Research Fund (BOF) at Ghent University and by PROPHET (A Personalized Prevention Roadmap for the Future Healthcare) which is funded by the European Commission under the Horizon Europe Research and Innovation Programme (grant agreement 101057721).

Notes

1 Nicole Mauer and Dimitra Panteli, 'Implementing Digital Solutions and AI – Public Debate on the Future Health Priorities of the European Union' (European Observatory on Health Systems and Policies 2023) https://eurohealthobservatory.who.int/publications/m/implementing-digital-solutions-and-ai accessed 6 March 2024; Digital Europe, 'DIGITALEUROPE Executive Council for Health's Recommendations for EU Digital Health Policy (2024-29)' (*DIGITALEUROPE*, 20 February 2024) https://www.digitaleurope.org/resources/digitaleurope-recommendations-eu-digital-health-policy-2024-29/ accessed 13 March 2024; European Commission, 'Speech by Commissioner Stella Kyriakides to the Future Of Health Summit – "Digitalisation as a Driver for Sustainable and Resilient Global Health"' (10 December 2023) https://ec.europa.eu/commission/presscorner/detail/fr/speech_23_4947 accessed 13 March 2024.
2 Essam H Houssein, Rehab E Mohamed and Abdelmgeid A Ali, 'Heart Disease Risk Factors Detection from Electronic Health Records Using Advanced NLP and Deep Learning Techniques' (2023) 13 *Scientific Reports* 7173.
3 Jessica E Stockdale, Pengyu Liu and Caroline Colijn, 'The Potential of Genomics for Infectious Disease Forecasting' (2022) 7 *Nature Microbiology* 1736.
4 Tania Pereira and others, 'Sharing Biomedical Data: Strengthening AI Development in Healthcare' (2021) 9 *Healthcare* 827.
5 Sari Palojoki, Lasse Lehtonen and Riikka Vuokko, 'Semantic Interoperability of Electronic Health Records: Systematic Review of Alternative Approaches for Enhancing Patient Information Availability' (2024) 12 *JMIR Medical Informatics* e53535.
6 TEHDAS (Joint Action Towards the European Health Data Space), 'Report on Secondary Use of Health Data through European Case Studies.' (28 February 2022) https://tehdas.eu/results/tehdas-suggests-options-to-overcome-data-barriers/ accessed 21 April 2023.
7 Johan Hansen and others, Assessment of the EU Member States' rules on health data in the light of GDPR (European Commission, Consumers, Health, Agriculture and Food Executive Agency Publications Office, 2021) 262.
8 Johan Hansen and others, Assessment of the EU Member States' rules on health data in the light of GDPR (European Commission, Consumers, Health, Agriculture and Food Executive Agency Publications Office, 2021) 262.
9 Santa Slokenberga, 'Setting the Foundations: Individual Rights, Public Interest, Scientific Research and Biobanking' in Santa Slokenberga, Olga Tzortzatou and

Jane Reichel (eds), *GDPR and Biobanking. Law, Governance, and Technology Series* (volume 43, Springer Cham 2021) 11.

10 Fruzsina Molnár-Gábor and others, 'Harmonization after the GDPR? Divergences in the Rules for Genetic and Health Data Sharing in Four Member States and Ways to Overcome Them by EU Measures: Insights from Germany, Greece, Latvia and Sweden' (2022) 84 *Seminars in Cancer Biology* 271.

11 Directorate-General for Health and Food Safety (European Commission), 'European Health Data Space' (17 November 2023) https://health.ec.europa.eu/ehealth-digital-health-and-care/european-health-data-space_en accessed 9 December 2023.

12 Laura Sikstrom and others, 'Conceptualising Fairness: Three Pillars for Medical Algorithms and Health Equity' (2022) 29 *BMJ Health & Care Informatics* e100459; Benedetta Giovanola and Simona Tiribelli, 'Beyond Bias and Discrimination: Redefining the AI Ethics Principle of Fairness in Healthcare Machine-Learning Algorithms' (2023) 38 *AI & Society* 549.

13 Patricia Cervera de la Cruz and Mahsa Shabani, 'Conceptualizing Fairness in the Secondary Use of Health Data for Research: A Scoping Review' (2023) *Accountability in Research*. https://doi.org/10.1080/08989621.2023.2271394 accessed 23 October 2023.

14 Annie Sorbie, 'Sharing Confidential Health Data for Research Purposes in the UK: Where Are "Publics" in the Public Interest?' (2020) 16 *Evidence & Policy* 249.

15 Mark J Taylor and Tess Whitton, 'Public Interest, Health Research and Data Protection Law: Establishing a Legitimate Trade-Off between Individual Control and Research Access to Health Data' (2020) 9 *Laws* 6.

16 EHDS Proposal Recital 1.

17 Maret Kruus, 'The Public Interest Requirement in the Secondary Use of Health Data in Scientific Research: The Examples of Estonia and Finland' (2023) 32 *Juridica International* 64.

18 Digital Europe, 'Making the Most of the GDPR to Advance Health Research' (*DIGITALEUROPE*, 6 November 2021) https://www.digitaleurope.org/resources/making-the-most-of-the-gdpr-to-advance-health-research/ accessed 28 March 2024.

19 EHDS Article 53.

20 EHDS Article 53(1)(e).

21 Regulation (EU) 2022/868 of the European Parliament and of the Council of 30 May 2022 on European data governance and amending Regulation (EU) 2018/1724 (Data Governance Act) (Text with EEA relevance) 2022 OJ L 152/1.

22 Angela Ballantyne, 'Adjusting the Focus: A Public Health Ethics Approach to Data Research' (2019) 33 *Bioethics* 357; David Townend, 'Conclusion: Harmonisation in Genomic and Health Data Sharing for Research: An Impossible Dream?' (2018) 137 *Human Genetics* 657; Angela Ballantyne and G Owen Schaefer, 'Consent and the Ethical Duty to Participate in Health Data Research' (2018) 44 *Journal of Medical Ethics* 392.

23 Stefanie Brückner and others, 'The Social Contract for Health and Wellness Data Sharing Needs a Trusted Standardized Consent' (2023) 1 *Mayo Clinic Proceedings: Digital Health* 527.

24 TEHDAS (Joint Action Towards the European Health Data Space), 'Citizens' Perception of and Engagement with Health Data Secondary Use and Sharing in Europe – A Literature Review' (2021) https://tehdas.eu/results/individuals-favour-data-sharing-and-use-if-benefits-are-clear/ accessed 22 April 2023.

25 Marieke Bak and others, 'You Can't Have AI Both Ways: Balancing Health Data Privacy and Access Fairly' (2022) 13 Frontiers in Genetics 929453.

26 Involve, Carnegie UK Trust and Understanding Patient Data, 'Data for Public Benefit: Balancing the Risks and Benefits of Data Sharing' (April 2018) https://understandingpatientdata.org.uk/data-public-benefit-risks-and-benefits-data-sharing accessed 23 April 2023; Reema Patel, 'The Foundations of Fairness for NHS Health Data Sharing' (Understanding Patient Data and Ada Lovelace Institute, 12 March 2020) https://www.adalovelaceinstitute.org/blog/the-foundations-of-fairness-for-nhs-health-data-sharing/ accessed 16 October 2023; Henrietta Hopkins and others,

'Putting Good into Practice: A Public Dialogue on Making Public Benefit Assessments When Using Health and Care Data' (Hopkins Van Mil, 2021) https://assets.publishing.service.gov.uk/media/6075700dd3bf7f4017cbef72/PGiP_Report_FINAL_1304.pdf accessed 7 May 2024; Mhairi Aitken and others, 'Who Benefits and How? Public Expectations of Public Benefits from Data-Intensive Health Research' (2018) 5 *Big Data & Society* 2053951718816724.

27 Taylor and Whitton (n 15).

28 Barbara Prainsack and Seliem El-Sayed, 'Beyond Individual Rights: How Data Solidarity Gives People Meaningful Control over Data' (2023) 23(11) *The American Journal of Bioethics* 36.

29 Involve, Carnegie UK Trust and Understanding Patient Data (n 26).

30 EHDS Article 57(1)(a).

31 EHDS Recital 30.

32 EHDSArticle 19(5).

33 Joint Statement, 'Stakeholder Coalition Calls for Legislative Refinement of the EHDS' (*DIGITALEUROPE*, 12 April 2023). https://www.digitaleurope.org/news/stakeholder-coalition-calls-for-legislative-refinement-of-the-ehds/ accessed 7 December 2023.

34 EHDS, Article 93(1).

35 EHDS Article 93(4).

36 Sam HA Muller, 'Patients' and Publics' Preferences for Data-Intensive Health Research Governance: Survey Study' (2022) 9(3) *JMIR Human Factors* e36797; Minerva C Rivas Velarde and others, 'Citizens' Views on Sharing Their Health Data: The Role of Competence, Reliability and Pursuing the Common Good' (2021) 22 *BMC Medical Ethics* 62; Karen Spencer and others, 'Patient Perspectives on Sharing Anonymized Personal Health Data Using a Digital System for Dynamic Consent and Research Feedback: A Qualitative Study' (2016) 18 *Journal of Medical Internet Research* e5011.

37 Cervera de la Cruz and Shabani (n 13).

38 World Medical Association, 'Declaration of Helsinki – Ethical Principles for Medical Research Involving Human Subjects' (2013) https://www.wma.net/policies-post/wma-declaration-of-helsinki-ethical-principles-for-medical-research-involving-human-subjects/ accessed 7 March 2024.

39 Council for International Organizations of Medical Sciences (CIOMS), *International Ethical Guidelines for Health-Related Research Involving Humans* (4th Edition, 2016) https://cioms.ch/publications/product/international-ethical-guidelines-for-health-related-research-involving-humans/ accessed 7 March 2024.

40 Eugenijus Gefenas and others, 'Controversies between Regulations of Research Ethics and Protection of Personal Data: Informed Consent at a Cross-Road' (2022) 25 *Medicine, Health Care and Philosophy* 23.

41 Data Protection Commission, 'Guidance on Legal Bases for Processing Personal Data' (Data Protection Commission 2019) https://www.dataprotection.ie/dpc-guidance/guidance-legal-bases-processing-personal-data accessed 23 August 2024.

42 European Data Protection Board (EDPB), 'Opinion 3/2019 Concerning the Questions and Answers on the Interplay between the Clinical Trials Regulation (CTR) and the General Data Protection Regulation (GDPR)' (2019) 23 January 2019.

43 Hansen and others (n 7).

44 Jiahong Chen, Edward S Dove and Himani Bhakuni, 'Explicit Consent and Alternative Data Protection Processing Grounds for Health Research' in Eleni Kosta, Ronald Leenes and Irene Kamara (eds), *Research Handbook on EU Data Protection Law* (Elgar, 2022).

45 European Commission, 'Commission Staff Working Document, Impact Assessment Report accompanying the document Proposal for a Regulation of the European Parliament and of the Council on the European Health Data Space' (3 May 2022) Swd(2022) 131 Final, 13.

46 European Commission, Proposal for a Regulation of the European Parliament and of the Council on the European Health Data Space 2022.Article 33 (5).
47 European Parliament, 'Amendments Adopted by the European Parliament on 13 December 2023 on the Proposal for a Regulation of the European Parliament and of the Council on the European Health Data Space (COM(2022)0197 – C9-0167/2022 – 2022/0140(COD))1'.
48 Francisca Nordfalk and Klaus Hoeyer, 'The Rise and Fall of an Opt-out System' (2020) 48 *Scandinavian Journal of Public Health* 400.
49 John Tazare and others, *NHS National Data Opt-Outs: Trends and Potential Consequences for Health Data Research* (2024) BJGP Open.
50 Finnish Social and Health Data Permit Authority (FINDATA), 'How Can I Prohibit the Secondary Use of My Data?' (Findata) https://findata.fi/en/faq/how-can-i-prohibit-the-secondary-use-of-my-data/ accessed 14 March 2024.
51 EHDS Article 71(2).
52 Martin Greenacre, 'Proposal on Health Data Access for Research Falters over Patient Consent' (*Science|Business*, 3 December 2024) https://sciencebusiness.net/news/data/proposal-health-data-access-research-falters-over-patient-consent accessed 13 March 2024.
53 Nordfalk and Hoeyer (n 48).
54 EHDS, Article 71(1).
55 EHDS Article 71(1).
56 EHDS Recital 54.
57 EHDS Recital 54.
58 Mari Eccles, 'Pharma, Medtech Lose Out in EU Deal on Health Data' *POLITICO* (20 March 2024) https://pro.politico.eu/news/177333 accessed 26 March 2024.
59 EHDS Recital 18.
60 Andrea Martani and others, 'Regulating the Secondary Use of Data for Research: Arguments Against Genetic Exceptionalism' (2019) 10 *Frontiers in Genetics* 1254.
61 Dixie B Baker, Jane Kaye and Sharon F Terry, 'Governance Through Privacy, Fairness, and Respect for Individuals' (2016) 4 *eGEMs* 1207.
62 Sven Zenker and others, 'Data Protection-Compliant Broad Consent for Secondary Use of Health Care Data and Human Biosamples for (Bio)Medical Research: Towards a New German National Standard' (2022) 131 *Journal of Biomedical Informatics* 104096.
63 Brückner and others (n 23).
64 '597/22 Entschließung des Bundesrates zur Ausgestaltung eines Gesundheits datennutzungsgesetzes' (*Bundesrat*, 22 November 2022) https://www.bundesrat.de/SharedDocs/beratungsvorgaenge/2022/0501-0600/0597-22.html accessed 11 December 2023 cited in Brückner and others (n 23).
65 Roberta Biasiotto and others, 'Public Preferences for Digital Health Data Sharing: Discrete Choice Experiment Study in 12 European Countries' (2023) 25 *Journal of Medical Internet Research* e47066.
66 Spencer and others (n 36).
67 Megan Prictor, Harriet JA Teare and Jane Kaye, 'Equitable Participation in Biobanks: The Risks and Benefits of a "Dynamic Consent" Approach' (2018) 6 *Frontiers in Public Health*. DOI: 10.3389/fpubh.2018.00253.
68 Luca Marelli and others, 'The European Health Data Space: Too Big To Succeed?' (2023) *Health Policy* 104861. DOI: 10.1016/j.healthpol.2023.104861.
69 Joint Statement (n 33).
70 Daiju Ueda and others, 'Fairness of Artificial Intelligence in Healthcare: Review and Recommendations' (2023) Japanese Journal of Radiology (2024) 42 *Japanese Journal of Radiology* 3.
71 Katharina Ó Cathaoir, 'In Search of Solidarity: Personalised Medicine in Denmark' (2019) (21–22) Nordisk socialrättslig tidskrift 65.
72 Brückner and others (n 23).

73 European Commission, 'Annex to the Commission Implementing Decision of 5.12.2023 on the Financing of the Programme for the Union's Action in the Field of Health ("EU4Health Programme") and the Adoption of the Work Programme for 2024' (12 May 2023). https://health.ec.europa.eu/publications/2024-eu4health-work-programme_en accessed 12 December 2023.
74 Sara LM Davis, 'The Trojan Horse' (2020) 22 Health and Human Rights 41.
75 Shanti Das, 'Private UK Health Data Donated for Medical Research Shared with Insurance Companies' *The Observer* (12 November 2023). https://www.theguardian.com/technology/2023/nov/12/private-uk-health-data-donated-medical-research-shared-insurance-companies accessed 13 November 2023.
76 European Data Protection Board (EDPB), '1.2 Billion Euro Fine for Facebook as a Result of EDPB Binding Decision' (22 May 2023) https://edpb.europa.eu/news/news/2023/12-billion-euro-fine-facebook-result-edpb-binding-decision_en accessed 11 December 2023; EDPB, 'The CNIL's Restricted Committee Imposes a Financial Penalty of 50 Million Euros against GOOGLE LLC' (21 January 2019). https://edpb.europa.eu/news/national-news/2019/cnils-restricted-committee-imposes-financial-penalty-50-million-euros_en accessed 11 December 2023.
77 Biasiotto and others (n 65); The European Consumer Organisation (BEUC), 'Consumer Attitudes to Health Data Sharing. Survey Results from Eight EU Countries.' (2023). https://www.beuc.eu/press-releases/consumers-uneasy-sharing-their-health-data-survey-shows; Ravi Aggarwal and others, 'Patient Perceptions on Data Sharing and Applying Artificial Intelligence to Health Care Data: Cross-Sectional Survey' (2021) 23 *Journal of Medical Internet Research* e26162.
78 Peter Walker, 'Why Has the NHS Patient Data-Sharing Scheme Been Pushed Back?' *The Guardian* (8 June 2021) https://www.theguardian.com/society/2021/jun/06/why-are-there-calls-for-a-pause-to-patient-data-sharing-scheme accessed 7 December 2023; Smitha Mundasad, 'NHS Data-Sharing Project Scrapped' *BBC News* (6 July 2016) https://www.bbc.com/news/health-36723486 accessed 7 December 2023.
79 Lotte Groth Jensen and Mette N Svendsen, 'Personalised Medicine in the Danish Welfare State: Political Visions for the Public Good' (2022) 32 *Critical Public Health* 713.
80 EHDS Article 54.
81 '5 Questions about Digital Sustainability To… Professor Barbara Prainsack' (*INNOPAY*, 12 May 2023) https://www.innopay.com/en/publications/5-questions-about-digital-sustainability-professor-barbara-prainsack accessed 11 December 2023.
82 Davis (n 74).
83 European Patients Forum, 'European Patients Forum Statement on EHDS' (November 2022). https://www.eu-patient.eu/news/latest-epf-news/2022/epf-statement-on-ehds/ accessed 6 March 2024.
84 EHDS Article 64.
85 EHDS Article 81.
86 Regulation (EU) 2022/2065 of the European Parliament and of the Council of 19 October 2022 on a Single Market For Digital Services and amending Directive 2000/31/EC (Digital Services Act) (Text with EEA relevance) 2022 (OJ L).
87 EHDS Article 64(5).
88 Article 9(2)(g). Emphasis added.
89 Paul Quinn, 'Research under the GDPR – a Level Playing Field for Public and Private Sector Research?' (2021) 17 Life Sciences, Society and Policy 4.
90 European Data Protection Supervisor (EDPS), 'Preliminary Opinion on Data Protection and Scientific Research.' (2020) 6 January 2020.
91 Mahsa Shabani and Pascal Borry, 'Rules for Processing Genetic Data for Research Purposes in View of the New EU General Data Protection Regulation' (2018) 26 *European Journal of Human Genetics* 149.
92 EHDS Article 53(e).
93 EHDS Recital 66.

94 Cervera de la Cruz and Shabani (n 13).
95 Article 61(5).
96 Article 94(2)(c).
97 Innopay (n 81).
98 I Glen Cohen and others, 'The Legal and Ethical Concerns That Arise from Using Complex Predictive Analytics in Health Care' (2014) 33 *Health Affairs* 1139.
99 Edouard Mathieu and others, 'Coronavirus Pandemic (COVID-19)' (2020) Our World in Data https://ourworldindata.org/covid-vaccinations accessed 6 March 2024.
100 The Lancet, 'The Pandemic Treaty: Shameful and Unjust' (2024) 403 *The Lancet* 781.
101 Ziad Obermeyer and others, 'Dissecting Racial Bias in an Algorithm Used to Manage the Health of Populations' (2019) 366 *Science* 447; Darshali A Vyas, Leo G Eisenstein and David S Jones, 'Hidden in Plain Sight – Reconsidering the Use of Race Correction in Clinical Algorithms' (2020) 383 *New England Journal of Medicine* 874; Poppy Noor, 'Can We Trust AI Not to Further Embed Racial Bias and Prejudice?' (2020) 368 *BMJ* m363.
102 Giovanola and Tiribelli (n 12).
103 EHDS Recital 59.
104 European Confederation of Pharmaceutical Entrepreneurs, 'The European Health Data Space Common Statement on the Amendment Proposals of the Council of the EU and the European Parliament' (Hogan Lovells, December 2023). https://www.hoganlovells.com/-/media/hogan-lovells/global/knowledge/publications/files/2024/common-statement-eucope_hogan-lovells-ehds_final_feb2024.pdf; European Federation of Pharmaceutical Industries and Associations, 'European Health Data Space: Key Aspects to Be Considered in the Trilogue Discussions' (31 January 2024). https://www.efpia.eu/news-events/the-efpia-view/statements-press-releases/european-health-data-space-key-aspects-to-be-considered-in-the-trilogue-discussions/ accessed 13 March 2024.
105 Francesco Lissoni and others, 'Academic Patenting in Europe: New Evidence from the KEINS Database' (2008) 17 Research Evaluation 87; Aldo Geuna and Lionel JJ Nesta, 'University Patenting and Its Effects on Academic Research: The Emerging European Evidence' (2006) 35(6) *Research Policy* 790.
106 EHDS Recital 55. Emphasis added.
107 Article 52(5).
108 European Federation of Pharmaceutical Industries and Associations (n 103).
109 EHDS Recital 53.
110 Petros Terzis, 'Onward for the Freedom of Others: Marching beyond the AI Ethics', Proceedings of the 2020 Conference on Fairness, Accountability, and Transparency (2020) 220.
111 Laurens Naudts, 'Algorithmic Governance: The Position of Fairness' (*Robotics & AI Law Society – RAILS*, 12 October 2019) https://ai-laws.org/2019/10/12/algorithmic-governance-the-position-of-fairness/ accessed 20 June 2023.

List of sources

Legislation and conventions

Regulation (EU) 2016/679 of the European Parliament and of the Council of 27 April 2016 on the protection of natural persons with regard to the processing of personal data and on the free movement of such data, and repealing Directive 95/46/EC (General Data Protection Regulation, GDPR) OJ L 119/1.

Regulation (EU) 2022/868 of the European Parliament and of the Council of 30 May 2022 on European data governance and amending Regulation (EU) 2018/1724 (Data Governance Act) (Text with EEA relevance) 2022 (OJ L).

'597/22 Entschließung des Bundesrates zur Ausgestaltung eines Gesundheitsdaten-nutzungsgesetzes' (*Bundesrat*, 22 November 2022) https://www.bundesrat.de/SharedDocs/beratungsvorgaenge/2022/0501-0600/0597-22.html accessed 11 December 2023

Policy Documents

Council for International Organizations of Medical Sciences (CIOMS), *International Ethical Guidelines for Health-Related Research Involving Humans* (4th Edition, 2016) https://cioms.ch/publications/product/international-ethical-guidelines-for-health-related-research-involving-humans/

Council of the European Union, 'Proposal for a Regulation on the European Health Data Space-Analysis of the final compromise text with a view to agreement' 2022/0140(COD)

European Data Protection Board (EDPB), 'Opinion 3/2019 Concerning the Questions and Answers on the Interplay between the Clinical Trials Regulation (CTR) and the General Data Protection Regulation (GDPR)' (2019). https://edpb.europa.eu/our-work-tools/our-documents/opinion-art-70/opinion-32019-concerning-questions-and-answers_en accessed 9 December 2023

European Data Protection Supervisor (EDPS), 'Preliminary Opinion on Data Protection and Scientific Research.' (2020) 20 January 2020 https://edps.europa.eu/sites/edp/files/publication/2001-06_opinion_research_en.pdf

European Parliament, 'Amendments Adopted by the European Parliament on 13 December 2023 on the Proposal for a Regulation of the European Parliament and of the Council on the European Health Data Space (COM(2022)0197 – C9-0167/2022 – 2022/0140(COD))1' (n.d.).

Proposal for a Regulation of the European Parliament and of The Council on the European Health Data Space (EHDS proposal) (n.d.). COM/2022/197 final.

TEHDAS (Joint Action Towards the European Health Data Space), 'Report on Secondary Use of Health Data through European Case Studies.' (28 February 2022). https://tehdas.eu/results/tehdas-suggests-options-to-overcome-data-barriers/ accessed 21 April 2023

TEHDAS (Joint Action Towards the European Health Data Space), 'Citizens' Perception of and Engagement with Health Data Secondary Use and Sharing in Europe – A Literature Review' (2021). https://tehdas.eu/results/individuals-favour-data-sharing-and-use-if-benefits-are-clear/ accessed 22 April 2023

World Medical Association, 'Declaration of Helsinki – Ethical Principles for Medical Research Involving Human Subjects' (n.d.). https://www.wma.net/policies-post/wma-declaration-of-helsinki-ethical-principles-for-medical-research-involving-human-subjects/

Literature and other secondary sources

'5 Questions about Digital Sustainability To… Professor Barbara Prainsack' (*INNOPAY*, 12 May 2023) https://www.innopay.com/en/publications/5-questions-about-digital-sustainability-professor-barbara-prainsack

'597/22 Entschließung des Bundesrates zur Ausgestaltung eines Gesundheitsdaten-nutzungsgesetzes' (*Bundesrat*, 22 November 2022) https://www.bundesrat.de/SharedDocs/beratungsvorgaenge/2022/0501-0600/0597-22.html

Aggarwal R and others, 'Patient Perceptions on Data Sharing and Applying Artificial Intelligence to Health Care Data: Cross-Sectional Survey' (2021) 23 *Journal of Medical Internet Research* e26162. DOI: 10.2196/26162

Aitken M and others, 'Who Benefits and How? Public Expectations of Public Benefits from Data-Intensive Health Research' (2018) 5 *Big Data & Society* 1–12. DOI: 10.1177/2053951718816724

Bak M and others, 'You Can't Have AI Both Ways: Balancing Health Data Privacy and Access Fairly' (2022) 13 *Frontiers in Genetics*. DOI 10.3389/fgene.2022.929453

Baker DB, Kaye J and Terry SF, 'Governance Through Privacy, Fairness, and Respect for Individuals' (2016) 4(2) *eGEMs* 7 DOI: 10.13063/2327-9214.1207

Ballantyne A, 'Adjusting the Focus: A Public Health Ethics Approach to Data Research' (2019) 33 *Bioethics* 357–366. DOI: 10.1111/bioe.12551

Ballantyne A and Schaefer GO, 'Consent and the Ethical Duty to Participate in Health Data Research' (2018) 44 *Journal of Medical Ethics* 392–396. DOI: 10.1136/medethics-2017-104550

Biasiotto R and others, 'Public Preferences for Digital Health Data Sharing: Discrete Choice Experiment Study in 12 European Countries' (2023) 25 *Journal of Medical Internet Research* e47066. DOI: 10.2196/47066

Brückner S and others, 'The Social Contract for Health and Wellness Data Sharing Needs a Trusted Standardized Consent' (2023) 1 *Mayo Clinic Proceedings: Digital Health* 527–533. DOI: 10.1016/j.mcpdig.2023.07.008

Cervera de la Cruz P and Shabani M, 'Conceptualizing Fairness in the Secondary Use of Health Data for Research: A Scoping Review' (2023) *Accountability in Research*. DOI: 10.1080/08989621.2023.2271394

Jiahong Chen, Edward S Dove and Himani Bhakuni, 'Explicit Consent and Alternative Data Protection Processing Grounds for Health Research' in Eleni Kosta, Ronald Leenes and Irene Kamara (eds), *Research Handbook on EU Data Protection Law* (Elgar, 2022) 474–502. DOI: 10.4337/9781800371682.00028

Cohen IG and others, 'The Legal And Ethical Concerns That Arise From Using Complex Predictive Analytics In Health Care' (2014) 33(7) *Health Affairs* 1139. DOI: 10.1377/hlthaff.2014.0048

Das S, 'Private UK Health Data Donated for Medical Research Shared with Insurance Companies' *The Observer* (12 November 2023). https://www.theguardian.com/technology/2023/nov/12/private-uk-health-data-donated-medical-research-shared-insurance-companies

Davis SLM, 'The Trojan Horse' (2020) 22(2) *Health and Human Rights* 41–48.

Digital Europe, 'Making the Most of the GDPR to Advance Health Research' (*DIGITALEUROPE*, 6 November 2021). https://www.digitaleurope.org/resources/making-the-most-of-the-gdpr-to-advance-health-research/

Digital Europe, 'DIGITALEUROPE Executive Council for Health's Recommendations for EU Digital Health Policy (2024-29)' (*DIGITALEUROPE*, 20 February 2024). https://www.digitaleurope.org/resources/digitaleurope-recommendations-eu-digital-health-policy-2024-29/ accessed 13 March 2024.

Directorate-General for Health and Food Safety (European Commission), 'European Health Data Space' (17 November 2023). https://health.ec.europa.eu/ehealth-digital-health-and-care/european-health-data-space_en

Eccles M, 'Pharma, Medtech Lose out in EU Deal on Health Data' *POLITICO* (20 March 2024). https://pro.politico.eu/news/177333

European Commission, 'Annex to the Commission Implementing Decision of 5.12.2023 on the Financing of the Programme for the Union's Action in the Field of Health ("EU4Health Programme") and the Adoption of the Work Programme for 2024' (12 May 2023). https://health.ec.europa.eu/publications/2024-eu4health-work-programme_en

European Commission, 'Speech by Commissioner Stella Kyriakides to the Future of Health Summit – "Digitalisation as a Driver for Sustainable and Resilient Global Health"' (*European Commission – European Commission*, 10 December 2023). https://ec.europa.eu/commission/presscorner/detail/fr/speech_23_4947

European Confederation of Pharmaceutical Entrepreneurs, 'The European Health Data Space Common Statement on the Amendment Proposals of the Council of the EU and the European Parliament.' (n.d.). https://www.hoganlovells.com/-/media/hogan-lovells/global/knowledge/publications/files/2024/common-statement-eucope_hogan-lovells-ehds_final_feb2024.pdf

European Data Protection Board (EDPB), 'The CNIL's Restricted Committee Imposes a Financial Penalty of 50 Million Euros against GOOGLE LLC' (21 January 2019). https://edpb.europa.eu/news/national-news/2019/cnils-restricted-committee-imposes-financial-penalty-50-million-euros_en

European Data Protection Board (EDPB), '1.2 Billion Euro Fine for Facebook as a Result of EDPB Binding Decision' (22 May 2023). https://edpb.europa.eu/news/news/2023/12-billion-euro-fine-facebook-result-edpb-binding-decision_en

European Federation of Pharmaceutical Industries and Associations, 'European Health Data Space: Key Aspects to Be Considered in the Trilogue Discussions' (31 January 2024). https://www.efpia.eu/news-events/the-efpia-view/statements-press-releases/european-health-data-space-key-aspects-to-be-considered-in-the-trilogue-discussions/

European Patients Forum, 'European Patients Forum Statement on EHDS' (November 2022). https://www.eu-patient.eu/news/latest-epf-news/2022/epf-statement-on-ehds/

Finnish Social and Health Data Permit Authority (FINDATA), 'How Can I Prohibit the Secondary Use of My Data?' (*Findata*, 2022). https://findata.fi/en/faq/how-can-i-prohibit-the-secondary-use-of-my-data/

Gefenas E and others, 'Controversies between Regulations of Research Ethics and Protection of Personal Data: Informed Consent at a Cross-Road' (2022) 25 *Medicine, Health Care and Philosophy* 23–30. DOI: 10.1007/s11019-021-10060-1

Geuna A and Nesta LJJ, 'University Patenting and Its Effects on Academic Research: The Emerging European Evidence' (2006) 35(6) *Research Policy* 790–807. DOI: 10.1016/j.respol.2006.04.005

Giovanola B and Tiribelli S, 'Beyond Bias and Discrimination: Redefining the AI Ethics Principle of Fairness in Healthcare Machine-Learning Algorithms' (2023) *AI & Society* 38, 549–563. DOI: 10.1007/s00146-022-01455-6

Greenacre M, 'Proposal on Health Data Access for Research Falters over Patient Consent' (*Science|Business*, 3 December 2024). https://sciencebusiness.net/news/data/proposal-health-data-access-research-falters-over-patient-consent

Hansen J., Wilson P., Verhoeve E., Korneman M., Kirwan M., Verheij R., van Veen EB, 'Assessment of the EU Member States' Rules on Health Data in the Light of GDPR' (2021) Publications Office. DOI: 10.2818/546193

Hopkins H and others, *Putting Good into Practice: A Public Dialogue on Making Public Benefit Assessments When Using Health and Care Data* (Hopkins Van Mil, 2021). https://assets.publishing.service.gov.uk/media/6075700dd3bf7f4017cbef72/PGiP_Report_FINAL_1304.pdf

Houssein EH, Mohamed RE and Ali AA, 'Heart Disease Risk Factors Detection from Electronic Health Records Using Advanced NLP and Deep Learning Techniques' (2023) 13 *Scientific Reports* 7173. DOI: 10.1038/s41598-023-34294-6

Involve, Carnegie UK Trust and Understanding Patient Data, 'Data for Public Benefit: Balancing the Risks and Benefits of Data Sharing' (April 2018). https://understandingpatientdata.org.uk/data-public-benefit-risks-and-benefits-data-sharing

Jensen LG and Svendsen MN, 'Personalised Medicine in the Danish Welfare State: Political Visions for the Public Good' (2022) 32(5) *Critical Public Health* 713–724. DOI: 10.1080/09581596.2021.1937524

Joint Statement, 'Stakeholder Coalition Calls for Legislative Refinement of the EHDS' (*DIGITALEUROPE*, 12 April 2023) https://www.digitaleurope.org/news/stakeholder-coalition-calls-for-legislative-refinement-of-the-ehds/

Kruus M, 'The Public Interest Requirement in the Secondary Use of Health Data in Scientific Research: The Examples of Estonia and Finland' (2023) 32 *Juridica International* 64–73. DOI: 10.12697/JI.2023.32.06

Lancet T, 'The Pandemic Treaty: Shameful and Unjust' (2024) 403(10429) *The Lancet* 781. DOI: 10.1016/S0140 6736(24)00410-0

Lissoni F and others, 'Academic Patenting in Europe: New Evidence from the KEINS Database' (2008) 17(2) *Research Evaluation* 87–102. DOI: 10.3152/095820208X287171

Marelli L and others, 'The European Health Data Space: Too big to Succeed?' (2023) 135 *Health Policy* 104861. DOI: 10.1016/j.healthpol.2023.104861

Martani A and others, 'Regulating the Secondary Use of Data for Research: Arguments Against Genetic Exceptionalism' (2019) *Frontiers in Genetics* 10, 1254. DOI: 10.3389/fgene.2019.01254

Mathieu E and others, 'Coronavirus Pandemic (COVID-19)' (2020) Our World in Data. https://ourworldindata.org/covid-vaccinations

Mauer N and Panteli D, 'Implementing Digital Solutions and AI – Public Debate on the Future Health Priorities of the European Union' (European Observatory on Health Systems and Policies 2023). https://eurohealthobservatory.who.int/publications/m/implementing-digital-solutions-and-ai

Molnár-Gábor F and others, 'Harmonization after the GDPR? Divergences in the Rules for Genetic and Health Data Sharing in Four Member States and Ways to Overcome Them by EU Measures: Insights from Germany, Greece, Latvia and Sweden' (2022) 84 *Seminars in Cancer Biology* 271–283. DOI: 10.1016/j.semcancer.2021.12.001

Muller SHA, 'Patients' and Publics' Preferences for Data-Intensive Health Research Governance: Survey Study' (2022) *JMIR Human Factors* 13. DOI: 10.1016/j.semcancer.2021.12.001

Naudts L, 'Algorithmic Governance: The Position of Fairness' (*Robotics & AI Law Society – RAILS*, 12 October 2019). https://ai-laws.org/2019/10/12/algorithmic-governance-the-position-of-fairness/

'NHS Data-Sharing Project Scrapped' *BBC News* (6 July 2016). https://www.bbc.com/news/health-36723486

Noor P, 'Can We Trust AI Not to Further Embed Racial Bias and Prejudice?' (2020) 368 *BMJ* m363. DOI: 10.1136/bmj.m363

Nordfalk F and Hoeyer K, 'The Rise and Fall of an Opt-out System' (2020) 48(4) *Scandinavian Journal of Public Health* 400–404. DOI: 10.1177/1403494817745189

Ó Cathaoir K, 'In Search of Solidarity: Personalised Medicine in Denmark' (2019) 21–22, *Nordisk socialrättslig tidskrift* 65–95.

Obermeyer Z and others, 'Dissecting Racial Bias in an Algorithm Used to Manage the Health of Populations' (2019) 366(6464) *Science* 447–453. DOI: 10.1126/science.aax234

Palojoki S and Vuokko R, 'Semantic Interoperability of EHRs: Review of Approaches for Enhancing the Goals of European Health Data Space' (Preprints, 26 April 2023). https://www.preprints.org/manuscript/202304.0957/v1

Patel R, 'The Foundations of Fairness for NHS Health Data Sharing' (Understanding Patient Data and Ada Lovelace Institute, 12 March 2020). https://www.adalovelaceinstitute.org/blog/the-foundations-of-fairness-for-nhs-health-data-sharing/

Pereira T and others, 'Sharing Biomedical Data: Strengthening AI Development in Healthcare' (2021) 9(7) *Healthcare* 827. DOI: 10.3390/healthcare9070827

Prainsack B and El-Sayed S, 'Beyond Individual Rights: How Data Solidarity Gives People Meaningful Control over Data' (2023) 23(11) *The American Journal of Bioethics* 36–39. DOI: 10.1080/15265161.2023.2256267

Prictor M, Teare HJA and Kaye J, 'Equitable Participation in Biobanks: The Risks and Benefits of a "Dynamic Consent" Approach' (2018) *Frontiers in Public Health* 6. DOI: 10.3389/fpubh.2018.00253

Quinn P, 'Research under the GDPR – A Level Playing Field for Public and Private Sector Research?' (2021) 17 *Life Sciences, Society and Policy* 4. DOI: 10.1186/s40504-021-00111-z

Rivas Velarde MC and others, 'Citizens' Views on Sharing Their Health Data: The Role of Competence, Reliability and Pursuing the Common Good' (2021) 22 *BMC Medical Ethics* 62. DOI: 10.1186/s12910-021-00633-3

Shabani M and Borry P, 'Rules for Processing Genetic Data for Research Purposes in View of the New EU General Data Protection Regulation' (2018) 26 *European Journal of Human Genetics* 149–156. DOI: 10.1038/s41431-017-0045-7

Sikstrom L and others, 'Conceptualising Fairness: Three Pillars for Medical Algorithms and Health Equity' (2022) 29 *BMJ Health & Care Informatics* e100459. DOI: 10.1136/bmjhci-2021-100459

Slokenberga S, 'Setting the Foundations: Individual Rights, Public Interest, Scientific Research and Biobanking' in Santa Slokenberga, Olga Tzortzatou and Jane Reichel (eds), *GDPR and Biobanking. Law, Governance, and Technology Series* (volume 43, Springer Cham 2021).

Sorbie A, 'Sharing Confidential Health Data for Research Purposes in the UK: Where Are "Publics" in the Public Interest?' (2020) 16(2) *Evidence & Policy* 249–265. DOI: 10.1332/174426419X15578209726839

Spencer K and others, 'Patient Perspectives on Sharing Anonymized Personal Health Data Using a Digital System for Dynamic Consent and Research Feedback: A Qualitative Study' (2016) 18(4) *Journal of Medical Internet Research* e5011. DOI: 10.2196/jmir.5011

Stockdale JE, Liu P and Colijn C, 'The Potential of Genomics for Infectious Disease Forecasting' (2022) 7 *Nature Microbiology* 1736–1743. DOI: 10.1038/s41564-022-01233-6

Taylor MJ and Whitton T, 'Public Interest, Health Research and Data Protection Law: Establishing a Legitimate Trade-Off between Individual Control and Research Access to Health Data' (2020) 9 *Laws* 6. DOI: 10.3390/laws9010006

Tazare J and others, *NHS National Data Opt-Outs: Trends and Potential Consequences for Health Data Research* (2024) *BJGP Open*. DOI: 10.3399/BJGPO.2024.0020

TEHDAS (Joint Action Towards the European Health Data Space), 'Citizens' Perception of and Engagement with Health Data Secondary Use and Sharing in Europe – A Literature Review.' (2021). https://tehdas.eu/results/individuals-favour-data-sharing-and-use-if-benefits-are-clear/

Terzis P, 'Onward for the Freedom of Others: Marching beyond the AI Ethics', Proceedings of the 2020 Conference on Fairness, Accountability, and Transparency (2020) 220–229. DOI: 10.1145/3351095.3373152

The European Consumer Organisation (BEUC), 'Consumer Attitudes to Health Data Sharing. Survey Results from Eight EU Countries.' (2023). https://www.beuc.eu/press-releases/consumers-uneasy-sharing-their-health-data-survey-shows

Townend D, 'Conclusion: Harmonisation in Genomic and Health Data Sharing for Research: An Impossible Dream?' (2018) 137 *Human Genetics* 657–664. DOI: 10.1007/s00439-018-1924-x

Ueda D and others, 'Fairness of Artificial Intelligence in Healthcare: Review and Recommendations' (2023) 42 *Japanese Journal of Radiology* 3–15. DOI: 10.1007/s11604-023-01474-3

Understanding Patient Data and Ada Lovelace Institute, 'The Foundations of Fairness for NHS Health Data Sharing' (March 2020). https://www.adalovelaceinstitute.org/blog/the-foundations-of-fairness-for-nhs-health-data-sharing/

Vyas DA, Eisenstein LG and Jones DS, 'Hidden in Plain Sight – Reconsidering the Use of Race Correction in Clinical Algorithms' (2020) 383 *New England Journal of Medicine* 874–882. DOI: 10.1056/NEJMms2004740

Walker P, 'Why Has the NHS Patient Data-Sharing Scheme Been Pushed Back?' (*The Guardian*, 8 June 2021). https://www.theguardian.com/society/2021/jun/06/why-are-there-calls-for-a-pause-to-patient-data-sharing-scheme

Zenker S and others, 'Data Protection-Compliant Broad Consent for Secondary Use of Health Care Data and Human Biosamples for (Bio)Medical Research: Towards a New German National Standard' (2022) 131 *Journal of Biomedical Informatics* 104096. DOI: 10.1016/j.jbi.2022.104096

8 The European Health Data Space

A New Paradigm for Secondary Uses of Health Data for Scientific Research?

Enrique Santamaría Echeverría

8.1 Introduction

Together with the General Data Protection Regulation (GDPR), the Regulation on the European Health Data Space (EHDS) will form the new regulatory and governance framework for the use of health data in the European Union. One of the objectives of the EHDS is to create a space in which health data, made available by data holders, can be accessed by data users for, among other purposes, secondary uses for scientific research. However, a key concern at the heart of this novel approach to the governance of health data is the lack of definitional clarity around the notion of scientific research, one of the core concepts on which the EHDS relies to govern the secondary use of health data.

As this chapter will demonstrate, the legal framework for the secondary use of health data for scientific research under the EHDS transforms the legal requirements under the GDPR for the secondary use of data as it risks opening the processing of health data for very undefined purposes and favours commercial uses of health data, thereby limiting the positive societal impact that the open use of health data can offer. Furthermore, as it stands, the EHDS deepens ongoing processes of research privatisation and science enclosure and further embeds in EU law and practice a profit-oriented culture surrounding scientific research.[1]

Against this background, the aim of this chapter is twofold. Firstly, it argues that the EHDS creates an imperfect or incomplete 'commons' – a type of governance of shared resources whereby users have a symmetric freedom to access the resource, i.e., health data for its secondary use in scientific research. Secondly, it puts forward a proposal to limit the (excessive) commercial uses of health data that the EHDS would enable.

For this purpose, Section 8.2 analyses some of the problems (and opportunities) arising from the scientific research regime for the secondary use of health data under the EHDS (hereafter scientific research regime). After this brief explanation, Section 8.3 presents an overview of different commons theories as a tool to analyse the scientific research regime under the EHDS. Section 8.4, drawing on relational theories of data governance and data solidarity,

DOI: 10.4324/9781003544111-10

presents a proposal to complete the EHDS commons model for the governance of health data. Section 8.5 concludes with recommendations for embedding data solidarity in the EHDS.

8.2 Scientific Research: Tensions Between the Private, the Public and the Common(s)

Until recently, research findings and scientific knowledge were considered integral components of the public domain. Fundamental research conducted by academic and other non-profit institutions received significant financial support from public funds and agencies, which typically mandated the public sharing of data. However, in the 1980s, there was a push for the privatisation of research,[2] resulting in what is now referred to as the 'enclosure of science' and the emergence of a profit-oriented culture surrounding scientific research.

Biomedical research, encompassing areas like genomics, proteomics, and metabolomics, has been notably impacted by this process of privatisation. Biomedical research, in broad terms, focuses on developing tools such as medicines, vaccines, and medical devices for disease prevention and treatment. This type of research heavily relies on two interconnected resources: health data and prior scientific knowledge.

The ongoing trend towards enclosure of science, driven by the current data-rush, identified these resources in biomedical research as fertile grounds for expansion. Indeed, the convergence of technologies like nanotechnology, biotechnology, information technology and cognitive science applied to the human body has given rise to a new network of external and internal body-monitoring devices (like wearables or medical and wellness devices), advanced techniques (such as AI and Big Data), and institutions like biobanks for the collection and processing of health data, both with and without consent. Alongside the privatisation of research, there is an ongoing political and legal effort to challenge the principles of resource privatisation in scientific research. The concept of the commons plays a pivotal role in this resistance.

In 1968, Garret Hardin in his now much-debated feature[3] analysed how actors' self-interest causes common resources to be overused and underinvested, eventually leading to their depletion. Hardin's article sparked at least two distinct, although intertwined, bodies of literature on the commons as responses to his advancements. The first response came from the field of political economy and the work of Elinor Ostrom and understands the commons as a type of governance for common pool resources (CPR). Ostrom developed an institutional analysis and development framework (AID) for the governance of these resources,[4] and since then, the framework has been adapted, developed, and remodelled to account for different types of commons and institutions for collective action.[5] The second set of responses came from legal scholarly literature and understands, broadly speaking, the commons as a type of resource to which an undefined set of users should have a symmetric access.[6] Within this stream of literature, the first and most notorious rejoinder to

Hardin came from Carol Rose and her work on inherent public property in the *Comedy of the Commons*.[7] From that moment onwards, within the same strand of scholarship, several theories have been further developed to understand the functioning of open commons (also called commons unmodified) and the public domain.[8] The work of prominent legal scholars such as Yochai Benkler,[9] Lawrence Lessig,[10] James Boyle[11] and Brett Frischmann[12] can also be framed within this line of work.[13]

Although these two strands of literature use very similar terminology for the articulation of their theories (for example, commons, the commons, commoning), their normative foundations and aims differ substantially. This has led to substantial confusion and misunderstandings around 'the commons'. For this reason, to understand the possible application of this concept to the governance of health data and the EHDS, 'the commons' requires a clear disambiguation. Let's begin by distinguishing between open commons (hereafter OC) and common pool resources commons (hereafter simply CPRC).

On the one hand, essential to OC is a general symmetric freedom to operate within the commons. In other words, nobody from an open undefined class of users is entitled to restrict access to the commons, and everybody from that class, all other conditions being equal, has the possibility to access and operate within the commons. From this perspective, OC are situated outside the property regime[14]: a regime characterised by asymmetric freedoms, whereby the possibility of exclusion *erga omnes* backed by the power of the state is its quintessential feature. OC can be the result of a top-down commons-oriented legal framework or can simply be socially constructed and maintained.

Benkler has identified a set of conditions in which resources in market economies are usefully managed as OC[15]:

a Efficient allocation of the resource, once provisioned, …, is not a paramount management concern; this includes (1) nonrival resources, (2) partially congestable resources and so on.
b Significant positive externalities are involved in the social value of the resource set.
c The resource is used as input into goods, services, innovations, or other sources of value.
d The resource is provisioned in a diverse set of market, public or social processes.

CPRC, on the other hand, may be defined as a commons inside but property outside: commons inside, insofar as the members of a very well-defined community, have, in principle, a similar symmetric freedom to access and operate within the commons; property outside as members can rely on the power of the state to prevent non-members from accessing the resources. The type of property on which CPRC rely is, however, neither public nor private but collective property. Moreover, unlike OC, CPRC usually manage natural resources. CPRC are also characterised by self-governance bottom-up arrangements, clear rules of membership and access, and resources with – naturally occurring or artificially created – high substractability[16] or rivalry and low excludability.[17]

Although OC and CPRC exhibit significant distinctions and adhere to separate rationales, they both share a common underlying assumption that relying solely on the state–market interface for resource governance is not always necessary nor sufficient.[18] Furthermore, at the heart of both types of commons lie two interconnected challenges: (a) the issue of how to share and circulate the resources being managed and (b) the dilemma of free riding, replenishing the commons, and fairly distributing the benefits it generates. In simpler terms, these challenges revolve around determining the conditions under which the commons can be accessed, the expected contributions back to the commons, and the principles governing the distribution of benefits.

Due to the inherent characteristics of data, these challenges become particularly intricate in the context of governing health data and the knowledge produced thereof. The following observations provide a detailed illustration of this complexity. Firstly, individual rights related to informed consent, privacy and data protection tend to restrict the sharing and repurposing (such as secondary uses) of data, making personal data highly exclusive. Secondly, health data and scientific knowledge are essentially non-subtractable and non-rival intangible resources generated through market, public or social processes. Thirdly, there is a circular relationship between health data and scientific knowledge: while data serves as the raw material for creating scientific knowledge, the latter acts as an input for further innovation and a source of positive societal benefits. The natural consequence of this interdependence is that when one of these resources is captured, enclosed or privatised, it has a detrimental impact on the existence of the other, while opening them up contributes to the growth and value of the other.[19]

In light of the foregoing, health data arguably constitutes a perfect case in point to illustrate Benkler's conditions in which resources can be managed as an OC: (i) because of their non-rivalrous nature, efficient allocation of health data is not a management concern: (ii) incredible positive externalities are involved in the social value of data; (iii) health data are the raw materials for scientific research, innovation, development and other activities of social value and, finally, (iv) health data is provisioned via market, public and social processes.

The next section analyses the scientific research regime under the EHDS in the light of commons theories.

8.3 From the GDPR to the EHDS: The Transformation of the Scientific Research Regime Into an Incomplete Open Commons

Under the GDPR, 'scientific research' was already considered, under certain circumstances, as a legitimate ground for the processing for secondary uses of sensitive data (including health data) without the data subject's consent. According to Article 9(2)i-j GDPR, data can be processed without such consent if necessary for reasons of public interest in the area of public health, for archiving purposes in the public interest, for scientific or historical research purposes, or for statistical purposes. The scope of the exemption spurred an animated discussion in scholarly literature on its meaning and reach.[20] What is 'research', and what is 'the public interest'? Is research in the interest of the public conducted exclusively by academics and healthcare bodies? Alternatively, can such research be carried out by industry (pharmaceutical, biotechnology, [medical] technology companies, and insurance providers), and, if so, how?[21] Some[22] argued that research in the public interest could be conducted by industry. Others advised circumspection and warned about the difficulties of differentiating between genuine research and studies that merely advance private interests.[23] These difficulties stem from the complex linkages between industry and academia, which revolve around, among others, funding, sponsorship, and the execution of joint research projects.[24] The EHDS transforms the GDPR framework for the secondary uses for scientific research. The core of this transformation can be distilled from Article 53, which lists the purposes for which electronic health data can be accessed by data users and prescribes the following:

1 Health data access bodies shall only grant access to electronic health data referred to in Article 51 for secondary use to a health data user where the processing of the data by that health data users is necessary for one of the following purposes: (e) *scientific research* related to health or care sectors that contributes to public health or health technology assessments, or ensures high levels of quality and safety of healthcare, of medicinal products or of medical devices, *with the aim of benefitting the end-users*, such as patients, health professionals and health administrators, including (i) development and innovation activities for products or services; (ii) training, testing and evaluation of algorithms, including in medical devices, in-vitro diagnostic medical devices, AI systems and digital health applications (emphasis added).

Furthermore, according to Recital 61, access for secondary uses should contribute to the 'general interest of the society'. In order to understand these two provisions, several questions immediately arise: how should the phrase 'with the aim of benefitting the end-users' be interpreted and what should be understood as general interest of the society'? Can the benefit of end-users be conflated with the more general idea of general interest of society?

Moreover, Recitals 52 and 54 partially modify the GDPR regime on (the limitations to) consent for secondary use (including research). On the one hand, Recital 52 prescribes that member states may 'no longer maintain or introduce' under Article 9(4) GDPR 'further conditions, including limitations and specific provisions requesting the consent of natural persons with regard to the processing for secondary use of personal electronic health data'. On the other hand, Recital 54 includes scientific research for important reasons of public interest as one of the purposes for which member states can establish mechanisms for public bodies to override the persons' right to opt-out from having their personal data made available for secondary use. Examples of scientific research in the public interest include research for addressing unmet medical needs, including rare diseases, or emerging health threats. On this particular point, one wonders why emerging health threats are included as a legitimate ground for secondary use under scientific research and not, for example under public interest in the area of public health (also included as a purpose for secondary use under Article 51). Beyond this, the EHDS seems to propose a new paradigm for the secondary use of health data for scientific research, no longer based on consent as a general rule, but on the notions of general interest of society and public interest,[25] without, however, providing many hints to their possible meaning.

Additionally, although the original proposal of the Commission for an EHDS listed (i) development and innovation activities for products or services; and (ii) training, testing and evaluating of algorithms, including in medical devices, in-vitro diagnostic medical devices, AI systems and digital health applications, as different legal bases other than scientific research, the final text includes them under the more general umbrella of scientific research. Such a change came accompanied by the inclusion in Recital 61 of a definition of scientific research, absent in the Commission's versions, and which mirrors the definition included in Recital 159 of the GDPR. According to Recital 61:

> The provision of the data should also support activities related to scientific research. The notion of scientific research purposes should be interpreted in a broad manner, including technological development and demonstration, fundamental research, applied research and privately funded research. Activities related to scientific research include innovation activities such as training of AI algorithms that could be used in healthcare or care of natural persons, as well as the evaluation and further development of existing algorithms and products for such purposes. It is necessary that the EHDS also contribute to fundamental research, and, although its benefits to end-users and patients might be less direct, such fundamental research is crucial for societal benefits in the longer term.

Beyond the fact that one may doubt the legitimacy of including private research as an activity in the general interest, the new inclusion of development and innovation and the training, testing, and evaluating of algorithms under scientific research could be a welcome change, as long as all types of data users abide to the stringent ethical structures and high epistemic standards[26] that have traditionally informed academic scientific research. In this regard, new additions in the compromise text regarding the requirements for data access applications and data permits are also very much welcome. On the former, Article 67(2)(j) EHDS prescribes that data access applications shall include 'where applicable, information on any assessment of ethical aspects of the processing, required under national law, which may serve to replace the health data applicant's own ethics assessment'; and on the latter, Article 68 mandates that health data access bodies shall decide to grant access to electronic health data only when the listed cumulative criteria are met, including

> d the health data applicant is qualified in relation to the intended purposes of data use and has appropriate expertise, including professional qualifications in the areas of healthcare, care, public health or research, consistent with ethical practice and applicable laws and regulations; ... (f) the information on the assessment of ethical aspects of the processing [...] where applicable, is in line with national law.

Furthermore, scientific research in the EHDS, in addition to the function already explained, i.e., a legitimate purpose for the secondary use of electronic health data, performs a second function: it constitutes one of the functional factors for the identification of the data holders which should make health data available for secondary use (Recital 59 and Article 2(2)t EHDS). In other words, entities or bodies performing research with regard to the health and care sectors shall make health data available for secondary use within the common European Health Data Space. The question that immediately arises is whether data users (defined in Article (2)(2)u) that rely on scientific research as the purpose to access data then immediately become data holders. In the Commission's version of the proposal, where innovation and training of algorithms were not considered to fall under the scientific research purpose, data users could rely on these to access data without falling within the scope of the EHDS as data holders.[27] However, with the changes regarding the definitions and scope of scientific research in the final text of the EHDS, it seems logical that users that are granted a permit for the purpose of scientific research for the purpose of, for example, training an algorithm, would then fall under the definition of data holders themselves.

Last but not least, unlike the GDPR, the EHDS relies on multiple and perhaps conflicting definitions of what constitutes health data, data concerning health and (personal) electronic (health) data. This multiplicity of definitions, as will become evident in the next lines, is problematic for the delimitation of the legal grounds for the purpose of secondary use for scientific research. First, Article 2(1)a EHDS relies on Article 4(15) of the GDPR for the definition of 'data concerning health', which in turn defines them as 'personal data related to the physical or mental health of a natural person, including the provision of health care services, which reveal information about his or her health status'. Second, Article 2(2)a defines 'personal electronic health data' to include genetic data (for example, Article 4(14) GDPR) and 'data concerning health' (in the sense Article 4(15) GDPR).

Thirdly, and to complete the picture, Article 51 EHDS, included in Chapter IV on secondary uses of electronic health data, provides a surprisingly broad list[28] of the minimum categories of electronic health data for secondary use, including electronic health data from electronic health records, data on factors impacting on health, including socio-economic, environmental and behavioural determinants of health, among many other categories. Finally, without providing a definition, Recital 56 seems to draw the contours for the secondary of electronic health data by proposing two conditions for their use: (a) electronic health data that can be processed for secondary use should be broad and flexible enough to accommodate the evolving needs of health data users and (b) remain limited to data related to health or known to influence health. From all these different categories, only personal electronic health data overlaps, with the addition of genetic data, with the GDPR's definition of data concerning health. All other novel categories go beyond it.

At the same time, additional questions arise. In the first place, why does Article 51 list the minimum categories of electronic data for secondary use, while the EHDS, generally, and Chapter IV, specifically, are aimed at regulating the secondary use of electronic *health* data? Additionally, how does Article 51 EHDS relate to Recital 56 and to Article 53 on the purposes for secondary use of electronic health data? Does electronic data that is not electronic health data fall outside the list of purposes of Article 53? Furthermore, Recital 52 EHDS requires that for the purpose of processing of electronic health data for secondary use, one of the legal bases set out in Article 6(1) points (a), (c), (e) or (f) GDPR, combined with Article 9(2) GDPR, should be required. Which of the categories under Article 51, which seems to include both electronic health data and other types of electronic data, should be processed according to the legal requirements set by Recital 52 EHDS? Lastly, why does Recital 56 take as a criterion the needs of health data users as the bar against which to measure the possible availability of health data for secondary use, instead of, for example, the use of data for the benefit of society, which seems to be the motivation behind the whole EHDS (see, for example, Recital 1)?

It would then appear that the EHDS aims to create a top-down open commons on health data. Indeed, the EHDS does tackle one of the problems identified above as central to the diverse theories on the commons: the problem of sharing and circulating managed resources: the scientific research regime under the EHDS framework performs the function of allowing health data to be shared and circulate. Furthermore, the EHDS also (partially) addresses the second set of problems central to commons theory: the question of freeriding, reseeding the commons and distributing its benefits. By subsuming the training and innovation purposes under the scientific research basis for the secondary use of data, the EHDS allows the automatic transformation of data users into data holders, therefore creating a symmetry in the availability of data for all actors in the data space. However, the EHDS misses a set of rules on the expectations in terms of giving back (reseeding) the commons and how the possible benefits arising from the use of health data ought to be distributed, particularly by big market players. Full supporters of the EHDS would argue that the regulation does impose a duty for data users to 'make public the results or output' of the secondary use of electronic health data.[29] It remains unclear, however, what constitutes results or output.

Moreover, the shift from a consent paradigm to a general interest of society or public interests seems to solve the problem of the highly excludable character of personal sensitive data. In other words, the data subject's prerogatives and rights over their data are overridden by the public or general interests of society. This move reverberates with an academic line of reasoning on the desirability to overcome individualistic accounts on privacy and data protection that transcend the traditional specific consent-based models,[30] and engages in new models of governance of health data for socially relevant activities (for example, the creation of new knowledge, innovation, and research). It is therefore possible to imagine OC for the secondary use of health, adding to the EHDS, in which the use of data contributes to the common good.[31] Determining the content of 'the common good' in this sense remains a highly complex problem. Due to the lack of definitional and functional clarity, the notions of general and public interest in the EHDS do not help in answering these problems. Using relational theories of governance, the next section aims at addressing this issue.

8.4 Data Solidarity

Relational theories of data governance may be useful for the conceptualisation of the common good in a health data OC. In general terms, relational theories of governance posit that data production in a digital economy puts individuals, groups and populations in relations with one another. In such (power) relations, both benefits and harms can arise, and inequalities and patterns of exploitation may be further deepened and reinforced. For this reason, data relations result in supra-individual legal interests that cannot be explained, nor represented by theories centred on individualist data subject rights.[32]

Specifically, in the context of health data governance, data solidarity – arguably a relational theory of data governance[33] – may play a role in representing supraindividual interests and in determining the content of the 'common good' in a health data open commons by setting standards and limits for socially worthwhile ends for data production and use.

Barbara Prainsack's and other prominent scholars' theories of data solidarity tackle precisely the problems of data capture and power imbalances in health data governance.[34] Prainsack's analysis is based on three pillars: (i) facilitating good data use; (ii) preventing and mitigating harm and (iii) returning profits for the public domain.[35] As such:

> If a data use likely creates significant public benefit and avoids undue risks, it should be facilitated. If a data use can be expected to benefit the public but also poses high risks, the risks must be reduced before it can go ahead. Profits from low-risk data use that only creates commercial value should be shared with communities that enabled that data use in the first place. Finally, when and where data use would create no significant public benefits yet poses high risks, it should be outlawed, along with the threat and cross-border enforcement of considerable fines.[36]

This formulation of data solidarity can contribute to solving two of the problems identified in this chapter as immanent to commons theory and to the EHDS: (a) the problem of sharing and circulating the managed resources and (b) the problem of freeriding, reseeding the commons and distributing its benefits. Regarding the first problem, the author pointed out the inadequacy of the function of the concepts of general interest and public interest in the EHDS framework as the rationales behind secondary uses of health data for scientific research. Regarding the second problem, the author pointed out how the EHDS framework is not sufficiently concerned with the issues of distributing the benefits and reseeding the commons with the results and outputs of the health data use.

Data solidarity contributes to solving both these problems. Starting with the second, data solidarity sets the normative standard to return the commercial profits of low public value (and high private value) to the public domain (in our terminology: to the commons). Regarding the first problem, data solidary would preclude the use of health data with low public value entailing high risks of harm, independent of the actors involved and independent of public–private value considerations. Hence, health data use for the public or general interest (in the EHDS terminology) involving a high risk of harm (for example, risk of discrimination) would be prohibited under a data-solidarity framework, unless risk of harm can be reduced to an acceptable level.

One issue remains highly debated: the abandonment of the consent-based legal framework for the secondary use of health data for scientific research. Although Prainsack has been vocal about the fact that a solidarity-based approach avoids communitarian ideas about privileging the public good over the interests of individuals,[37] one may wonder whether, for example, the use of individuals' data without consent to avoid causing harm to another individual (or group) may be permissible under a data-solidarity approach. In other words, is (broad) consent for health data use a condition sine qua non for their use under a data solidarity framework? Although scholars have already answered this question in the negative,[38] and the EHDS proposes a new normative stand, the author does not venture yet a definitive response. Arguably, the use of health data without consent should be permissible if the use of data delivers high public (or common) value and the processing does entail a high risk of harm. In the same line, Calderai has argued for a revision of the contract between science and society in which citizenship, and no longer consent, constitutes the normative justification for the use of personal data for scientific purposes.[39]

8.5 Conclusion

This chapter demonstrated how the new scientific research regime under the EHDS entails a paradigm shift from a consent-based approach to one that could be termed as a general or public interest approach. However, this new model lacks a definition or procedural mechanisms to determine what should be understood as public and general interests. As such, the EHDS constitutes an incomplete attempt to create open commons for the purpose of the secondary uses of health data for scientific research at the EU level. To begin addressing the regulatory lacunas, this chapter suggests that a complete open commons on health data for scientific research could be created by using data solidarity as a relational theory to determine the rules in data sharing and data access, to avoid freeriding and to reseed the commons. Data solidarity would act in this proposal as the cornerstone on which the common good is built to nurture and complete the transformations the EHDS would entail. Therefore, at least the following changes and additions are necessary: firstly, clear guidelines on how to identify what constitutes public interest; secondly, in the case of data uses for private interests, the establishment of rules on how the results of the data use can benefit public interests. For this purpose, and within the limits of the principle of subsidiarity, mechanisms associated to (mandatory) licenses, pricing, benefit sharing, and data disclosure can be imagined. The details on how to find the best mechanisms for re-seeding the commons remains a problem for further (empirical) research.

Notes

1 On the privatisation and the enclosure of science movement see Section 8.2 below.
2 Jerome H Reichman and Paul F Uhlir, 'A Contractually Reconstructed Research Commons for Scientific Data in a Highly Protectionist Intellectual Property Environment' (2003) 66(1/2) *Law and Contemporary Problems* 315.
3 Garrett Hardin, 'The Tragedy of the Commons' (2009) 1 *Journal of Natural Resources Policy Research* 243.
4 Elinor Ostrom, *Governing the commons: The evolution of institutions for collective action* (Cambridge University Press 1990); Elinor Ostrom, 'Background on the institutional analysis and development framework' (2011) 39 *Policy Studies Journal* 7.
5 Tine De Moor, 'From common pastures to global commons: A historical perspective on interdisciplinary approaches to commons' (2011) 19 *Natures Sciences Societies* 422; Tine de Moor, 'What do we have in common? A comparative framework for old and new literature on the commons' (2012) 57 *International Review of Social History* 269.
6 Italian scholarly literature has been extraordinarily prolific in the legal study of the commons. See for example: Stefano Rodotà, 'The role of common goods in fostering shared responsibility, linking sustainable social cohesion to the reduction of inequalities' (International University College of Turin, 2-11, 2011); Ugo Mattei, Rocco Alessio Albanese and Ryan J Fisher, 'Commons as possessions: The path to protection of the commons in the ECHR system' (2019) 25 *European Law Journal* 230; Ugo Mattei, 'I beni comuni fra economia, diritto e filosofia' (2013) 7 *Spazio filosofico* 111; Ugo Mattei, *The state, the market, and some preliminary question about the commons* (International University College of Turin, 2011) http://ideas.iuctorino.it/RePEc/iuc-rpaper/1-11_Mattei.pdf accessed 9 May 2024; Ugo Mattei, 'First thoughts for a phenomenology of the commons' in Roberto Morea, Chantal Delmas (eds), *Socialisation and commons in Europe: Constructing an alternative project* (transform! 2016) 75; Antonio Gambaro, 'Note in tema di beni comuni' (2013) 1 *Aedon* 11; Maria Rosaria Marella, 'Beni comuni: oltre l'opposizione natura/

cultura' (2012) 113 *Lettera Internacionales* 9; Maria Rosaria Marella, 'Per un Diritto dei Beni Comuni' in Maria Rosaria Marella (ed), *Oltre il ePubblico ee il Privato* (Ombre Corte 2013) 9.

7 Carol Rose, 'The comedy of the commons: Custom, commerce, and inherently public property' (1986) 53 *The University of Chicago Law Review* 711.

8 James Boyle, *The public domain: Enclosing the commons of the mind* (Yale University Press, 2008).

9 Yochai Benkler, *The wealth of networks. How social production transforms markets and freedom* (Yale University Press 2006); Yochai Benkler, 'Between Spanish Huertas and the open road' in Brett M Frischmann, Michael J Madison, Katherine J Strandburg (eds), *Governing knowledge commons* (Oxford University Press 2014) 69; Yochai Benkler, 'The political economy of commons' (2003) IV *Upgrade: The European Journal for the Informatics Professional* 6; Yochai Benkler, 'Open Access and Information Commons' in Francesco Parisi (ed), *The Oxford handbook of law and economics: Private and commercial law* (vol. 2, Oxford University Press 2017) 256.

10 Lawrence Lessig, 'Keynote address. Code and the commons' (Conference on Media Convergence, Fordham University Law School 1999).

11 Boyle (n 9).

12 Brett M Frischmann, *Infrastructure: The social value of shared resources* (Oxford University Press 2012).

13 In the field of political philosophy, a third body of literature considers the commons (and communing) as a means for radical political and economic change. See for example: Michael Hardt and Antonio Negri, *Commonwealth* (Harvard University Press 2009); M De Angelis, *Omnia sunt communia: On the commons and the transformation to postcapitalism* (Bloomsbury Publishing 2017); Pierre Dardot and Christian Laval, *Commun: Essai sur la révolution au XXIe siècle* (La découverte 2014); Peter Linebaugh, *The Magna Carta Manifesto* (University of California Press 2008); Peter Linebaugh, *Stop, thief!: The commons, enclosures, and resistance* (Pm Press 2014). In this chapter, I will not focus on this theoretical corpus.

14 Even if one may formally find different underlying titles of property, it is the case of some types of infrastructure falling under the public property regime.

15 Benkler (n 10) 90.

16 Charlotte Hess and Elinor Ostrom, *Understanding knowledge as a commons: From theory to practice* (MIT Press 2007) 5.

17 De Moor (n 6) 426.

18 David Bollier, 'The growth of the commons paradigm.' (2007) 27 *Understanding Knowledge as a Commons: From Theory to Practice* 33.

19 Bollier, 'The growth of the commons paradigm,' 34.

20 See generally, European Data Protection Supervisor, 'A preliminary opinion on data protection and scientific research' (2020) 6 January 2020; European Data Protection Supervisor, 'Preliminary Opinion 8/2020 on the European Health Data Space' (2020) 17 November 2020; MLC Foundation and Med Law consult, 'GDPR and research. A basic overview' (2017) www.medlaw.nl/wp-content/uploads/2018/01/GDPRrshexemptionsv.1.4.pdf accessed 9 May 2024; Giovanni Comandè and Giulia Schneider, 'Can the GDPR make data flow for research easier? Yes it can, by differentiating! A careful reading of the GDPR shows how EU data protection law leaves open some significant flexibilities for data protection-sound research activities' (2021) *Computer Law and Security Review* 41; Mary Donnelly and Maeve McDonagh, 'Health research, consent and the GDPR exemption' (2019) 26 *European Journal of Health Law* 97; European Data Protection Supervisor, 'Opinion 3/2020 on the European Strategy for data' (2020) 16 June 2020; Mark J

Taylor and Tess Whitton, 'Public interest, health research and data protection law: Establishing a legitimate trade-off between individual control and research access to health data' (2020) 9 *Laws* 6; Paul Quinn, 'Research under the GDPR – A level playing field for public and private sector research?' (2021) 17 *Life Sciences, Society and Policy* 4; Regina Becker and others, 'Secondary Use of Personal Health Data: When is it "further Processing" under the GDPR, and what are the implications for data controllers?' (2023) 30 *European Journal of Health Law* 129; Victoria Chico, 'The impact of the general data protection regulation on health research' (2018) 128 *British Medical Bulletin* 109.

21 On the interplay between the concepts of scientific research and public interests see Santa Slokenberga, 'Setting the foundations: Individual rights, public interest, scientific research and biobanking' in Santa Slokenberga, Olga Tzortzatou and Jane Reichel (eds), *GDPR and biobanking. Law, governance, and technology series* (vol. 43, Springer 2021) 11. Slokenberga is critical of the authority of the European Data Protection Supervisor and its interpretation of the notion of scientific research.

22 Johan Hansen and others, 'Assessment of the EU Member States' rules on health data in the light of GDPR' (European Commission, Consumers, Health, Agriculture and Food Executive Agency. Publications Office 113, 2021) 57.

23 European Data Protection Supervisor (n 20) 3.

24 European Data Protection Supervisor (n 20) 8.

25 For an analysis of lawfulness in secondary use of health data in the GDPR, DGA and EHDS with reference to the distinction between general interest and public interests see Mahsa Shabani and Sami Yilmaz, 'Lawfulness in secondary uses of health data' (2022) *Technology and Regulation* 128.

26 For the scientific research regime arising from the EHDS see Santa Slokenberga, 'Scientific research regime 2.0? Transformations of the research regime and the protection of the data subject that the proposed EHDS regulation promises to bring along' (2022) *Technology and Regulation* 135. See also Enrique Santamaria Echeverría, 'Governing health data for research, development, and innovation: The missteps of the European Health Data Space Proposal' https://blog.petrieflom.law.harvard.edu/2023/03/23/governing-health-data-for-research-development-and-innovation-the-missteps-of-the-european-health-data-space-proposal/ accessed 5 June 2023.

27 On the asymmetries created by the EHDS see Petros Terzis, 'Compromises and asymmetries in the European Health Data Space' (2022) 30(3) *European Journal of Health Law* 345.

28 For the list of what constitutes health data, see EHDS rec 56 and art 51.

29 EHDS Art 61(4).

30 Barbara J Evans, 'Genomic data commons' in Katherine J. Strandburg, Brett M Frischmann and Michael J Madison (eds), *Governing Medical Knowledge Commons* (Cambridge University Press 2017) 74, 97.

31 Recently, theories on the common good have been applied to health innovation. See for example, Mariana Mazzucato, 'A collective response to our global challenges: A common good and "market-shaping" approach' (Working Paper Series (IIPP WP 2023-01) www.ucl.ac.uk/bartlett/public-purpose/wp2023-01 accessed 8 May 2023; The WHO Council on the Economics of Health for All, 'Governing health innovation for the common good' (World Health Organization 2021).

32 A beautifully crafted relational theory of data governance is Salomé Viljoen's proposal for data as a democratic medium. See Salomé Viljoen, 'A relational theory of data governance' (2021) 131 *Yale Law Journal* 573.

33 On solidarity-based perspectives as relational see Barbara Prainsack, 'The "We" in the "Me": Solidarity and health care in the era of personalized medicine' (2018) 43 *Science Technology and Human Values* 21.

34 See generally: Barbara Prainsack and Alena Buyx, 'Solidarity in practice I: Governing health databases' in Barbara Prainsack and Alena Buyx (eds), *Solidarity in Biomedicine and Beyond* (Cambridge University Press 2017) 97-122; Barbara Prainsack, 'Data donation: How to resist the iLeviathan' in Jenny Krutzinna and Luciano Floridi (eds), *The Ethics of Medical Data Donation* (Philosophical Studies Series, vol 137, Springer 2019) 9; Barbara Prainsack and Seliem El-Sayed, 'Beyond individual rights: How data solidarity gives people meaningful control over data' (2023) 23 *American Journal of Bioethics* 36; Barbara Prainsack, 'Data solidarity: A blueprint for governing health futures' (2022) 4 *The Lancet* 773.
35 Barbara Prainsack and Alena Buyx 'Data solidarity: A blueprint for governing health futures'.
36 Prainsack and El-Seyed, (n 35) 38.
37 Prainsack, 'Beyond individual rights' (n 34) 36.
38 Evans (n 31).
39 Valentina Calderai, 'The Self and the Commodified Self. Biotechnologies before the Bare Life' (2023) book chapter on file with the author.

List of Sources

Treaties, Secondary Law and Conventions

Regulation (EU) 2016/679 of the European Parliament and of the Council of 27 April 2016 on the protection of natural persons with regard to the processing of personal data and on the free movement of such data, and repealing Directive 95/46/EC (General Data Protection Regulation) (Text with EEA relevance) OJ L 119/1.

Regulation (EU) 2022/868 of the European Parliament and of the Council of 30 May 2022 on European data governance and amending Regulation (EU) 2018/1724 (Data Governance Act) (Text with EEA relevance) OJ L 152/1.

Official Documents

Council of the European Union, 'Proposal for a Regulation of the European Parliament and of the Council on the European Health Data Space' (COM/2022/197 final) 2022/0140 (COD).

European Data Protection Supervisor, 'A Preliminary opinion on data protection and scientific research' (2020a).

European Data Protection Supervisor, 'Preliminary opinion 8/2020 on the European Health Data Space' (2020b).

European Data Protection Supervisor, 'Opinion 3/2020 on the European strategy for data' (2020c).

Literature and Other Secondary Sources

Becker R and others, 'Secondary use of personal health data: When is it "further Processing" under the GDPR, and what are the implications for data controllers?' (2023) 30 *European Journal of Health Law* 129. DOI: 10.1163/15718093-bja10094

Benkler Y, 'The political economy of commons' (2003) IV *Upgrade* 6. www.benkler.org/commons.pdf

Benkler Y, *The wealth of networks. How social production transforms markets and freedom* (Yale University Press 2006).

Benkler Y, 'Between Spanish Huertas and the open road' In Frischmann BM, Madison MJ, Strandburg KJ (eds), *Governing knowledge commons* (Oxford University Press 2014).

Benkler Y, 'Open access and information commons' in Parisi F (ed), *The Oxford handbook of law and economics: private and commercial law* (Volume 2, Oxford University Press 2017).

Bollier D, 'The growth of the commons paradigm' in Charlotte Hess and Elinor Ostrom (eds) *Understanding knowledge as a commons: From theory to practice* (MIT Press 2007).

Boyle J, *The public domain: Enclosing the commons of the mind* (Yale University Press 2008).

Calderai V, 'The self and the commodified self. Biotechnologies before the bare life' (2023) book chapter in file with the author.

Chico V, 'The impact of the general data protection regulation on health research' (2018) 128 *British Medical Bulletin* 109. DOI: 10.1093/bmb/ldy038

Comandè G and Schneider G, 'Can the GDPR make data flow for research easier? Yes it can, by differentiating! A careful reading of the GDPR shows how EU data protection law leaves open some significant flexibilities for data protection-sound research activities' (2021) *Computer Law and Security Review* 41. DOI: 10.1016/j.clsr.2021.105539

Dardot P and Laval C, *Commun: essai sur la révolution au XXIe siècle* (La découverte 2014).

De Angelis M, *Omnia sunt communia: On the commons and the transformation to post-capitalism* (Bloomsbury Publishing 2017).

De Moor T, 'From common pastures to global commons: A historical perspective on interdisciplinary approaches to commons' (2011) 19 *Natures Sciences Societes* 422. www.cairn.info/revue-natures-sciences-societes-2011-4-page-422.htm

De Moor T, 'What do we have in common? A comparative framework for old and new literature on the commons' (2012) 57 *International Review of Social History* 269. DOI: 10.1017/S002085901200020X

Donnelly M and McDonagh M, 'Health research, consent and the GDPR exemption' (2019) 26 *European Journal of Health Law* 97. DOI: 10.1163/15718093-12262427

Evans BJ, 'Genomic data commons' (2017) *Governing Medical Knowledge Commons* 74. DOI: 10.1017/9781316544587.005

Frischmann BM, *Infrastructure: The social value of shared resources* (Oxford University Press, 2012).

Gambaro A, 'Note in tema di beni comuni' (2013) 1 *Aedon* 11.

Hansen J and others, 'Assessment of the EU Member States' rules on health data in the light of GDPR' (European Commission, Consumers, Health, Agriculture and Food Executive Agency Publications Office 113, 2021).

Hardin G, 'The tragedy of the commons' (2009) 1 *Journal of Natural Resources Policy Research* 243.

Hardt M and Negri A, *Commonwealth* (Harvard University Press, 2009).

Hess C and Ostrom E, *Understanding knowledge as a commons: From theory to practice* (MIT press 2007).

Lessig L, 'Keynote Address. Code and the Commons' (Conference on Media Convergence, Fordham University Law School 1999).

Linebaugh P, *The Magna Carta Manifesto* (University of California Press 2008).

Linebaugh P, *Stop, thief!: The commons, enclosures, and resistance* (Pm Press 2014).

Marella MR, 'Beni comuni: oltre l'opposizione natura/cultura' (2012) 113 *Lettera Internacionales* 9.

Linebaugh P, 'Per un Diritto dei Beni Comuni' in Maria Rosaria Marella (ed), *Oltre il Pubblico e il Privato* (Ombre Corte 2013).

Mattei U, *The state, the market, and some preliminary question about the commons* (International University College of Turin 2011). http://ideas.iuctorino.it/RePEc/iuc-rpaper/1-11_Mattei.pdf

Mattei U, 'First thoughts for a phenomenology of the commons' in Roberto Morea, Chantal Delmas (eds), *Socialisation and Commons in Europe: constructing an alternative project* (transform! 2016).

Mattei U, 'I beni comuni fra economia, diritto e filosofia' (2013) 7 *Spazio filosofico* 111.

Mattei U, Albanese RA and Fisher RJ, 'Commons as possessions: The path to protection of the commons in the ECHR system' (2019) 25(3) *European Law Journal* 230. DOI: 10.1111/eulj.12320

Mazzucato M, 'A collective response to our global challenges: A common good and "market-shaping" approach' (Working Paper Series (IIPP WP 2023-01) https://www.ucl.ac.uk/bartlett/public-purpose/wp2023-01

MLC Foundation and Med Law Consult, 'GDPR and research. A basic overview' (2017). www.medlaw.nl/wp-content/uploads/2018/01/GDPRrshexemptionsv.1.4.pdf

Ostrom E, *Governing the Commons: The evolution of institutions for collective action* (Cambridge University Press 1990).

Ostrom E, 'Background on the institutional analysis and development framework' (2011) 39 *Policy Studies Journal* 7. DOI: 10.1111/j.1541-0072.2010.00394.x

Prainsack B, 'The "We" in the "Me": Solidarity and health care in the era of personalized medicine' (2018) 43 *Science Technology and Human Values* 21. DOI: 10.1177/016224391773613

Prainsack B, 'Data donation: How to resist the iLeviathan' in Krutzinna J and Floridi L (eds), *The Ethics of Medical Data Donation* (Philosophical Studies Series, vol. 137, Springer, 2019).

Prainsack B, 'Data solidarity: A blueprint for governing health futures' (2022) 4 *The Lancet* 773. DOI: 10.1016/S2589-7500(22)00189-3

Prainsack B and Buyx A, 'Solidarity in practice I: Governing health databases' in Prainsack B and Buyx A (eds), *Solidarity in biomedicine and beyond* (Cambridge University Press 2017) 97–122.

Prainsack B and El-Sayed S, 'Beyond individual rights: How data solidarity gives people meaningful control over data' (2023) 23 *American Journal of Bioethics* 36. DOI: 10.1080/15265161.2023.2256267

Quinn P, 'Research under the GDPR – a level playing field for public and private sector research?' (2021) 17 *Life Sciences, Society and Policy* 4. DOI: 10.1186/s40504-021-00111-z

Reichman JH and Uhlir PF, 'A contractually reconstructed research commons for scientific data in a highly protectionist intellectual property environment' (2003) 66(1/2) *Law and Contemporary Problems* 315. https://scholarship.law.duke.edu/lcp/vol66/iss1/12

Rodotà S, *The role of common goods in fostering shared responsibility, linking sustainable social cohesion to the reduction of inequalities* (International University College of Turin, no 2–11, 2011).

Rose C, 'The comedy of the commons: Custom, commerce, and inherently public property' (1986) 53 *The University of Chicago Law Review* 711.

Santamaria Echeverría E, 'Governing Health Data for Research, Development, and Innovation: The Missteps of the European Health Data Space Proposal' https://blog.petrieflom.law.harvard.edu/2023/03/23/governing-health-data-for-research-development-and-innovation-the-missteps-of-the-european-health-data-space-proposal/

Shabani M and Yilmaz S, 'Lawfulness in secondary uses of health data' (2022) *Technology and Regulation* 128. DOI: 10.26116/techreg.2022.013

Slokenberga S, 'Setting the foundations: Individual rights, public interest, scientific research and biobanking' in Santa Slokenberga, Olga Tzortzatou and Jane Reichel (eds), *GDPR and biobanking. Law, governance, and technology series* (Vol. 43, Springer 2021).

Slokenberga S, 'Scientific research regime 2.0? Transformations of the research regime and the protection of the data subject that the proposed EHDS regulation promises to bring along' (2022) *Technology and Regulation* 135. DOI: 10.26116/techreg.2022.014
Taylor MJ and Whitton T, 'Public interest, health research and data protection law: Establishing a legitimate trade-off between individual control and research access to health data' (2020) 9 *Laws* 6. DOI: 10.3390/laws9010006
Terzis P, 'Compromises and asymmetries in the European Health Data Space' (2022) 30(3) *European Journal of Health Law* 345. DOI: 10.1163/15718093-bja10099
The WHO Council on the Economics of Health for All, 'Governing health innovation for the common good' (World Health Organization 2021).
Viljoen S, 'A relational theory of data governance' (2021) 131 *Yale Law Journal* 573. https://www.yalelawjournal.org/feature/a-relational-theory-of-data-governance

Part III

Adequate safeguards and data governance through health data access bodies

9 Secondary use of health data in the EHDS

Public interest and the role of HDABs

Tjaša Petročnik

9.1 Introduction: harnessing the potential of health data sharing

In recent years, the EU has developed its governance of data, including in the health domain,[1] where it has long been established that (data) 'sharing is caring'[2] and that 'health data generated in different contexts are of significant long-term and multifaceted utility, well beyond the specific clinical, diagnostic, or research use for which they were initially collected'.[3] Yet, while healthcare is generally seen as a data-rich sector, health data re-use is limited in practice due to its inherent sensitivity, as well as due to fragmented digital standards and national divergences in the implementation of data protection rules.[4]

Against this background, the European Commission in May 2022 tabled its long-awaited legislative proposal for a regulation on the European Health Data Space (EHDS), with a goal to harness health data for tackling societal challenges, specifically in relation to health(care),[5] and establish 'common rules, standards, infrastructures and a governance framework with a view to facilitating access to electronic health data for the purposes of primary and secondary use of these data'.[6] With regard to the latter – the use of health data for purposes other than the direct provision of healthcare,[7] which is also the focus of this contribution – the EHDS is to 'make full use'[8] of health data's potential as a 'treasure trove for scientists, researchers, innovators and policy-makers working on the next life-saving treatment'.[9] Arguably, its underlying rationale is the idea that broad access to and (re-)use of health data can lead to better understanding, management, and treatment of disease, more efficient, safer, and patient-friendly health(care) interventions, systems, and policies, and better health outcomes for individuals and populations.[10] Therefore, the 'added value that health data sharing has for the public interest is enormous'.[11]

To promote and coordinate health data sharing for secondary use, the EHDS envisions a new entity in each of the member states:[12] the Health Data Access Body (HDAB). As the '*de facto* health data managers and administrators'[13] in secondary use, HDABs can be expected to play a key role in delivering upon the promises of the EHDS, thus calling for a critical discussion on their position and the tasks they will perform. Therefore, this contribution scrutinises the newly established regime for secondary use of health data and HDABs

DOI: 10.4324/9781003544111-12

as the focal points for realising the EHDS aspirations for secondary use and the public interest. To do this, first, the relevant provisions on the structure and tasks of HDABs are outlined. Then, the public interest narrative underpinning the EHDS is examined, followed by analysis of the changes in health data governance brought along by the EHDS. The chapter concludes by providing recommendations, suggesting that HDABs should explicitly assume their role as health data custodians to more directly contribute to the EHDS' (implied) public interest aspirations.

9.2 HDABs and the secondary use of health data in the EHDS

The EHDS aims to provide an EU-wide framework for sharing health data. It construes secondary use broadly; namely, the regulation covers a wide variety of electronic health data[14] and an array of purposes for which secondary use is allowed, while prohibiting certain uses detrimental to individuals or the society.[15] In terms of data users, any public or private party that intends 'to pursue one of these purposes may request and gain lawful access to health data'.[16] Following a consultation process, the European Commission with its EHDS proposal opted for an authorisation and compensation scheme for the secondary use of health data,[17] instructing each member state to set up one or more HDABs[18] tasked with granting access to health data and promoting its secondary use. This indicates that HDABs, once functioning, will occupy the central position in the regime for secondary use, taking place as follows: a prospective data user applies to access health data and the HDAB processes and reviews their application.[19] In case of a positive assessment, the HDAB issues a data permit that spells out the conditions for secondary use,[20] requests health data from the data holder,[21] and then provides access to it to the data user in an anonymised format[22] through a secure processing environment.[23] HDABs should reject any application that does not meet the requirements of Chapter IV of the regulation[24] and justify its decision to the applicant.[25] Lastly, if a data user does not adhere to the data permit, the HDAB can revoke it or issue a fine or exclude from the EHDS the non-compliant parties.[26]

In addition to issuing data permits and processing health data for the requested purposes, HDABs also have other tasks. Among other things, they are to maintain a national dataset catalogue based on the information from health data holders and to make public health data applications and permits, non-compliance measures, and results of secondary use.[27] Furthermore, they are to abide by certain information requirements, cooperate with and supervise data holders and users, and cooperate among each other on national and EU levels, as well as with other competent authorities.[28] According to the regulation, HDABs can be formed as new or existing public sector bodies or services.[29] They are considered independent entities, subject to financial monitoring and review, and their staff shall avoid any conflict of interest.[30] Whereas the member states are to ensure that HDABs have the necessary resources for their functioning,[31] a part of the costs of operation will also be covered by charging fees for secondary use.[32] Finally, the EHDS establishes the technical infrastructure to support secondary use (HealthData@EU),[33] in which HDABs take part.[34] On the EU level, the coordination concerning these and other EHDS developments will be ensured through the EHDS Board.[35]

9.3 The EHDS and public interest aspirations: promoting a trickle-down approach to secondary use of health data?

In public policies, drawing upon the notion of public interest is commonplace. It is no different in the case of the EHDS, where a closer look at the framework can reveal how the regulator understands the EHDS' objectives in relation to the general or public interest concerning the secondary use of health data. First, the European Strategy for Data, from which the EHDS regulation emanates, asserts that the European Commission should promote the development of European data spaces, complementing the applicable horizonal regulatory frameworks, 'in strategic economic sectors and domains of *public interest* [emphasis added]',[36] including healthcare. Next, the overarching message from the Commission is that health data will work 'for people and science'.[37] The EHDS states that its objective, when it comes to secondary use, is to improve access to and control over health data for 'purposes in the healthcare and care sector that would *benefit society*, such as research, innovation, policy-making, health threats preparedness and response, including preventing and addressing future pandemics, patient safety, personalised medicine, official statistics or regulatory activities [emphasis added]'.[38] In Recital 61, the regulator maintains that access to data for secondary use should contribute to the *general interest* of the society. Article 53 then specifies the array of purposes for which secondary use is allowed, including some specifically invoking the notion of public interest. The EHDS assigns to HDABs tasks *in the public interest* in the sense of the GDPR,[39] whereas the GDPR itself in Recital 53 underlines that health data in particular can only be processed for purposes necessary to benefit the health of individuals or society.

From these instances, it is evident that the EHDS considers that secondary use should be societally beneficial and/or in the general or *public interest*. While the initial Commission's EHDS proposal was rather unclear on what constitutes said public interest, despite several references to this notion,[40] the political agreement on the EHDS now provides more clarity by qualifying that in particular, secondary use for research and development should benefit society in the form of new medicines, medical devices, and other health care products and services at affordable prices, as well as to improved access to these products and services, invoking both direct and indirect benefits of scientific research.[41]

In the literature, public interest is presented, and often criticised, as a vague and abstract concept.[42] Scholarship puts forward various conceptualisations, ranging from public interest being a representation of an aggregate of individual interests reconciled through competition and negotiation to public interest signifying an embodiment of a common, collective, or public good distinct from (the sum of) private interests,[43] pointing to the interest or welfare of the public or society as a whole.[44] In other words, an interest becomes 'public' 'if and when a broader group of (potential) individuals draws benefits from it'.[45] Importantly, the notion of public interest is suggested to be linked to legitimacy[46] and can be seen as providing normative justification or a policy assessment benchmark.[47] In the case of the EHDS, the Commission seemed to conceive its public interest aspirations concerning the secondary use of health data in a rather constrained manner. It can be inferred from the preparatory works, as well as from the objective of the proposal itself, that the EHDS was put forward as a mechanism to improve access to and sharing of quality health data, while leaving it to the data users themselves to implement secondary uses that would deliver upon the intended benefits.[48]

On the one hand, this seems consistent with the more narrow, liberal conception of public interest, where the state needs to ensure the necessary conditions for the market to function well and where the societal value arises from the aggregate actions of individuals.[49] Indeed, the EHDS is arguably intended as a tool to open up the health data market and incentivise health data availability and exchange.[50] This is also evident in the legal bases chosen for the EHDS, Articles 16 and 114 TFEU, which cover data protection and internal market, respectively, and corresponds to the EU's 'constitutional asymmetry'[51] that characterises its role in healthcare: while the EU has limited powers in terms of social welfare, it has a strong regime for enforcing the free movement rules.[52] In the context of the EHDS, this in turn seems to promote what this chapter suggests is a 'trickle-down' approach to health data (re-)use,[53] reflecting a conviction that merely opening up the health data market for data users will in itself result in certain (health) benefits that will then reach patients and healthcare systems in need of them. With this, 'the EU seems set to continue the well-worn path of focusing on innovation benefits and market value',[54] couching public interest in market-oriented terms, which presuppose that economic efficiency will lead to innovation that will then spill-over into health benefits.[55]

Such stance, while in line with the EU's market-building aims, could, on the other hand, represent a problem from the perspective of (public) acceptance, since, adapted from Selznick's definition, regulation is 'the use of the concept of the public interest as a justification for regulatory intervention into private activity, limiting the exercise of private power, in pursuit of objectives *valued by the community* [emphasis added]'.[56] While people are in general supportive of opening up access to health data, 'this goodwill does not equal a blank cheque',[57] as health data re-use is considered acceptable only if it is likely to create (a clear) public benefit without posing high risks to individuals or society.[58] With the question of public benefit therefore being central to the secondary use of health data, this chapter submits HDABs' role is especially important, as they are positioned in the centre of managing and overseeing the secondary use of health data in the EHDS to ensure its effective use.[59] In this role, HDABs will have to engage with and manage the expectations and incentives to generate, share, and re-use health data of all the different parties involved therein.[60]

In this light, how HDABs will relate to the regulation's ambitions – namely, in what sense they will relate and contribute to the public interest and the benefits poised to materialise from secondary use – is thus at the heart of the discussion of their position in the EHDS.

9.4 Analysis: the secondary use regime and public interest

9.4.1 Data protection principles and the secondary use of health data in the EHDS

Due to its sensitivity, health data enjoys special legal protection under the current data protection regime and can only be processed in specific cases. The GDPR acknowledges that health data re-use can benefit healthcare provision and research,[61] providing for a degree of flexibility when health data is (re-) used for scientific research.[62] The implementation of the GDPR provisions on this matter, however, led to a patchwork of applicable rules across the EU member states.[63] Against this, the EHDS provides a harmonised regime for the collection and processing of electronic health data for the secondary use, building upon the possibilities granted by the GDPR.[64] While the EHDS states that health data for secondary use is to be provided in an anonymised format, unless the use of pseudonymised data is justified,[65] the present analysis is grounded in data protection principles of lawfulness, fairness, and transparency[66] as they arguably form a basis of the approach devised under the EHDS.

Firstly, as regards lawfulness,[67] HDABs, in deciding on the data access applications, have to assess, among other things, the intended use of health data, including for which purpose(s) outlined in Article 53 and, as added in the text of the political agreement, the expected benefits,[68] if the requested data is necessary, adequate, and proportionate for the intended purpose,[69] the adequacy of the applicable data protection safeguards, as well as the legal basis in the sense of the GDPR that the applicant relies upon.[70] Namely, the EHDS provides a legal basis and safeguards in accordance with Articles 9(2)(g), (h), (i), and (j) of the GDPR,[71] whereas the data applicant will need to demonstrate a legal basis pursuant Article 6 GDPR. Specifically, the revised Recital 52 states that data applicants are to demonstrate a legal basis in accordance with Article 6 GDPR; if the data user relies on paragraph (1), points (e) or (f) of the same article, the EHDS regulation should provide the required safeguards under Article 9(2) GDPR. In the light of this, the EHDS evidently constructs the secondary use of health data broadly,[72] corralling diverse purposes together, despite them being distinct in their nature, the party performing them, the objectives they pursue, and the epistemological, methodological, and ethico-legal standards they are subject to.[73] This might result in a rather complex assessment,[74] and the issues of such an approach were especially obvious in the Commission's EHDS proposal. In response to it, the EDPB and EDPS noted that the purposes included in (proposed) Articles 34(1)(f) and (g) were particularly problematic, as they referred to the development and innovation activities and training, testing, and evaluation of algorithms contributing to public health, respectively. In their view, these purposes should be further delineated and their sufficient connection with public health and/or social security established.[75] Moreover, their joint opinion stressed that the purposes of secondary use, as proposed, fall under different grounds for exception in Article 9(2) GPDR, which is not reflected in the criteria for HDABs to assess data applications and issue data permits.[76]

As pointed out, the GDPR's research regime is grounded in the epistemic and methodological standards applicable to scientific research and its societal importance,[77] yet the initial EHDS proposal seemed to include under this category broadly defined research and innovation purposes that were set to enjoy the relatively permissive regime of the EHDS.[78] Such a choice could be problematic from the perspective of lawfulness, raising issues for HDABs when evaluating and distinguishing purposes of secondary use in the general or public interest and mere experimental, data-intensive AI projects,[79] against the lack of clear and specific criteria,[80] and, moreover, could pose an issue when deliberating on how legitimate a proposed activity is in light of the overarching goal of the EHDS to enable access to health data for societally beneficial purposes. The legislature seemingly took this on board and restructured the provision on allowed purposes of secondary use that will need to be compliant with Article 6(1) GDPR; these now include activities in public interest in the area of public and occupational health; policy-making and regulatory activities to support the health or care sector; health statistics; health training and education; scientific research contributing to public health or health technology assessments, under which the development and innovation activities and training, testing, and evaluation of algorithms are subsumed; and improving the delivery of healthcare, adding that the first three purposes are only reserved for public sector bodies. Consequently, the activities that were considered most problematic in the initial proposal will arguably need to be assessed against the tenets of scientific research.

Secondly, the fairness principle is another cornerstone of the right to data protection,[81] with both procedural and substantive roles.[82] Its procedural role refers to data controllers complying with requirements that ensure effective implementation of the data protection principles, like the provision of information. The EHDS seems to understand fairness in a similar, procedural manner, as fairness is mentioned in relation to HDABs and their transparency obligations, further discussed below.[83] Regarding the substantive dimension of fairness, the notion is commonly associated with a balancing exercise among the interests of the data subject and controller or other relevant interests.[84] As posited, in the general context of health data (re-)use, a definite understanding of fairness is lacking and is usually considered to be context-dependent,[85] but it mainly refers to (overcoming) the tension between individual control or autonomy and promoting the broader public interest in health data sharing and re-use. While this also seems the underlying logic of the EHDS, problematic from the vantage point of fairness can be cases in which public interest that overrides individual autonomy is unspecified or defined broadly, since public interest as a justification for secondary use cannot be boundless.[86] Considering the initially broadly constructed purposes of secondary use, which could cause issues also for HDABs' decision-making, the EHDS now provides some more clarity on how access to data for secondary use should contribute to the general interest of society, referring to 'new medicines, medical devices, health care products and services at affordable and fair prices'. This point might be particularly relevant in HDABs' assessments of the data applications, but it inevitably invites to an extent a normative discussion. Moreover, the opt-out clause was included in the EHDS regulation, as acknowledged in Recital 54, with cases in which opt-out can be overridden, identified, as an attempt to reach a fairer balance in this regard.

Thirdly, the GDPR principle of transparency refers to data controllers' obligation to keep data subjects informed about how their data is used before, during, and after the data processing.[87] This information should be easily accessible and easy to understand.[88] In terms of transparency, HDABs hold a central role: on the one hand, they are essential for ensuring the availability of information to (prospective) data users, by maintaining a national dataset catalogue on the source and nature of health data and the conditions for making it available.[89] On the other hand, HDABs also assume transparency duties towards the individuals. It was argued that the EHDS proposal weakened the transparency in secondary uses of health data.[90] Namely, transparency is a difficult principle to implement in the domain of digital health, in light of technological opacity, corporate secrecy, and general lack of understanding of the functioning of AI.[91] In addition, concrete exceptions to data subject rights in terms of information provision are already in place under the GDPR scientific research regime.[92] Thus, the impression was that the EHDS proposal watered down transparency even more, since it only required HDABs to provide general-level information on secondary use. The EHDS now addresses this by mandating the provision of information about granted permits, measures to protect the rights of natural persons and how they can exercise their rights, for example, as regards opting-out, and the outcomes of secondary use, as a complement to Article 14 GDPR. Regarding transparency obligations to natural persons, HDABs will need to maintain an easily searchable website on conditions for the secondary use, including a record of who has been granted access to which datasets to allow natural persons to understand whether their data have been used for secondary use. The EHDS proposal foresaw an exception to general information provision of HDABs for when 'the results of the research could assist in the treatment of the natural person concerned'.[93] The EHDS now in Article 58(3) requires that natural persons are informed about significant findings related to their health through data holders. When the data user informs the HDAB about the said finding, the latter shall contact the data holder that is to inform the natural person or their treating physician.

The general information as envisioned in the initial proposal might have been considered justified on cost-efficiency reasons, as well as in light of the proposal's data protection safeguards.[94] Still, we were left with the question of practical implications for transparency. Pursuant to the EHDS proposal, individuals would have only a limited idea about data flows in the context of the EHDS and, furthermore, little room to exercise oversight and negotiate their position therein.[95] This could risk undermining data subject rights,[96] and, as pointed out, also seemed contrary to one of the EHDS' own objectives: the empowerment of natural persons 'in relation to the availability and control of their electronic health data'.[97] The final text on the EHDS now includes a more granular level of information on secondary use and, as a means to give some level of control back to natural persons, and also introduces the right to opt-out of secondary data use, subject to exceptions.[98] Practical implementation will show whether such transparency requirements are sufficient in fostering meaningful communication or if they serve more to 'nudge' individuals towards the goals of the regulator to open up the health data market. The latter would mean that the public interest acts not 'as an end in itself, but rather as a means towards the end of making more data-intensive health research [and innovation, author's note] possible'.[99]

Lastly, the GDPR refers to accountability as the responsibility for compliance, and demonstrating compliance, with the data protection principles. According to the GDPR, accountability lies with the data controller,[100] who must, for that purpose, implement appropriate technical and organisational measures that give effect to the substantive data protection principles.[101] As suggested in the literature, meaningful accountability would imply effective deliberation on the basis of information provided with direct beneficiaries and the public, measures for correcting any possible process failures,[102] and effective public participation.[103] In the context of the EHDS, HDABs are positioned as a focal point of ensuring a high(er) level of accountability as regards health data processing;[104] they have obligations to make public the information that is relevant to society as a whole, beyond just affected individuals, as they need to make public information on all issued data permits and data requests and applications, measures related to non-compliance, and the results of secondary use, as communicated by the data users.[105] Furthermore, the EHDS tasks HDABs with reporting duties, instructing them to publicise on their website a biennial activity report, also to be sent to the Commission and the EHDS Board, on the nature of data applications, the fulfilment of regulatory and contractual commitments by data holders and users, information on processing times, revenues, fines, and audits carried out, etc.[106] From the viewpoint of accountability, this might be considered a positive measure.[107] As suggested however, the derogation from providing specific information, at least as conceived in the Commission's proposal, might in turn deprive interested parties, like the civil society or journalists, from accessing timely information on the secondary use of health data and therefore limit their public oversight role[108] and thus their capacity to assess whether this particular policy action successfully fulfils its objectives. Again, the roll-out in practice will show whether the publication and reporting measures as contained in the EHDS regulation allow for appropriate public oversight.

Importantly, the EHDS also instructs HDABs to work with the relevant stakeholders in healthcare, including representatives of patients and representatives of data holders and users, like healthcare providers, researchers, and ethics committees in the exercise of their tasks,[109] and report on their activities carried out in relation to engagement and consultation of the stakeholders.[110] While this seems key to advancing accountability, the regulation does not further suggest what HDABs' cooperation with the stakeholders should entail in practice. Thus, while it could be argued that the EHDS 'shows a positive evolution in the direction of stakeholder involvement, /... the latter/ risks being turned in an empty promise'[111] if said cooperation is not defined more concretely. On a positive side, the EHDS in Article 93 now also establishes a stakeholder forum, active on the EHDS Board level, which is to be considered a welcome step from the accountability perspective.

9.4.2 Institutional aspects of access to health data for secondary use

Already under the GDPR regime, various health data access mechanisms exist in (some of) the Member States. These include research ethics committee or data access committee approvals or a DPA authorisation. Another option in place is for the data controller to provide access to the required health data directly.[112] In other words, having a procedure in place to access health data for secondary use is nothing new. The EHDS now introduces an HDAB to manage access to health data for secondary use and thus centralises the governance of health data access within a particular Member State,[113] attempting to unify this process on the EU level.

From an efficiency perspective, such an approach is sensible, since researchers, innovators, policymakers, and regulators will now be able to have 'access to quality data for their work in a secure way, with a trusted governance and at lower costs than relying on consent'.[114] However, it also needs to be noted that the tasks envisioned for the HDABs are resource- and knowledge-intensive. To handle data applications, for example, the personnel needs to possess the necessary administrative and legal expertise, as well as the domain-specific knowledge of health data and its possible uses.[115] Experience from Finland, whose agency FinData served as an inspiration for the governance of the secondary use in the EHDS,[116] demonstrates that there is a steep learning curve with setting up such a body, that demands of data users are high, a variety of possible data types and processing methods can be applied for, and dissatisfaction can emerge with regards to the handling times.[117] The EHDS sets out a wide array of responsibilities for HDABs, which necessitate HDABs to be sufficiently staffed and otherwise supported to be effective and responsive. Developments in Ireland as regards GDPR enforcement are in this regard illustrative of the issues that can emerge when insufficient resources are allocated to the responsible authorities, since the Irish data protection authority is accused by some to represent a bottleneck in data protection enforcement.[118] The multitasking nature of HDABs is further problematised by Reichel in this book.

In the light of this, and considering some member states have more experience with data access mechanisms and more (institutional) capital in dealing with health data re-use than others,[119] there is hence a significant risk of inconsistency in HDABs' approach(es) across the EU in relation to the institutional aspects of the governance of secondary use.[120] This could then have negative implications on the interpretation and realisation of its overall aspirations, including those pertaining to public interest, as the EHDS could end up being implemented in a fragmented or incoherent manner, making the governance of the secondary use of health data less effective. An additional issue to take into account is the relationship between HDABs and the above-mentioned existing data access mechanisms.[121] While they could represent a relevant source of expertise, the question is if and how will their established procedures and knowledge be integrated into the workings of HDABs. Next, what kind of institutional culture HDABs will themselves develop – or what is the culture, objectives, and working methods they will adapt to, if organised as a part of an existing body – and how will this shape HDAB's understanding of secondary use in relation to public interest is also relevant.

Finally, the institutional transformations brought about by the EHDS raise another point. Since the EHDS establishes an administrative procedure, with data permits serving as a barrier to entry into a regulated activity,[122] it places a deliberation on secondary use in the general or public interest within a bureaucratic system. Thus far, this deliberation was entrusted to specialised committees (see above), bound by professional and other domain-relevant norms; the EHDS now shifts the locus of power and decision-making into the hands of an administrative agency, the HDAB,[123] placing it further outside of a civic or political context.[124] Thus, an absence of a clear substantive guidance on what constitutes secondary use in the general or public interest, and a lack of stakeholder involvement, could result either in an 'anything goes' situation or in a situation where individual public officials employ their own personal values in decision-making, or, more fundamentally, in a situation in which a non-elected agency rules on what is in the interest of the public and what not.[125] Neither of these options seem particularly satisfactory.

9.4.3 HDABs and the political economy of health data: capturing the benefits of secondary use

Since '/o/pening up informational resources means exposing them to the power structures governing the networked information ecosystem',[126] the role of the HDABs in the broader context of the ever more concentrated digital economy that rests upon intensified data sourcing needs to be examined,[127] as they are set to be key facilitators of health data flows into it.[128] From the public interest perspective, one key question that emerges is: how and for whom will the benefits of the secondary use materialise and how will they be shared with the 'public'? The EHDS establishes a duty for health data users to make public the results of output of the secondary use within 18 months and inform the HDABs about them that are in turn to make these results public. While the text of the proposal was not concrete as to what is meant by 'research results or output', the regulation now lists as an example scientific publications. When appropriate, data holders should, in addition to a link to publication, also provide to the HDAB a lay summary.[129] It seems that the EHDS is satisfied with the public deriving indirect benefits from the outputs of secondary use and does not envision more substantial benefit-sharing arrangements for the population affected or for health systems more broadly.[130]

Another issue that concerns the position of the HDABs in the political economy of health data is the functioning of the data-driven markets themselves. As access to data is one of the conditions for companies to effectively compete on digital markets,[131] opening up the data market could be seen in a positive light.[132] From this vantage point, the EHDS counters data concentration tendencies and makes data-driven markets more contestable through data sharing.[133] The issue here is how the EHDS regime for secondary use of health data will play out in practice. Namely, permit applications can be quite burdensome, especially for smaller entities, whereas those with the resources required for bearing the (administrative) load of applying for data access might benefit more, and more often, from such a regime.[134] Note that the text of the political agreement on the EHDS calls for the Commission to support the harmonisation of the applications, to minimise their burden. Nonetheless, those already powerful might ultimately gain access to even more data and generate important competitive advantages over the less powerful entities.[135]

With its focus on data uses, rather than on those using health data,[136] the EHDS moreover seems to widely open the doors for accessing 'troves of broadly defined' health data to any entity with infrastructural and technological capabilities wishing to develop health AI, 'by merely pleading its case about its algorithmic project and the measures it will put in place to protect people's data'.[137] This includes 'Big Tech' corporations like Apple or Google, not native to the field of healthcare, but firmly establishing their presence therein.[138] While the EHDS regulation seems to remedy the concerns expressed in relation to the Commission's initial proposal, namely that 'Big Tech' initiatives could 'easily align with rather ill-defined notions of "general interest"',[139] by including research and development of health AI under 'scientific research' with the aim of benefitting the end-users, it still, in essence, facilitates access to health data that might end up reinforcing the data power of 'Big Tech' firms, allowing them to further leverage it in the health domain.[140] With benefit understood loosely, without a clear mandate to 'give back', as examined by Santamaría in this book, HDABs would become the main enablers of such a regime, putting under question public interest justifications of the EHDS.

As shown, navigating the landscape of secondary use might be a challenge for the HDABs. Again, while the EHDS now provides more precision, compared to the text of the proposal, as to what are the envisioned societally beneficial purposes contained in the secondary use of health data, the HDABs will need to tread carefully not to inflate or overstep the public expectations as regards data sharing practices,[141] as well as their own decision-making powers. Namely, if the trust of the public is harmed, for instance if the risk-benefit distribution in health data re-use is perceived as unfair, individuals might withdraw their support for data sharing activities[142] or lose confidence in healthcare and research altogether, which would negatively affect individual and population health.[143]

9.5 Conclusions and recommendations

While generating public benefit by enabling secondary use of health data 'lies at the heart of the EHDS',[144] this contribution concurs with Marelli and others who suggested that in its proposal stage, the 'key concepts and provisions that should support and help realize this aim /... were/ still vague and underdeveloped'.[145] While the (legally non-binding) recitals of the political agreement now provide some further indications on what constitutes public interest in the context of the EHDS, the question remains as to whether these updates are enough to guarantee public acceptance and trust as necessary foundations to secondary use of health data. As public interest (in secondary use of health data) can be understood being 'both /in/ the robust protection of individual privacy and uses of data that stand to result in wider public benefit',[146] especially as regards the latter, HDABs are critically positioned to manage the rather broad purposes of secondary use under the assumption that the accessibility of health data will lead to the materialisation of (health) benefits for the public.[147] While the qualification as to what are the supposed societal benefits in the text of the political agreement is a welcome development, especially in light of changes introduced to Article 53, the EHDS in its essence remains a mechanism to incentivise health data markets. The public might thus need to be satisfied with the EHDS indirectly contributing to the societal objectives of the data sharing paradigm as they relate to health protection and improvement, and more directly supporting the market efficiency and innovation claims.

Conversely, the identified vacuum between the direct and indirect aspirations of secondary use could also present an opportunity to envision the role of HDABs as promoting what Prainsack refers to as *desirable* secondary use of health data; in the light of this, HDABs should assume their role to counter the concerns related to the trickle-down approach by guaranteeing that secondary use is only allowed 'if it can be plausibly assumed that the data use will have clear benefits for either many [people], for society as a whole, or for future generations, and no person or group will experience significant [and undue] harm'[148] from it. Thus, HDABs would proactively assume their role as health data custodians maintaining the 'social licence' for data-intensive research and innovation,[149] instead of acting merely as administrators of a system promoting a trickle-down approach to secondary use of health data. In line with the desirable use approach, such licence refers to enabling the health data market while ensuring that data privacy and security are respected, which is what the EHDS already dedicates attention to, but it also refers to measures that more directly counter the imbalances and promote public good and welfare.[150] Consequently, HDABs would represent the key to build, maintain, and promote the necessary level of trust,[151] as their loyalty would more explicitly lie with the interests of the individuals and the society[152] in their respective national contexts.

For this, firstly, the scope of secondary use of health data in the public interest is to be clearly articulated in advance,[153] to enable HDABs to operate with a shared understanding of what types of secondary use of health data are, in fact, in the public interest.[154] As Slokenberga argued, '/i/f the EU is claiming an enhanced role in the area, it needs to be ready to assume the responsibility that follows it',[155] indicating that this is the task for the regulator. The (HDABs') assessment of the public interest should indeed be case-specific and thus the secondary use provisions not overly prescriptive, but at a minimum, as also suggested by the EDPB-EDPS joint opinion on the Commission's proposal, the allowed purposes of secondary use in Article 53 should be sufficiently linked to public interest and to (public) health. The text of the political agreement on the EHDS to an extent remedied this, including by bringing development and innovation and training and testing of AI under the auspices and logic of scientific research and by providing examples of concrete societal benefits stemming from secondary use in Recital 61. Yet, there is perhaps more scope to consider, in addition to guaranteeing procedural fairness and transparency, further substantive principles of, for instance, reciprocity, non-exploitation, public good, participation, and inclusivity,[156] conducive to the materialisation of societal benefits from secondary use in relation to health specifically. Translating these principles into practice should be done on the HDABs level on a case-by-case basis, to truly ensure fairness, affordability, and enhanced access to the outcomes of secondary use. Such stronger link to EHDS' health benefits might be particularly relevant in light of EU's ambitions to establish a European Health Union and the calls for 'more Europe' in health matters.[157]

Apart from that, the EHDS already offers some possibilities for such custodian role for HDABs to be realised. In the first instance, this pertains to the HDABs' role in issuing data permits and to their relationship towards the data users. As posited, the main question here revolves around if and how will the value generated from health data assets flow back into the health and care sector,[158] broadly defined, since a significant part of health data intended for secondary use originates therefrom. While the political agreement on the EHDS mandates data access applications also to refer to expected benefits, HDABs should be especially mindful in assessments to how the data user intends the benefits will materialise and could, for example in the conditions spelled out in the data permit, refer to benefit-sharing arrangements. This could for instance concern specifying, in dialogue with the data users, open access requirements, measures for affordable access to innovative treatments or products and services developed through secondary use, the promotion of sharing of know-how, access to intellectual property, or even measures like redistribution of financial profits back into the public domain.[159] Next, HDABs should, in their supervisory capacity, proactively rely on the options they have available to deter from non-desirable uses,[160] and explore mechanisms for harm mitigation and compensation.[161] Notably, the text of the political agreement introduces the rights to lodge a complaint and to compensation for those that suffered damage as a result of an infringement of the regulation, which is to be considered a positive development.

Article 68 of the EHDS now importantly introduces cumulative criteria to issue a data permit, which instruct that the intended purpose matches one of the purposes listed in Article 53(1); that the requested data is necessary, adequate, and proportionate to said purpose; that processing complies with a legal basis under the GDPR; that the applicant is qualified to carry out the intended purpose and demonstrates sufficient measures to prevent health data misuse; and that ethical assessment is included where applicable. Still, to remedy concerns regarding fairness, for private companies and 'Big Tech' firms specifically, HDABs could require a demonstration in concrete terms that access to health data will be for purposes other than purely commercial and how they abide by the relevant ethical, epistemic, and methodological standards.[162] Lastly, HDABs should support data application process and in their work proactively lean into the option to prioritise among applications, as indicated in Recital 74, but for instance focus on those that address health inequalities or the needs of vulnerable or traditionally excluded population groups, etc.[163]

Some recommendations can also be formulated as regards the involvement of the interested parties and stakeholders in HDABs' work, most notably the data holders, natural persons, and the general public, to strengthen acceptability and oversight. In this regard, the transparency expected of the HDABs is welcome as it enables individuals and the society a sense of oversight and maintains a level of reciprocity,[164] but this information should be as specific as possible. Even then, information campaigns in themselves do not necessarily imply a genuine two-way communication required to maintain public trust.[165] In this sense, the 'rather passive reference to cooperation with stakeholders' indicates that there is further scope for the EHDS to enable more active ways for citizens' engagement,[166] in order to understand and meaningfully respond to their needs, interests, and concerns.[167] Diverse strategies of consulting, educating, and enabling participation are possible. The literature suggests involving individuals in the governance of secondary use by including them in the data access bodies directly, but also via public talks and deliberations, forums, or citizen juries, or in the form of encouraging collective data governance approaches.[168] HDABs as health data custodians could thus be instrumental for facilitating a more bottom-up approach to health data governance,[169] conducive to a genuine dialogue among all the involved parties that could contribute to desirable secondary use of health data.

While the EHDS now opens the doors for implementing these recommendations, it is imperative that the provisions contained therein are implemented to lead EHDS to truly work 'for people and science', and the HDABs will be key for this. On the practical level, all this will require ample resources, skills and expertise, as well as sensitivity to the matters at hand. Indeed, the HDABs already have a lot on their plates and the enhanced health data custodian role would significantly add to the tasks. Whether this is a realistic expectation or not, remains to be seen. To make it more manageable, the EHDS Board could in this sense be instrumental for overcoming the possible fragmentation, ensuring cooperation and coherent governance, and supporting the capabilities of HDABs in this proposed role towards all the involved parties in secondary use of health data and the public. In this regard, one of the positive outcomes of the political agreement is the introduction of the stakeholders' forum to advise the EHDS Board, which could also importantly contribute to increasing public participation and trust.

Acknowledgements

My research has been part of the Digital Legal Studies research initiative, funded through the Law Sector Plan of the Dutch Ministry of Education, Culture and Science. I am thankful to the editors for their thoughtful comments on this chapter and to Taner Kuru, Kyle McKibbin, Giorgio Monti, Siddharth Peter de Souza, and Thomas Tombal for their helpful feedback on an earlier draft.

Notes

1 Denis Horgan and others, 'European Health Data Space – An opportunity now to grasp the future of data-driven healthcare' (2022) 10 *Healthcare* 1629.
2 Tim Hulsen, 'Sharing is caring—Data sharing initiatives in healthcare' (2020) 17 *International Journal of Environmental* Research and Public Health 3046.
3 Regina Becker and others, 'Secondary use of personal health data: When is it 'Further Processing' under the GDPR, and what are the implications for data controllers?' (2022) 30 *European Journal of Health Law* 129, 131.
4 See Tjaša Petročnik, 'Health data between improving health(Care) and fuelling the data economy: editorial' (2022) 2022 *Technology and Regulation* 124, 125. See also 'EDPB-EDPS Joint Opinion 03/2022 on the Proposal for a Regulation on the European Health Data Space' (2022) https://edpb.europa.eu/our-work-tools/our-documents/edpbedps-joint-opinion/edpb.edps-joint-opinion-032022-proposal_en accessed on 3 November 2023.
5 European Commission, 'A European strategy for data' (Communication) (2020) 66 final, 2–3.
6 European Commission, 'Proposal for a regulation – The European Health Data Space' COM(2022) 197 final, Article 1.
7 EHDS Recital 1.
8 European Commission, 'A European Health Data Space: harnessing the power of health data for people, patients and innovation' COM(2022) 196 final.
9 European Commission, 'European health union: A European Health Data Space for people and science' (2022) https://ec.europa.eu/commission/presscorner/detail/en/IP_22_2711 accessed on 3 November 2023.
10 See, for example, Roberta Pastorino and others, 'Benefits and challenges of big data in healthcare: An overview of the European initiatives' (2019) 29 *The European Journal of Public Health* 23; Mahsa Shabani, 'Will the European health data space change data sharing rules?' (2022) 375 *Science* 1357, 1357.

11 See BEUC, 'Consumer attitudes to health data sharing. Survey results from eight EU countries' (2023) https://www.beuc.eu/sites/default/files/publications/BEUC-X-2023-051_consumer_attitudes_to_health_data.pdf accessed on 3 November 2023.
12 EHDS Recital 64. See also Mahsa Shabani and Sami Yilmaz, 'Lawfulness in secondary use of health data: Interplay between three regulatory frameworks of GDPR, DGA & EHDS' (2022) 2022 *Technology and Regulation* 128, 132.
13 Petros Terzis, 'Compromises and asymmetries in the European health data space' (2022) 30 *European Journal of Health Law* 345, 350.
14 See EHDS Article 51.
15 EHDS Articles 53 and 54.
16 See further Marlies Saelaert and others, 'Expanding citizen engagement in the secondary use of health data: An opportunity for national health data access bodies to realise the intentions of the European Health Data Space' (2023) 81(168) *Archives of Public Health.* DOI: 10.1186/s13690-023-01182-4. https://link.springer.com/article/10.1186/s13690-023-01182-4.
17 European Parliament, 'European health data space' (2022) https://www.europarl.europa.eu/RegData/etudes/BRIE/2022/733646/EPRS_BRI(2022)733646_EN.pdf accessed on 3 November 2023, p. 8.
18 EHDS Article 55(1).
19 EHDSArticle 67.
20 See EHDS Recital 52 and Article 68(10).
21 EHDS Article 68(7).
22 Unless access to pseudonymised data is justified, EHDS Recital 72 and Article 66.
23 EHDS Articles 57 and 73.
24 EHDS Article 68(3).
25 EHDS Article 68(9).
26 EHDS Article 63.
27 EHDS Article 57(1)(j).
28 EHDS Article 57.
29 EHDS Article 55(1).
30 EHDS Article 55. See also Terzis (n 13) 349.
31 EHDS Article 55(2).
32 EHDS Article 62.
33 See EHDS Article 75.
34 EHDS Recital 80.
35 EHDS Articles 92 and 94. See also Article 82 and Terzis (n 13) 352.
36 European strategy for data (n 5) 21-2.
37 European Commission (n 9).
38 EHDS Recital 1.
39 EHDS Recital 52.
40 See also Shabani and Yilmaz (n 12) 132. See generally Alexander J. Belohlavek, 'Public Policy and Public Interest in International Law and EU Law' (2012) *CYIL – Czech Yearbook of International Law: Public Policy and Ordre Public*. Juris Publishing.
41 EHDS Recital 61.
42 Eric R. Boot, 'Public Interest' (*Oxford Research Encyclopedia of Politics*, 2022) https://oxfordre.com/politics/display/10.1093/acrefore/9780190228637.001.0001/acrefore-9780190228637-e-2044 accessed on 3 November 2023. See also Anthony Downs, 'The public interest: Its meaning in a democracy' (1962) 29 *Social Research* 1, 1–2.
43 Marc A. Rodwin, 'Patient data: Property, privacy & the public interest' (2010) 36 *American Journal of Law & Medicine* 586, 617–618. See further Jeanise Dalli, 'Public Interest', in Valentina Colcelli and others (eds), *GDPR Requirements for Biobanking Activities Across Europe* (Springer, 2023).

44 Belohlavek (n 40). See also Iskander De Bruycker, 'Politicization and the public interest: When do the elites in Brussels address public interests in EU policy debates?' (2017) 18 *European Union Politics* 603.
45 Belohlavek (n 40).
46 See further Andrew Moravcsik and Andrea Sangiovanni, 'On Democracy and 'Public Interest' in the European Union' (2003) Center for European Studies Working Paper No. 93.
47 Boot (n 42); Downs (n 42), 1–2, 4.
48 European Commission, 'Commission Staff Working Document, Impact Assessment Report accompanying the document Proposal for a Regulation of the European Parliament and of the Council on the European Health Data Space' (3 May 2022) Swd(2022) 131 final.
49 Rodwin (n 43), 617–618.
50 See further Nadya Purtova and Gijs van Maanen, 'Data as an economic good, data as a commons, and data governance' (2023) *Law, Innovation and Technology*. DOI: 10.1080/17579961.2023.2265270.
51 Fritz Scharpf, 'The European social model: coping with the challenges of diversity' (2002) 40 *Journal of Common Market Studies* 645.
52 See, for example, Anniek de Ruijter, *EU Health Law & Policy. The Expansion of EU Power in Public Health and Health Care* (Oxford University Press 2019). As further posited, the EU has consistently relied on its internal market provisions to shape and legislate healthcare matters. Eleanor Brooks, Anniek de Ruijter and Scott L. Greer, 'Covid-19 and European Union health policy: from crisis to collective action', in Bart Vanhercke, Slavina Spasova, and Boris Fronteddu (eds), *Social policy in the European Union: State of play 2020. Facing the pandemic* (ETUI 2021), 37.
53 On 'trickle-down' approach, see, for example, Philippe Aghion and Patrick Bolton, 'A theory of trickle-down growth and development' (1997) 64 *Review of Economic Studies* 151.
54 Klein in Nicole Gross and Susi Geiger, 'Choreographing for public value in digital health?' (2023) 10 *Big Data & Society*. DOI: 10.1177/20539517231220622.
55 See in Giulia Schneider, *Health data pools under European Data Protection and competition law. Health as a digital business* (Springer Cham, 2022), 204.
56 In Mike Feintuck, *'The Public Interest' in Regulation* (Oxford University Press, 2004), 179.
57 Saelaert and others (n 16). See also Andrea Martani and others, 'A role-model for data policies? Qualitative study on the governance of health data in Denmark' (2022) 11 *Health Policy and Technology* 100683.
58 Luca Marelli and others, 'The European health data space: Too big to succeed?' (2023) 135 *Health Policy*, DOI: 10.1016/j.healthpol.2023.104861. See also Angela Ballantyne and others, 'Sharing precision medicine data with private industry: Outcomes of a citizens' jury in Singapore' (2022) 9 *Big Data & Society*. DOI: 10.1177/20539517221108988.
59 See further Jan Piasecki and Phaik Yeong Cheah, 'Ownership of individual-level health data, data sharing, and data Governance' (2022) 23 *BMC Medical Ethics* 104.
60 David Fåhraeus, Jane Reichel, and Santa Slokenberga, 'The European Health Data Space: Challenges and opportunities' (SIEPS, 2024). https://sieps.se/en/publications/2024/the-european-health-data-space/ accessed on 8 February 2024.
61 European Parliament and the Council Regulation 2016/679 of 27 April 2016 on the Protection of Natural Persons with Regard to the Processing of Personal Data and on the Free Movement of such Data (General Data Protection Regulation) [2016] OJ L 119/1, Recitals 52–53. See also Terzis (n 13) 346.
62 See GDPR Recital 159. See also Ciara Staunton, Santa Slokenberga, and Deborah Mascalzoni, 'The GDPR and the research exemption: Considerations on the necessary safeguards for research biobanks' (2019) 27 *European Journal of Human Genetics* 1159.

63 Patricia Cervera de la Cruz and Mahsa Shabani, 'Conceptualizing fairness in the secondary use of health data for research: A scoping review' (2023) *Accountability in Research*. DOI: 10.1080/08989621.2023.2271394; Mary Donnelly and Maeve McDonagh, 'Health research, consent and the GDPR exemption' (2019) 26 *European Journal of Health Law* 97; Tugce Schmitt, 'What does it take to create a European Health Data Space? International commitments and national realities' (2023) 179 *Evidence in Healthcare*. DOI: 10.1016/j.zefq.2023.03.011.
64 EHDS proposal (n 6) 15. See also Terzis (n 13) 347.
65 EHDS Article 66. For the issues associated therewith, see Veronique Cimina, 'The proposal for a European Health Data Space: Between pursued objectives and data protection challenges' (2023) *ERA Forum*. DOI: 10.1007/s12027-023-00764-7.
66 GDPR Article 5(1)(a).
67 GDPR Article 6(1).
68 See EHDS Article 67(2)(c).
69 EHDS Article 68(1).
70 EHDS Recital 73, Article 68. See also Article 67(4).
71 EHDS Recital 52.
72 EHDS Recital 61.
73 See Santa Slokenberga, 'Scientific research regime 2.0? Transformations of the research regime and the protection of the data subject that the proposed EHDS regulation promises to bring along' (2022) Technology and Regulation 135, 145–156; Shabani and Yilmaz (n 12), 132–133. See also Enrique Santamaría, 'Governing health data for research, development, and innovation: The missteps of the European Health Data Space Proposal' (*Bill of Health*, 23 March 2023) https://blog.petrieflom.law.harvard.edu/2023/03/23/governing-health-data-for-research-development-and-innovation-the-missteps-of-the-european-health-data-space-proposal/ accessed on 3 November 2023.
74 See further Reichel in Chapter 10 of this anthology.
75 EDPB-EDPS Joint opinion (n 4) 22.
76 EDPB-EDPS Joint opinion (n 4) 23.
77 Terzis (n 13) 359. See also EDPS in Luca Marelli, Giuseppe Testa, and Ine Van Hoyweghen, 'Big Tech platforms in health research: Re-purposing big data governance in light of the General Data Protection Regulation's research exemption' (2021) 8 *Big Data & Society*. DOI: 10.1177/20539517211018783.
78 Luca Marelli and others (n 58).
79 Terzis (n 13) 359.
80 See further Sam H. A. Muller and others, 'The social licence for data-intensive health research: Towards co-creation, public value and trust' (2021) 22 *BMC Med Ethics* 110.
81 Cervera de la Cruz and Shabani (n 63).
82 Gianclaudio Malgieri, 'The Concept of Fairness in the GDPR: A Linguistic and Contextual Interpretation' (2020). Proceedings of FAT* '20, January 27–30, 2020. ACM, New York, NY, USA. See also European Data Protection Board, 'Guidelines 4/2019 on Article 25 Data Protection by Design and by Default. Version 2.0' (2020), 17-8.
83 EHDS proposal Recital 44.
84 Jef Ausloos, *The Right to Erasure in EU Data Protection Law* (Oxford University Press 2020); Silvia De Conca, 'The present looks nothing like the Jetsons: Deceptive design in virtual assistants and the protection of the rights of users' (2023) 51 *Computer Law & Security Review*. DOI: 10.1016/j.clsr.2023.105866. See also Cervera de la Cruz and Shabani (n 63).
85 See further Cervera de la Cruz and Shabani (n 63), providing a useful account how literature conceptualises fairness in the secondary use of health data.

86 Although some authors might defend a broad conception of public interest, on the account of 'progress in science /…/ rarely /being/ linear'. See Ballantyne and Schaefer in Cervera de la Cruz and Shabani (n 63).
87 GDPR Articles 12–15.
88 GDPR Recital 39.
89 EHDS Article 57(1)(j)(i).
90 Shabani and Yilmaz (n 12) 133.
91 Luca Marelli, Elisa Lievevrouw, and Ine Van Hoyweghen, 'Fit for purpose? The GDPR and the governance of European digital health' (2020) 41 *Policy Studies* 447.
92 GDPR Article 14(5).
93 See EHDS Proposal Recital 44. See also Cimina (n 65); Fåhraeus, Reichel, and Slokenberga (n 60), 10.
94 See Luca Marelli and others (n 58); Terzis (n 13), 360.
95 Shabani (n 10) 1359. See also Fåhraeus, Reichel, and Slokenberga (n 60) 10.
96 Slokenberga (n 73) 144. See also Luca Marelli and others (n 58).
97 See EHDS proposal Article 1(2)(a). See also Saelaert and others (n 16).
98 See EHDS Article 71.
99 See in Muller and others (n 80), who discuss secondary use of health data not in the EHDS, but in the general context of ethical data governance.
100 GDPR Article 5(2).
101 GDPR Article 24, taking into account the nature, scope, context, and purposes of processing, and the risks to the rights and freedoms of natural persons. See also Article 29 Data Protection Working Party, 'Opinion 3/2010 on the principle of accountability' (2010) 00062/10/EN. WP 173, https://ec.europa.eu/justice/article-29/documentation/opinion-recommendation/files/2010/wp173_en.pdf5-6. See further Paul de Hert and Guillermo Lazcoz, 'When GDPR-principles blind each other: Accountability, not transparency, at the heart of algorithmic governance' (2022) 8 *European Data Protection Law Review* 31.
102 De Hert and Lazcoz (n 101).
103 See Future and Instrat in Petros Terzis and (Enrique) OE Santamaría Echeverria, 'Interoperability and Governance in the European Health Data Space Regulation' (2023) *Medical Law International* 09685332231165692, 7–8.
104 EHDS proposal p 15.
105 EHDS Article 57(1)(j) (ii)-(v).
106 See EHDS Article 59.
107 Cervera de la Cruz and Shabani (n 63).
108 Terzis (n 13) 361.
109 EHDS Articles 55(2), (4) and 57(2)(b).
110 EHDS Article 59(1)(f).
111 Teodora Lalova-Spinks, Janos Meszaros, and Isabelle Huys, 'The application of data altruism in clinical research through empirical and legal analysis lenses' (2023) 10 *Frontiers in Medicine*. DOI: 10.3389/fmed.2023.1141685.
112 Mahsa Shabani, Gauthier Chassang, and Luca Marelli, 'The Impact of the GDPR on the governance of biobank research', in Santa Slokenberga, Olga Tzortzatou, and Jane Reichel (eds), *GDPR and Biobanking. Law, Governance and Technology Series, 43* (Springer 2021) 51–53. See also DG Health and Food Safety, 'Assessment of the EU Member States' rules on health data in the light of GDPR' (Publications Office of the European Union 2021) 98.
113 Terzis (n 13) 352.
114 EHDS proposal p 13. See also EHDS Impact Assessment Report (n 48).
115 See Ville Aula, 'Institutions, infrastructures, and data friction – Reforming secondary use of health data in Finland' (2019) 6 *Big Data & Society* 205395171987598, 2–3, 8. This expertise is currently not specifically addressed in the EHDS proposal. See EDPB-EDPS Joint Opinion (n 4) 24.

116 EHDS Impact Assessment Report (n 48).
117 'Common European Data Spaces and The Data Economy 03_11_2022' (*EU Data Landscape*, 2022) https://www.youtube.com/watch?v=Tl_IhR8woJ4 accessed on 10 May 2023; Fåhraeus, Reichel, and Slokenberga (n 60) 19.
118 Luca Bertuzzi, 'Ireland's privacy watchdog accused of paralysing GDPR enforcement' (*Euractiv*, 13 September 2021) https://www.euractiv.com/section/data-protection/news/irelands-privacy-watchdog-accused-of-paralysing-gdpr-enforcement/ accessed on 3 November 2023.
119 See Balint Ferencz and Bettina Buki, 'Three ways of secure data reusability in Europe: German research data centres, Finnish FinData and the French secure access data centre' (2022) 1 *ELTE Law Journal* 81; Sarah Wadmann and Klaus Hoeyer, 'Dangers of the digital fit: Rethinking seamlessness and social sustainability in data-intensive healthcare' (2018) 5 *Big Data & Society*. DOI: 10.1177/2053951717752964.
120 See Kjetil A Van Der Wel and others, 'A gold mine, but still no klondike: Nordic register data in health inequalities research' (2019) 47 *Scandinavian Journal of Public Health* 618.
121 Shabani and Yilmaz (n 12), 132.
122 Eric Biber and J.B. Ruhl, 'The permit power revisited: The theory and practice of regulatory permits in the administrative state' (2014) 64 *Duke Law Review* 133, 144. See also Richard A. Epstein, 'The permit power meets the constitution' (1995) 81 *Iowa Law Review* 407, 414–415.
123 Biber and Ruhl (n 122) 137–138.
124 See Aula (n 115) 10.
125 See Downs (n 42) 14–15.
126 Keller and Tarkowski in Terzis and Santamaría Echeverria (n 103) 6.
127 Marelli, Lievevrouw, and Van Hoyweghen (n 91). See also Pantelis Koutroumpis, 'Data as markets – It is time to talk (re)distribution' (*UNESCO Inclusive Policy Lab*, 22 Jun 2021) https://en.unesco.org/inclusivepolicylab/analytics/data-markets-%E2%80%93-it-time-talk-redistribution accessed on 3 November 2023.
128 Terzis (n 13) 350. See also Karoliina Snell, Heta Tarkkala, and Aaro Tupasela, 'A solidarity paradox – Welfare state data in global health data economy' (2023) 27 *Health* 664.
129 EHDS Recital 66, 57(1)(j)(v) and 61.
130 Terzis and Santamaría Echeverria (n 103). See also Shabani (n 10) 1359.
131 Inge Graef and Jens Pruefer, 'Governance of data sharing: A law and economics proposal' (2021) TILEC Discussion Paper 2021-001, 6.
132 Graef and Pruefer (n 131) 16. See also Bertin Martens, 'An economic perspective on data and platform market power' (2021) JRC Digital Economy Working Paper 2020–09.
133 Fåhraeus, Reichel, and Slokenberga (n 60) 15.
134 Biber and Ruhl (n 122) 180–181.
135 See, for example, Fåhraeus, Reichel, and Slokenberga (n 60) 15; Martani and others (n 57).
136 Shabani and Yilmaz (n 12) 132.
137 Terzis (n 13), 356–357. See also '[Opinion] EU plans allow big tech to exploit your medical records, without permission' (*EUobserver*, 21 April 2023) https://euobserver.com/opinion/156943 accessed on 12 May 2023.
138 See Jathan Sadowski, Salomé Viljoen, and Meredith Whittaker, 'Everyone should decide how their digital data are used—Not just tech companies' (2021) 595 *Nature* 169; Tamar Sharon, 'Blind-sided by privacy? Digital contact tracing, the Apple/Google API and big tech's newfound role as global health policy makers' (2021) 23 *Ethics and Information Technology* 45.
139 Marelli and others (n 58).
140 Terzis (n 13) 363. See also Barbara Prainsack, 'The political economy of digital data: Introduction to the special issue' (2020) 41 *Policy Studies* 439.

141 Ballantyne and others (n 58); Lea L. Skovgaard, Sarah Wadmann and Klaus Hoeyer, 'A review of attitudes towards the reuse of health data among people in the European Union: The primacy of purpose and the common good' (2019) 123 *Health Policy (Amsterdam, Netherlands)* 564.
142 Angela Ballantyne, 'How should we think about clinical data ownership?' (2020) 46 *Journal of Medical Ethics* 289. See also Muller and others (n 80).
143 Slokenberga (n 73) 145–146. See also Angela Ballantyne and G Owen Schaefer, 'Consent and the ethical duty to participate in health data research' (2018) 44 *Journal of Medical Ethics* 392, 394; Marelli and others (n 58).
144 Marelli and others (n 58).
145 Marelli and others (n 58).
146 Laurie and Stevens in Angela Ballantyne and G. Owen Schaefer, 'Public interest in health data research: Laying out the conceptual groundwork' (2020) 46 *Journal of Medical Ethics* 610.
147 See further Purtova and van Maanen (n 50).
148 Barbara Prainsack, 'Research for personalised medicine: Time for solidarity' (2017) 36 *Medicine & Law* 87, 94.
149 Muller and others (n 80).
150 See also in Judy Allen, Carolyn Adams, and Felicity Flack, 'The role of data custodians in establishing and maintaining social licence for health research' (2019) 33 *Bioethics* 502. In this regard, its governance could account for broader implications of health data (re-)use and facilitate a level of collective control. See similar in Marelli, Testa, and Van Hoyweghen (n 77).
151 The Commission in the EHDS proposal envisions ensuring trust through responsible data uses and respect for fundamental rights. Fåhraeus, Reichel, and Slokenberga (n 60), 18. Thus, in addition to this, the HDABs could serve to attest that secondary use is acceptable and in line with the values and expectations of the individuals, stakeholders, and the general public. See generally in Muller and others (n 80).
152 See also in Sara Rosenbaum, 'Data governance and stewardship: Designing data stewardship entities and advancing data access' (2010) 45 *Health Services Research* 1442.
153 See in De Bruycker (n 44).
154 Cervera de la Cruz and Shabani (n 63).
155 Slokenberga (n 73) 146.
156 Muller and others (n 80). See also Allen, Adams, and Flack (n 150).
157 See Martin McKee and Anniek de Ruijter, 'The path to a European Health Union' (2024) 36 *The Lancet Regional Health – Europe*. DOI: 10.1016/j.lanepe.2023.100794. See also Jillian Deutsch, 'Coronavirus prompts calls for 'more Europe' on health care' (*Politico*, 30 April 2020) https://www.politico.eu/article/is-it-time-to-make-health-an-eu-competence/ accessed on 5 February 2024.
158 Marelli and others (n 58).
159 See Cervera de la Cruz and Shabani (n 63); Marelli and others (n 58).
160 Fåhraeus, Reichel, and Slokenberga (n 60) 15.
161 See Aisling McMahon, Alena Buyx, and Barbara Prainsack, 'Big data governance needs more collective responsibility: The role of harm mitigation in the governance of data use in medicine and beyond' (2020) 28 *Medical Law Review* 155. Furthermore, the risk mitigation should, in this sense, pertain not only to addressing the actual risks, but also those *perceived* by the public to alleviate their concerns. Muller and others (n 80).
162 Ballantyne and others (n 58); Rosenbaum (n 152). See also Giedre Peseckyte, 'Doctors concerned about medical ethics in European health data space' (*Euractiv*, 9 November 2022) https://www.euractiv.com/section/health-consumers/news/doctors-concerned-about-medical-ethics-in-european-health-data-space/ accessed on 3 November 2023.

163 Ballantyne and Schaefer (n 143) 394–395. See also Ballantyne and others (n 58).
164 Allen, Adams, and Flack (n 150).
165 See Allen, Adams, and Flack (n 150).
166 Saelaert and others (n 16).
167 To this end, see Louise C. Druedahl and Sofia Kälvemark Sporrong, 'Patient perspectives on data sharing', in Marcelo Corrales Compagnucci and others (eds), *The law and ethics of data sharing in health sciences* (Springer Singapore 2024).
168 Cervera de la Cruz and Shabani (n 63); Muller and others (n 80); Saelaert and others (n 16).
169 See generally also in Muller and others (n 80).

List of sources

'CORRIGENDUM to the position of the European Parliament adopted at first reading on 24 April 2024 with a view to the adoption of Regulation (EU) 2024/... of the European Parliament and of the Council on the European Health Data Space' P9_TA(2024)0331 (COM(2022)0197 – C9-0167/2022 – 2022/0140(COD)), 27.11.2024 (European Health Data Space Regulation - EHDS).

Legislation

European Parliament and the Council Regulation 2016/679 of 27 April 2016 on the Protection of Natural Persons with Regard to the Processing of Personal Data and on the Free Movement of such Data (General Data Protection Regulation) [2016] OJ L 119/1.
European Parliament and the Council Regulation 2016/679 of 27 April 2016 on the Protection of Natural Persons with Regard to the Processing of Personal Data and on the Free Movement of such Data (General Data Protection Regulation) [2016] OJ L 119/1.

Official documents

'EDPB-EDPS Joint Opinion 03/2022 on the Proposal for a Regulation on the European Health Data Space' (2022) https://edpb.europa.eu/our-work-tools/our-documents/edpbedps-joint-opinion/edpb.edps-joint-opinion-032022-proposal_en accessed on 3 November 2023
Article 29 Data Protection Working Party, 'Opinion 3/2010 on the principle of accountability' (2010) 00062/10/EN. WP 173.
European Commission, 'A European Health Data Space: harnessing the power of health data for people, patients and innovation' (Communication) (2022a) 196 final.
European Commission, 'A European strategy for data' (Communication) (2020) 66 final.
European Commission, 'Proposal for a regulation – The European Health Data Space' COM(2022b) 197 final.
European Data Protection Board, 'Guidelines 4/2019 on Article 25 Data Protection by Design and by Default. Version 2.0' (2020).

Literature and other secondary sources

Aghion P, Bolton P, 'A theory of trickle-down growth and development' (1997) 64 *Review of Economic Studies* 151.
Allen J, Adams C, and Flack F, 'The role of data custodians in establishing and maintaining social licence for health research' (2019) 33 *Bioethics* 502.
Aula V, 'Institutions, infrastructures, and data friction – Reforming secondary use of health data in Finland' (2019) 6 *Big Data & Society* 205395171987598.
Ausloos J, *The right to erasure in EU data protection law* (Oxford University Press 2020).
Ballantyne A, Schaefer G O, 'Consent and the ethical duty to participate in health data research' (2018) *Journal of Medical Ethics* 44, 392.

Ballantyne A, 'How should we think about clinical data ownership?' (2020) *Journal of Medical Ethics* 46, 289.

Ballantyne A, Schaefer G O, 'Public interest in health data research: Laying out the conceptual groundwork' (2020) *Journal of Medical Ethics* 46, 610.

Ballantyne B and others, 'Sharing precision medicine data with private industry: Outcomes of a citizens' jury in Singapore' (2022) *Big Data & Society* 9. DOI: 10.1177/20539517221108988

Becker R and others, 'Secondary use of personal health data: When is it 'further processing' under the GDPR, and what are the implications for data controllers?' (2022) *European Journal of Health Law* 30, 129. DOI: 10.1163/15718093-bja10094

Belohlavek A J, 'Public policy and public interest in international law and EU Law' (2012) *CYIL – Czech Yearbook of International Law: Public Policy and Ordre Public*. Juris Publishing, New York.

Bertuzzi L, 'Ireland's privacy watchdog accused of paralysing GDPR enforcement' (*Euractiv*, 13 September 2021). https://www.euractiv.com/section/data-protection/news/irelands-privacy-watchdog-accused-of-paralysing-gdpr-enforcement/, accessed on 3 November.

BEUC, 'Consumer attitudes to health data sharing. Survey results from eight EU countries' (2023). https://www.beuc.eu/sites/default/files/publications/BEUC-X-2023-051_consumer_attitudes_to_health_data.pdf accessed on 3 November 2023.

Biber E, Ruhl J B, 'The permit power revisited: The theory and practice of regulatory permits in the administrative state' (2014) 64 *Duke Law Review* 133.

Boot E R, *Public interest* (Oxford Research Encyclopedia of Politics, 2022) https://oxfordre.com/politics/display/10.1093/acrefore/9780190228637.001.0001/acrefore-9780190228637-e-2044 accessed on 3 November 2023.

Brooks E, de Ruijter A, Greer S L, 'Covid-19 and European Union health policy: From crisis to collective action', in Bart Vanhercke, Slavina Spasova, and Boris Fronteddu (eds), *Social policy in the European Union: state of play 2020*. Facing the pandemic (ETUI 2021).

De Bruycker I, 'Politicization and the public interest: When do the elites in Brussels address public interests in EU policy debates?' (2017) 18 *European Union Politics* 603.

Cervera de la Cruz P, Shabani M (2023) 'Conceptualizing fairness in the secondary use of health data for research: A scoping review'. *Accountability in Research*. DOI: 10.1080/08989621.2023.2271394

Cimina V, 'The proposal for a European Health Data Space: Between pursued objectives and data protection challenges' (2023) *ERA Forum*. DOI: 10.1007/s12027-023-00764-7

European Commission, 'Commission staff working document, impact assessment report accompanying the document Proposal for a Regulation of the European Parliament and of the Council on the European Health Data Space' (3 May 2022c) Swd(2022) 131 final.

'Common European Data Spaces and The Data Economy 03_11_2022' (*EU Data Landscape*, 2022). https://www.youtube.com/watch?v=Tl_IhR8woJ4 accessed on 10 May 2023.

De Conca S, 'The present looks nothing like the Jetsons: Deceptive design in virtual assistants and the protection of the rights of users' (2023) *Computer Law & Security Review* 51. DOI: 10.1016/j.clsr.2023.105866

Dalli J, 'Public interest', in Valentina Colcelli and others (eds), *GDPR requirements for biobanking activities across Europe* (Springer, 2023).

Deutsch J, *Coronavirus prompts calls for 'more Europe' on health care* (*Politico*, 30 April 2020). https://www.politico.eu/article/is-it-time-to-make-health-an-eu-competence/ accessed on 5 February 2024.

DG Health and Food Safety, 'Assessment of the EU member states' rules on health data in the light of GDPR' (Publications Office of the European Union, 2021).

Donnelly M, McDonagh M, 'Health research, consent and the GDPR exemption' (2019) 26 *European Journal of Health Law* 97.

Downs A, 'The public interest: Its meaning in a democracy' (1962) 29 *Social Research* 1.
Druedahl L. C., Kälvemark Sporrong S, 'Patient perspectives on data sharing', in Marcelo Corrales Compagnucci and others (eds), *The law and ethics of data sharing in health sciences* (Springer Singapore, 2024).
Epstein R A, 'The permit power meets the constitution' (1995) 81 *Iowa Law Review* 407.
European Commission, 'European Health Union: A European Health Data Space for people and science' (2022d). https://ec.europa.eu/commission/presscorner/detail/en/IP_22_2711 accessed on 3 November 2023.
European Parliament, 'European Health Data Space' (2022). https://www.europarl.europa.eu/RegData/etudes/BRIE/2022/733646/EPRS_BRI(2022)733646_EN.pdf accessed on 3 November 2023.
Fåhraeus D, Reichel J, Slokenberga S, 'The European Health Data space: Challenges and opportunities' (*SIEPS*, 2024). https://sieps.se/en/publications/2024/the-european-health-data-space/ accessed on 8 February 2024.
Ferencz B, Buki B, 'Three ways of secure data reusability in Europe: German research data centres, Finnish FinData and the French secure access data centre' (2022) 1 *ELTE Law Journal* 81.
Feintuck M, *The Public Interest' in Regulation* (Oxford University Press 2004).
Graef I, Pruefer J, 'Governance of data sharing: A law and economics proposal' (2021) TILEC Discussion Paper 2021-001.
Gross N, Geiger S, 'Choreographing for public value in digital health?' (2023) *Big Data & Society* 10. DOI: 10.1177/20539517231220622
de Hert P, Lazcoz G, 'When GDPR-principles blind each other: Accountability, not transparency, at the heart of algorithmic governance' (2022) 8 *European Data Protection Law Review* 31.
Horga Dn and others, 'European Health Data Space – An opportunity now to grasp the future of data-driven healthcare' (2022) 10 *Healthcare* 1629. DOI: 10.3390/healthcare10091629
Hulsen T, 'Sharing is caring—Data sharing initiatives in healthcare' (2020) 17 *International Journal of Environmental Research and Public Health* 3046. DOI: 10.3390/ijerph17093046
Koutroumpis P, 'Data as markets – It is time to talk (re)distribution' (*UNESCO Inclusive Policy Lab*, 22 June 2021). https://en.unesco.org/inclusivepolicylab/analytics/data-markets-%E2%80%93-it-time-talk-redistribution accessed on 3 November 2023
Lalova-Spinks T, Meszaros J, Huys I, 'The application of data altruism in clinical research through empirical and legal analysis lenses' (2023) *Frontiers in Medicine* 10. DOI: 10.3389/fmed.2023.1141685
Malgieri G, 'The concept of fairness in the GDPR: A linguistic and contextual interpretation' (2020). Proceedings of FAT* '20, January 27–30, 2020, ACM, New York, NY, USA.
Marelli L, Lievevrouw L, Van Hoyweghen I, 'Fit for purpose? The GDPR and the governance of European digital health' (2020) 41 *Policy Studies* 447. DOI: 10.1080/01442872.2020.1724929
Marelli L, Testa G, Van Hoyweghen I, 'Big Tech platforms in health research: Repurposing big data governance in light of the General Data Protection Regulation's research exemption' (2021) 8 *Big Data & Society*. DOI: 10.1177/20539517211018783
Marelli L and others, 'The European health data space: Too big to succeed?' (2023) 135 *Health Policy*. DOI: 10.1016/j.healthpol.2023.104861
Martani A and others, 'A role-model for data policies? Qualitative study on the governance of health data in Denmark' (2022) 11 *Health Policy and Technology* 100683. DOI: 10.1016/j.hlpt.2022.100683
Martens B, 'An economic perspective on data and platform market power' (2021) JRC Digital Economy Working Paper 2020-09.
McKee M, de Ruijter A, 'The path to a European Health Union' (2024) 36 *The Lancet Regional Health – Europe*. DOI: 10.1016/j.lanepe.2023.100794

McMahon A, Buyx A, Prainsack B, 'Big data governance needs more collective responsibility: The role of harm mitigation in the governance of data use in medicine and beyond' (2020) 28 *Medical Law Review* 155. DOI: 10.1093/medlaw/fwz016

Moravcsik A, Sangiovanni A, 'On democracy and "Public Interest" in the European Union' (2003) Center for European Studies Working Paper No. 93.

Muller S H and others, 'The social licence for data-intensive health research: Towards co-creation, public value and trust' (2021) 22 *BMC Med Ethics* 110. DOI: 10.1186/s12910-021-00677-5

'[Opinion] EU plans allow Big Tech to exploit your medical records, without permission' (*EUobserver*, 21 April 2023). https://euobserver.com/opinion/156943 accessed on 12 May 2023.

Pastorino R and others, 'Benefits and challenges of big data in healthcare: An overview of the European Initiatives' (2019) 29 *The European Journal of Public Health* 23. DOI: 10.1093/eurpub/ckz168

Peseckyte G, 'Doctors concerned about medical ethics in European health data space' (*Euractiv*, 9 November 2022). https://www.euractiv.com/section/health-consumers/news/doctors-concerned-about-medical-ethics-in-european-health-data-space/ accessed on 3 November 2023.

Petročnik T, 'Health data between improving health(care) and fuelling the data economy: Editorial' (2022) 2022 *Technology and Regulation* 124. DOI: 10.26116/techreg.2022.012

Piasecki J, Cheah P Y, 'Ownership of individual-level health data, data sharing, and data governance' (2022) 23 *BMC Medical Ethics* 104. DOI: 10.1186/s12910-022-00848-y

Prainsack B, 'Research for personalised medicine: Time for solidarity' (2017) 36 *Medicine & Law* 87.

Prainsack B, 'The political economy of digital data: Introduction to the special issue' (2020) 41 *Policy Studies* 439. DOI: 10.1080/01442872.2020.1723519

Purtova N, van Maanen G, 'Data as an economic good, data as a commons, and data governance' (2023) *Law, Innovation and Technology*. DOI: 10.1080/17579961.2023.2265270

Rodwin M A, 'Patient data: Property, privacy & the public interest' (2010) 36 *American Journal of Law & Medicine* 586. DOI: 10.1177/009885881003600403

Rosenbaum S, 'Data governance and stewardship: Designing data stewardship entities and advancing data access' (2010) 45 *Health Services Research* 1442. DOI: 10.1111/j.1475-6773.2010.01140.x

de Ruijter A, *EU health law & policy. The expansion of EU power in public health and health care* (Oxford University Press, 2019).

Sadowski J, Viljoen S, Whittaker M, 'Everyone should decide how their digital data are used – Not just tech companies' (2021) 595 *Nature* 169. DOI: 10.1038/d41586-021-01812-3

Saelaert M and others, 'Expanding citizen engagement in the secondary use of health data: An opportunity for national health data access bodies to realise the intentions of the European Health Data Space' (2023) 81 *Archives of Public Health*. DOI: 10.1186/s13690-023-01182-4

Santamaría E, 'Governing health data for research, development, and innovation: The missteps of the european health data space proposal' (*Bill of Health*, 23 March 2023). https://blog.petrieflom.law.harvard.edu/2023/03/23/governing-health-data-for-research-development-and-innovation-the-missteps-of-the-european-health-data-space-proposal/ accessed on 3 November 2023.

Scharpf F, 'The European social model: Coping with the challenges of diversity' (2002) 40 *Journal of Common Market Studies* 645.

Schmitt T, 'What does it take to create a European Health Data Space? International commitments and national realities' (2023) 179 *Evidence in Healthcare*. DOI: 10.1016/j.zefq.2023.03.011

Schneider G, *Health data pools under european data protection and competition law. Health as a digital business* (Springer Cham, 2022).

Shabani M, Chassang G, Marelli L, 'The impact of the GDPR on the governance of biobank research', in Santa Slokenberga, Olga Tzortzatou, and Jane Reichel (eds), *GDPR and biobanking. Law, governance and technology series*, 43 (Springer 2021). DOI: 10.1007/978-3-030-49388-2_4

Shabani M, 'Will the European Health Data Space change data sharing rules?' (2022) 375 *Science* 1357. DOI: 10.1126/science.abn4874

Shabani M, Yilmaz S, 'Lawfulness in secondary use of health data: Interplay between three regulatory frameworks of GDPR, DGA & EHDS' (2022) *Technology and Regulation* 128. DOI: 10.26116/techreg.2022.013

Sharon T, 'Blind-sided by privacy? Digital contact tracing, the Apple/Google API and Big Tech's newfound role as global health policy makers' (2021) 23 *Ethics and Information Technology* 45. DOI: 10.1007/s10676-020-09547-x

Skovgaard L L, Wadmann S, Hoeyer K, 'A review of attitudes towards the reuse of health data among people in the European Union: The primacy of purpose and the common good' (2019) 123 *Health Policy (Amsterdam, Netherlands)* 564. DOI: 10.1016/j.healthpol.2019.03.012

Slokenberga S, 'Setting the foundations: Individual rights, public interest, scientific research and biobanking', in Santa Slokenberga, Olga Tzortzatou, and Jane Reichel (eds), *GDPR and biobanking. Law, governance and technology series*, 43 (Springer, 2021). DOI: 10.1007/978-3-030-49388-2_2

Slokenberga S, 'Scientific research regime 2.0? Transformations of the research regime and the protection of the data subject that the proposed EHDS regulation promises to bring along' (2022) 2022 *Technology and Regulation* 135. DOI: 10.26116/techreg.2022.014

Snell K, Tarkkala H, Tupasela A, 'A solidarity paradox – Welfare state data in global health data economy' (2023) 27 *Health* 664. DOI: 10.1177/13634593211069320

Staunton C, Slokenberga S, Mascalzoni D, 'The GDPR and the research exemption: Considerations on the necessary safeguards for research biobanks' (2019) 27 *European Journal of Human Genetics* 1159. DOI: 10.1038/s41431-019-0386-5

Terzis P, 'Compromises and asymmetries in the European Health Data Space' (2022) *European Journal of Health Law* 1. DOI: 10.1163/15718093-bja10099

Terzis P, Santamaría Echeverria E O E, 'Interoperability and governance in the European Health Data Space Regulation' (2023) *Medical Law International* 09685332231165692. DOI 10.1177/09685332231165692

Wadmann S, Hoeyer K, 'Dangers of the digital fit: Rethinking seamlessness and social sustainability in data-intensive healthcare' (2018) 5 *Big Data & Society*. DOI: 10.1177/2053951717752964

Van Der Wel K A and others, 'A gold mine, but still no klondike: Nordic register data in health inequalities research' (2019) 47 *Scandinavian Journal of Public Health* 618. DOI: 10.1177/1403494819858046

10 Administrative tools for balancing societal and individual interests

Data protection safeguards and administrative procedural guarantees in secondary use in the European Health Data Space

Jane Reichel

10.1 Introduction

In its EU Strategy for Data, the Commission draws up a vision of a European space for free movement of data, where the General Data Protection Regulation (GDPR)[1] serves as a solid framework for digital trust.[2] The European Health Data Space (EHDS) is the first sectoral data space, with the aim of 'unleashing the data' in order to pursue important societal benefits.[3] An obstacle to this aim is the administrative governance systems for health data in the member states. According to the Commission, the differences in the implementation of the GDPR between the member states have resulted in 'fragmented and divergent legal and administrative rules, frameworks, processes, standards and infrastructure for reusing health data'.[4] One aim of the EHDS is therefore to create a legal framework consisting of trusted governance mechanisms within the EU and the member states.[5] The EHDS is thus to provide harmonised and tailored legal and technical solutions for accessing electronic health data for secondary use, taking into account the GDPR categorisation of health data as a special category of data in need of extra layers of safeguards in order to protect individual rights.[6]

The idea of using health data as an asset for society is not new. Health data stored in archives, registries and data pools have long been important assets for building the modern welfare state and improving public health, social infrastructures and health care.[7] In order to protect the individual whose data is stored in the archives, registries and data pools, specific safeguards are introduced to balance the societal interest against the interest of the individuals. This chapter analyses the efficiency of the governance structure for access of data for secondary use in the EHDS regulation[8] from the perspective of protecting rights and interests of the individuals concerned via two sets of administrative tools to balance these competing interests.

The first set of tools consists of sector-specific requirements for legal, technical and organisational safeguards to protect the right to informational privacy under Article 8 of the European Convention on Human Rights, and more specifically

DOI: 10.4324/9781003544111-13

data protection under Article 8 of the EU Charter of Fundamental Rights (the Charter) and the GDPR. These safeguards may consist of technical mechanisms to ensure data minimisation, such as anonymisation or pseudonymisation, or legal mechanisms, such as requirements of approvals or licenses, purpose limitations, secrecy and confidentiality. The aim is accordingly to allow for the processing of health data while minimising the risk of breaches of privacy for the natural persons concerned, i.e., the data subjects, when personal data are processed. The focus will be on the role and function of the safeguards in the assessment of applications for access to electronic health data for secondary use.

The second category consists of general administrative guarantees for protecting individual interests in the handling of their matters before a public administration, i.e., the right to good administration under the general principle of good administration that has also found expression in Article 41 of the Charter. The right to good administration includes a general right to have one's affairs handled impartially, fairly and within a reasonable time, corresponding to the public authorities' duty to care, and the right to be heard, the right of access to files and the right to a reasoned decision. These procedural rights aim to ensure that the interests of the individuals concerned are being handled correctly and to allow individuals to be involved in and have insight into the handling of their matters. In connection with this, the relevant interests can be identified first and foremost as data protection, but also as intellectual property (IP) and trade secrets.[9] Natural and legal persons concerned in a legally relevant manner should for example be able to ensure that all relevant aspects are included in the assessment, and be given opportunities to present their views on a matter before a decision is made. If not, they should be able to initiate a review of the decision before a court, Article 47 of the Charter.

The administrative balancing tools are to be used by the health data access bodies (HDABs) when assessing applications for access to electronic health data. The role and function of these bodies are thus also relevant in an analysis of the context in which the balancing tools are to be applied, as are the relations between the national bodies, the EHDS Board and the Commission. The main question raised in this chapter is the following: has the EHDS managed to define administrative balancing tools for the fragmented legal landscape of secondary use of health data in the EU and its member states, which can overcome the legal uncertainties regarding secondary use of electronic health data and barriers thereto?

The chapter is organised as follows. Section 10.2 deals with the implementation of the basic division of competence of regulating administrative safeguards and guarantees in EU and national law, as well as the general safeguards and procedures related to these matters in the EHDS. Section 10.3 includes an in-depth evaluation of the allocation of regulatory powers for legal safeguards and guarantees for handling individual applications in the EHDS, whereas Section 10.4 discusses the different roles and functions of the HDABs. Section 10.5 includes a summary of the findings in the chapter, including conclusions.

10.2 General administrative safeguards and guarantees in EU law and the EHDS

10.2.1 Points of departure for regulating data protection safeguards and administrative guarantees

According to the doctrine of institutional and procedural autonomy, it is up to the member states to appoint public authorities competent to manage specific policy areas under EU law, and – in the absence of EU regulation – to decide what procedures public authorities and courts are to apply, on the condition that they are effective and applied equivalently.[10] The locution 'in the absence of EU law' includes all relevant EU legal sources, i.e., primary and secondary law and general principles of EU law.[11] The EU does not have any independent legislative competence to regulate the internal administrative organisation or procedures of the member states but may merely support, coordinate or supplement the actions of the member states in the area of administrative cooperation.[12] However, institutional and procedural rules are regularly enacted on a sector-specific legislative basis, with the argument that common rules are needed to achieve the goals set out in sector-specific areas.[13] Already from the very beginning of the establishment of the EU, it was recognised that administrative cooperation between the EU and its member states was necessary, not least in the area of sharing administratively relevant data.[14] In the last decades, the EU has, to an increasing extent, introduced common mechanisms for the enforcement, application and supervision of EU law, for EU and national competent authorities to use in cooperation, in more or less fully developed composite procedures.[15]

A core aspect of the EU administrative rules is focused on the management of information in administrative cooperation and handling of individual matters.[16] There are therefore numerous rules in the European composite administration on the gathering and exchange of information. In the past decade, technical advancements have provided for both new possibilities and challenges.[17] Yet national law remains relevant – at least in relation to data which is protected by data protection legislation, confidentiality rules or as IP. As seen in the introduction, the legal landscape for secondary use of health data, however, is fragmented, which the Commission had identified as an obstacle to the free movement of health data.[18]

In regard to safeguards for data protection, the GDPR is the main EU framework for digital trust,[19] laying down general requirements for the member states to ensure that data subjects' rights are upheld and that personal data are processed in a secure setting.[20] Generally, the GDPR allows member states some room for adapting the safeguards to their national traditions and legal context, meaning that the national solutions may differ here too.[21] Specific requirements for safeguards may also be introduced in sector-specific law, as is seen in the EHDS, discussed in the following section.

In secondary law on administrative procedures, the focus is often directed at the formal steps in the handling of administrative matters. Recurring features are duties of information-sharing between competent national authorities in general, as well as in individual cases,[22] minimum criteria for what parameters to include in assessments,[23] and timelines for public authorities to handle matters.[24] Because many EU sources on administrative and judicial procedures, as well as data protection safeguards in the GDPR, are drafted in an open manner – leaving quite a lot of room to be filled by national law – the relationship between EU and national data protection safeguards and administrative guarantees is often complex.

In addition, the member states are also required to uphold the general principles of law elaborated by the Court of Justice of the European Union in its case law.[25] Accordingly, under the principles of good administration, member states are obliged to investigate matters carefully under the duty to care,[26] the right to be heard,[27] to provide reasoned decisions,[28] and to uphold other administrative principles, such as the principle of legitimate expectations, even though these are not explicitly mentioned in secondary law.[29] As with requirements in secondary law, the application of these principles does not require that national procedures are abandoned, but rather that they are applied in such a way that the sought-after legal protection is guaranteed in an effective manner.[30] The Court of Justice held in *Åkerberg Fransson*, in regard to the principle of *ne bis in idem*, that national procedures can be applied 'provided that the level of protection provided for by the Charter, as interpreted by the Court, and the primacy, unity and effectiveness of European Union law, are not thereby compromised'.[31]

10.2.2 General data protection safeguards in the EHDS

According to the EHDS proposal put forward by the Commission, 'strong safeguards and security measures will be implemented to ensure that the fundamental rights of data protection are fully protected'.[32] The EHDS Regulation accordingly sets out a number of general safeguards, to be built into the relevant legal and technical solutions. The most central of these are data minimisation, technical safeguards for secure processing, purpose limitations and an opt-out mechanism for natural persons from the processing of personal health data.[33]

Data minimisation rules are given a particularly prominent place in the EHDS, meaning that electronic health data are primarily to be processed in an anonymised format. Pseudonymised data are only to be made available if the purpose of the planned processing otherwise cannot be achieved.[34] If pseudonymised data are to be provided, the encryption key is to be available to the HDAB only.[35]

Another central category of safeguards is technical safeguards for secure processing. Access to electronic health data for secondary use should be given through a secure processing environment, which the HDAB is to provide.[36] The HDAB providing the service should remain in control of the access to the electronic health data at all times, and grant relevant access to data users. Only non-personal data which do not contain any electronic health data should be extracted by the data users from that secure processing environment.[37] All secondary use access to electronic health data should be granted through a secure processing environment, and the principle 'bring questions to data instead of moving data' should be applied whenever possible.[38] For multi-country application, where electronic health data need to be accessed across borders, the Commission is to establish an infrastructure, HealthData@EU, in which the national HDABs and other trusted partners will be authorised participants.[39]

The limitation of permitted purposes in the EHDS is a further safeguard, aiming to ensure that the arrangements for making electronic health data available are only accessible for data users with legitimate purposes benefitting society. It defines eight permissible purposes for which electronic health data can be processed for secondary use. They include public and occupational health interests, policy making and regulatory activities, official statistics and scientific research, including the training, testing and evaluating of algorithms and AI systems.[40] There are five purposes that are explicitly prohibited, including making certain decisions detrimental to a natural person, advertising or marketing activities, developing harmful products or services and activities in conflict with ethical provisions pursuant to national law.[41]

10.2.3 Available and efficient administrative application procedures for secondary data use in the EHDS

One of the most central parts of the EHDS for secondary use is the introduction of an elaborate scheme for providing access to electronic health data at the national level, in order to ensure an efficient governance structure for access to data. The regulation lays down two tracks for accessing health data. The main track is via a data access application for a data permit in accordance with Article 67. A simplified form of access can be given via a data request set out in Article 69, merely providing access to anonymised statistical data, without access to the underlying electronic health data. Both tracks go via the HDAB, where the procedure for assessing the data access application, in order to issue a data permit, requires a more in-depth assessment, as discussed below. By derogation, if data are sought from a single data holder in a single member state, the HDAB can refer the application directly to that data holder, if it has been designated a 'trusted data holder'.[42] The trusted data holders are to apply the same assessment requirements as the HDAB.[43] An accelerated application procedure is also provided for public sector bodies and Union institutions, bodies, offices and agencies with a legal mandate in the field of public health.[44] In this chapter, the focus will be on the main track for the data access application.

The EHDS is in line with the type of procedural rules in secondary EU law described above, laying down formal steps in the handling of an administrative matter. The main steps for the procedure for assessing a data access application, in order to issue a data permit, are set out in Articles 67 and 68. The applicant must submit eight categories of information: the purposes for which the data are requested, a detailed explanation of the intended use and expected benefits, a description of the requested data and whether pseudonymised data are requested, the safeguards planned to prevent any misuse and to protect the rights and interests of the health data holder and of the natural persons concerned, and, where applicable, information on any assessment of ethical aspects of the processing. The eighth point requires the applicant to demonstrate that 'all other requirements in this Chapter are fulfilled'.[45]

The HDAB is then to assess whether the requirements are met, taking into account the risks to national defence, security, public security and public order, as well as the risk of undermining confidential data in the governmental databases of regulatory authorities.[46] The HDAB will also decide on general and specific conditions for each data permit.[47] The HDAB should issue a decision on a permit within three months of receiving a complete application, with the possibility of an extension of three additional months, depending on the urgency and complexity of the application and the volume of requests.[48] After a data permit has been issued, the data holder must put the electronic health data at the disposal of the HDAB within three months, with a possible extension of another three months,[49] after which the HDAB should make them available to the data user within two months, unless it specifies a longer timeframe.[50]

The EHDS foresees that health data applicants may want to access electronic health data from data holders in more than one member state and has therefore devised a specific procedure for the assessment of such applications, in accordance with the single application principle.[51] With a single application, the applicant can thus be able to obtain authorisation from multiple HDABs in different member states. However, each HDAB will remain responsible for deciding to grant or refuse access to the health data within its remit.[52]

Lastly, it may be noted that the EHDS also includes rules on sanctions and penalties for data holders and data users, in case of breaches of their obligations. Data holders that fail to put the electronic health data at the disposal of the HDAB within the deadline can be fined for each day of delay.[53] In case of repeated breaches, a data holder may be banned from participation in the EHDS for a period of up to five years.[54] Data users that do not comply with the regulation and with the data permit may have their permit revoked and can also be banned from any access to electronic health data for a period of up to five years.[55] Furthermore, and more severely, data holders and data users can be subjected to administrative fines of up to 20,000,000 EUR or in the case of an undertaking, up to 4% of the total worldwide annual turnover of the preceding financial year, whichever is higher.[56] These procedures will be discussed below.

10.3 Allocation of regulatory powers: EU or national rules on administrative safeguards and protective tools?

10.3.1 Exhaustive procedures, minimum rules or national regulatory responsibility?

The question to be discussed in this section is what administrative law tools are available for balancing the general and individual interests under the EHDS, and where the power to regulate these tools is allocated. As seen above, some of these tools are laid down in the EHDS, whereas others follow from national law.

In relation to the process of assessing applications for data permits, the question may be raised of to what extent the procedure laid down in the EHDS is comprehensively regulated, and if it may be complemented by national law. It seems clear that this question cannot be answered in a definitive manner, as the answer will differ between different steps in the procedure. In regard to the rules on time limits for both the HDAB and the data holders, they must be understood to be exhaustive, with no possibility for deviations in national law. The same applies to the definitions of what data are to be accessible and the aforementioned rules on purpose limitations and conditions for access. Accordingly, it is stated in the preamble that member states may no longer maintain or introduce further conditions, limitations or specific provisions requesting the consent of natural persons in accordance with Article 9(4) GDPR, except those that are explicitly mentioned in Article 51(4) EHDS.[57] However, the assessments of the safeguards planned in the individual applications for data permits will have to be complemented by national law, in accordance with the delegated structure of defining appropriate safeguards in the GDPR. These will be discussed in Section 10.3.2.

Furthermore, the EHDS contains only limited rules on the right to good administration, the duty of care, the participation of the parties concerned, the right to reasoned decisions, and the right of access to an effective legal remedy. It must be presumed that national law on the matter will be applicable, as will be discussed in Section 10.3.3.

10.3.2 Legal, technical and organisational safeguards in the assessments of data access applications

Generally, the GDPR itself does not define the exact requirements for the processing of personal data in a specific context but requires that safeguards are in place, be they legal, technical or organisational.[58] As seen in Section 10.2.2, the EHDS contains several strong data protection safeguards, rules on data minimisation, technical safeguards for secure processing, purpose limitations and an opt-out mechanism for natural persons. As for the exact content of these safeguards, this will vary depending on the sector-specific area, as well as the national law applicable. For example, the research exception in Article 89.1 GDPR requires specific safeguards to be adopted.[59] However, the EHDS regulation sets out certain limitations to what safeguards the member states may require. In a medical research context, two mechanisms are widely used, namely the informed consent of the data subject and an ethical approval from a competent research ethics committee.[60] As the EHDS does not rely on the informed consent of the data subject as a legal basis for processing of data, instead relying on different grounds depending on who is doing the processing,[61] national requirements on informed consent are no longer to be upheld.[62] As seen above, natural persons are given a right to opt out from the processing of their personal health data for secondary use.[63] As regards ethical approval, the EHDS foresees that this assessment will be aligned with that conducted by the HDAB ahead of granting a data permit.[64]

Processing for other purposes than research, such as innovation, policy-making, patient safety, official statistics or regulatory activities, will be governed under other sets of safeguards.[65] With the importance attributed to the principle of proportionality in balancing the interest of protection of the rights of the data subject and the interest of access to information and free movement of data, the level of protection will be context-dependent.[66]

Secrecy and confidentiality rules are another category of legal safeguards that may be used in order to protect both the privacy of individuals (in medical research and elsewhere) and the rights of IP right holders and businesses. Unlike what is the case for data protection rules, there are no generally applicable EU rules on secrecy, although there are many examples of secondary EU law requiring member states to ensure the confidentiality of information circulated under EU law.[67] The EHDS also sets out a procedure for protecting IP rights and trade secrets.[68] As a first step, the data holder should inform the HDAB of any data in their possession containing content or information protected by IP rights, already when communicating the dataset descriptions pursuant to Article 60(3).[69] The HDAB is to take 'all specific appropriate and proportionate measures, including legal, organisational, and technical ones', to protect the relevant rights, for example via contractual arrangements between health data holders and health data users. If a serious risk of infringement of rights remains, access to the health data may be denied.[70] Here too, national traditions and cultures vary, meaning that the available measures will also be likely to vary.

In summary, the HDABs may face a complex task in assessing the applications for data permits. The HDABs will be tasked with assessing all categories of electronic health data available under the EHDS, which includes a wide variety of data divided into 15 different categories,[71] for any of the eight permitted purposes.[72] Even if all processing of health data were to take place locally, in accordance with local law, the data users could come from all over the world, with different traditions regarding the means of processing and of applying safeguards. This may be especially cumbersome in the assessment of multi-country applications.[73] However, trusted data holders assessing single data applications will only assess applications for health data that they are storing themselves.[74]

10.3.3 Administrative and judicial procedural guarantees in the assessments of data access applications

Turning to the second category of tools to balance general and individual interests under the EHDS, this section will focus on the EU rules and principles available to ensure administrative and judicial procedural guarantees, the right to good administration and the right to an effective remedy within the handling of a data access application. The question is thus to what extent the EHDS lays down rules on the duty to care for the HDAB or the trusted data holder, the right to be heard, the right of access to files and the right to a reasoned decisions for the parties concerned, as well as the right of access to effective judicial remedies.[75] It should be said that the provisions in the EHDS are limited and not always consistent. Five sections involving sub-principles to the general principle of good administration in individual decision-making procedures have been introduced, as well as a general reference to 'appropriate procedural safeguards, including effective judicial remedies and due process' in relation to administrative fines.

First, the procedure for applying for a data permit contains elements of the principle of the duty of care and the right to timely processing in accordance with the rules on time limits. These limits describe how soon the HDAB must handle a data access application, how soon the data holder must provide the data after a permit has been issued and again, and how soon the HDAB must make the data available to the data user.[76] Furthermore, data applicants are given a right to a reasoned decision, if a data access application is refused. However, there is no explicit right to a reasoned decision if the conditions in the data permit should be considered unreasonably strict.

The procedures for investigating breaches of obligations under the EHDS also include some elements of the principle of a duty of care, as they require the HDAB to take 'appropriate and proportionate' measures aimed at the data users.[77] In regard to measures aimed at the data holder, these must be 'transparent and proportionate'.[78] Both data holders and data users are further to be given a right to be heard before any measures are taken against them.[79] Both data holders and data users are to be provided reasons for the measures imposed.[80] The Commission's proposal included a right to effective judicial remedy, which was not included in the EHDS.[81]

In regard to procedural safeguards applicable when handling matters of administrative fines, the EHDS uses a different regulatory model. It makes a blanket reference to EU and member state law, in order for the exercise of power by the HDAB to be subject to appropriate procedural safeguards, including effective judicial remedies and due process.[82] This regulatory model is in line with the general obligation laid on the member states, to uphold the general principles of EU law even when relevant secondary law does not include corresponding rules.[83] Accordingly, the scant rules on administrative and judicial guarantees in the EHDS could be complemented by national rules. However, the regulatory model becomes especially opaque when parts of the procedure are regulated in the form of minimum rules, as is the case for the application procedure with its elements of the right to good administration, and other parts are to be fully regulated under undefined legal principles. It is not obvious to what extent the application procedure can be regulated by national law, or if it is to be exhaustively regulated through the rules described above.

One aspect that can be seen as particularly relevant in this regard is the scope of application of the procedural rules *ratione personae*. Who may be identified as concerned in such a manner that they can trigger the right to good administration and the right to an effective remedy, and at what point in the procedure does this status arise? It follows from the above that the administrative procedure on a data access application only involves the applicant and the HDAB, whereas the data holder is not involved at all until after the data permit is issued. At this stage, the data holder must put the electronic health data at the disposal of the HDAB within three months, with a possible extension for another three months.[84] If the data holder does not comply, it can be fined for each day of delay.[85] There is accordingly no participatory procedure before a data permit is issued to allow the data holder to present its views on the possibility to give access to the data that it is holding, in regard to legal restriction due to data protection rules, IP rights or confidentiality. However, the preamble does seem to presuppose that the data holder could be involved in the application procedure, as it is stated that 'the HDABs and, where relevant data holders, should assist data users in the selection of the suitable datasets or data sources for the intended purpose of secondary use'.[86] The EHDS accordingly foresees that the data holder could assist in the application procedure, but not that it could be given a possibility to state its views on the outcome. Only when the HDAB is investigating the breach of obligations is a right to be heard provided. Moreover, in the final version of the regulation, no right to an effective remedy is ensured.

The deletion of any explicit right to an effective remedy from the final version of the EHDS may be compared to what is seen with the Data Governance Act, which provides an effective right to redress for any natural or legal person directly affected by a decision on a request for re-use of data under the Act.[87] This review could be performed by an 'impartial body with the appropriate expertise', meaning that there is no right to an effective remedy before a court.[88] The EHDS does not provide the individuals who have an interest in the data, either as data subjects or as holders of data protected by IP rights and trade secrets (which can of course be the data holders themselves), any role in the application procedure, nor any right to redress or effective remedy.

In as far as the procedural rules are not to be seen as exhaustive, the ambiguities in regard to the scope of application of the rights may be resolved in accordance with national laws, providing broader administrative and judicial guarantees than the rules in the EHDS. As with the legal, technical and organisational safeguards, administrative and judicial procedures differ between member states. There is a common understanding on standards, principles and rules at a basic level, but there are important differences in the actual implementation, scope of application and content.[89] Thus, it can be foreseen that the data access applications may be handled rather differently in different member states.

Importantly, the right to good administration is traditionally a right to be exercised in an administrative procedure before a public authority, whereas the EHDS foresees that a data access application may also be submitted to a trusted data holder, which may be a private entity, either commercial or non for profit.[90]

On the one hand, the trusted data holder procedure becomes less complex in this two-party setting, involving only the data holder and the data applicant. On the other hand, the implementation of the administrative guarantees that the EHDS includes – for example the different time limits and penalties for not respecting them – may be more difficult to uphold in a procedure with only private parties. The procedures also differ in the sense that in reality, the trusted data holder will have an independent say in the assessment that it would not have if the HDAB were involved. In these cases, it might be beneficial for data applicants if the EHDS provided for a clear right to an effective remedy if a trusted data holder does not give access to data in accordance with the EHDS.

The important differences in administrative and judicial guarantees that can be foreseen may, in themselves, be seen as contradictory to the ambitions of the Commission to enable swift and efficient access to electronic health data, in order to achieve the aim to 'unleash the data'.[91] In the preamble to the EHDS, it is stated that 'in order to ensure that all HDABs issue permits in a similar way, it is necessary to establish a standard common process for the issuance of data permits, with similar requests in different Member States'.[92] The Commission should therefore support the harmonisation of data applications and requests.[93] This may be especially relevant in multi-country applications, which will be discussed in the following.

10.4 The roles of HDABs – facilitators, collaborators and overseers

10.4.1 The different roles of the health data access bodies

Two sets of administrative balancing tools available to the HDAB were discussed above – data protection safeguards and administrative and judicial guarantees – focusing on the allocation of the regulatory responsibilities between EU law and national law. The question discussed here is how the roles and functions of the HDABs are to be understood.[94]

When analysing the discretion and room for manoeuvre of the HDABs to interpret EU and national law, i.e., the context in which the balancing tools are to be applied, it is relevant to take into account what tasks and functions the bodies are given in the EHDS. First, it may be underlined that one important task for the HDABs is to 'contribute to the consistent application of this Regulation throughout the Union', which is to be done by cooperating with the Commission and the Data Protection Authorities (DPAs) under the GDPR, among others.[95] The EHDS also seems to cast the HDABs as multi-tasking organs, with several distinctive features. They can to some extent be described as facilitators, supporting and increasing access to electronic health data. The facilitator feature is not clearly expressed in the tasks of the HDABs but can to a certain extent be read into their role. It is only expressly recognised in relation to multi-country data applications, where the HDABs are tasked with facilitating cross-border access, in close collaboration with each other and with the Commission.[96] This feature is presented in Section 10.4.2.

The HDABs are also to collaborate closely data users and, when providing a secure processing environment. In the EHDS proposal, the HDABs and data users were to be joint data controllers, requiring active involvement on the part of the HDABs in the actual data processing. This role has been removed in the final text of the EHDS and the functions have been separated. The remaining collaborative functions are discussed in Section 10.4.3.

HDABs also function as overseers, to some extent together with DPAs, ensuring compliance with the EHDS. Here, the competence to decide on penalties and administrative fines for both data holders and data users, described above, is key. These issues are further discussed in Section 10.4.4.

Lastly, it may be mentioned that the HDABs have some, limited obligations vis-à-vis the natural persons whose health data are being processed, regardless of whether they can be considered data subjects under the GDPR. The obligations are mostly of a general nature, directed at the public at large, not individual data subjects. The HDABs are to provide information on the conditions under which electronic health data are made available for secondary use. This shall include information on technical and organisational measures undertaken to protect the rights of natural persons, the applicable rights of natural persons in relation to the secondary use and how rights under the GDPR may be exercised, as well as the results of the outcomes of the projects for which the health data were used.[97] If an HDAB is informed of a significant finding related to the health of a natural person, the HDAB is to inform the data holder about that finding. The data holder, in turn, is to inform the natural person or the relevant health professionals, in accordance with national law.[98]

10.4.2 HDABs as facilitators in multi-country applications

Although the overall aim of the EHDS is to improve access to electronic health data for the benefit of society,[99] it does not expressly state that this is an aim for the HDABs to pursue. Instead, the EHDS defines the role of the HDABs in more neutral terms in Articles 55 and 57, with the granting of access to electronic health data on application as their most prominent task. However, in the preamble, it is noted that the establishment of HDABs is 'an essential component for promoting the secondary use of health-related data'.[100]

As seen above, the EHDS explicitly tasks the HDABs with facilitating access to health data in one situation, namely multi-country applications.[101] The preamble acknowledges that going through the authorisation process in multiple member states can be repetitive and cumbersome, and that the stated purpose of the single application procedure is to reduce the administrative burden and barriers for data users.[102] The data applicant will be able to obtain authorisation from multiple HDABs in different member states with one single application. However, this will not result in just one permit. Each HDAB remains responsible for assessing access to the data held in their member state.[103] The HDABs are to communicate via HealthData@EU, a secure infrastructure for participants authorised under the EHDS.[104] The Commission will operate HealthData@EU and support and facilitate the information exchange necessary.[105]

How the assessment of the different parts of the application is to be carried out is not quite clear, but in order to meet the goal of easing the administrative burden, it must be assumed that the HDABs are to coordinate their work. The EHDS Board is also tasked with facilitating the cooperation and information exchange between member states, for instance in coordinating the practices of HDABs, and to issue written contributions and exchange best practices on matters related to this coordination.[106] The HDABs are to be represented in the EHDS Board and will thus take part in that work.[107] The Commission further has a general role in supporting capacity building in the member states.[108]

However, the procedure for multi-country applications in the EHDS must be described as vague, with no elements of actual composite decision-making. The single application will not result in just one data permit. On the other hand, the EHDS foresees that the coordinated assessment could ease the acceptance of a decision in other member states, as it is held that 'a data permit issued by one concerned HDAB may benefit from mutual recognition by the other concerned HDABs'.[109] For this to work in practice, the HDABs would probably need to actively interpret national laws in the light of the aim of the EHDS, to facilitate access to electronic health data.

10.4.3 HDABs as collaborators with data holders and data users

Although the EHDS – unlike the EHDS proposal – no longer allocates joint controllership to HDABs and data users, it is clear that the parties must cooperate. In order to separate the roles of the HDAB, the data holder and the data user, the EHDS sets out a model for how the roles of controller and processor are to be allocated during the transfer of data, in so far as they constitute personal data according to the GDPR, i.e., are not fully anonymised.[110] The data holder should be deemed to be the controller for the disclosure of the requested data to the HDAB, whereas the HDAB should be deemed to be the controller for the data processing when 'fulfilling its tasks pursuant to this Regulation'.[111] In the preamble, this is described as 'when preparing the data and making them available to the health data user'.[112] After this, it is the data user that is deemed to be the controller for the processing of data in pseudonymised form in the secure processing environment pursuant to its data permit. The HDAB is then deemed to be a processor on behalf of the data user. If data are accessed from a trusted data holder directly, the data holder should be deemed to be acting as a controller and processor under the same terms.[113]

It is expected that the Commission will establish a template for controller–processor agreements for the HDABs and data users.[114]

10.4.4 HDABs as overseers

The third and last role of the HDABs to be analysed here is that as overseers of compliance on the part of data holders and data users. The HDABs are to monitor and supervise the compliance of data users and data holders with the requirements laid down in the regulation.[115] As presented above, the EHDS includes rules on penalties for both data holders and data users, which the HDABs are responsible for enforcing. In a late stage in the legislative procedures, the HDABs were given a mandate to issue substantial administrative fines against data holders and data users, which must be considered to alter their cooperative relationships to some extent.

If the supervisory functions involve processing of personal health data, the relevant provisions in the GDPR would apply. According to the preamble, the supervisory authorities under the GDPR would then be the only authorities competent to enforce those rules.[116] In such a case, the HDAB is to inform the competent DPA and provide all the relevant information.[117] Furthermore, in regard to the possibility for member states to introduce an opt-out mechanism from the processing of personal health data for secondary use, the EHDS allocates the supervisory responsibilities for this to the DPAs.[118]

10.5 Summary and conclusions: what are the conditions for balancing general and individual interests under the EHDS regulation?

The main aim behind the EHDS is to improve access to health data and to enable their use for the benefit of society.[119] Thus, there is a societal interest in making the data easily accessible, which is to be secured by the introduction of available and efficient administrative procedures for data applicants. The EHDS should also strive to uphold the rights and interests of the natural and legal persons involved, mainly related to data protection, IP rights and trade secrets. This will be another task for the competent public authorities.[120]

In this chapter, the analysis has focused on the tools provided in the EHDS for balancing these two interests. The main question to be answered is if the EHDS regulation has managed to define administrative balancing tools for societal and individual interests within the fragmented legal landscape for secondary use of health data in the EU and its member states, which may overcome the legal uncertainties regarding secondary use of electronic health data and barriers thereto.

The answer to the question could be yes or no, depending on whether you see the EHDS as a half-full or half-empty glass. Important steps have certainly been taken. The EHDS provides for strong general data protection safeguards by only allowing access to electronic health data in anonymised or pseudonymised form in a secure processing environment. For the latter type of data, the aim is that the principle 'bring questions to data instead of moving data' is to be applied, as far as possible. Furthermore, in regard to the main road to access electronic health data – the data access application for a data permit – the EHDS provides for an efficient governance structure by laying down a step-by-step procedure. There is also clear allocation of responsibilities for the different roles, and there are timelines, penalties and administrative fines to ensure compliance.

However, there is a risk that the efficiency of the step-by-step procedure laid down will be efficient only on paper. The actual assessment of the requirements of data protection safeguards for granting a data permit is regulated only at a minimum level, with the gaps to be filled by national law. These rules will accordingly vary between member states. It is for the data user to propose safeguards to be implemented in each individual case and for the HDAB to assess if these fulfil the requirements of national law. The HDABs must accordingly assess the sector-specific rules for all the 15 categories of health data available under the EHDS, in relation to any of eight permitted purposes. This must be described as a complex administrative endeavour. In Finland, where a similar centralised health data access regime has been introduced, there are reports that the procedure is both lengthy and expensive.[121]

The applicable administrative procedures are also regulated at a minimum level. A data user may submit a single application for multi-country access. The HDABs are then supposed to collaborate in their assessment under the lead of the HDAB of the data user's choice. However, there are no actual composite decision-making procedures. The collaboration is only informal and will not lead to only one data permit. Instead, the EHDS recommends member states to apply the principle of mutual recognition in relation to the other HDABs concerned. Whether or not this will work in practice is difficult to say.

Furthermore, the roles of the natural and legal persons involved in the procedure are unclear. As for administrative guarantees for good administration, the EHDS does contain some minimum rules, mainly in regard to procedures on penalties and restrictive measures. In the most important procedures, on administrative fines, the regulation simply refers to "appropriate procedural safeguards" in EU and national law, which casts some doubt over how the other procedural rules are to be interpreted. To what extent are the procedural rules of the EHDS exhaustive and to what extent might they be complemented by other sources? For example, should the HDAB provide a right for the data holder to be heard before a data permit is granted by an HDAB, if this follows from national law? Beyond protecting the rights and interests of the individuals concerned, such procedural guarantees might actually render the assessment more adequate, as it is the data holder that has detailed knowledge of the electronic health data and the legal constraints that may apply. On the other hand, the explicit aim to render the access to health data less fragmented would be challenged.

The EHDS thus seems to leave quite some room for manoeuvre. National legislators can lay down rules for the HDABs or trusted data holders in applying the administrative balancing tools in individual cases. The HDABs may thus have quite a lot of freedom in performing the balancing in individual cases. It is relevant to analyse how the roles and functions of the HDABs have been formulated. Indeed, the roles of the HDABs are diverse. The most prominent task is to neutrally and objectively assess applications for data permits, ensuring that the safeguards planned are adequate to prevent misuse of data and to protect the rights and interests of the data holders and the natural persons concerned. However, in regard to multi-country applications, the HDABs have been explicitly tasked with facilitating access. Furthermore, the HDABs are to collaborate with data holders and data users when providing a secure processing environment but will at the same time monitor and supervise them and may subject them to substantive fines. In the final version of the EHDS, a specific task was introduced for the member states to ensure that any conflict of interest between the different tasks of HDABs is avoided.[122] This could be interpreted as an admission of the complexity of the roles and functions of the HDABs.

In order for the EHDS to overcome the legal uncertainties regarding secondary use of health data and barriers thereto within the EU, there seems to be a need to streamline how the room for manoeuvre of the HDABs and any discretionary power is to be used. The EHDS envisions that the HDABs will cooperate amongst themselves and with the Commission and the EHDS Board, sharing best practices and developing standards and common processes. This could foster a culture of openness and accessibility, which in itself could be seen as commendable.[123] The cooperation also extends to the DPAs under the GDPR, as well as administrative bodies under the Data Governance Act, the Data Act[124] and the AI Act.[125] All in all, this creates a multifaceted and complex administrative organisational model.

There are signs that the EU is beginning to take some small steps towards filling in some gaps. The Commission has recently proposed harmonised administrative rules to be applied in the one-stop-shop procedure under the GDPR, a composite decision-making procedure for collaboration between DPAs in multi-country enforcement of the GDPR.[126] The proposal focuses on the administrative procedural guarantees for the rights of complainants and for parties under investigation, implementing existing rights under the Charter, as well as streamlining cooperation and procedures.[127] As the EHDS is to be applied in close connection to the GDPR, this may also affect EHDS-related matters, at least indirectly and in certain cases. In a sensitive area like health data, this may be seen as challenging. On the other hand, the uncertainty regarding how assessments are to be regulated is a problem in itself. If the EU legislator is not willing to go down the road of a concretely formalised composite procedure, it would perhaps be better to let the administrative balancing tools remain in the context of national law after all.

Notes

1 European Parliament and of the Council Regulation 2016/679 of 27 April 2016 on the Protection of Natural Persons with Regard to the Processing of Personal Data and on the Free Movement of such Data (General Data Protection Regulation) [2016] OJ L 119/1.

2 Commission, 'A European strategy for data' (Communication) (2020) 66 final, hereinafter a European Strategy for Data, 4. See further Commission, 'A European Health Data Space: Harnessing the Power of Health Data for People, Patients and Innovation' (Communication) COM(2022) 196 final, 3.

3 A European strategy for data (n 2) 1; Commission communication COM(2022) 196 final (n 2), 2, 3, 13 and 18; Commission Proposal for a Regulation of the European Parliament and of the Council on the European Health Data Space, COM(2022) 197 final, Recital 38 in the preamble to the proposed regulation (hereinafter EHDS proposal); Corrigendum to the position of the European Parliament adopted at first reading on 24 April 2024 with a view to the adoption of Regulation (EU) 2024/... of the European Parliament and of the Council on the European Health Data Space', (COM(2022)0197 – C9-0167/2022 – 2022/0140(COD)), 27 November 2024 (hereinafter EHDS).

4 Commission communication COM(2022) 196 final (n 2) 6.

5 EHDS proposal 1–2.

6 EHDS proposal 3–4; GDPR Article 9.1.

7 Jane Reichel and Johanna Chamberlain, 'Public Registries as Tools for Realising the Swedish Welfare State – Can the State Still Be Trusted?' (2021) 6 *Public Governance, Administration and Finances Law Review*, 35, 35–36.

8 See note 3.

9 See Tjaša Petročnik 'Secondary use of health data in the EHDS: public interest and the role of HDABs' in this volume.

10 The principle of the institutional autonomy of the Member States was introduced in case 51-54/71 *International Fruit Company v Produktschap voor groenten en fruit* EU:C:1971:128, 4; The principle of procedural autonomy was introduced in case 33/76 *Rewe-Zentralfinanz eG and Rewe-Zentral AG v Landwirtschaftskammer für das Saarland*, EU:C:1976:167, 5.

11 In regard to general principles, see for example C-349/07 *Sopropé – Organizações de Calçado Lda v Fazenda Pública* EU:C:2008:746, para 37 et seq; C-222/86 *Unectef v Heylens* EU:C:1987:442, paras 15–16, discussed below.

12 Consolidated version of the Treaty on the Functioning of the European Union [2012] OJ C 326/47, Articles 6 and 197 (hereinafter TFEU).

13 Compare Mariolina Eliantonio, 'Proceduralisation of EU Law Through the Backdoor: Legitimacy, Rationale and Future Prospects' (2015) 8 *Review of European Administrative Law* 177, 178, focusing on procedural rules for national courts.

14 An early example is the Administrative Commission on Social Security for Migrant Workers, established in 1958, see further Henrik Wenander, 'A Network of Social Security Bodies – European Administrative Cooperation under Regulation (EC) No 883/2004' (2013) 6 *Review of European Administrative Law* 39, 47.

15 Jürgen Schwarze, *European Administrative Law* (rev. ed, Sweet and Maxwell, 2006) cxiii; Herwig C H Hofmann and Alex Türk, 'The Development of Integrated Administration in the EU and its Consequences' (2007) 13 *European Law Journal* 253; Craig, P. et al. *ReNEUAL Model Rules on EU Administrative Procedure* (OUP 2017).

16 Diana-Urania Galetta, Herwig G.H. Hofmann and Jens-Peter Schneider, 'Information Exchange in the European Administrative Union: An Introduction' (2014) 20 *European Public Law*, 65, 66 et seq.

17 Jens-Peter Schneider, 'Basic Structures of Information Management in the European Administrative Union' (2014) 1 *European Public Law*, 90 et seq; Deirdre Curtin and Filipe Brito Bastos, 'Interoperable Information Sharing and the Five Novel Frontiers of EU Governance: A Special Issue' (2020) 26 *European Public Law* 59, 65.

18 Commission communication COM(2022) 196 final (n 2) 6.

19 A European Strategy for Data (n 2) 4.

20 Herwig C.H. Hofmann and Lisette Mustert, 'Data Protection' in M Scholten (ed), *Research Handbook on the Enforcement of EU law* (Edward Elgar Publishing 2023).

21 Jane Reichel, Allocation of Regulatory Responsibilities: Who Will Balance Individual Rights, the Public Interest and Biobank Research Under the GDPR? in S Slokenberga, O Tzortzatou and J Reichel (eds.), *GDPR and Biobanking. Individual Rights, Public Interest and Research Regulation across Europe* (Springer 2021), 422 *et seq*.

22 Schneider (n 17) 90 et seq. See, for example, Articles 81 and 87 European Parliament and the Council Directive 2014/65/EU of 15 May 2014 on markets in financial instruments and amending Directive 2002/92/EC and Directive 2011/61/EU (recast) [2014] OJ L 173/349.

23 See, for example, Article 5.1 European Parliament and the Council Directive 2004/38/EC 29 April 2004 on the right of citizens of the Union and their family members to move and reside freely within the territory of the Member States amending Regulation (EEC) No 1612/68 and repealing Directives 64/221/EEC, 68/360/EEC, 72/194/EEC, 73/148/EEC, 75/34/EEC, 75/35/EEC, 90/364/EEC, 90/365/EEC and 93/96/EEC [2004] OJ L 158/77, stating that 'no entry visa or equivalent formality may be imposed on Union citizens'.

24 European Parliament and the Council Regulation (EU) 2022/868 of 30 May 2022 on European data governance and amending Regulation (EU) 2018/1724 (Data Governance Act) [2022] OJ L 152/1, Article 9.1.

25 This follows explicitly from Article 51, Charter of Fundamental Rights of the European Union [2012] OJ C 326/391.

26 C-340/89 *Irène Vlassopoulou v Ministerium für Justiz, Bundes- und Europaangelegenheiten Baden-Württemberg* EU:C:1991:193, para 16–18; C-604/12 *H. N. v. Minister for Justice, Equality and Law Reform* EU:C:2014:302, paras 49–50. See, in general, Diana-Urania Galetta, Herwig C.H. Hofmann, Oriol Mir Puigpelat and Jacques Ziller, 'The General Principles of EU Administrative Procedural Law. An In-Depth Analysis' (2015) 5 *Rivista Italiana di diritto pubblico Comunitario* 1420.

27 *Sopropé* (n 11) para 37 et seq.

28 C-222/86 *Unectef v Heylens* EU:C:1987:442, paras 15–16.

29 C-453/00 *Kühne & Heitz NV v Produktschap voor Pluimvee en Eieren* EU:C:2004:17, para 27; C-119/05 *Ministero dell'Industria, del Commercio e dell'Artigianato v Lucchini SpA* EU:C:2007:434 para 59 et seq; C-568/11 *Agroferm A/S v Ministeriet for Fødevarer, Landbrug og Fiskeri* EU:C:2013:407, para 49 et seq.

30 C-46/16 Valsts ieņēmumu dienests v "LS Customs Services", SIA ECLI:EU:C:2017:839, para 46.

31 C-617/10 *Åklagaren v. Åkerberg Fransson* EU:C:2013:105, para 29.

32 EHDS proposal (n 3) 15.

33 See further Eila El Asry, Juli Mansnérus, Sandra Liede 'Striking the Balance: Genomic Data, Consent and Altruism in the European Health Data Space' in this volume.

34 EHDS Articles 66(2)–(3).

35 EHDS Article 66(3).

36 EHDS Article 73(1) and Recital 72.

37 EHDS Articles 73(1)–(2).

38 EHDS Recital 80.

39 EHDS Article 75.

40 EHDS Articles 53(1) a–f.

41 EHDS Article 54.

42 EHDS Articles 72(1)–(2).

43 EHDS Article 72(4).

44 EHDS Article 68(6).

45 EHDS Articles 68(1) a–h.

46 EHDS Articles 68(2) a–b.

47 EHDS Article 68(10).

48 EHDS Article 68(4).

49 EHDS Article 60(2).

50 EHDS Article 68(7).

51 EHDS Article 67(3).

52 EHDS Article 68(5).

53 EHDS Article 63(4).

54 EHDS Article 63(4).

55 EHDS Article 63(3).
56 EHDS Articles 64(4–5).
57 EHDS Recital 52.
58 See for example Articles 6.4 (e), 9.2 (b), (d), (h), 10, 13.1(f), 14.1(f) and 5 (b), 15.2, 23.2 (d), (f), 25.1, 30.1 (e), (c), 35.7 (d), 36.3 (c) GDPR, among others.
59 See Magdalena Kogut-Czarkowska, Mahsa Shabani 'Federated Networks and Secondary Uses of Health Data – Challenges in Ensuring Appropriate Safeguards for Sharing Health Data Under the GDPR and EHDS' in this volume.
60 Olga Tzortzatou-Nanopoulou, Kaya Akyüz, Melanie Goisauf, Łukasz Kozera, Signe Mežinska, Michaela Th Mayrhofer, Santa Slokenberga, Jane Reichel, Talisiea Croxton, Alexandra Ziaka and Marina Makri, 'Ethical, Legal, and Social Implications in Research Biobanking: A Checklist for Navigating Complexity' (2023) *Dev World Bioeth*. Epub ahead of print. PMID: 37428947, 4.
61 EHDS Recital 52 of the preamble to the EHDS regulation states that one of the legal bases set out in Article 6(1), points (a), (c), (e) or (f), GDPR combined with Article 9(2) GDPR should be required.
62 EHDS Recital 52. On consent in this volume see Patricia Cervera de la Cruz, Mahsa Shabani 'Fair Enough? Exploring the Role of Fairness in Secondary Uses of Health Data in the European Health Data Space in this volume.'
63 Patricia Cervera de la Cruz, Mahsa Shabani 'Fair Enough? Exploring the Role of Fairness in Secondary Uses of Health Data in the European Health Data Space in this volume.'
64 EHDS Article 55(2).
65 GDPR Articles 9(2) (g), (h) and (i).
66 GDPR Recital 4, Articles 6.3-4 GDPR; C-439/19 *B joined parties:Latvijas Republikas Saeima*, EU:2021:1054, para 122.
67 Carl Fredrik Bergström and Mikael Ruotsi, *Grundlag i gungning? En ESO-rapport om EU och den svenska offentlighetsprincipen* (ESO 2018:1), 125 et seq.
68 EHDS Article 52.
69 EHDS Article 52(2).
70 EHDS Articles 52(3–5).
71 EHDS Article 51.
72 EHDS Article 53.
73 Quentin Fontaine and Jan Clinck, 'The European Health Data Space Proposal: A First Look at the Newest Piece of the EU Data Sharing Puzzle' (2022) 6 EHPL 87.
74 EHDS Article 72.
75 For the content of these rules, see Galetta et al. (n 16).
76 EHDS Articles 60(2) and, 46(3–4).
77 EHDS Article 63(3).
78 EHDS Article 63(4).
79 EHDS Article 63(2).
80 EHDS Article 63(5).
81 EHDS proposal Article 43(9).
82 EHDS Article 64(7).
83 Section 10.2.1, *Sopropé* (n 11) para 37 et seq.
84 EHDS Article 60(2).
85 EHDS Article 63(4).
86 EHDS Recital 73.
87 Compare with Article 9(2) Data Governance Act.
88 Article 9(2) Data Governance Act.
89 Paul Craig, *EU Administrative Law* (OUP 2018) 265.
90 EHDS Recital 59.
91 A European strategy for data 1.
92 EHDS Recital 73.
93 EHDS Recitals 73–74.

94 See also Chapter Tjaša Petročnik, 'Secondary use of health data in the EHDS: public interest and the role of HDABs' in this volume.
95 EHDS Article 55(1).
96 EHDS Article 57(1)i.
97 EHDS Article 58(1).
98 EHDS Article 58(3).
99 EHDS Recital 1.
100 EHDS Recital 64.
101 EHDS Article 57(1).
102 EHDS Recital 83.
103 EHDS Article 68(5).
104 EHDS Article 75(7).
105 EHDS Article 75(8).
106 EHDS Articles 94(2) a and b.
107 EHDS Article 92(1).
108 EHDS Article 82.
109 EHDS Article 68(5).
110 EHDS Articles 74(1–2) and Recitals 72 and 79.
111 EHDS Article 74(1).
112 EHDS Recital 79.
113 EHDS Article 74(2).
114 EHDS Article 74(3).
115 EHDS Article 57(1)a(ii).
116 EHDS Recital 65.
117 EHDS Article 63(1).
118 EHDS Article 65.
119 EHDS Recital 1 and the EHDS proposal 2.
120 See especially EHDS proposal 15.
121 Aleksi Reito and others, 'Toisiolaki – lääketieteellisen tutkimuksen mahdollistaja vai tukahduttaja?' (2022) *Suom Lääkäril*, 77, www.laakarilehti.fi/e30589, English summary: Enabler or Suppressor? – Survey on the Effects of the Act on the Secondary Use of Health and Social Data on Medical Research.
122 EHDS Article 55(2).
123 Jane Reichel, 'The European Strategy for Data and Trust in EU Governance – the Case of Access to Publicly held Data' (2023) 4 *CERIDAP* 129.
124 European Parliament and the Council Regulation 2023/2854 of 13 December 2023 on harmonised rules on fair access to and use of data and amending Regulation (EU) 2017/2394 and Directive (EU) 2020/1828 (Data Act) [2023] OJ L2854/ 2854.
125 Regulation (EU) 2024/1689 of the European Parliament and of the Council of 13 June 2024 laying down harmonised rules on artificial intelligence; see Tjaša Petročnik 'Secondary use of health data in the EHDS: public interest and the role of HDABs' in this volume.
126 Commission, 'Proposal for a Regulation of the European Parliament and of the Council Laying Down Additional Procedural Rules Relating to the Enforcement of Regulation (EU) 2016/679' (Communication) COM(2023) 348 final.
127 Commission, Proposal for Additional Procedural Rules Relating to the Enforcement of Regulation (n 126), 2, 9.

Bibliography

Legislative acts

Charter of Fundamental Rights of the European Union [2012] OJ C 326/391.
Consolidated version of the Treaty on the Functioning of the European Union [2012] OJ C 326/47.

Council of Europe, European Convention on Human Rights as amended by Protocols Nos. 11, 14 and 15, supplemented by Protocols Nos. 1, 4, 6, 7, 12, 13 and 16, [4 November 1950], CETS 5.

European Parliament and the Council Directive 2004/38/EC 29 April 2004 on the right of citizens of the Union and their family members to move and reside freely within the territory of the Member States amending Regulation (EEC) No 1612/68 and repealing Directives 64/221/EEC, 68/360/EEC, 72/194/EEC, 73/148/EEC, 75/34/EEC, 75/35/EEC, 90/364/EEC, 90/365/EEC and 93/96/EEC [2004] OJ L 158/77.

European Parliament and the Council Directive 2014/65/EU of 15 May 2014 on markets in financial instruments and amending Directive 2002/92/EC and Directive 2011/61/EU (recast).

European Parliament and the Council Regulation 2016/679 of 27 April 2016 on the Protection of Natural Persons with Regard to the Processing of Personal Data and on the Free Movement of such Data (General Data Protection Regulation) [2016] OJ L 119/1.

European Parliament and the Council Regulation 2023/2854 of 13 December 2023 on harmonised rules on fair access to and use of data and amending Regulation (EU) 2017/2394 and Directive (EU) 2020/1828 (Data Act) [2023] OJ L2854/ 2854.

European Parliament and the Council Regulation (EU) 2022/868 of 30 May 2022 on European data governance and amending Regulation (EU) 2018/1724 (Data Governance Act) [2022] OJ L 152/1.

Official documents

Commission, 'A European strategy for data' (Communication) (2020) 66 final.

Commission, 'A European Health Data Space: Harnessing the Power of Health Data for People, Patients and Innovation' (Communication) COM(2022) 196 final.

Commission, 'Proposal for a Regulation of the European Parliament and of The Council on the European Health Data Space' (EHDS proposal) (Communication) COM(2022) 197 final.

Commission, 'Proposal for a Regulation of the European Parliament and of the Council Laying Down Additional Procedural Rules Relating to the Enforcement of Regulation (EU) 2016/679' (Communication) COM(2023) 348 final.

Council of the European Union, 'Proposal for a Regulation on the European Health Data Space – Analysis of the final compromise text with a view to agreement' 2022/0140(COD) (hereinafter EHDS compromise text).

Literature

Bergström C F and Ruotsi M, Grundlag i gungning? En ESO-rapport om EU och den svenska offentlighetsprincipen (ESO 2018:1).

Craig P, *EU Administrative Law* (OUP 2018) 265.

Craig P, et al. *ReNEUAL Model Rules on EU Administrative Procedure* (OUP 2017).

Curtin D and Bastos P B, 'Interoperable Information Sharing and the Five Novel Frontiers of EU Governance: A Special Issue' (2020) 26 *European Public Law* 59.

Eliantonio M, 'Proceduralisation of EU Law Through the Backdoor: Legitimacy, Rationale and Future Prospects' (2015) 8 *Review of European Administrative Law* 177.

Fontaine Q and Clinck J, 'The European Health Data Space Proposal: A First Look at the Newest Piece of the EU Data Sharing Puzzle' (2022) 6 *EHPL* 87.

Galetta D-U, Hofmann H C H, Puigpelat O M and Ziller J, 'The General Principles of EU Administrative Procedural Law. An In-Depth Analysis' (2015) *Rivista Italiana di diritto pubblico Comunitario* 1420.

Galetta D-U, Hofmann H C H and Schneider J-P, 'Information Exchange in the European Administrative Union: An Introduction' (2014) 20 *European Public Law* 65.

Hofmann H C H and Mustert L, 'Data Protection' in M Scholten (ed), *Research Handbook on the Enforcement of EU law* (Edward Elgar Publishing 2023).

Hofmann H C H and Türk A, 'The Development of Integrated Administration in the EU and its Consequences' (2007) 13 *European Law Journal* 253.

Reichel J, Allocation of Regulatory Responsibilities: *Who Will Balance Individual Rights, the Public Interest and Biobank Research Under the GDPR?* in Slokenberga S, Tzortzatou O and Reichel J (eds.), *GDPR and Biobanking. Individual Rights, Public Interest and Research Regulation across Europe* (Springer 2021). DOI: 10.1007/978-3-030-49388-2_23

Reichel J, 'The European Strategy for Data and Trust in EU Governance – the Case of Access to Publicly held Data' (2023) 4 *CERIDAP* 129.

Reichel J and Chamberlain J, 'Public Registries as Tools for Realising the Swedish Welfare State – Can the State Still Be Trusted?' (2021) 6 *Public Governance, Administration and Finances Law Review* 35, 35–36. DOI: 10.53116/pgaflr.2021.2.4

Reito A and others, 'Toisiolaki – lääketieteellisen tutkimuksen mahdollistaja vai tukahduttaja?' (2022) Suom Lääkäril, 77, www.laakarilehti.fi/e30589

Schneider J-P, 'Basic Structures of Information Management in the European Administrative Union' (2014) 1 *European Public Law* 90.

Schwarze J, *European Administrative Law* (rev. ed, Sweet and Maxwell 2006).

Tzortzatou-Nanopoulou O, Akyüz K, Goisauf M, Kozera Ł, Mežinska S, Mayrhofer M Th, Slokenberga S, Reichel J, Croxton T, Ziaka A and Makri M, 'Ethical, Legal, and Social Implications in Research Biobanking: A Checklist for Navigating Complexity' (2023) *Developing World Bioethics*. DOI: 10.1111/dewb.12411

Wenander H, 'A Network of Social Security Bodies – European Administrative Cooperation under Regulation (EC) No 883/2004' (2013) *Review of European Administrative Law*, 6, 39.

Case law

51-54/71 *International Fruit Company v. Produktschap voor groenten en fruit* EU:C:1971:128.

33/76 *Rewe-Zentralfinanz eG and Rewe-Zentral AG v Landwirtschaftskammer für das Saarland* EU:C:1976:167.

C-222/86 *Unectef v Heylens* EU:C:1987:442.

C-340/89 *Irène Vlassopoulou v Ministerium für Justiz, Bundes- und Europaangelegenheiten Baden-Württemberg* EU:C:1991:193.

C-453/00 *Kühne & Heitz NV v Produktschap voor Pluimvee en Eieren* EU:C:2004:17.

C-119/05 *Ministero dell'Industria, del Commercio e dell'Artigianato v Lucchini SpA* EU:C:2007:434.

C-349/07 *Sopropé – Organizações de Calçado Lda v Fazenda Pública* EU:C:2008:746.

C-617/10 *Åklagaren v. Åkerberg Fransson* EU:C:2013:105.

C-568/11 *Agroferm A/S v Ministeriet for Fødevarer, Landbrug og Fiskeri* EU:C:2013:407.

C-604/12 *H. N. v. Minister for Justice, Equality and Law Reform* EU:C:2014:302.

C-46/16 Valsts ieņēmumu dienests v "LS Customs Services", SIA EU:C:2017:839.

C-439/19 *B other party: Latvijas Republikas Saeima* EU:2021:1054.

11 Federated networks and secondary uses of health data

Challenges in ensuring appropriate safeguards for sharing health data under the GDPR and EHDS

Magdalena Kogut-Czarkowska and Mahsa Shabani

11.1 Introduction

Sharing and accessing diverse types of health data across borders play a crucial role in advancing biomedical research,[1] developing targeted therapies[2] and enhancing diagnostic tools.[3] Traditionally, the research community has relied on large, centralised repositories such as disease-specific databases to publish and exchange health data for scientific purposes. However, this centralised model faced challenges such as compliance with stringent and fragmented legal frameworks and lack of adequate incentives to share data,[4] among other obstacles. These barriers to data sharing prompted the exploration of alternative approaches.[5]

One way to address the challenges associated with traditional health data sharing is through technical solutions, such as the use of decentralised approaches that allow data holders to store data in a local hub rather than a centralised repository. Federated networks are a prominent example of such de-centralised approaches to data sharing, which would offer secure environment for data use.[6] Unlike centralised data pools, federated networks enable data holders (such as hospitals or biobanks acting as controllers of health data) to retain control over data re-use,[7] as the data remains within the secure environment of the data holder and is not duplicated. The features of federated networks seem to introduce a transformative approach to data sharing, addressing both practical and regulatory restrictions associated with the centralised approaches.

On the policy and regulatory level, the concept of data federation rapidly evolved into a new paradigm and made its way into national data sharing infrastructures[8] and multiple EU initiatives. Some examples include GAIA-X federated data infrastructure for Europe, European Genome-phenome Archive (EGA) work on decentralising genetic and phenotypic databases, which originally were a centralised resource, European Cancer Imaging Initiative and various projects supported by EU funding, among others. The imperative to facilitate and expand cross-border exchange of health data through secure, federated repositories was embedded into the 2020 European strategy for data[9] paving the way for the European flagship initiative, the European Health Data Space (EHDS).[10]

DOI: 10.4324/9781003544111-14

Despite the growing focus on de-centralised approaches, particularly federated networks, there remains a lack of comprehensive legal analysis regarding federated infrastructures concerning regulatory requirements for sharing and reusing health data for research purposes.[11] This includes relevant requirements outlined in the General Data Protection Regulation (GDPR)[12] and the EHDS.

It is crucial to first investigate, whether federated networks have been integrated and explained in the recent EU policies and regulatory frameworks for health data sharing and secondary uses, including those related to the EHDS as part of transformation in secondary uses of health data. Second, clarifications are required on the expected function of federated networks within the framework of applicable data protection regulations. In response, this chapter discusses whether and how federated networks can be considered as a form of appropriate safeguards, as recognised by the GDPR, and further supported by the EHDS. Indeed, under the GDPR, the adoption of appropriate security measures, including technical measures, is recognised by Article 89(1), which should be read in conjunction with Article 9(2)(j) when special categories of data, including health data, are to be processed for, inter alia, research purposes. For its part, the EHDS continues to support the need for safeguards and sees its role in establishing them for responsible secondary uses of health data. For this analysis, this chapter specifically examines three aspects, namely whether federated networks can be considered as a tool for data minimisation, their compliance with relevant data protection requirements, and their impact on the protection of fundamental rights and interests of data subjects.

The results of this investigation should provide invaluable insights into whether federated networks should be considered for use under the EHDS. This consideration aligns with the aim of the EHDS to introduce sufficient safeguards for the utilisation of health data for secondary purposes, including for scientific purposes.

11.2 Federated networks in the context of health data sharing

The term federated network was coined already in 1979,[13] and followed by the first conceptual model of federated architecture for office information management described in 1985.[14] With technological advancements, the concept evolved, yet at its core remaining a model consisting of multiple databases or repositories where the data is stored. This model is often contrasted with a centralised one, where the data is copied from the original location and stored in a central storage.[15] Although federated networks can be used for various purposes, in the context of health research, this concept is associated with research infrastructure which allows data users, mostly being researchers in the health field (such as developers of AI tools for healthcare), to seamlessly conduct research using data from multiple repositories. Repositories are connected by a centralised infrastructure or – at least – an agreement on data sharing or governance principles.[16] The individual repositories are sometimes called the nodes[17] or hubs.[18] The entities or persons that are responsible for the nodes are referred to as data custodians,[19] controllers,[20] owners[21] or stewards.[22] To facilitate data use, the federated network may include an interface which allows the users to search for or access data across various nodes as if they were using a single database.[23]

Currently, numerous federated networks are designed to conduct AI model training in a federated manner, a process commonly referred to as federated learning.[24] In federated learning (also referred to as model-to-data[25]), the data stays in their place of generation or storage and are never transferred to the central location (cloud or server). The training of the AI model takes place locally in individual nodes, and the parameters of each local model are aggregated into a global model.[26] This process is sometimes depicted as 'bringing questions to data rather than moving data'.[27]

In scientific literature, the term federated network is often interchangeably used with federated repository,[28] federated data sharing,[29] federated infrastructure,[30] federated data systems,[31] federation of data[32] or simply federation[33] and others. While this concept is frequently explored from architectural, health[34] or even sociotechnical[35] perspectives, the legal sources on the topic scarce. As shown in Table 11.1, although prominent policy documents and regulatory frameworks reference federated networks or similarconcepts, a comprehensive legal analysis of the concept is absent from these documents.

11.3 Federated networks as appropriate safeguards

11.3.1 Appropriate safeguards under Article 89(1) GDPR

Compliance with Article 89(1) GDPR, read in conjunction with Article 9(2)(j), is pivotal for sharing and using personal data for health scientific research. The provisions mandate that the processing of personal data for scientific purposes adheres to appropriate safeguards, in accordance with the GDPR, to protect the rights and freedoms of the data subjects. The safeguards shall ensure that technical and organisational measures are in place in particular in order to ensure respect for the principle of data minimisation. The lack of a legal definition for the term appropriate safeguards in the GDPR, coupled with the opaque wording of Article 89(1), has drawn much criticism[51,52] and fuelled various interpretations of the requirements for establishing these safeguards.

Safeguards must comply with the GDPR, and Article 89(1) highlights two examples: pseudonymisation and anonymisation. However, no criteria for assessing other measures as potential safeguards are provided. Moreover, the provision has not been interpreted by the EU Court of Justice, and the EU regulatory guidance remains incomplete. Opinions of the EDPS and the EDPB[53] list various examples of safeguards, such as conducting a data protection impact assessment (DPIA), appointment of data protection officer (DPO), notifying a data breach without undue delay, guaranteeing data security and data minimisation through anonymisation or pseudonymisation, access limitations and obtaining the informed consent of research participants as an ethical

Table 11.1 References to federated networks in selected legal, policy and regulatory documents relating to use of personal data for scientific purposes

Type of document	*Name of the document*	*References to federated networks*
Policy document	A European strategy for data[36]	States that the data sharing infrastructures 'should support the creation of European data pools enabling Big Data analytics and machine learning, in a manner compliant with data protection legislation and competition law, allowing the emergence of data-driven ecosystems. These pools may be organised in a centralised or a distributed way'. A footnote explains: 'In the latter case the data are not moved to a central place in order to analyse them together with other data assets. The analytical tools come to the data, not the other way around. This makes it easier to keep the data secure and to ensure control over who accesses, what data, for what purposes.'
EU law or EU law proposal	GDPRData Governance Act (DGA)[37]	Terms federated or federated networks not found.
	EHDS[38]	Does not define or use of the term federated network, however the infrastructure foreseen for secondary data sharing, HealthData@EU, will by design not be a central one, but rather will a network of existing databases. The impact assessment report[39] accompanying EHDS refers to the proposed model as 'federated governance structure'. Recital 80 EHDS states that due to the sensitivity of health data, concepts such as 'bring questions to data instead of moving data' should be respected whenever possible. Article 76(2) allows registries or databases from a number of Member States which 'organise themselves into a single network of registries or databases at Union level', to designate a coordinator to ensure the provision of data from the registries' network for secondary use. Article 96(1) also mentions federated EU dataset catalogue connecting the national dataset catalogues.

Guidelines issued by EU advisory and supervisory bodies in the area of data protection and security – European Data Protection Supervisor (EDPS), the European Data Protection Board (EDBP) or the European Union Agency for Cybersecurity (ENISA)	Joint Opinion 03/2021 on the Proposal for a Regulation of the European Parliament and of the Council on European data governance Data Governance Act,[40] EDPS and EDPB opinions on EHDS[41,42] Opinion on Data Strategy for Europe[43]	The term federated networks not found.
	EDPS Preliminary Opinion on data protection and scientific research[44]	The term federating appears only in a footnote and pertains to a citation of EC press release, without analysing it further.
Other guidance and materials on websites of EU agencies and bodies	EDPS website[45]	Website includes a short note on federated learning[46] and on federated social media platforms,[47] however does not include an analysis on federated databases for data sharing.
	Documents published by ENISA	The term federated appears in the context of federated identity[48] and federated cloud environments.[49] Document on Engineering personal data protection in EU Data Spaces[50] identifies building blocks for ensuring personal data protection in data spaces, however does not mention federated networks.

requirement. However, the authorities do not provide a rationale for their selection, nor do they establish criteria for evaluating other potential safeguards. In 2021, the EDPB acknowledged the complexity and importance of explaining the meaning of the term and referred to future guidance for a detailed analysis.[54] This guidance has yet to be issued.

Challenges also arise when differentiating between the appropriate safeguards and the technical and organisational measures which are also mentioned in Article 89(1). Some approaches emphasize understanding safeguards through their objectives, citing the second sentence of the provision ('those safeguards shall ensure that technical and organisational measures are in place in particular in order to ensure respect for the principle of data minimisation') as an indirect definition of the safeguards. In this context, the Study on the appropriate safeguards[55] examined technical and organisational measures outlined in regulatory documents across selected EU countries. This led to a narrow understanding of the safeguards, with focus on principles of data minimisation and data security. Other scholars adapt a broader approach, built around the contextual purpose of the safeguards, which is to uphold the data subjects' rights and freedoms defined under European human rights law,[56] i.e., the European Convention of Human Rights (ECHR)[57] and the Charter Fundamental Rights of the European Union (EU Charter).[58] For example, Staunton, Slokenberga and Mascalzoni[59] argue that data protection is much more than a technical issue requiring technical solutions and point out that 'safeguards must respond to the multitude of legal, ethical and social risks that are associated with the sharing of data'. In turn, they extract informed consent (as an ethical requirement in research), independent review and oversight, accountable processes to govern access and use of samples and data, clear and transparent policies and processes, security, and training and education as possible appropriate safeguards for biobank, databank and genetic research.

These varied views lead to large diversity of cited examples of safeguards, ranging from strictly technical measures, such as encryption or data access logs,[60] to organisational or legal practices, such as implementation of procedures to support the exercise of data subjects' rights, use of anonymous or pseudonymous data, appointment of a data protection officer, feedback mechanisms on the results of scientific research, professional accreditations of persons involved in research, creating a specific supervisory body for research endeavour, or the creation of a code of conduct.[61]

It is also not clear which (if any) authority is responsible for designating the safeguards and in which manner they need to be introduced. One interpretation hinges on Recital 156 GDPR, which states, 'Member States should provide for appropriate safeguards for the processing of personal data for … scientific or historical research purposes', suggesting that it is the member states[62] that should define the appropriate safeguards in their national laws. Examples of such safeguards are provided for in the Swedish national legislation on ethical approvals[63] and Section 64 of UK's Digital Economy Act 2017 (pre-Brexit).[64] One may however argue that if researchers can only rely on EU countries to specify the safeguards, absence of national legislation would prevent making use of research exemption rules. Some thus suggest that also the parties that conduct research may design appropriate safeguards after taking into consideration the risks relevant to the processing activity.[65,66] Researchers (as controllers) can thus implement the safeguards based on the principles stemming from the GDPR (such as data minimisation, proportionality and security)[67] or on principles beyond data protection, such as ethical requirements ensuring protections for the research participant.[68] The EDPS in the preliminary opinion on data protection and scientific research also emphasises that the safeguards to be implemented by data controllers and processors should depend on the risk to individuals, however does not take a clear stance on the provenance of the safeguards.

In summary, it can be acknowledged that there is currently no consensus over the interpretation of Article 89(1). It can be argued, however, that GDPR clearly states that safeguards must remain in accordance with GDPR, and that while appropriate safeguards need to lead to implementation of technical and organisational measures, their objective is the protection of rights and freedoms of the data subjects. In turn, the technical and organisational measures imposed by the safeguards must ensure *at least* the principle of data minimisation (including necessity and proportionality), and possibly other Article 5 GDPR principles such as data security and data protection by design and by default. Hence, safeguards deemed appropriate must: (i) ensure the implementation of technical and organisational measures that support these principles, (ii) comply with the GDPR, and (iii) safeguard the rights and freedoms of data subjects.

11.3.2 Safeguards for secondary use of health data under the EHDS proposal

Notably, the EHDS does refer to appropriate safeguards as recognised under Article 89(1) GDPR. In fact, the act uses the term sufficient safeguards in Recital 4 when stating:

> Given the sensitivity of personal health data, this Regulation seeks to provide sufficient safeguards at both Union and national level to ensure a high degree of data protection, security, confidentiality and ethical use. Such safeguards are necessary to promote trust in safe handling of electronic health data of natural persons for primary use and secondary use as defined in this Regulation.

Moreover, Recital 52 states that the EHDS provides a legal basis in accordance with GDPR for the secondary use of personal electronic health data, *including the safeguards* to permit the processing of special categories of data, required under Article 9(2), points (g) to (j) GDPR, in terms of lawful purposes, trusted governance for providing access to health data (through the involvement of health data access bodies) and processing in a secure environment, as well as arrangements for data processing, set out in the data permit. A breakdown of the EHDS safeguards is provided by Jane Reichel in Chapter 10.

As mentioned in Table 11.1, the EHDS does not refer to data federation. Still, when comparing the proposed framework for secondary uses of health data with the core elements of federated networks, a number of similarities emerge. First and foremost, the EHDS does not anticipate the creation of a large centralised electronic health data pool. On the contrary, the data will be stored by the respective health data holders and only released following the issuance of a data permit. This is similar to the concept of data nodes which are the constituting elements of federated networks. Furthermore, the EHDS restricts access to data through a secure processing environment and prohibits copying personal health data from this environment. The concept of accessing data without transferring it, while adhering to the GDPR principle of data minimisation, is integral to many federated infrastructures, as discussed further below. Given these similarities, it is worth examining the safeguards provided by existing federated networks, not only in the context of the GDPR but also in view of the framework of the EHDS. Conversely, looking at federated networks and their approach to aligning with the requirements of appropriate safeguards outlined in Article 89(1) GDPR may also enhance understanding of the EHDS framework.

11.4 Can federated networks be considered as appropriate safeguards?

11.4.1 Federated networks and data minimisation

Safeguards must ensure that technical and organisational measures are implemented to uphold, in particular, the principle of data minimisation. This principle stipulates that personal data must be adequate, relevant and limited to what is necessary in relation to the purposes for which they are processed (Article 5(1)(c) GDPR). Recital 156 also mentions necessity and proportionality, which support the principle of data minimisation. Data pseudonymisation and anonymisation are mentioned in Article 89(1) as examples of practices that translate the principle of data minimisation into concrete measures. The use of the term in particular in Article 89(1) emphasises that the measures should serve to support the principle of data minimisation but does not exclude that they may also ensure other GDPR principles, such as the principle of integrity and confidentiality (also known as data security, Article 5(1)(f) GDPR) and data protection by design and by default (Article 25 GDPR). Moreover, the role of those principles in addressing the requirements of Article 89(1) was emphasised in the EDPB guidelines.[69] These principles require technical and organisational measures to secure the data to be considered in the design of processing operations. This ensures that privacy and data protection principles are safeguarded from the outset, with the highest possible level of privacy protection by default (for example, limiting the number of persons who have access to the data).

In federated networks, data remains stored on a local node with its original owner (data custodian) and is not copied to a central database. In this way, the data storage model avoids duplication of personal data to the central repository,[70] at the point of deposit for further reuse. The data is also typically pseudonymised or anonymised by the node owner. These measures could be viewed as supporting the principle of data minimisation by design and by default as recognised by the GDPR and further supported by the EHDS. It has also been claimed that data in the node is to be held 'as securely as the local infrastructure will allow'.[71] However, in practice, the individual node holders may not have sufficient resources nor skills to ensure data security of their node. Furthermore, data breaches may occur during data communication.[72] Hence, whether the measures in the federated network will respect the principle of integrity and confidentiality will depend on the participants of the network, in particular the node holders, and the features of connecting infrastructure.

Data minimisation, integrity and confidentiality principles also need to be considered from the perspective of the data users' access to data. Depending on the model of federated networks, access to the data may be provided in various ways. Direct access to data means that the user can visit the data and analyse each database separately but are only allowed to take summary statistics or aggregated information from the database. It has been claimed that direct access limits copying and transmission of data, reduces security risks and allows continuous monitoring of user activity.[73] Yet, if, during the direct access, the users can view the data in the node (for example, through an Internet browser), at least temporary copies of personal data will be generated.[74] Therefore, the impact of possible temporary copying of database content during direct access must be evaluated against data minimisation and data security principles. Federated networks may need to find additional measures to address the risks associated with such access, such as data access monitoring, data use agreements and logging of user activity.[75]

Arguably, indirect access to data may be a remedy that better addresses the requirement of data confidentiality and limits the scope of data processing. Indirect access mandates that while data remain behind secure firewalls at all times, users submit algorithms or queries and receive summary or performance statistics, which are vetted and executed by the data provider.[76] Thus, this is associated with a higher level of data security. However, this feature may reduce the usability of the data. If the users do not have access to data, they cannot verify its quality and check the harmonisation of data in different federated nodes, which may translate to errors and research challenges.[77] Therefore, although restrictive indirect data access may uphold the principles of data minimisation, integrity and confidentiality, a balance still needs to be achieved, to ensure that the data remains suitable for research purposes. Moreover, the use of health data for AI training, including in federated learning, may pose its own security challenges, such as the potential for a partially trained model to still reveal information about the training data.[78]

In summary, the storage of data in federated nodes, as opposed to copying the data to a central repository, can be perceived as ensuring data minimisation. However, questions arise whether accessing data in the federated node inherently has advantages in terms of minimising the data. This will depend on the levels of permissions that users have within the specific federated database. Moreover, deployment of multiple nodes in the network may bring about additional privacy threats.

Under the EHDS, the principle of data minimisation is ensured at various levels, such as by the requirement of anonymisation or pseudonymisation of the electronic health data made available for secondary use (Articles 66(2) and 3), provision of access only to electronic health data which is relevant for the purpose of processing indicated in the data access application by the data user (Article 66(1)), and by limiting access to electronic health data to access through secure processing environments (Article 73(1)). These environments resemble those federated networks, in which the data cannot be copied by the user, and at all times remains in the node. The technical, information security and interoperability requirements for the secure processing environments will be further elaborated by the Commission by way of implementing acts. The questions on minimising the risk of unauthorised processing of data during direct and indirect access which are outlined for federated networks may inform the development of such requirements for secure environments under EHDS.

11.4.2 Federated networks and compliance with GDPR and the relevant points from the EHDS

The second condition of the appropriate safeguards according to Article 89(1) GDPR is that they need to comply with the GDPR. This, in turn, raises the question of whether the use of federated networks for sharing of health data can be considered a GDPR compliant measure. Some of the GDPR requirements relevant to the sharing and use of personal data for scientific research include defining and complying with the responsibilities of the relevant role of a controller or processor of the data (Articles 5(2), 24 and 28 GDPR, among others), demonstrating a legal basis for data processing (Articles 6 and 9 GDPR), complying with restrictions on data transfers outside the European Economic Area (EEA) to countries that do not provide an adequate level of data protection (Chapter V of GDPR), and ensuring data accuracy (Article 5(1)(c) GDPR). Below, we discuss how sharing personal data across federated networks may impact compliance with these requirements.

11.4.2.1 Federated networks and roles and responsibilities of various parties regarding controllership over data

The data custodians and data users, as well as any other parties involved in the federated networks (such as providers of elements of its infrastructure), need to understand their role in data processing under the GDPR. The possible roles are controller (Article 4(7)), which determines the purposes and means of processing (Article 4(7) GDPR) including joint controller (Article 26), and processor (Article 4(8)), which processes personal data on behalf of the controller (Article 4(8) GDPR). These roles cannot be contractually modified, as they depend on the law or factual circumstances.[79] The role determines the responsibilities of the participant of the network. For example, a controller must ensure a legal basis for the processing. A processor does not need to demonstrate such legal basis but must observe the restrictions of the data processing agreements and instructions of the controller (Article 28 GDPR). The identification of the controllers and processors for each processing operation is a prerequisite for the preparation of privacy notices (pursuant to Articles 13 or 14), records of processing operations (Article 30), agreements between entities involved in processing operations (for example, data processing agreements pursuant to Article 28(3) or joint controller arrangement under Article 26) and other documents necessary to demonstrate compliance with the GDPR.

The development of a federated network requires complex multi-party discussions and various converging decisions to be made, taking into account the entire data lifecycle. These decisions relate to various issues such as categories of data to be shared in the federated network, tools to be used for storage, data management and access, collaboration of various components of the infrastructure to ensure data security, data access levels and policies. Such decisions are often beyond the control of any single data custodian and must be made jointly by all data custodians in close coordination with the infrastructure component providers. The scope of these decisions and the manner in which they are made may affect the assessment of the GPDR roles of federated network stakeholders.

Under CJEU jurisprudence[80] and the EDPB Guidelines,[81] the controller does not necessarily have to possess a copy of the data it controls or even have access to it, as long as it gives instructions in relation to the processing. Thus, the argument that since the data is not moved from the node to a new user, the node owner remains the controller and the existence of the federation does not change that role[82] may not always be true. Furthermore, harmonisation of data access rules (discussed below) may tip the assessment of the GDPR role of the custodians from individual controllers to joint controllership. To complicate matters further, if the nodes delegate the decisions to approve users of the federated networks to a central authority (such as data access committee), depending on the terms of reference and access procedures,[83] the authority may become a controller of the data in the federated networks or act as a processor on behalf of the node custodians. Users who use data for their own purposes will typically be independent controllers.[84] However, this qualification may change if they have common scientific goals with the data custodians or other users.

Proper qualification as a controller has various implications under the GDPR. For example, actors qualified as controllers are responsible for ensuring the legal basis for processing (Articles 6 and 9), informing data subjects (Articles 13 and 14), implementing the principles of data protection by design and by default (Article 25 GDPR) and reporting data breaches (Article 33). Establishing common governance over the data in the federated network complicates the issue of legal responsibility. For example, how should the data access governance structure be explained to data subjects in a privacy notice? If a single gatekeeper allows users to access all data in the repository, who is liable if a malicious user leaks the data? Which participant in the federated networks should report the breach to the authorities and take corrective action? As put by Bak and others, 'because this responsibility is spread out over multiple partners instead of being allocated to a central controller, the risk that no one takes proper responsibility for data governance is increased'.[85]

In light of the above, planning a federated network to determine steps for GDPR compliance requires early discussion and assessment of stakeholder roles, followed by a written agreement that addresses established roles and responsibilities.[86] The agreement should cover both responsibilities to data subjects and obligations of potential users of the data. In practice, however, it may be difficult to identify and allocate responsibilities, and nodes may have conflicting perceptions of their qualifications. The matrix can become even more complex when additional parties are involved in building the shared infrastructure or providing certain components of it (such as user access and authorisation services).

Difficulties in proper assignment of GDPR roles and diverging views on this matter are clearly shown in the legislative process of EHDS. In the EHDS proposal, both the data users and health data access bodies (HDABs) were considered joint controllers of the electronic health data processed in accordance with the data permit. During the legislative process, this position was amended to state now that the health data holder and HDABs are simply controllers for a specific part of the process of secondary use of health data and according to their respective roles, without reference to joint controllership (Article 74).

11.4.2.2 Federated networks and nature of data processing

Counterintuitively, although the term "sharing of data" suggests a single action, multiple operations are required to enable health data sharing with users in federated networks. These operations involve both the data custodians and the data users. This is an important consideration, because under the GDPR, the processing of personal data by the controller requires a legal basis under Article 6 and, for special categories of data (such as health data), identification of an exception under Article 9(1) GDPR. The various steps taken by data controllers and data users when sharing and using personal data in the federated networks need to be examined to determine whether they could be considered as processing, which requires a legal basis.

Processing of personal data is defined broadly in the GDPR as any operation or set of operations which is performed on personal data or on sets of personal data, whether or not by automated means, such as collection, recording, organisation, structuring, storage, adaptation or alteration, retrieval, consultation, use, disclosure by transmission, dissemination or otherwise making available, alignment or combination, restriction, erasure or destruction (Article 4(2) GDPR).

Custodians are typically responsible for collecting and preparing the data (for example, pseudonymising it and adapting it to the agreed standards) and keeping it stored in the node. The collection, adaptation, and storage of data are clear examples of processing under the Article 4(2) GDPR definition and, therefore, require the custodian to establish a legal basis for these activities. In turn, the user typically performs a search for data stored in the nodes before accessing the data. Searching the central data catalogue or reviewing the metadata of each node without using the actual data is not an operation on the data itself, and therefore does not constitute data processing under the GDPR. Once the user finds a suitable dataset and is given access to it, they can start using that data for their research purposes. The use of the data is also mentioned as an example of processing in Article 4(2) GDPR. Some federated networks allow the users to query or process data in the local node,[87] but without providing direct access to the data. For example, a user's AI model can visit[88] the data during federated learning. The user initiates this activity and as a result the data is used to fulfil the user's scientific goals. Given the broad definition of processing under GDPR, which includes any use of personal data, we agree with the view[89] that the data analysis performed at the local node is a data processing operation. Similarly, conducting federated AI training on personal data is subject to GDPR.[90] Moreover, while the federated network may not facilitate direct user interaction with the data, it is ultimately the user who determines the purpose for which the data is queried for scientific research and the means (for example, specific query) by which it is done. In turn, the user acting as controller for the use of health data in their research activity must demonstrate a legal basis for this processing.

Consequently, the processing of data for storage in the federated node by the data holder would be considered a different processing purpose than the access and use of the same data by one or more data users (researchers). In order to comply with the GDPR, all controllers involved in the processing of data in the federated network must ensure an appropriate legal basis for their processing operations. In practice, a single consent from the data subject may not sufficiently cover multiple operations that are often performed by different actors in the federated networks, so alternative approaches (such as dynamic consent[91]) may need to be implemented to ensure that all controllers can demonstrate a valid legal basis for their processing.

The EHDS provides an interesting insight into this discussion. According to Recital 52, the EHDS will provide the legal basis (and obligation) for the data holder to disclose the requested electronic health data to the HDAB and secure the legal basis for the processing performed by these administrative bodies. However, to obtain a data permit, the data applicant will have to demonstrate a legal basis pursuant to Article 6 GDPR. This recital highlights the complexity of ensuring a legal basis for all participants in the data sharing framework, even when governance rules are imposed by a legislative act such as the EHDS.

11.4.2.3 Other challenges in deployment of federated networks

Federated networks may also not comply with other GDPR principles, such as the need to respect the data accuracy principle, as well as broader issues such as infrastructure sustainability. Under Article 5(1)(d) GDPR, the data must be accurate and, where necessary, kept up to date. This raises the question of whether federated networks can ensure the accuracy and quality of research data. This is not a straightforward issue. Some doubt whether error-free data sets are even possible, especially in the medical field.[92] Dealing with distributed structures adds another layer of complexity. Federated networks consist of many distributed data sources (nodes). If the data within a node is restricted to the custodian's access, only the custodian can vouch for its accuracy. As a result, attempting to verify all data nodes by an outside entity becomes infeasible. As a practical solution, the participating nodes may establish a process of validating datasets, define measures to evaluate their quality and even *ex ante* accountability measures.[93] Still, such an overarching agreement on how the data will be collected and prepared may trigger the qualification of nodes as joint controllers, as further discussed above.

Compliance with Chapter V of GDPR when transferring personal data to countries outside the European Economic Area which do not provide for adequate level of data protection (non-adequate third countries) is also an area for consideration. These strict legal conditions drive the question of whether accessing data through the federated network constitutes a data transfer. While comprehensive analysis of this topic remains beyond the scope of this chapter, given the broad interpretation of data transfers by the recent EDPB guidelines,[94] such qualification is not excluded.

Sustainability and continued reliability of data sources in federated networks also require further consideration. Users should be able to document the data sources for their results so that these results can be verified and reproduced. Often the structure of the network is fluid and the data in the nodes may be altered or removed by its custodians. This has implications for reproductivity of the research results. To become an attractive resource for the potential users, the node custodians must agree on the rules of withdrawing or modifying the data in the network, and those rules should be transparent and allow the users to plan and document their research.

As shown in this part of the chapter, the answer to the question of whether federated networks are GDPR compliant is multifaceted and depends on different decisions made during the implementation of the network. While there does not appear to be any feature of the federated network model that inherently violates the requirements of the GDPR, given the different possible implementations of the federated approach, GDPR compliance must be carefully considered and documented during the planning and implementation of the network.

The EHDS addresses some of the key points indicated above. It provides for data quality and utility labels (Article 78) which can be used by the data users to find a dataset that fits their needs. Moreover, it provides additional restrictions regarding access to non-personal health data from third countries (Article

61). Finally, the inclusion of obligations to make health data available for secondary use (Article 41) may shift perspectives on the long-term sustainability of existing data repositories, provided they align with the requirements of the EHDS.

11.4.3 Federated networks and protection of rights and freedoms of the data subjects

According to the third overarching requirement of Article 89(1) GDPR, the appropriate safeguards should protect the rights and freedoms of the data subject. These rights and freedoms can be viewed, in a broad sense, as deriving directly from human rights law. For example, in discussing the safeguards mandated by the legislative measures implemented by the DEA, J. Bell[95] has referred to European human rights law, in particular Article 8 of ECHR and Articles 7 and 8 of the EU Charter and related case law to assess the enforcement mechanisms behind the legislative measures.

However, the requirement to respect the rights and freedoms of natural persons can also be understood in a narrower sense, as referring to the right of protection of personal data. In particular, Recital 75 of GDPR lists examples of the risks to the rights and freedoms which may result from personal data processing, including among others, physical, material or non-material damage, where the processing may give rise to discrimination, identity theft or fraud, financial loss, damage to the reputation, loss of confidentiality of personal data protected by professional secrecy, unauthorised reversal of pseudonymisation, or any other significant economic or social disadvantage. Many of those risks are associated with data subjects' loss of control over their personal data. In the context of use of data for research purposes, mitigating such risks is often associated with not only compliance with GDPR but also with ethical standards, such as Oviedo Convention[96] or OECD Guidelines on Human Biobanks and Genetic Research Databases.[97]

As mentioned above, participation in a federated network is tied to an agreement which the data custodian must accept when joining a federated network. We argue that the content of this agreement can be a key factor in ensuring that the rights and freedoms of the data subjects are respected. Specifically, the measures to address risks to the rights and freedoms of data subjects should be evaluated when designing the data access governance rules to be adopted by the network of custodians. Data access governance regulates who are the users who have access to data, for what purposes and under what conditions.[98] Through an agreement on data governance, each node custodian may cede some of its autonomy to a central authority or to rules of common governance. This may include connecting the federated node to a central infrastructure[99] or, in a loosely defined federated network, adhering to agreements on common rules or standards[100] (for example, on data or technology). Common rules should determine how the access to the data in the node is granted. These rules should be designed not only in compliance with GDPR but also to respect the ethical standards mentioned above.

When establishing conditions for data access, it is important to consider not only the legitimate interests of potential data users in pursuing their scientific goals but also to protect the rights and freedoms of data subjects. Delegating the authority to make data access decisions to a common governance body[101] of the federated network (such as data access committee, DAC) may serve to streamline the process. It is argued that collective bodies, such as DACs are better suited to assess the data use requests objectively and transparently.[102] However, to ensure that the DAC decision making process is sufficiently independent from professional interests of the data custodians and potential users, the DAC should consist of a diverse group of stakeholders, with different expertise. It is particularly important to include representatives from patient organisations to ensure that the perspectives and needs of patients are effectively represented.[103] Moreover, the transparency of the data access process could be supported by technical solutions where federated networks collect and make public certain information about data usage.[104] Furthermore, the legal terms on the data access accepted by the data user can also be an instrument to ensure protections for the rights and freedoms of data subjects by providing legally binding rules on confidentiality, security measures to be adopted by the data user and restrictions on attempting to re-identify the data subjects.[105] Data use conditions for data users should also take into consideration any restrictions stemming from data subjects' informed consent or ethics approvals.

When in effect, the EHDS will change the rules of the game for seeking health data for scientific research by introducing harmonised rules for accessing data for secondary use. Yet, before its adoption, existing federated networks are challenged with the design of their own data governance framework, in a way that minimises privacy risks and fosters research goals. Decisions on such framework can be informed by some of the safeguarding elements which are provided in the EHDS, in particular standard common processes for data access applications (Article 67), conditions imposed on the data user in the data permit (Article 68) and reporting requirements for HDABs to ensure the transparency of the process (Article 59). One notable difference, however, is that while federated networks may deploy various governance bodies, including data access committees, under the EHDS the data access decision hinges, in principle, on the health data access bodies. The mechanisms aimed to shield the rights and freedoms of the patients under the EHDS framework are evaluated by others in this book.

11.5 Conclusions

Federated networks have emerged as a response to challenges in sharing health data. They offer advantages such as cost reduction through shared infrastructure and precise control over data access permissions at various levels.[106] From a legal perspective, properly implemented federated networks comply with GDPR requirements and support data minimisation and security.

However, it is premature to declare them a universal solution for complex legal demands for data sharing. Federated networks must be evaluated on a case-by-case basis, and further research is needed to define GDPR-compliant characteristics. Depending on the implementation, roles and responsibilities of stakeholders within the federated infrastructure can vary, affecting the ability to assess whether their technical and organisational measures can support GDPR principles of data minimisation (Article 5(1)(c)), data accuracy (Article 5(1)(d)) or integrity and confidentiality (Article 5(1)(f)). The sustainability and reliability of data sources in federated networks also warrant further examination, as they may affect data security and accountability. There is also a need for further exploration into how the means to protect the rights and freedoms of data subjects should be reflected in the rules of data governance and usage within the network. The absence of standardised guidelines for constructing these networks within health infrastructures for data sharing complicates the assessment of federated networks as appropriate safeguards under Article 89(1) GDPR.

Understanding the benefits and risks associated with sharing data in federated networks may inform legislative decisions and create a more robust EHDS framework. At the same time, some safeguards foreseen by the EHDS should be carefully evaluated by existing and future federated networks. These safeguards may serve as guiding examples to improve GDPR compliance and balance the interests and obligations of data subjects, data holders, and data users.

Another point of consideration is to what extent the framework of health data sharing provided for in the EHDS will be mandatory and exclusive. EHDS provides that the regulation 'shall not affect access to electronic health data for secondary use agreed in the framework of contractual or administrative arrangements between public or private entities' (Article 1(8)). This suggests that existing health data repositories (either centralised or federated) may be allowed to function based on contractual agreements and provide their own governance rules for reuse of deposited data. Nevertheless, federated network developers should pay close attention to the EHDS proposal to understand the potential impact on their sharing model, as well as for (indirect) guidance on how to address the legal challenges inherent in multi-stakeholder data sharing.

Acknowledgements/Funding

The work of MKC was funded by the European Union's research and innovation programme under grant agreement number 952179 – INCISIVE and grant agreement number 101095382 – FLUTE.

Notes

1 Sarah J. MacEachern and Nils D. Forkert, 'Machine learning for precision medicine' (2021) 64(4) *Genome* 416.
2 Anna D. Barker and Jerry SH Lee, 'Translating 'Big Data' in oncology for clinical benefit: progress or paralysis' (2022) 82(11) *Cancer Res.* 2072.
3 Eric J Topol, 'High-performance medicine: the convergence of human and artificial intelligence' (2019) 25(1) *Nat. Med.* 44.

4 David Peloquin and others, 'Disruptive and avoidable: GDPR challenges to secondary research uses of data' (2020) 28(6) *Eur. J. Hum. Genet.* 697; Olga Tzortzatou and others, 'Biobanking Across Europe Post-GDPR: A Deliberately Fragmented Landscape' in Santa Slokenberga, Olga Tzortzatou and Jane Reichel (eds), *GDPR and Biobanking: Individual Rights, Public Interest and Research Regulation across Europe* (Springer Nature, 2021).; Birgit Wouters and others, 'Putting the GDPR into practice: Difficulties and uncertainties experienced in the conduct of big data health research' (2021) 7 *Eur. Data Prot. L. Rev.* 206.

5 World Economic Forum, 'Sharing sensitive health data in a federated data consortium model: An eight-step guide' (2020) https://www.weforum.org/reports/sharing-sensitive-health-data-in-a-federated-data-consortium-model-an-eight-step-guide/ accessed on 28 September 2023.

6 Alexander Bernier and others, 'Reconciling the biomedical data commons and the GDPR: three lessons from the EUCAN ELSI collaboratory' (2023) *Eur. J. Hum. Genet.* 1.

7 James Casaletto and others 'Federated analysis for privacy-preserving data sharing: a technical and legal primer' (2023) 24 *Annu. Rev. Genomics Hum. Genet.* 347.

8 Raivo Ruusalepp, 'A comparative study of international approaches to enabling the sharing of research data' (2008) https://era.ed.ac.uk/bitstream/handle/1842/3361/Ruusalepp%20Data_Sharing_Report.pdf?sequence=1 accessed on 28 September 2023.

9 European Commission, 'A European strategy for data' (Communication) (2020) 66 final.

10 European Commission, 'Proposal for a regulation – The European Health Data Space' COM(2022) 197 final. On 24 April 2024 the European Parliament passed a legislative resolution with a view to the adoption of Regulation (EU) 2024/… of the European Parliament and of the Council on the European Health Data Space P9_TC1-COD(2022)0140 (EHDS compromise text).

11 For example, Peloquin (n 4); Casaletto (n 7); Rita T. Lawlor, 'The impact of GDPR on data sharing for European cancer research' (2023) 24(1) *Lancet Oncol.* 6; Regina Becker and others, 'Applying GDPR roles and responsibilities to scientific data sharing' (2022) 12(3) *Int. Data Priv. Law* 207.

12 European Parliament and the Council Regulation 2016/679 of 27 April 2016 on the Protection of Natural Persons with Regard to the Processing of Personal Data and on the Free Movement of such Data (General Data Protection Regulation) [2016] OJ L 119/1.

13 Amit P. Sheth and James A. Larson, 'Federated database systems for managing distributed, heterogeneous, and autonomous databases' (1990) 22(3) *ACM Comput. Surv.* 183.

14 Dennis Heimbigner and Dennis McLeod, 'A federated architecture for information management' (1985) 3(3) *ACM Trans. Inf. Syst.* 253.

15 Adrian Thorogood and others, 'International federation of genomic medicine databases using GA4GH standards' (2021) 1(2) *Cell Genomics* 100032.

16 Christine Suver and others, 'Bringing code to data: Do not forget governance' (2020) 22(7) *JMIR* e18087.

17 World Economic Forum, 'Federated data systems: balancing innovation and trust in the use of sensitive data' (2019) https://www3.weforum.org/docs/WEF_Federated_Data_Systems_2019.pdf accessed on 9 November 2023.

18 Stéphane Goldstein, 'The evolving landscape of Federated Research Data Infrastructures Knowledge Exchange', (2017) *Zenodo*.

19 Yannick Marcon and others, 'Orchestrating privacy-protected big data analyses of data from different resources with R and DataSHIELD' (2021) 17(3) *PLoS Comput. Biol.* e1008880.

20 Richard Milne and others, 'A concentric circles view of health data relations facilitates understanding of sociotechnical challenges for learning health systems and the role of federated data networks' (2022) 5 *Front. Big Data* 945739.
21 Rolf Gedeborg and others, 'Federated analyses of multiple data sources in drug safety studies' (2023) 32(3) *Pharmacoepidemiol Drug Saf.* 279.
22 Suver and others (n 16).
23 Global Alliance for Genomics and Health, 'A federated ecosystem for sharing genomic, clinical data' (2016) 352(6291) *Science* 1278.
24 Brendan McMahan and others, 'Communication-efficient learning of deep networks from decentralized data' (2017) 54 Proceedings of the 20th International Conference on Artificial Intelligence and Statistics, PMLR.
25 Suver and others (n 16).
26 Alissa Brauneck and others, 'Federated Machine Learning, Privacy-Enhancing Technologies, and Data Protection Laws in Medical Research: Scoping Review' (2023) 25 *JMIR* 41588.
27 Gary Saunders and others, 'Leveraging European infrastructures to access 1 million human genomes by 2022' (2019) 20(11) *Nat. Rev. Genet.* 693.
28 J. Damián Segrelles Quilis and others, 'A federated cloud architecture for processing of cancer images on a distributed storage' (2023) 139 *Future Gener. Comput. Syst.* 38.
29 Kari A. Stephens and others, 'Implementing partnership-driven clinical federated electronic health record data sharing networks' (2016) 93 *Int. J. Med. Inform.* 26.
30 Goldstein (n 18).
31 Suver and others (n 16).
32 Marc Fiume and others, 'Federated discovery and sharing of genomic data using Beacons' (2019) 37 *Nat. Biotechnol.* 220.
33 Luís António Bastião Silva, 'Federated architecture for biomedical data integration' (Dissertation, Universidade de Aveiro 2015) http://hdl.handle.net/10773/15759 accessed on 14 May 2024.
34 Griffin M. Weber, 'Federated queries of clinical data repositories: Scaling to a national network' (2015) 55 *J. Biomed. Informat.* 231.
35 Marcelline R. Harris, Lisa A. Ferguson, and Airong Luo, 'Infrastructuring an organizational node for a federated research and data network: A case study from a sociotechnical perspective' (2021) 5(1) *J. Clin. Transl. Sci.* e186.
36 European Strategy for Data (n 9).
37 Regulation (EU) 2022/868 of the European Parliament and of the Council of 30 May 2022 on European data governance and amending Regulation (EU) 2018/1724 (Data Governance Act) [2022] OJ L 152/1.
38 EHDS.
39 European Commission, 'Commission Staff Working Document, Impact Assessment Report accompanying the document Proposal for a Regulation of the European Parliament and of the Council on the European Health Data Space' (3 May 2022) Swd(2022) 131 final.
40 EDPB-EDPS Joint Opinion 03/2021 on the Proposal for a regulation of the European Parliament and of the Council on European data governance (Data Governance Act), adopted on 10 March 2021.
41 EDPS, Preliminary Opinion 8/2020 on the European Health Data Space, adopted on 17 November 2020.
42 EDPB-EDPS Joint Opinion 03/2022 on the Proposal for a Regulation on the European Health Data Space, adopted on 12 July 2022.
43 EDPS, Opinion 3/2020 on the European strategy for data, adopted on 16 June 2020.
44 EDPS, A Preliminary Opinion on data protection and scientific research, adopted on 6 January 2020.

45 EDPS website https://edps.europa.eu/_en accessed on 25 October 2023.
46 Federated Learning https://edps.europa.eu/press-publications/publications/techsonar/federated-learning_en accessed on 5 January 2024.
47 TechDispatch #1/2022 – Federated Social Media Platforms https://edps.europa.eu/data-protection/our-work/publications/techdispatch/2022-07-26-techdispatch-12022-federated-social-media-platforms_en accessed on 5 January 2024.
48 ENISA 'Engineering Personal Data Sharing Emerging Use Cases and Technologies' January 2023 https://www.enisa.europa.eu/publications/engineering-personal-data-sharing accessed on 5 January 2024.
49 ENISA 'Fog And Edge Computing in 5G Security Opportunities And Challenges' March 2023.
https://www.enisa.europa.eu/publications/fog-and-edge-computing-in-5g accessed on 5 January 2024.
50 ENISA, 'Engineering personal data protection in EU Data Spaces' January 2023 https://www.enisa.europa.eu/publications/engineering-personal-data-protection-in-eu-data-spaces accessed on 5 January 2024.
51 Kart Pormeister, 'Genetic data and the research exemption: is the GDPR going too far?' (2017) 7 *Int. Data Priv. Law* 137.
52 Jessica Bell and others, 'Balancing Data Subjects' Rights and Public Interest Research' (2019) 5 *European Data Protection Law Review* 43.
53 EDPS, Opinion on safeguards and derogations under Article 89 GDPR in the context of a proposal for a Regulation on integrated farm statistics, adopted 20 November 2017; EDPS, A Preliminary Opinion on data protection and scientific research (n 44); EDPB, Response to the Request from the European Commission for Clarifications on the Consistent Application of the GDPR, Focusing on Health Research, adopted on 2 February 2021.
54 EDPS, opinion on safeguards and derogations under Article 89 GDPR.
55 Els Kindt and others, 'Study on the Appropriate Safeguards under Article 89(1) GDPR for the Processing of Personal Data for Scientific Research. Final Report' (2021, EDPS/2019/02–08).
56 Bell and others (n 52).
57 Convention for the Protection of Human Rights and Fundamental Freedoms, Rome, 1950 Council of Europe European Treaty Series 5.
58 Charter of Fundamental Rights of the European Union [2012] OJ C 326/391.
59 Ciara Staunton, Santa Slokenberga and Deborah Mascalzoni, 'The GDPR and the research exemption: considerations on the necessary safeguards for research biobanks' (2019) 27(8) *European J. Hum. Gen.* 1159.
60 Christopher Kuner and others (eds), *The EU General Data Protection Regulation (GDPR): A Commentary* (Oxford Academic, online edn, 2020).
61 Anne-Marie Duguet and Jean Herveg, 'Safeguards and Derogations Relating to Processing for Scientific Purposes: Art. 89 Analysis for Biobank Research' in Santa Slokenberga, Olga Tzortzatou and Jane Reichel (eds) *GDPR and Biobanking: Individual Rights, Public Interest and Research Regulation across Europe* (Springer Nature 2021); Christopher F. Mondschein and Cosimo Monda 'The EU's General Data Protection Regulation (GDPR) in a research context' in Pieter Kubben, Michel Dumontier and Andre Dekker (eds), *Fundamentals of Clinical Data Science* (Springer Nature 2019).
62 Annagrazia Altavilla and others, 'The secondary use of paediatric data under GDPR: looking for new safeguards for research' (2019) 3 *EPLR* 156.
63 Jane Reichel, 'The GDPR and processing of personal data for research purposes: what about case law?' (2021) 27(1) *European Pub. Law* 167.
64 Bell and others (n 52).
65 Kuner (n 60).

66 Mondschein and Monda (n 61).
67 Giulia Schneider, 'Health data pools under European policy and data protection law: research as a new efficiency defence?' (2020) 11 *JIPITEC* 49 https://www.jipitec.eu/archive/issues/jipitec-11-1-2020/5082 accessed on 14 May 2024.
68 Ciara Staunton and others, 'Appropriate safeguards and Art. 89 of the GDPR: considerations for biobank, databank and genetic research' (2022) 13 *Front. Gen.*
69 EDPB Guidelines 03/2020 on the processing of data concerning health for the purpose of scientific research in the context of the COVID-19 outbreak, adopted 21 April 2020.
70 Stephanie Rossello, Luis Muñoz-González, and Roberto Díaz Morales, 'Data protection by design in AI? The case of federated learning' (2021) 166 *Computerrecht* 273. https://ssrn.com/abstract=3879613 accessed on 14 May 2024.
71 Milne and others (n 20).
72 Brauneck and others (n 26).
73 Thorogood and others (n 15).
74 C-360/13 *Public Relations Consultants Association Ltd v Newspaper Licensing Agency Ltd and Others* ECLI:EU:C:2014:1195.
75 Maria Alvarellos and others, 'Democratizing clinical-genomic data: How federated platforms can promote benefits sharing in genomics' (2023) 13 *Front. Genet.* 3725.
76 Thorogood and others (n 15).
77 Suver and others (n 16).
78 Bjørn Aslak Juliussen and others, 'The third country problem under the GDPR: enhancing protection of data transfers with technology' (2023) 13(3) *Int. Data Priv. Law* 225.
79 EDPB Guidelines 07/2020 on the concepts of controller and processor in the GDPR, adopted on 07 July 2021.
80 C-25/17 *Jehovan todistajat – uskonnollinen yhdyskunta* ECLI:EU:C:2018:551; C-40/17 *Fashion ID GmbH & Co.KG v Verbraucherzentrale NRW eV* ECLI:EU:C:2019:629.
81 EDPB Guidelines 07/2020 (n 79).
82 Milne and others (n 20).
83 Foundation 29 *Health Data: the Playbook* https://www.healthdata29.org/playbook accessed on 10 November 2023.
84 Becker and others (n 11).
85 Marieke Bak and others 'Federated learning is not a cure-all for data ethics' (2024) *Nat Mach Intell* ***6**, pages 370–372 (2024).*
86 Gedeborg and others (n 21).
87 Harry Hallock and others, 'Federated networks for distributed analysis of health data' (2021) 9 *Front Public Health* 712569.
88 Thorogood and others (n 15).
89 Gedeborg and others (n 21).
90 Rossello, Muñoz-González, and Morales (n 70).
91 Jane Kaye and others, 'Dynamic consent: a patient interface for twenty-first century research networks' (2015) 23(2) *Eur. J. Hum. Gen.* 141.
92 Brauneck and others (n 26).
93 Brauneck and others (n 26).
94 EDPB, Guidelines 05/2021 on the Interplay between the application of Article 3 and the provisions on international transfers as per Chapter V of the GDPR, adopted 14 February 2023.
95 Bell and others (n 52).
96 Council of Europe, Convention for the Protection of Huan Rights and of the Huan Being with regard to the Application of Biology and Medicine (Convention on Human Rights and Biomedicine or the Oviedo Convention).

97 Organization for Economic Cooperation and Development, 'OECD guidelines on human biobanks and genetic research databases' (2009).
98 Mahsa Shabani, Adrian Thorogood and Madeleine Murtagh, 'Data access governance' in Graeme Laurie and others (eds), *The Cambridge Handbook of Health Research Regulation* (Cambridge University Press, 2021).
99 World Economic Forum (n 17).
100 Thorogood and others (n 15).
101 Alvarellos and others (n 75).
102 Thijs Devriendt and others, 'Data sharing platforms: instruments to inform and shape science policy on data sharing? (2022) 127(6) *Scientometrics* 3007.
103 Milne and others (n 20).
104 Devriendt and others (n 102).
105 Shabani, Thorogood and Murtagh (n 98).
106 World Economic Forum (n 17).

List of sources

EU treaties, legislative acts and international conventions

Charter of Fundamental Rights of the European Union [2012] OJ C 326/391.

Council of Europe, Convention for the Protection of Human Rights and Fundamental Freedoms, Rome, 1950 European Treaty Series 5.

Council of Europe, Convention for the Protection of Human Rights and of the Human Being with regard to the Application of Biology and Medicine (Convention on Human Rights and Biomedicine or the Oviedo Convention) European Treaty Series 164, [1997].

European Parliament and the Council Regulation 2016/679 of 27 April 2016 on the Protection of Natural Persons with Regard to the Processing of Personal Data and on the Free Movement of such Data (General Data Protection Regulation) [2016] OJ L 119/1.

European Parliament and the Council Regulation (EU) 2022/868 of the European Parliament and of the Council of 30 May 2022 on European data governance and amending Regulation (EU) 2018/1724 (Data Governance Act) [2022] OJ L 152/1.

Official documents

EDPB, Guidelines 03/2020 on the processing of data concerning health for the purpose of scientific research in the context of the COVID-19 outbreak, adopted on 21 April 2020.

EDPB, Response to the request from the European Commission for clarifications on the consistent application of the GDPR, focusing on health research, adopted on 2 February 2021.

EDPB, Guidelines 07/2020 on the concepts of controller and processor in the GDPR, adopted on 07 July 2021.

EDPB, Guidelines 05/2021 on the interplay between the application of Art. 3 and the provisions on international transfers as per Chapter V of the GDPR, adopted on 14 February 2023.

EDPB-EDPS, Joint Opinion 03/2021 on the Proposal for a regulation of the European Parliament and of the Council on European data governance (Data Governance Act), adopted on 10 March 2021.

EDPB-EDPS, Joint Opinion 03/2022 on the Proposal for a Regulation on the European Health Data Space, adopted on 12 July 2022.

EDPS, Opinion on safeguards and derogations under Article 89 GDPR in the context of a proposal for a Regulation on integrated farm statistics, adopted on 20 November 2017.

EDPS, A Preliminary Opinion on data protection and scientific research, adopted on 6 January 2020.

EDPS, Opinion 3/2020 on the European strategy for data, adopted on 16 June 2020.

EDPS, Preliminary Opinion 8/2020 on the European Health Data Space, adopted on 17 November 2020.

EDPS https://edps.europa.eu/_en accessed on 25 October 2023.

ENISA 'Engineering Personal Data Sharing Emerging Use Cases and Technologies' January 2023 https://www.enisa.europa.eu/publications/engineering-personal-data-sharing accessed on 5 January 2024.

ENISA 'Fog And Edge Computing in 5G Security Opportunities And Challenges' March 2023 https://www.enisa.europa.eu/publications/fog-and-edge-computing-in-5g accessed on 5 January 2024.

ENISA, 'Engineering Personal Data Protection in EU Data Spaces' January 2023 https://www.enisa.europa.eu/publications/engineering-personal-data-protection-in-eu-data-spaces accessed on 5 January 2024.

European Commission, 'A European strategy for data' (Communication) (2020) 66 final.

European Commission, Proposal for a regulation – The European Health Data Space COM(2022) 197 final.

European Commission, 'Commission Staff Working Document, Impact Assessment Report accompanying the document Proposal for a Regulation of the European Parliament and of the Council on the European Health Data Space' (3 May 2022) Swd(2022) 131 final.

European Parliament position adopted at first reading on 24 April 2024 with a view to the adoption of Regulation (EU) 2024/... of the European Parliament and of the Council on the European Health Data Space P9_TC1-COD(2022)0140.

Literature

Altavilla A and others, 'The Secondary Use of Paediatric Data under GDPR: Looking for New Safeguards for Research' (2019) 3 *EPLR* 156. DOI:10.21552/eplr/2019/4/6

Alvarellos M and others, 'Democratizing Clinical-Genomic Data: How Federated Platforms Can Promote Benefits Sharing in Genomics' (2023) 13 *Frontiers in Genetics* 3725. DOI: 10.3389/fgene.2022.104545

Bak M and others, 'Federated Learning Is Not a Cure-All for Data Ethics' (2024) *Nat Mach Intell* 1. DOI:10.1038/s42256-024-00813-x

Barker A and Lee J, 'Translating 'Big Data' in Oncology for Clinical Benefit: Progress or Paralysis' (2022) 82(11) *Cancer Research* 2072. DOI: 10.1139/gen-2020-0131

Becker R and others, 'Applying GDPR Roles and Responsibilities to Scientific Data Sharing' (2022) 12(3) *Int. Data Priv. Law* 207. DOI: 10.2139/SSRN.3851128

Bell J and others, 'Balancing Data Subjects' Rights and Public Interest Research' (2019) 5 *Eur. Data Prot. Law Rev.* 43. DOI:10.21552/EDPL/2019/1/8

Bernier A and others, 'Reconciling the Biomedical Data Commons and the GDPR: Three Lessons From the EUCAN ELSI Collaboratory' (2023) 1 *European Journal of Human Genetics* DOI:10.1038/s41431-023-01403-y.

Brauneck A and others, 'Federated Machine Learning, Privacy-Enhancing Technologies, and Data Protection Laws in Medical Research: Scoping Review' (2023) 25 *JMIR* 41588. DOI:10.2196/41588

Casaletto J and others, 'Federated Analysis for Privacy-Preserving Data Sharing: A Technical and Legal Primer' (2023) 24 *Annual Review of Genomics and Human Genetics* 347. DOI:10.1146/annurev-genom-110122-084756

Suver Ch and others, 'Bringing code to data: Do not forget governance' (2020) 22(7) *JMIR* e18087. DOI:10.2196/preprints.18087

Devriendt T and others, 'Data Sharing Platforms: Instruments to Inform and Shape Science Policy on Data Sharing? (2022) 127(6) *Scientometrics* 3007. DOI:10.1007/s11192-022-04361-2

Duguet AM and Herveg J, 'Safeguards and Derogations Relating to Processing for Scientific Purposes: Art. 89 Analysis for Biobank Research' in Slokenberga, S, Tzortzatou, O and Reichel, J (eds) *GDPR and Biobanking: Individual Rights, Public Interest and Research Regulation across Europe* (Springer Nature, 2021). DOI:10.1007/978-3-030-49388-2_7

Federated Learning https://edps.europa.eu/press-publications/publications/techsonar/federated-learning_en accessed on 5 January 2024.

Fiume M and others, 'Federated Discovery and Sharing of Genomic Data Using Beacons' (2019) *Nature Biotechnology* 37, 220. DOI:10.1038/s41587-019-0046-x

Foundation 29 Health Data: The Playbook https://www.healthdata29.org/playbook accessed on 10 November 2023.

Gedeborg R and others, 'Federated Analyses of Multiple Data Sources in Drug Safety Studies' (2023) 32(3) *Pharmacoepidemiology and Drug Safety* 279. DOI:10.1002/pds.5587

Global Alliance for Genomics and Health, 'A Federated Ecosystem for Sharing Genomic, Clinical Data' (2016) 352(6291) *Science* 1278. DOI: 10.1126/science.aaf6162

Goldstein S, 'The Evolving Landscape of Federated Research Data Infrastructures Knowledge Exchange', (2017). DOI:10.5281/ZENODO.1064730

Hallock H and others, 'Federated Networks for Distributed Analysis of Health Data' (2021) *Frontiers in Public Health* 9, 712569. DOI:10.3389/fpubh.2021.712569

Harris M, Ferguson L and Luo A, 'Infrastructuring an Organizational Node for a Federated Research and Data Network: A Case Study From a Sociotechnical Perspective' (2021) *J. Clin. Transl. Sci.* 5(1), e186. DOI:10.1017/cts.2021.846

Heimbigner D and McLeod D, 'A Federated Architecture for Information Management' (1985) 3(3) *ACM Transactions on Information Systems* 253. DOI:10.1145/4229.4233

Juliussen BA and others, 'The Third Country Problem Under the GDPR: Enhancing Protection of Data Transfers With Technology' (2023) 13(3) *Int. Data Priv. Law* 225. DOI:10.1093/idpl/ipad013

Kaye J and others, 'Dynamic Consent: A Patient interface for Twenty-First Century Research Networks' (2015) 23(2) *European Journal of Human Genetics* 141. DOI:10.1038/ejhg.2014.71

Kindt E and others, 'Study on the Appropriate Safeguards under Article 89(1) GDPR for the Processing of Personal Data for Scientific Research. Final Report' (2021, EDPS/2019/02–08).

Kuner Ch and others (eds), *The EU General Data Protection Regulation (GDPR): A Commentary* (Oxford Academic, online edn, 2020).

Lawlor R, 'The Impact of GDPR on Data Sharing for European Cancer Research' (2023) 24(1) *The Lancet Oncology* 6. DOI: 10.1016/S1470-2045(22)00653-2

MacEachern S and Forkert N, 'Machine Learning for Precision Medicine' (2021) 64(4) *Genome* 416. DOI: 10.1139/gen-2020-0131

Marcon Y and others, 'Orchestrating Privacy-Protected Big Data Analyses of Data From Different Resources with R and DataSHIELD' (2021) 17(3) *PLoS Computational Biology* e1008880. DOI:10.1371/journal.pcbi.1008880

McMahan B and others, 'Communication-Efficient Learning of Deep Networks From Decentralized Data.' (2017) Proceedings of the 20th International Conference on Artificial Intelligence and Statistics, PMLR. 54. DOI: 10.48550/arXiv.1602.05629

Milne R and others, 'A Concentric Circles View of Health Data Relations Facilitates Understanding of Sociotechnical Challenges for Learning Health Systems and the Role of Federated Data Networks' (2022) *Front. Big Data* 5, 945739. DOI:10.3389/fdata.2022.945739

Mondschein Ch and Monda C, 'The EU's General Data Protection Regulation (GDPR) in a Research Context' in Kubben, P, Dumontier, P and Dekker, A (eds), *Fundamentals of clinical data science*'. (Springer Nature, 2019). DOI:10.1007/978-3-319-99713-1_5

Organization for Economic Cooperation and Development, 'OECD Guidelines on Human Biobanks and Genetic Research Databases' (2009).

Peloquin D and others, 'Disruptive and Avoidable: GDPR Challenges to Secondary Research Uses of Data' (2020) 28(6) *European Journal of Human Genetics* 697. DOI:10.1038/s41431-020-0596-x

Pormeister K, 'Genetic Data and the Research Exemption: Is the GDPR Going too Far?' (2017) 7 *Int. Data Priv. Law* 137. DOI: 10.1093/IDPL/IPX006

Reichel J, 'The GDPR and Processing of Personal Data for Research Purposes: What About Case Law?' (2021) 27(1) *Eur. Public Law* 167. DOI: 10.54648/euro2021007

Rossello S, Muñoz-González L and Díaz Morales R, 'Data protection by design in AI? The case of federated learning' (2021) 166 *Computerrecht* 273. https://ssrn.com/abstract=3879613 accessed on 14 May 2024.

Ruusalepp R, 'A Comparative Study of International Approaches to Enabling the Sharing of Research Data' (2008) https://era.ed.ac.uk/bitstream/handle/1842/3361/Ruusalepp%20Data_Sharing_Report.pdf?sequence=1 accessed on 28 September 2023

Saunders G and others, 'Leveraging European Infrastructures to Access 1 Million Human Genomes by 2022' (2019) 20(11) *Nature Reviews. Genetics* 693. DOI: 10.1038/s41576-019-0156-9.

Schneider G, 'Health Data Pools Under European Policy and Data Protection Law: Research as a New Efficiency Defence?' (2020) 11 JIPITEC 49. https://www.jipitec.eu/archive/issues/jipitec-11-1-2020/5082 accessed on 14 May 2024.

Segrelles Quilis D and others, 'A Federated Cloud Architecture for Processing of Cancer Images on a Distributed Storage' (2023) 139 *Future Gener. Comput. Syst.* 38. DOI: 10.1016/j.future.2022.09.019

Shabani M, Thorogood A and Murtagh M, 'Data access governance' in Graeme Laurie and others (eds), *The Cambridge Handbook of Health Research Regulation* (Cambridge University Press, 2021). DOI: 10.1017/9781108620024.023

Sheth A and Larson J, 'Federated Database Systems for Managing Distributed, Heterogeneous, and Autonomous Databases' (1990) 22(3) *ACM Computing Surveys* 183. DOI:10.1145/96602.96604

Silva L, 'Federated Architecture for Biomedical Data Integration' (Dissertation, Universidade de Aveiro 2015) http://hdl.handle.net/10773/15759 accessed on 14 May 2024.

Staunton C and others, 'Appropriate Safeguards and Art. 89 of the GDPR: Considerations for Biobank, Databank and Genetic Research' (2022) 13 *Frontiers in Genetics*. DOI: 10.3389/fgene.2022.719317

Staunton C, Slokenberga S and Mascalzoni D, 'The GDPR and the Research Exemption: Considerations on the Necessary Safeguards for Research Biobanks' (2019) 27(8) *European Journal of Human Genetics* 1159. DOI: 10.1038/s41431-019-0386-5

Stephens K and others, 'Implementing Partnership-Driven Clinical Federated Electronic Health Record Data Sharing Networks' (2016) 93 *International Journal of Medical Informatics* 26. DOI:10.1016/j.ijmedinf.2016.05.008

TechDispatch #1/2022 – Federated Social Media Platforms, https://edps.europa.eu/data-protection/our-work/publications/techdispatch/2022-07-26-techdispatch-12022-federated-social-media-platforms_en accessed on 5 January 2024.

Thorogood A and others, 'International Federation of Genomic Medicine Databases Using GA4GH Standards' (2021) 1(2) *Cell Genom.* 100032. DOI:10.1016/j.xgen.2021.100032

Topol E, 'High-Performance Medicine: The Convergence of Human and Artificial Intelligence' (2019) 25(1) *Nature Medicine* 44. DOI:10.1038/s41591-018-0300-7

Tzortzatou O and others, 'Biobanking Across Europe Post-GDPR: A Deliberately Fragmented Landscape' in Slokenberga, S, Tzortzatou, O and Reichel, J (eds), *GDPR and Biobanking: Individual Rights, Public Interest and Research Regulation across Europe* (Springer Nature, 2021). DOI:10.1007/978-3-030-49388-2_22

Weber G, 'Federated Queries of Clinical Data Repositories: Scaling to a National Network' (2015) 55 *Journal of Biomedical Informatics* 231. DOI:10.1016/j.jbi.2015.04.012

World Economic Forum, 'Federated Data Systems: Balancing Innovation and Trust in the Use of Sensitive Data' (2019), https://www3.weforum.org/docs/WEF_Federated_Data_Systems_2019.pdf accessed on 9 November 2023.

World Economic Forum, 'Sharing Sensitive Health Data in a Federated Data Consortium Model: An Eight-Step Guide' (2020). https://www.weforum.org/reports/sharing-sensitive-health-data-in-a-federated-data-consortium-model-an-eight-step-guide/ accessed on 28 September 2023.

Wouters B and others, 'Putting the GDPR Into Practice: Difficulties and Uncertainties Experienced in the Conduct of Big Data Health Research' (2021) 7 *Eur. Data Prot. L. Rev*. 206. DOI: 10.21552/edpl/2021/2/9

Case law

C-360/13 *Public Relations Consultants Association Ltd v Newspaper Licensing Agency Ltd and Others* ECLI:EU:C:2014:1195.

C-25/17 *Jehovan todistajat – uskonnollinen yhdyskunta* ECLI:EU:C:2018:551.

C-40/17 *Fashion ID GmbH & Co.KG v Verbraucherzentrale NRW eV Fashion ID* ECLI:EU:C:2019:629.

12 EHDS

Transforming the role of technological platforms for health data analysis

Hrefna D. Gunnarsdóttir

12.1 Introduction

One of the novelties of the European Health Data Space (EHDS) is the infrastructure that it introduces to improve natural persons' access and control over their electronic health data (EHD). It also aims to better achieve other purposes such as to facilitate research use of health data and to harmonise the legal and technological health data framework for the benefit of the internal market.[1] These aims are to be achieved via *inter alia* introducing labels for unified coding and registration of health data, new procedural requirements and facilitated access to data for secondary use (such as research and innovation) via *Secure Processing Environments* (SPEs).[2] The EHDS may, as a result, transform the role of already existing technological platforms that are being used for health data analysis.

This chapter analyses aspects of the EHDS in relation to already established technological platforms which allow researchers to analyse health data for scientific purposes while protecting the interests of the individuals from which the data origins. One of these platforms is *DataShield* (*Data Aggregation Through Anonymous Summary-statistics from Harmonised Individual-level Databases*).[3] Data Shield is used to undertake scientific research with health data. The research analysis takes place on a centralised server which has access to local servers on which the health data is stored. It allows for a simultaneous comparison of multiple data sets, including large and diverse data collections without disclosing individual-level data.[4] In this chapter, DataShield will be used as an example.[5] The chapter starts with providing a closer look at the software. It then lays out the requirements that the EHDS regulation introduces in relation to the format of EHD, exploring how these changes may influence data analysis supported by such already-established technological platforms. The EHDS's procedural requirements on secondary use for research purposes will then be analysed and discussed in the context of the future role of such platforms. This includes whether platforms enabling health data analysis on centralised servers without disclosing individual-level data may be utilised to achieve the goals of the EHDS to facilitate scientific research while preserving individuals' rights and what role the platforms may have in light of the development of SPEs.

DOI: 10.4324/9781003544111-15

12.2 Platform for health data analysis

While the EHDS builds upon the General Data Protection Regulation (GDPR), it also aims to respond to some of the challenges that have been associated with the requirements of the GDPR.[6] Despite the aims to the contrary, researchers encountered hindrances in using health data for scientific purposes after the GDPR was adopted, including when transferring such data. Certain routine research practices with health data, some of vital importance such as in response to the pandemic or the continuous development of precision medicine, came to halt.[7]

Technological platforms have however been developed to provide researchers and scientists, patients and others that provide access to their sensitive data for research purposes, with as safe digital environment for data processing as possible. By using platforms that have been considered 'safe' for data analysis or to allow the data to be discoverable, researchers and scientists have been able to get access to registries and other data sets holding health data (or other types of sensitive, personal data). All while resting in the assurance that the platform has been considered secure (enough) because, for example, it does not disclose individual-level data.

One such technological platform is *DataShield* (*Data Aggregation Through Anonymous Summary-statistics from Harmonised Individual-level Databases*), a software tool that started to be developed in 2009.[8] The platform can be used when single or multiple individual-data sources need to be analysed.[9] It allows for a 'pooled analysis' which is a method often used in epidemiology. Pooled analysis means that individual data is statistically re-analysed.[10] Such analysis can either be a meta-analysis of already collected individual data sources[11] or prospectively planned data collection – the latter meaning that the collection of the individual data is planned in advance to 'avoid large differences between the studies' providing the primary data.[12] However, when the pooled analysis is undertaken on data sources that have already been collected, such pre-planning does not take place. In these instances, the method entails in its essence that the scientists using the platform are granted access to existing individual-level data which has been collected in other research projects or for other purposes than research, such as health care services or a national register.

With the DataShield platform, the pooled analysis takes place on a centralised server that has access to local servers on which the individual-level data (the primary data) is stored. This individual-level data is therefore never physically transferred or shared. It has indeed been argued that one of the benefits of using the platform for analysing multiple, large datasets in health and biosciences is that the platform does not disclose any individual-level data and that the analysis can take place without 'physically pooling' the local data sets.[13]

With the use of the platform, the data sets themselves thus continue to stay on the local servers and within their respective jurisdictions. Additionally, the platform allows the parties who are responsible for the local data sets to stay in control over who is granted access. The researchers that are granted access can, via the platform, 'pass commands' to the servers and obtain an outcome, which, as stated earlier, is not believed to disclose any individual-level data.[14] As a result, the platform has been considered an appropriate technological platform to simultaneously compare multiple data sets, including large and diverse data collections.[15]

The platform has furthermore been considered an attractive option for researchers as *their* use of the platform has not been perceived as subject to the GDPR.[16] This is because the researchers, as the end users of the platform, are only meant to receive 'non-disclosive summary statistics [which has been] computed at each data center [and] sent to the remote research institution that requested the analysis where they are aggregated to produce the final result'.[17] Various ethico-legal considerations can be highlighted in this context, of which three will be briefly noted here: *Firstly*, even though the researchers as end users of the platform may not be considered subject to the GDPR in this context, the data holders operating the local servers and providing the access to their databases continue to be subject to the GDPR. *Secondly*, the reliance on the platform and the position that the technology is sufficiently secure to 'circumvent' the GDPR certainly raises questions as to who, how and at what intervals the safety of the technology is assessed. Considering the constant and rapid technological developments, it must be under continuous scrutiny by software developers. An additional question of transparency arises, as to, for example, the criteria used to assess the safety of the platform, how regularly it is tested and whether such tests fulfil the security requirements of the GDPR. *Lastly*, it should be noted that even if the end use of the platform is not considered subject to the GDPR, the researchers may be bound by other applicable rules, including in the jurisdictions in which the databases are stored. These could for example entail legal requirements about ethical assessments under which the research proposal shall be evaluated and to apply for the permits necessary to access the local databases via the platform.

12.3 Foreseeable impact of the EHDS on the use of the platform

With the introduction of the EHDS, the current governance system for the use of health data for research purposes has been transformed. The EHDS is the first of various 'data spaces' that the Commission intends to establish in the foreseeable future to further enhance the digital economy of the member states.[18]

The EHDS divides health data processing into 'primary' and 'secondary' uses of EHD. The former refers to the processing needed when an individual interacts with the health care and relevant social and administrative services.[19] The latter refers to use for other purposes, including research.[20] Prior to the EHDS, processing for both primary and secondary use has been challenged by lack of interoperability of how data is collected, registered and stored in local systems as well as variations in national laws about health data governance.[21] The EHDS addresses these challenges by *inter alia* introducing rights and rules of primary use of EHD (Chapters II and III of EHDS) and rules about secondary use of health data (Chapter IV of EHDS), transforming Europe's health data governance in various ways.

It should however be noted that many of the rules presented in the EHDS in Chapters II and III about primary data clearly influence the use of data for secondary purposes. A foreseeable impact that the EHDS may have on the use of already established technological platforms for health data analysis is the EHDS's requirements intended to facilitate interoperability of EHDs. The EHDS lays out format requirements of data that is to be registered as EHD. If sufficiently implemented by the data holders operating an EHD database, this may positively influence the data analysis process itself which has hereto lacked efficiency due to the challenges associated with the variations of data in the pooled datasets. Other foreseeable influence of the EHDS on the use of such platforms may stem from requirements aimed at ensuring security, and procedural rules applicable to secondary use of data. The remainder of this chapter will thus analyse these three aspects of the EHDS, namely EHDS's requirements aimed at facilitating interoperability (Section 12.3.1); EHDS's requirements aimed at ensuring security (Section 12.3.2); and EHDS's procedural requirements on secondary use for research purposes (Section 12.3.3).

12.3.1 EHDS's requirements aimed at facilitating interoperability

EHDS's goal to ensure interoperability of health data in the region may have a beneficial impact on the use of already existing technological platforms. The EHDS does for example lay out how various types of EHD (electronic health records, genetic data, and population-based health data) are to be coded and registered in a harmonised manner.[22] Albeit all data shall be made available, data of certain quality can be granted a 'quality and utility label'.[23] The data that is granted such a label should fulfil requirements in relation to documentation, technical quality, management process, coverage, information about access, provision and data enrichments. The Commission is furthermore empowered with an authority to adopt delegated acts to amend, modify or remove the requirements for the label.[24]

If sufficiently implemented, the EHDS may have a real, positive impact on data analysis that takes place via platforms for health data analysis. Scientists are currently encountering major challenges when analysing multiple, existing databases for a pooled analysis (i.e., not including pre-planned collection of data). This is because the databases may not be uniformly managed, and there may be variations in how the data is registered. One of the initial steps of a pooled analysis with such already collected individual data sources is thus to formulate an inclusion criterion. When the databases that fit the criteria have been identified and access has been granted, the data needs to be standardised. This initial work can be both time-consuming and challenging for researchers and takes place prior to any further analysis of the data.[25]

EHDS's structure on quality and utility label should provide researchers, who have had to spend valuable time sorting through and standardising accessed data, better information when choosing datasets for their analysis, and access to data that will (hopefully) have less variables in how it is registered and coded.

In this context, two considerations can be raised. Firstly, the EHDS entails requirements which manufacturers of wellness applications should fulfil for the data collected through these applications to be eligible for a label. These are found in Article 47 and Article 49 of EHDS, c.f. Annex II.[26] Health data from wellness application may hold data that can be valuable for research that benefits peoples' health.[27] Labelling of health data collected with wellness application would allow researchers to implement such data in their research when appropriate, and better assess, choose and sort the datasets that are to be analysed. Data from wellness applications may however not entail the same quality as can be achieved from other types of health data. Additionally, wellness application data can also be produced in larger volume and thus not necessarily be compliant with the data minimisation principle. As such, balanced approach to the labelling of wellness applications is necessary, and the format and content of the label for wellness applications need to both address the drawbacks of such data and be clearly distinct from the quality label of EHDs.

A second factor of relevance to researchers that use existing technological platforms is whether the health data that is of interest to the researcher is collected, registered and coded prior or after the adoption of the EHDS. Data that has accumulated prior to the adoption of the EHDS may not have been registered electronically and may have been coded in line with existing national specification of health data. It remains to be seen to what extent MSs will have the capacity to re-visit the registration and coding of health data collected prior to the adoption and implementation of EHDS's harmonised specification system. As a result, the interoperability of health data may continue to be limited to data collected after the adoption and sufficient implementation of the EHDS.

12.3.2 EHDS's requirements aimed at ensuring security

Under the EHDS, access for secondary use should, as a main principle, be provided in an anonymised form. Only if it has been sufficiently demonstrated that the purposes cannot be achieved with anonymised data, access to pseudonymised EHR can be granted.[28] The anonymisation (or pseudonymisation) should be carried out 'as early as possible in the chain of making data available for secondary use'.[29] Both the health data access bodies (HDAB, which role is further discussed in the next section of this chapter) and the data holders are expected to be able to carry out the anonymisation (or pseudonymisation) that is necessary.[30]

This should in principle be beneficial for the use of technological platforms for health data analysis. In the current operations of the example platform (DataShield), the user gives an analysis command to an R server on which the data is stored and receives a non-disclosive summary statistics in return (and thus should not receive any individual-level data). However, researchers that apply for access permits or undergo legally required ethical assessments with their proposals have experienced an uncertainty when they have had to confirm, prove or maintain that the software is as safe as it is perceived or said to be.[31] Under the EHDS, the responsibility of not disclosing individual-level data will not lie with the researcher in the same manner. The responsibility to ensure that data is anonymised (or pseudonymised) will indeed be carried by another actor earlier in the 'chain' of actors that are involved as the data travels from a natural person whose data is being collected to a secondary use researcher.

It is foreseeable that these requirements will have an impact on already established technological platforms. Under the EHDS, the researcher's request for access to health data for secondary use will, as a main principle, be limited to datasets which have already been anonymised (or pseudonymised) by the data holders or the health data access bodies.[32] The researchers will thus not solely have to rely on a software of the data analysis platform of choice as there will be other actors that are responsible to apply state-of-the-art anonymisation or pseudonymisation of datasets. As a result, there may thus be certain transfer of responsibility from the researchers to confirm that the technology that they use for data analysis is safe, to other actors involved in the health data economy. Upon applying for permits or going through legally required ethical assessments, researchers may thus be relieved from the burden of having to hold the necessary knowledge of legal and technological nature to responsibly confirm that the software is sufficiently secure to use for health data analysis.

Another transformative influence could be on the market with software solutions. Technological platforms that have hereto gained their popularity because they were considered GDPR compliant, safe and secure data analytical tools may have to demonstrate other, prestigious benefits to keep their uniqueness in a digital market which, in principle, should mainly operate with anonymised data.

12.3.3 EHDS's procedural requirements on secondary use for research purposes

The EHDS lays out procedural requirements on how EHD can be further used for various purposes, including for secondary research. These procedural requirements will have an impact on researchers' use of already established technological platforms. The reason being that the EHDS's procedural requirements are intended to apply to all actors requesting access to health data. This is irrespective of the fact that the health data is, as a main rule, already supposed to be anonymised. The use of already established technological platforms that have been developed to not disclose any individual-level data will thus be subject to new procedural requirements that are laid out in the EHDS.

Data access applications shall be submitted to a health data access body (HDAB),[33] a new entity which shall be established in the MSs.[34] The HDAB is responsible for processing the application regardless of whether access is requested from one data holder in a single MS or from multiple health data holders in more than one MS. When using technological platforms for pooled analysis, i.e., when access is requested from several data holders resulting in a combination of multiple datasets from different MSs, such an application shall thus be submitted to and processed by an HDAB albeit it is sufficient to submit an application with a *single* HDAB.[35]

If the secondary use of data is intended for one or more of the purposes laid out in the proposed Article 53, an access application can be submitted. The purposes listed in the proposed provisions relate to research, innovation, statistics, education, policy making and regulation, and bodies that either have a public mandate to carry out tasks in the health or care sectors or improve delivery of care.[36] The information that should be provided with an application to an HDAB is laid out in the proposed Article 67 EHDS, c.f. Article 53 EHDS. In addition to providing details about the applicant and the purpose for which the access is requested, the applicant shall describe the requested EHD and whether access is requested to anonymised or pseudonymised data; description of any data already held by the applicant and which is intended to be stored in an SPE; description of safeguards, justification of period during which the EHD is needed; tools and computing resources; ethical aspects of the processing (where relevant); and any opt-out mechanism that may be required by MS's law.[37]

Prior to the EHDS, research projects undertaken with the support of technological platforms may have been subject to a (variety) of legally required ethical assessments and permits that are applicable under domestic laws of each of the MSs.[38] Researchers have however not been considered subject to any *regional* legal instrument regarding the use of technological platforms such as DataShield. The EHDS's procedural requirements will come as an addition to the national requirements, as it imposes new, regional procedural rules which will be applicable to health data access, including researchers who have hereto been using platforms that have been considered non-disclosive of any individual-level data.

A second consideration could be mentioned in this regard. That is how Article 67(4) of EHDS differentiates between anonymised and pseudonymised data, placing an additional requirement on those who intend to access electronic health data in the latter form. Those who access pseudonymised data need to describe the lawful basis of the intended processing (i.e., Article 6(1) GDPR) and provide information about how the processing will apply with Union and national law on data protection and privacy.[39] The EHDS does however not entail references or requirements to describe the ethical aspects of the intended processing, which continues to be subject to the domestic laws of each of the MS.

12.4 What roles could the platform play in a new governance system?

Based on the DataShield example, some broader lines can be drawn about the impact that the EHDS may have on the use of existing technological platforms which are being used for health data analysis. In this chapter, two considerations will be highlighted. That is how technological platforms can achieve the goals of the EHDS, and how the role of such platforms may change under the EHDS.

There is little doubt that technological platforms which are used for health data analysis have played an important role hereto with facilitating certain scientific endeavours while striving to protect natural persons by not disclosing any individual-level data. Their teams hold both the knowledge and experience to develop and maintain an up-to-date solution for research that protects the natural persons from which the data is collected. With the EHDS's main principle of only providing access to anonymised data via SPEs, this way of undertaking research with health data may however be about to become the norm rather than the exemption. The EHDS use of SPEs may thus fundamentally change the role, or more precisely – the uniqueness – of the services that technological platforms such as DataShield have provided to researchers with health data. The role of such software tools may thus have to change accordingly. In light of the knowledge and experience held by the developers of these technological platforms, it may however become beneficial to aim to fulfil the requirements that the EHDS lays out for authorising SPEs.

According to Article 73 of the EHDS, health data access bodies 'shall provide access to electronic health data … only through a secure processing environment which is subject to technical and organisational measures and security and interoperability requirements'.[40] EHDS's security measures are then further laid out in sub-paragraphs (a)–(f). For technological platforms to continue to contribute to a transformed health data governance model, it needs to be considered whether the intention is that the HDAB only *oversees* the SPEs (as opposed to operating their own system).

Recital 54 of EHDS indicates that third parties may have a role to play in this regard. The recital states that 'where the secure environment is managed by a third party', the SPE should fulfil the requirements laid out in Article 28 of the GDPR as well as Chapter V (on transfers of personal data to third countries or international organisations) of the GDPR where applicable. Since the GDPR's definition of a 'third party' applies to the EDHS, c.f. Art. 2 EHDS, private entities which develop technological environments that fulfil the necessary requirements may be considered for SPEs. This would be similar to, for example, the Finnish model that has been in place since mid-year 2022. Albeit the Finnish Social and Health Data Permit Authority (Findata) has a primary processing environment (Kapseli)[41], other environments that fulfil Finland's requirements for secure data processing can be granted an approval to be used to safely access and process data (see further Chapter 6 of this volume).[42] Article 73 of the EHDS, read in conjunction with Recital 77, may thus provide an opportunity for already established technological platforms to develop to the extent that the security requirements are fulfilled. As a result, such platforms may have an opportunity to become *one of the SPEs* that the HDAB (or where relevant, trusted data holders) use to provide access to data for research and innovation. Thus, using the knowledge and experience that these platforms have gathered in facilitating research while protecting natural persons rights contribute to the new European health data governance system.

In this context, it should however be noted that the concept of SPEs may have to be clarified and articulated further[43] including which security measures are necessary to become an authorised SPE. Here, it should be highlighted that Recital 77 places the responsibility on the Commission to assist the member states to develop 'common security standards' in order to ensure security and interoperability 'of the various secure environments'.[44] While this wording may not come across as directly referring to harmonised rules on security standards, Article 73(5) of the EHDS states that by two years from the date of entry into force of this Regulation, the 'Commission shall, by means of implementing acts, lay dow the technical, organisational, information security, confidentiality, data protection and interoperability requirements' for the SPEs.[45]

It is indeed argued here that such regional standards are necessary, particularly for researchers that undertake pooled analysis or any regional or international collaborations in their research. If MSs were given the flexibility to decide which standards apply to SPEs, researchers undertaking pooled analysis could potentially face a situation where a particular, useful SPE would be authorised in one MS from which data is used and not in another. This would not only be contrary to EHDS's general aim to facilitate science in the region while safeguarding individuals' rights. It would also – keeping in mind how researchers undertaking studies in more than one MS should only need a permission from one HDAB – place an unnecessary burden on that single HDAB to assess whether a particular SPE would be eligible in all the MS that provide data for the research.

The final consideration that will be drawn up in this context is in relation to the already existing, and the foreseeably enlarging market of (third party) technological platforms that are or will be authorised as SPEs. From the client's (such as the researcher) point of view, it will be of vital importance to receive correct information about the services which are provided to the researchers when using a particular platform. In the absence of regionally harmonised standards, it will be burdensome for customers to differentiate whether an authorisation of a particular SPE is limited to specific MSs or can be relied on regionally.

Lastly, it could be argued that the EHDS's requirement to use an authorised SPEs does indeed transform the role of already existing technological platforms such as DataShield, partly forcing the software developers to seriously consider moving into a developing phase to become one of the SPEs. The reason being that some of the MS have already assessed and authorised third party technological platforms under local rules on 'secure environments'. Some of these third parties also provide various tools to analyse the data, making them an attractive option for researchers as a one-stop shop for both accessing data from an authorised environment that also provides the necessary technological means for the data analysis. Platforms which only provide the latter, but are not an authorised SPE, could thus be forced to transform their services in light of the emphasis that the EHDS lays on the role of SPEs. Work is currently being undertaken to investigate, analyse and systematise which factors should be considered elements in SPEs.[46] It can thus be expected that such further development will continue to influence already existing technological platforms.[47]

12.5 Conclusion

The EHDS can be expected to transform the foreseeable efficiency of already established technological platforms such as DataShield. The reason being that the coding and registering of primary data will be labelled allowing researchers to better assess and choose the datasets used for data analytics. The EHDS's requirement that accessed data should, as a main principle, already be anonymous may influence the pressure felt by software developers and particularly the researchers, to confirm, maintain and ensure that the platform in use will not disclose individual-level data. For the technological platform as such, this could also mean that the uniqueness of their services will not be the same as before. In any event, investment in infrastructure, whether it is in relation to data interoperability or security, will strengthen the operations and analysis of already existing data analysis software. Current challenges in relation to the variability of data, such as the time consuming standardisation of data that fits the inclusion criteria prior to analysis, may be avoided as the data available for science becomes standardised by the data providers.

From a procedural point of view, the researchers using already established technological platforms for health data analysis will be subject to new rules other than those that they may have had to comply with in domestic legislation of certain MSs. The EHDS lays out various steps that need to be undertaken to access health data, in addition to any national legislation such as legally required ethical assessments.

Lastly, it is argued that technological platform developers hold knowledge and experience valuable to achieving the goals of facilitating scientific research while protecting natural persons' rights. This knowledge and experience could become beneficial for the aims of the EHDS if they will be allowed to, and be successful in, fulfilling the standards set to become authorised secure processing environments for secondary use of electronic health data. In this context, it is argued that regionally harmonised standards for such environments are necessary.

Acknowledgements

The work for this chapter is part of the UCPH Data+ project: *Bringing the analyses to the data using DataShield: Exploration of an infrastructure with in-built protection of privacy for federated analyses of sensitive health data*. Insights into the work of the scientists were provided by Anne-Marie Nybo Andersen, Professor at the Section of Epidemiology, Department of Public Health, University of Copenhagen, and Research Assistant Line Marie Toft Dyhr from the same institute. The author would like to thank them for their valuable insights into the application and use of the DataShield platform for epidemiology studies.

Notes

1 European Parliament, 'Corrigendum to the position of the European Parliament adopted at first reading on 24 April 2024 with a view to the adoption of Regulation (EU) 2024/... of the European Parliament and of the Council of the European Health Data Space' P9_TA(2024)0331, 2024, cor01 (hereinafter EHDS). Council of the European Union, 'Proposal for a Regulation on the European Health Data Space – Analysis of the final compromise text with a view to agreement' 2022/0140(COD) (compromise text) Recital 1. See also René Raab and others, 'Federated Electronic Health Records for the European Health Data Space' (2023) 5 *The Lancet Digital Health* e840.

2 See for example EHDS Recitals 46, 52, and 77.

3 'DataSHIELD Secure Bioscience Collaboration' (23 July 2020) https://www.datashield.org/ accessed 17 March 2024.

4 Amadou Gaye and others, 'DataSHIELD: Taking the Analysis to the Data, Not the Data to the Analysis' (2014) 43 *International Journal of Epidemiology* 1929; Rebecca C Wilson and others, 'DataSHIELD – New Directions and Dimensions' (2017) 16 *Data Science Journal* 21; Yannick Marcon and others, 'Orchestrating Privacy-Protected Big Data Analyses of Data from Different Resources with R and DataSHIELD' (2021) 17 *PLOS Computational Biology* e1008880.

5 According to Tomasoni et al.'s 'best ... knowledge, DataShield is the only community-driven open-source framework for privacy-aware data analysis currently available.' Danilo Tomasoni, Rosario Lombardo and Mario Lauria, 'Strengths and Limitations of Non-Disclosive Data Analysis: A Comparison of Breast Cancer Survival Classifiers Using VisualSHIELD' (2024) 15 *Frontiers in Genetics* 1270387, 2.

6 European Parliament and the Council Regulation 2016/679 of 27 April 2016 on the Protection of Natural Persons with Regard to the Processing of Personal Data and on the Free Movement of Such Data (General Data Protection Regulation) [2016] OJ L 119/1.

7 Ciara Staunton and others, 'Ethical and Social Reflections on the Proposed European Health Data Space' (2024) 32 *European Journal of Human Genetics* 498; Laura Bradford, Mateo Aboy and Kathleen Liddell, 'Standard Contractual Clauses for Cross-Border Transfers of Health Data after *Schrems II*' (2021) 8 *Journal of Law and the Biosciences* lsab007; Laura Bradford, Mateo Aboy and Kathleen Liddell, 'International Transfers of Health Data between the EU and USA: A Sector-Specific Approach for the USA to Ensure an "Adequate" Level of Protection' (2020) 7 *Journal of Law and the Biosciences* lsaa055; David Peloquin and others, 'Disruptive and Avoidable: GDPR Challenges to Secondary Research Uses of Data' (2020) 28 *European Journal of Human Genetics* 697.

8 The uptake so far can be estimated by the list of current DataShield implementations, which can be found here 'About' (*DataSHIELD*, 27 January 2021) 130 https://datashield.org/about accessed 22 March 2024; Ben Goldacre and Jessica Morley, 'Better, Broader, Safer: Using Health Data for Research and Analysis. A Review Commissioned by the Secretary of State for Health and Social Care.' (2022) Department of Health and Social Care 130 state furthermore: Federated analytics is readily achievable and has already been successfully implemented on NHS data in some form, delivering a range of completed analytic outputs in open code projects such as OpenSAFELY and DataShield (the latter in particular with a large existing user-base).

9 Michael Wolfson and others, 'DataSHIELD: Resolving a Conflict in Contemporary Bioscience-Performing a Pooled Analysis of Individual-Level Data without Sharing the Data' (2010) 39 *International Journal of Epidemiology* 1372.

10 M Blettner and others, 'Traditional Reviews, Meta-Analyses and Pooled Analyses in Epidemiology.' (1999) 28 *International Journal of Epidemiology* 1, 2. This can include 'inclusion criteria for all studies, a unified definition of the variables, and new statistical modelling. With a large sample size the effect of rare exposures can also be examined, which is often not possible in single studies. New hypotheses may

be formulated with these types of pooled analyses and specific subgroups, such as age groups, may also be analysed.' See M Blettner and others, 2–3.

11 Referred to as either: 'pooled analyses of … primary data or meta-analyses of individual data, see Stephanie A Smith-Warner and others, 'Methods for Pooling Results of Epidemiologic Studies: The Pooling Project of Prospective Studies of Diet and Cancer' (2006) 163 American Journal of Epidemiology 1053, 1054.

12 Blettner and others (n 9) 3.

13 This seem to be the position of authors involved in the development of the platform as well as independent reviewers carrying out risk assessments for projects that intend to use the platform. For the former see Wilson and others (n 4) 2 citing also; Wilson and others (n 4); Gaye and others (n 4); Wilson is now a Principal Investigator and current Lead of the DataShield project, see here: Administrator, 'Meet The Team' (*DataSHIELD*, 14 September 2020) https://www.datashield.org/about/meet-the-team accessed 22 March 2024.

14 Marcon and others (n 4).

15 Tomasoni, Lombardo and Lauria (n 5); Ben Goldacre and Jessica Morley (n 7).

16 Wilson and others (n 4); See also Marcon and others (n 4) 1. For a practical example, see p 9 and onwards.

17 Tomasoni, Lombardo and Lauria (n 5) 2.

18 See introduction of the EHDS compromise text (n 1).

19 EHDS Article 2(2)(d).

20 EHDS Article 2(2)(e); See also J Scott Marcus and others, 'The European Health Data Space – Study Requested by the ITRE Committee' (Directorate – General for Internal Policies 2022) PE 740.054 11.

21 David Fåhraeus, Jane Reichel and Santa Slokenberga, 'The European Health Data Space: Challenges and Opportunities' (2024) February 2024 *Sieps Swedish Institute for European Policy Studies* 1, 2.

22 See for example EHDS Recitals 46 and 51, Articles 15 and 36.

23 EHDS Article 78.

24 See particularly EHDS Articles 78(3) and (4).

25 Interview with a researcher using DataShield for their health data analysis, 12 October 2023. See also Smith-Warner and others (n 10) 1054.

26 EHDS Articles 47 and 49. See also Recitals 49–51 therein.

27 Catherine Boutet and Ning-Zi Sun, 'Fitness App for Resident Wellness during COVID-19' (2022) 56 *Medical Education* 559.

28 See EHDS Articles 66(2) and (3).

29 See EHDS Recital 72.

30 See EHDS Recital 72 and (for example) Article 55(3).

31 Interview with a researcher using DataShield for their health data analysis, 12 October 2023. See also Susan E Wallace, 'What Does Anonymization Mean? DataSHIELD and the Need for Consensus on Anonymization Terminology' (2016) 14 *Biopreservation and Biobanking* 224.

32 Albeit it should be noted that Recital 72 states that these tasks can be delegated to data processors, see EHDS Recital 72.

33 EHDS Article 67(1).

34 Staunton (n 6) 3; Santa Slokenberga, 'Scientific Research Regime 2.0? Transformations of the Research Regime and the Protection of the Data Subject That the Proposed EHDS Regulation Promises to Bring Along' (2022) 2022 *Technology and Regulation* 135.

35 EHDS Article 67(3).

36 EHDS Article 53.

37 EHDS Article 67(2).

38 For an insight into how differences between national laws can impact research collaboration between countries (in Europe) see Katharina Ó Cathaoir, Hrefna Dögg Gunnarsdóttir and Mette Hartlev, 'The Journey of Research Data: Accessing Nordic Health Data for the Purposes of Developing an Algorithm' *Medical Law International* 23. DOI: 10.1177/09685332211046179.

39 EHDS Article 67(4).
40 EHDS Article 73(1). See also European Parliament and the Council Regulation (EU) 2022/868 of 30 May 2022 on European data governance and amending Regulation (EU) 2018/1724 (Data Governance Act) [2022] OJ L 152/1, Articles 2(2), 5, and 7.
41 'Kapseli®' (*Findata*) https://findata.fi/en/kapseli/ accessed 30 January 2024.
42 Finnish Social and Health Data Permit Authority (Findata), Regulation by the Health and Social Data Permit Authority: Requirements for other service providers' secure operating environments 2022; Finnish Social and Health Data Permit Authority (Findata), Annex 1: Requirements for a Secure Operating Environment 1.
43 'Initial Reactions to the European Health Data Space Proposal' (Digital Europe 2022) https://cdn.digitaleurope.org/uploads/2022/07/Initial-reactions-to-the-EHDS-DIGITALEUROPE-28072022.pdf.
44 EHDS Recital 77.
45 EHDS Article 73(4). The provisions further refers to Article 98(2) EHDS, c.f. Article 4 of European Parliament and the Council Regulation (EU) No 182/2011 of 16 February 2011 laying down the rules and general principles concerning mechanisms for control by Member States of the Commission's exercise of implementing powers [2011] OJ L 55/13.
46 Irene Schlünder, Michaela Th Mayrhofer and Erdina Ene, 'Elements of Secure Processing Environments (Workshop Report) V1.0' (Zenodo 2023) https://zenodo.org/records/8341642 accessed 18 February 2024; Romain David and others, '"Be Sustainable": EOSC-Life Recommendations for Implementation of FAIR Principles in Life Science Data Handling' (2023) 42 *The EMBO Journal* e115008; Erkki Soini, Taru Hallinen and Janne Martikainen, 'RWD31 Secure Processing Environments (SPE) Are Needed for the Cybersecure Collection and Secondary Use of Personal, Health, and Social Data' (2022) 25 *Value in Health* S453.
47 It should also be noted that during the legislative process some stakeholders called for an exemption to be introduced to the EHDS when 'secondary use of health data cannot be processed' via a SPE that is provided by HDAB. COCIR recommended for example: 'Article 50 [now 73] should reflect on specific situations. If due to the research or product development specifics it is technically not possible to complete health data processing in the secure environment, provided by the health data access bodies, other secure processing safeguards should be introduced and used to ensure safeguard of personal information, as well as compliance with the GDPR', 'COCIR Feedback – Proposal for a European Health Data Space' (COCIR Advancing healthcare 2022) 4 https://www.cocir.org/fileadmin/Position_Papers_2022/20220727_COCIR_Feedback_EHDS.pdf accessed 18 February 2024.

List of sources

Legislative acts

European Parliament and the Council Regulation (EU) 2022/868 of 30 May 2022 on European data governance and amending Regulation (EU) 2018/1724 (Data Governance Act) [2022] OJ L 152/1.

European Parliament and the Council Regulation (EU) No 182/2011 of 16 February 2011 laying down the rules and general principles concerning mechanisms for control by Member States of the Commission's exercise of implementing powers [2011] OJ L 55/13.

European Parliament and the Council Regulation 2016/679 of 27 April 2016 on the Protection of Natural Persons with Regard to the Processing of Personal Data and on the Free Movement of such Data (General Data Protection Regulation) [2016] OJ L 119/1.

Official documents

Council of the European Union, 'Proposal for a Regulation on the European Health Data Space – Analysis of the final compromise text with a view to agreement' 2022/0140(COD).

Council of the European Union, 'Proposal for a Regulation on the European Health Data Space – Analysis of the final compromise text with a view to agreement' 2024 (8571/22 ADD1-8) 1.

European Data Protection Board, Guidelines 1/2018 on the certification and identifying certification criteria in accordance with Articles 42 and 43 of the Regulation – Version 3.0 2019 1.

European Data Protection Board and European Data Protection Supervisor, EDPB-EDPS Joint Opinion 03/2022 on the Proposal for a Regulation on the European Health Data Space 2022 1.

European Data Protection Board and European Data Protection Supervisor, EDPB-EDPS Joint Opinion 03/2022 on the Proposal for a Regulation on the European Health Data Space 2022 1.

European Parliament, 'Corrigendum to the position of the European Parliament adopted at first reading on 24 April 2024 with a view to the adoption of Regulation (EU) 2024/… of the European Parliament and of the Council of the European Health Data Space' P9_TA(2024)0331, 2024, cor01.

Finnish Social and Health Data Permit Authority (Findata), Annex 1: Requirements for a Secure Operating Environment 1. 2022.

Goldacre B and Morley J, 'Better, Broader, Safer: Using Health Data for Research and Analysis. A Review Commissioned by the Secretary of State for Health and Social Care.' (2022) Department of Health and Social Care.

Marcus JS and others, 'The European Health Data Space – Study Requested by the ITRE Committee' (Directorate – General for Internal Policies 2022) PE 740.054 11.

Literature

Blettner M and others, 'Traditional Reviews, Meta-Analyses and Pooled Analyses in Epidemiology.' (1999) 28 *International Journal of Epidemiology* 1. DOI: 10.1093/ije/28.1.1

Boutet C and Sun N, 'Fitness App for Resident Wellness during COVID-19' (2022) 56 *Medical Education* 559. DOI: 10.1111/medu.14755

Bradford L, Aboy M and Liddell K, 'International Transfers of Health Data between the EU and USA: A Sector-Specific Approach for the USA to Ensure an "Adequate" Level of Protection' (2020) 7 *Journal of Law and the Biosciences* lsaa055. DOI: 10.1093/jlb/lsaa055

Bradford L, Aboy M and Liddell K, 'Standard Contractual Clauses for Cross-Border Transfers of Health Data after *Schrems II*' (2021) 8 *Journal of Law and the Biosciences* lsab007. DOI: 10.1093/jlb/lsab007

David R and others, '"Be Sustainable": EOSC-Life Recommendations for Implementation of FAIR Principles in Life Science Data Handling' (2023) 42 *The EMBO Journal* e115008. DOI: 10.15252/embj.2023115008

Fåhraeus D, Reichel J and Slokenberga S, 'The European Health Data Space: Challenges and Opportunities' (2024) February 2024 *Sieps Swedish Institute for European Policy Studies* 1.

Gaye A and others, 'DataSHIELD: Taking the Analysis to the Data, Not the Data to the Analysis' (2014) 43 *International Journal of Epidemiology* 1929. DOI: 10.1093/ije/dyu188

Marcon Y and others, 'Orchestrating Privacy-Protected Big Data Analyses of Data from Different Resources with R and DataSHIELD' (2021) 17 *PLOS Computational Biology* e1008880. DOI: 10.1371/journal.pcbi.1008880

Ó Cathaoir K, Gunnarsdóttir HD and Hartlev M, 'The Journey of Research Data: Accessing Nordic Health Data for the Purposes of Developing an Algorithm' *Medical Law International* 23. DOI: 10.1177/09685332211046179

Peloquin D and others, 'Disruptive and Avoidable: GDPR Challenges to Secondary Research Uses of Data' (2020) 28 *European Journal of Human Genetics* 697. DOI: 10.1038/s41431-020-0596-x

Raab R and others, 'Federated Electronic Health Records for the European Health Data Space' (2023) 5 *The Lancet Digital Health* e840. DOI: 10.1016/S2589-7500(23)00156-5

Slokenberga S, 'Scientific Research Regime 2.0? Transformations of the Research Regime and the Protection of the Data Subject That the Proposed EHDS Regulation Promises to Bring Along' (2022) 2022 *Technology and Regulation* 135. DOI: 10.26116/techreg.2022.014

Smith-Warner SA and others, 'Methods for Pooling Results of Epidemiologic Studies: The Pooling Project of Prospective Studies of Diet and Cancer' (2006) 163 *American Journal of Epidemiology* 1053. DOI: 10.1093/aje/kwj127

Soini E, Hallinen T and Martikainen J, 'RWD31 Secure Processing Environments (SPE) Are Needed for the Cybersecure Collection and Secondary Use of Personal, Health, and Social Data' (2022) 25 *Value in Health* S453. DOI: 10.1016/j.jval.2022.09.2256

Staunton C and others, 'Ethical and Social Reflections on the Proposed European Health Data Space' (2024) 32 *European Journal of Human Genetics* 498. DOI: 10.1038/s41431-024-01543-9

Tomasoni D, Lombardo R and Lauria M, 'Strengths and Limitations of Non-Disclosive Data Analysis: A Comparison of Breast Cancer Survival Classifiers Using VisualSHIELD' (2024) 15 *Frontiers in Genetics* 1270387. DOI: 10.3389/fgene.2024.1270387

Wallace SE, 'What Does Anonymization Mean? DataSHIELD and the Need for Consensus on Anonymization Terminology' (2016) 14 *Biopreservation and Biobanking* 224. DOI: 10.1089/bio.2015.0119

Wilson RC and others, 'DataSHIELD – New Directions and Dimensions' (2017) 16 *Data Science Journal* 21.

Wolfson M and others, 'DataSHIELD: Resolving a Conflict in Contemporary Bioscience--Performing a Pooled Analysis of Individual-Level Data without Sharing the Data' (2010) 39 *International Journal of Epidemiology* 1372. DOI: 10.1093/ije/dyq111

Other

'About' (*DataSHIELD*, 27 January 2021). https://datashield.org/about accessed 22 March 2024.

Administrator, 'Meet The Team' (*DataSHIELD*, 14 September 2020) https://www.datashield.org/about/meet-the-team accessed 22 March 2024.

'COCIR Feedback – Proposal for a European Health Data Space' (COCIR Advancing healthcare 2022) https://www.cocir.org/fileadmin/Position_Papers_2022/20220727_COCIR_Feedback_EHDS.pdf accessed 18 February 2024.

'DataSHIELD Secure Bioscience Collaboration' (23 July 2020) https://www.datashield.org/ accessed 17 March 2024.

'Initial Reactions to the European Health Data Space Proposal' (Digital Europe 2022) https://cdn.digitaleurope.org/uploads/2022/07/Initial-reactions-to-the-EHDS-DIGITALEUROPE-28072022.pdf

'Kapseli®' (*Findata*) https://findata.fi/en/kapseli/ accessed 30 January 2024.

Schlünder I, Mayrhofer MT and Ene E, 'Elements of Secure Processing Environments (Workshop Report) V1.0' (*Zenodo* 2023) https://zenodo.org/records/8341642 accessed 18 February 2024.

13 Conclusion

Tracing key transformations in light of the primary and secondary use

Mahsa Shabani, Santa Slokenberga and Katharina Ó Cathaoir

13.1 Some general remarks on transformation

Transformation is a central theme of this volume. We have asked the authors to reflect on to what extent the EHDS is transforming their field of study. We have not been prescriptive in how we understand the concept of transformation but we understand it to go beyond simple add-ons and instead result in marked change for the field, such as through new rights and obligations, new organs or bodies, or new opportunities and visions. Authors have adopted varied and nuanced approaches though the status quo established by the GDPR runs as a red thread throughout the volume. There can be no doubt that the latter has had a transformative effect on the secondary use of health data, and we wait to see whether the EHDS will have similar reverberations.

The book consists of 11 substantive chapters, each discussing a unique aspect of health data processing, either for primary or secondary uses, and investigating how the European Health Data Space (EHDS) Regulation can play a transformative role in regulating such health data processing. The focus of Chapters 2–4 is on data processing for primary purposes and collection of data through wellness applications, and the expected impact of EHDS on specific rights of patients and individuals such as their rights to access, rectification and insertion of information in their Electronic Health Records (EHR). In these chapters, the EHDS is expected to have direct, tangible impacts for patients and data subjects. In contrast, Chapters 5–11 investigated various aspects related to secondary uses of health data, including those related to consent, the boundaries of scientific research, fairness, and administrative and technical solutions for safeguarding individuals' rights. In these cases, the impact of the EHDS is designed to be indirect through using health data to improve the functioning of healthcare systems and further research and innovation across the EU.

In the following, we discuss the main findings of each chapter, in light of the overarching theme of transformation by the EHDS.

DOI: 10.4324/9781003544111-16

13.2 EHDS and transforming patients' rights in relation to primary use

Chapters 2–4 discussed the impact of the EHDS on existing patient (and data subject) rights in relation to electronic health data, including the right to access EHR and the right to insert information in the EHR. It is worth noting that the point of departure for such analyses was firstly assessing the adequacy of the status quo and secondly how the EHDS could address the identified shortcomings. The chapters showed that in doing so, attention must be paid to the considerable differences among member states regarding how digitalised their healthcare systems currently are and how the EHDS may change or improve the existing systems. In countries such as Denmark, which already benefit from established EHR systems, the transforming role of the EHDS rights may not be as significant, whereas in countries with less digitised healthcare systems, like Ireland, the EHDS will be transformative.

That said, the relevant provisions of the EHDS may still further facilitate exercising such rights in all member states, in particular across borders. For example, as Ó Cathaoir highlighted in Chapter 2, imposing a binding obligation on member states to establish MyHealth@EU as an interoperability platform for digital health and the Commission's role in issuing specifications for a mandatory European exchange format establishes a harmonised and binding framework for such data exchange compared to the previous voluntary regime under the Patients' Rights Directive. The same goes for the obligation to record in the EHR, given that health professionals must register at least priority categories of health data in an EHR.

In this regard, the right of individuals to object to access to their health record by anyone except the original data controller can strengthen patients' self-determination over their data. Crucially, where patients make use of the provision, they will not be able to enjoy the benefits of EHR. Another example is the right of access, where the EHDS probably does not provide patients with access to more extensive information than the GDPR when interpreted in line with the case law of the CJEU but will facilitate access through the mandatory infrastructure and precision of the right provided for. In addition, the EHDS provides for a right to request rectification of EHR data, which again is not absolute and is subject to limitations. Other rights include the right to restrict healthcare workers' access to one's record and the right to information on who has accessed one's record.

Thus, one can argue that the bases of such health data protection rights had been already established in the GDPR. As such, as Ó Cathaoir emphasises, in line with the European Data Protection Board (EDPB) and the European Data Protection Supervisor (EDPS), the rights conferred by the EHDS to individuals concerning their personal data are essentially 'add-ons' to those established by the GDPR. However, as described, these enhancements are anticipated to significantly boost patients' rights, granting them increased access to and control over their EHR, thereby reshaping patients' control of their data throughout the EU. Thus, Chapter II of EHDS can be considered to amount to both GDPR+ and a transformation for patients' rights.

Notably, some of the specifications regarding each right, such as, how to manage the right to object, the scope of the right to rectification, or access through proxy services have been left to the member states to decide, which again may result in fragmentation. In that sense, one can conclude that while the EHDS will provide patients with increased control over their electronic health data, there is a significant risk of fragmentation given that the specificity of the rights and that relevant exceptions are largely left to member states.

In terms of innovation in patients' rights in the EHDS compared to the GDPR, one can refer to the individual's right to insert information into EHR. Considering the increasing amount of user-generated health data, such as those generated through wearables, mhealth apps, and Direct-to-Consumer (DTC) testing such as DTC genetic testing, establishing such right under the EHDS seems to be beneficial. This can, on the one hand, increase the richness of EHR and, on the other hand, strengthen patients' control over information in their EHR, in line with other relevant rights such as rights to access, rectification and portability which have been previously established under the GDPR and other applicable national laws.

However, as Phillips argues in Chapter 3, adding extra sources of health data to EHR can bring about questions regarding roles and responsibilities of healthcare professionals on how to deal with reliability and accuracy of such patient-inserted data. Should they treat them as primary sources of health data generated in traditional healthcare settings? What should they do with inaccurate information? Notably, if large numbers of people begin to add this information to their EHR, this is likely to place a strain on the healthcare systems of individual member states. To illustrate the discussion, Phillips uses the case of DTC genetic testing results and explains potential risks, which may stem from an individual's engagement with that industry and desire to add genetic data to their EHR.

Implementing the EHDS provisions regarding the right to insert data will require some preliminary work, such as harmonised standards and determining what is health related- and non-health related information, which may fall outside the remit of the EHDS. This is particularly the case in contexts like genetic testing. As Phillips recommends, further consultation is required regarding the implementation of the right to insert information to EHR, and it would be ideal if, together with educational initiatives for patients, guidelines, best practices and codes of conduct were developed to assist health professionals in dealing with information that is inserted by their patients and their representatives.

The discussions on EHR, data sources, and relevant patient rights also bring about another important question related to patients' informed and meaningful control over primary data collected from outside traditional health settings. Holmberg, in Chapter 4, takes on this question by focusing on health data collected through wellness applications. To start such analysis, it is crucial to first have a clear definition of what is considered a wellness application and whether or not these applications also fall under the remit of the Medical

Device Regulation. The final text of the EHDS provides the first definition of wellness applications in EU law and avoids using vague terms as previous iterations did, and as such takes an important step forward in clarifying the applicable scope of the regulation of such apps.

To ensure that health data processing through user-generated data will align with individuals' rights to control their data, special attention needs to be paid to how consent has been obtained in the context of wellness applications. Holmberg discusses the role of the EHDS in how wellness apps have been regulated from the stand point of addressing the power imbalance between the manufacturers and the users. As she concludes in her chapter, while the EHDS establishes mandatory labelling which will regulate some aspects such as interoperability of wellness apps with EHRs, still there is room for strengthening the role of valid consent in data processing in this context to better respect the rights of the users in how their data has been processed or shared for secondary purposes. This is particularly important considering the underlying concerns about power imbalances between app developers and users, especially users who are suffering from physical or psychological conditions.

13.3 EHDS and transforming secondary uses of the health data landscape

13.3.1 Secondary uses and potential conflicts with patients' rights

One of the major transformative roles of the EHDS is to recognise medical information collected for primary use such as those stemming from EHR as a source of data also for secondary use purposes. Notably, such health data are often subject to strict confidentiality protections and regulated through national patient rights and other relevant regulations. In response, in Chapter 5, Spajić analyses the legal position of confidentiality in European law, focusing on judgements of the European Court of Human Rights and a textual analysis of the GDPR. Turning to the EHDS, she highlights that the Regulation appears to have neglected the fact that data from electronic health records are gathered in the medical setting and thereby subject to the duty of medical confidentiality.

In addition, when the appropriate legal basis for such data processing is concerned, further delineations need to be made regarding the purposes laid down in Article 53 of EHDS and those included in Article 9 of GDPR. As Spajić mentions, a main question is whether Article 9(2)(h) GDPR will continue to constitute an adequate legal basis for healthcare professionals for processing patient data in light of the new obligations under the EHDS to share data with health data access bodies. Like other authors, Spajić reminds the reader that as healthcare provision is a national competence, the EHDS will interact with – and potentially clash with – domestic legislation and norms, such as the right to patient confidentiality.

13.3.2 Distancing from consent as a legal basis for secondary uses: a welcome approach?

The existing literature and legal analyses on the relevant provisions of the GDPR, especially those related to the legal bases for processing personal data (Article 6) and processing of special categories of personal data including health data (Article 9), have shown a lack of clarification and at times lack of harmonisation across member states on the adequate legal bases for secondary uses of health data. With recent developments in the EU digital policy and regulatory frameworks, including the adoption of the Data Governance Act (DGA) and the EHDS Regulation, expectations have been high for clarifying what is the most suitable legal basis for secondary use of health data. Needless to say, consent as a legal basis for secondary uses has already been debated in relation to the GDPR, and a pressing question here is whether the EHDS and other relevant regulations such as DGA will bring about a transformation on consent as a legal basis.

In Chapter 6, El Asry, Mansnérus and Liede explore this question and compare consent-based altruism, as provided for under the DGA, with the approach to secondary use under the EHDS. In the case of the latter, secondary use will generally not be based on the data subject's consent but instead on another legal basis under the GDPR. Distancing from consent as a legal basis for secondary uses has proven contentious during the negotiation of the EHDS with the various legislative drafts recommending different approaches. While the Regulation eventually favoured use of opt-outs under some conditions for secondary uses of health data and not consent as a legal basis, as Chapter 6 argues, the implementation of such rules is expected to be influenced by the past experiences of member states in how they have made use of such option. For example, in the context of genomics and genetics, which have often been considered as more sensitive due to higher risks of reidentification and the predictive power of such data for individuals and their family members, the previous experiences and approaches of member states could be informative. For example, drawing on experience from Finland, the authors reveal that consent has proven contentious in discussions on establishing a national genome centre (which has so far proven unsuccessful) and on mandating secondary use. Consequently, in Finland, this has led to consent being viewed as an inappropriate legal basis when it comes to the secondary use of genetic data. This is an important point as EHDS has still left some room for member states to decide on how strict their rules should be on more sensitive types of health data for secondary uses, such as genomic data. While this will allow member states to build their own regulatory framework in line with domestic preferences, it can again lead to fragmentation among member states.

13.3.3 Scientific research and commercial access: are EHDS rules clear and fair enough?

The EHDS admittedly broadens the scope of allowed secondary uses of health data and includes purposes such as development and innovation, and training, testing and developing algorithms under scientific research. The EHDS is predominantly agnostic to the public or private nature of such data access for scientific research purposes and only makes some distinctions in this regard on the conditions to override the right to opt-out (see Recital 54). This consideration has sparked many discussions on how potential concerns about access by commercial entities and for commercial purposes should be addressed. As Santamaría Echeverría discusses in Chapter 8, one of the goals of the EHDS can be seen as building an open commons, which can be defined as 'a type of governance of shared resources whereby users have a symmetric freedom to access the resource'. However, as he argues, the model offered by the EHDS amounts to an incomplete open commons. While the Regulation tackles certain problems, others are overlooked or underdeveloped. In particular, the shift from consent to general or public interest is problematic, while the latter concepts remain insufficiently defined, as is the concept of health data and 'making public the results or output' of secondary use. This is a point that Cervera de la Cruz and Shabani also stress in Chapter 7, where they discuss the historical concerns related to access by commercial parties for public trust. Similarly, the public interest is central to Petročnik's contribution in Chapter 9, where she argues that its broad construction in the EHDS could lead to public officials (employed in HDABs) adopting their own personal conception of what is in the interest of the public.

As secondary uses of health data should be in compliance with overarching principles such as fairness, adequate rules should be put in place. This includes those related to benefit sharing, as Cervera de la Cruz and Shabani stress, to ensure the ultimate benefits of access to health data come back to society. In addition, they demand that in order to ensure that access is fair for all data users, commercial data holders should not exploit their claims over IP rights and trade secrets in order to obstruct access to their datasets. Similarly, private actors accessing data should also be obligated to make data available for secondary use.

To address the shortcomings of the EHDS, Santamaría Echeverría argues for a shift to a relational approach governed by data solidarity. Drawing on the work of Barbara Prainsack, the author proposes requirements for returning commercial profits of low public value to the public domain and prohibiting secondary use involving a high risk of harm.

Furthermore, concerns about fairness in secondary uses go beyond those related to commercial uses. To bring further clarity on what fairness means in this context, Cervera De La Cruz and Shabani investigate how far the provisions of the EHDS align with the fairness principle in secondary uses of health data. They discuss, among other things, that in order to comply with the fairness principle, it is crucial that public interest as a legal and ethical basis for secondary uses of health data should be further clarified. This is particularly essential when individual and public interests clash in the secondary uses of health data, and there is a need to balance public and individual interests. They also stress the role of the oversight bodies in ensuring that the incoming data access requests have sufficiently justified the public interest aspect.

13.3.4 Is EHDS playing a transformative role regarding governance of health data in terms of technical safeguards, administrative tools and oversight mechanisms?

Under the GDPR, one of the important considerations has been on adopting adequate technical and organisational safeguards when processing data for scientific research purposes, among others (Article 89). By developing new digital policies and relevant regulatory frameworks, such as the EHDS, it is interesting to explore whether any transformation has taken place in this aspect.

An important new entity to be discussed under new administrative tools is oversight by the health data access bodies (HDABs) in the context of secondary uses of health data and their role in ensuring secondary uses are for public interest purposes. Oversight bodies such as data access committees historically played a gatekeeping role in how sensitive data can be accessed and under which terms and conditions. So far, data access committees, depending on the size and infrastructure of data holders, either worked locally or in a centralised manner. With the EHDS, the intention is now to move towards a centralised approach to further harmonise the governance of data access. The analysis of Petročnik demonstrates that HDABs are put in a challenging position by the legislature in how they are tasked to navigate the expectations of the interested public(s). There is a risk of inconsistencies in HDABs approaches, which could result in the EHDS being applied in a fragmented manner. While Reichel in the next chapter sees HDABs as serving more modest functions as facilitators, overseers and collaborators, Petročnik suggests envisioning HDABs as health data custodians, placing their loyalty to the interests of the individuals and society as a whole.

In Chapter 10, Reichel focuses on whether the EHDS Regulation has managed to define administrative balancing tools for the fragmented legal landscape of secondary use of health data in the EU and its member states. According to the author, one could say that the heart of the EHDS is furthering the societal interest in making the data easily accessible and upholding the rights and interests of the natural and legal persons involved. This task is not easy in a fragmented regulatory landscape, where complex data governance synergies exist between the EU and the member states and confined powers in administrative law.

In her chapter, Reichel examines whether the EHDS Regulation managed to define administrative balancing tools for the fragmented legal landscape of secondary use of health data in the EU and its member states, which can overcome the legal uncertainties regarding the secondary use of electronic health data and barriers thereto. The answer to this question is not straightforward. According to Reichel, it could be answered in the affirmative if one accounts for the strong safeguards that the EHDS provides for the rights and interests at stake. However, it could also be answered in the negative if one accounts for the formulation of these rules and their operationalisation in practice. A case in point is the assessment of the requirements for granting a data permit. This is regulated at a minimum level only and leaves gaps for further regulation at the national level. Moreover, the implementation could differ for different categories of electronic health data, making assessing compliance rather challenging. In addition to that, questions about cost and time also emerge.

Reichel draws attention to the potential that the EHDS will raise questions in the field of administrative law, given the EU's limited competencies. She suggests that further regulatory specifications across the 27 EU member states could be a step towards overcoming legal uncertainties and removing barriers of sharing. However, the author suspects that the administrative balancing tools set out in the EHDS will generate further questions, and it remains to be seen how these will play out in different national legal cultures. For example, a right to effective remedy was omitted in the final text of the Regulation, meaning that access to this right will likely vary among member states subject to domestic law.

In Chapter 11, Kogut and Shabani focus on one example of safeguards when secondary uses of health data has been planned, namely use of federated networks for data sharing. They explore whether the use of federated networks has been included in the recent EU digital policy and regulatory documents. They conclude that while such documents have broadly recommended use of decentralised approaches or use of trusted environments for data sharing, the specific focus on federated networks has not been the case. They subsequently discuss that the position of technical solutions such as federated networks can be assessed in view of their role in fulfilling various data protection principles. In that sense, for example, federated networks can be seen as facilitating respect for data minimisation as one of the pillars of data protection under the GDPR. That said, adequacy and suitability of each safeguard method must be assessed case-by-case, as they provoke many questions regarding the roles and responsibilities of various parties regarding controllership, the nature of data processing, and the rights and freedoms of the data subjects.

In turn, in Chapter 12, Gunnarsdóttir explores whether the EHDS is transforming the role of technological platforms for health data analysis. One major challenge in scientific research has been collaborative research, which entails work on personal data stored in various sites and various states. To facilitate collaboration and the achievement of scientific goals, technological solutions, including technological platforms, have commonly been used. One such is DataShield that allows pooled analysis to take place on a centralised server that has access to local servers on which the individual level data is stored. Gunnarsdóttir explores selected aspects of the EHDS requirements in light of such already established technological platforms, using DataShield as an example.

She highlights the integrated nature of the EHDS, whereby requirements set out for the primary use of electronic health data, electronic health record systems and wellness applications spill over to the secondary use framework. That, in turn, contributes to researchers being able to better assess and choose the datasets used for data analytics. She argues that the EHDS can be expected to transform the foreseeable efficiency of already established technological platforms such as DataShield. The users of these platforms, however, will unavoidably need to be familiar with the new requirements set out in the EHDS, and that could imply practical changes, too. The common focus of the platform developers to balance between achieving the goals of facilitating scientific research while protecting natural persons' rights is an asset for achieving the aims of the EHDS. A question is whether and how this asset will be used.

13.4 Future research

This book has provided a timely contribution on the transformation of electronic health data governance in the EU and beyond. The chapters have reflected on various points regarding primary and secondary uses of health data which have been discussed on the policy and scholarly levels during the legislative process. The contributions also made connections between the expected outcome and impact of the EHDS in view of the existing and emerging EU digital policies and regulations such as the GDPR and the Data Governance Act.

While the authors had the opportunity to include the final text of the regulation, the implementation phase is still to be unfolded in the coming months and years. As has been noted on many occasions in this book, despite the ultimate goal of the legislature being to harmonise governance of health data processing, still considerable room has been left to the member states in how to determine the details on establishing primary and secondary uses systems. In that sense, future research is needed to explore the potential divergences across member states in the implementation phase, in aspects such as the opt-out.

Introduction of new entities such as centralised HDABs, trusted data holders and health specific data authorities among national level will also bring about new questions regarding their interaction with the existing general data protection authorities, and research ethics oversight bodies such as ethics committees. Future research should assess how this interplay will take shape on national and EU level, and the potential overlaps among their respective competences.

At a broader health policy level, the introduction of the EHDS will provide an opportunity to assess the long-term impacts of the increased role of EU law in the health sector, via governance of health data processing for primary and secondary purposes. As it has been pointed out on several occasions in this book, the COVID-19 global pandemic has acted as an influencing factor in demanding the EU to play a stronger role in this landscape. It remains to be seen whether in view of the implementation of the EHDS, this will be seen as a success story to be followed in the other areas of healthcare. In addition, as the EHDS will appear as the first example of a data space, it can play an important role in how future data spaces in the other sectors such as transportation data, financial data and the like will be established.

In sum, further legal and policy analyses of the EHDS should be informed by the realities of health data processing in each member state and across the

EU, influenced by existing infrastructure, available resources, incentives and at times competing interests and rights of the relevant stakeholders, including patients, healthcare professionals, healthcare institutions, researchers, commercial entities and policy makers.

Acknowledgements

SS's work has been supported by WASP HS 'AI and Automated Systems and the Right to Health – Revisiting Law Accounting for the Exploitation of Users Preferences and Values', 2021–2025 and PROMOT – the project has received funding from the Canadian Institutes of Health Research (CIHR), and in partnership with L'Agence Nationale de la Recherche (France), Health Research Board (Dublin, Ireland), Instituto de Salud Carlos III (Spain), IRSC – IG, Swedish Research Council (Sweden), and Swiss National Science Foundation (Switzerland) – partners of the EJP RD, under grant agreement No. 02424 – 000. The EJP RD initiative has received funding from the European Union's Horizon 2020 research and innovation programme under grant agreement No. 825575.

Index

Pages in **bold** refer to tables.

For Product Safety Concerns and Information please contact our EU
representative GPSR@taylorandfrancis.com
Taylor & Francis Verlag GmbH, Kaufingerstraße 24, 80331 München, Germany

www.ingramcontent.com/pod-product-compliance
Lightning Source LLC
LaVergne TN
LVHW021121300926
849160LV00010B/804
9781032896847